Law and Language in the Middle Ages

Medieval Law and Its Practice

Edited by

John Hudson (*St Andrews*)

VOLUME 25

The titles published in this series are listed at *brill.com/mlip*

Law and Language in the Middle Ages

Edited by

Jenny Benham, Matthew McHaffie and Helle Vogt

BRILL

LEIDEN | BOSTON

Cover illustration: Law and grammatical miscellany from Ireland (c.1564), image courtesy of The British Library.

Library of Congress Cataloging-in-Publication Data

Names: Benham, Jenny, editor. | McHaffie, Matthew (Matthew W.), editor. | Vogt, Helle, editor.
Title: Law and language in the Middle Ages / Edited by Jenny Benham, Matthew McHaffie and Helle Vogt.
Description: Leiden : Brill, 2018. | Series: Medieval law and its practice ; 25 | Includes bibliographical references and index.
Identifiers: LCCN 2018024208 (print) | LCCN 2018025783 (ebook) | ISBN 9789004375765 (E-Book) | ISBN 9789004342675 (hardback : alk. paper)
Subjects: LCSH: Law—Language. | Law, Medieval. | Law—Europe—History.
Classification: LCC K213 (ebook) | LCC K213 .L394 2018 (print) | DDC 340/.14—dc23
LC record available at https://lccn.loc.gov/2018024208

Typeface for the Latin, Greek, and Cyrillic scripts: "Brill". See and download: brill.com/brill-typeface.

ISSN 1873-8176
ISBN 978-90-04-34267-5 (hardback)
ISBN 978-90-04-37576-5 (e-book)

This book is printed on acid-free paper and produced in a sustainable manner.

Contents

Notes on Contributors

Jenny Benham
School of History, Archaeology and Religion, Cardiff University.

Michael H. Gelting
Danish National Archives, Copenhagen.

Dirk Heirbaut
Ghent Legal History Institute, Faculty of Law and Criminology, Ghent University.

Carole Hough
English Language and Linguistics, School of Critical Studies, University of Glasgow.

Anders Leegard Knudsen
Diplomatarium Danicum (Society for Danish Language and Literature), Copenhagen.

Anette Kremer
Faculty of Humanities and Cultural Studies, University of Bamberg.

Ada Maria Kuskowski
Department of History, University of Pennsylvania.

André Evangelista Marques
Institute of Medieval Studies, University of Lisbon.

Matthew McHaffie
Department of History, King's College London.

Bruce O'Brien
History and American Studies, University of Mary Washington.

Paul Russell
Department of Anglo-Saxon, Norse and Celtic, University of Cambridge.

Werner Schäfke
Faculty of Law, University of Copenhagen.

Vincenz Schwab
Faculty of Humanities and Cultural Studies, University of Bamberg.

Helle Vogt
Centre for Privacy Studies, Faculty of Law, University of Copenhagen.

List of Illustrations

Figures

Tables

Map

Introduction

Jenny Benham, Matthew McHaffie, and Helle Vogt

Law and language, as modern scholars are increasingly aware, were central to medieval society. Indeed, all communities generate their own legal cultures, and in all historical contexts law uses language at every level on which it operates. Even when explicit rules are or remain identical across time and space, they are not necessarily reflected by the same legal practices, because they are produced, interpreted, and applied according to different social concepts and experiences. It was in the translation, performance, and application of law and juridical discourse that the encounter and negotiation between legal culture and the culture of society at large took place in the medieval period. Translation and interpretation inevitably affected not only how medieval people represented themselves in public, in order to take advantage of perceived norms or to present arguments of moral or political legitimacy, but also how such images have been transmitted to posterity. Observing the transformation of language and law through these encounters over a long period and across a wide geographical area is, therefore, one of the best ways to track key factors governing the lives of the medieval people we study.

The study of law and language in the medieval period continues to be of great interest to scholars and the general public alike, primarily because the medieval period has been seen as formative for both law and language; a time when the various languages and legal systems of the Europe of today emerged. As a consequence, scholars have shown a great interest in examining the ways in which particular languages emerged historically as dominant in particular geographical locales, often in conjunction with the formation of modern nation-states and their laws and legal systems.[1] Such studies follows a long tradition as even the tenth-century German chronicler Regino of Prüm considered that law and language were two of four characteristics that could

1 For but a few examples of this historiography, see Pierre Bourdieu, *Language and Symbolic Power. Edited and Introduced by John B. Thompson*, trans. Gina Raymond and Matthew Adamson (Cambridge: 1991); Jonathan Steinberg, 'The Historian and the *questione della lingua*', in *The Social History of Language*, ed. Peter Burke and Roy Porter (Cambridge: 1987), pp. 198–209; Michel de Certeau, Dominique Julia, and Jacques Revel, *Une politique de la langue. La revolution française et les patois* (Paris: 1975); Xing Yu, *Language and State. An Inquiry into the Progress of Civilization* (Lanham, MA: 2017).

 | DOI 10.1163/9789004375765_002

be used to determine how peoples differed from one another.[2] Nevertheless, as the Middle Ages was a period before the formation of fully-fledged nation-states, it is important to develop new paradigms for the study of law and language of that period. Indeed, the study of medieval law more generally has been challenged by the theoretical and methodological innovations that have transformed almost every sector of our profession over the last forty years or so. Scholars interested in ethnicity, gender, sexuality, subalternity, translation, and new modes of intellectual history have not only diversified the field of medieval legal studies and the role of language within it, but also the way in which we use and interpret our legal sources. Despite this, more focused studies on law and language have often continued to adhere closely to national and/or disciplinary boundaries, and have, additionally, focused primarily on the history of legal terminology.[3] Law, of course, is a technical subject with a specialized vocabulary defining practices, procedures, and terms that are often tricky to interpret and translate, whether into medieval or modern languages. While scholars often acknowledge that histories of law, texts, and legal practice across the medieval west have an intricate web of connections and relationships that are well attested in contemporary documentary sources, these are rarely explored by researchers because of boundaries created by languages and scholarly traditions. Hence, while the last few decades have seen a great range of scholarship devoted to the translation and interpretation of medieval law, much still remains to be done.

Studies on language generally tend to agree on one thing: language expresses relations of power. As summed up by John B. Thompson in his introductory remarks to Pierre Bourdieu's *Language and Symbolic Power*:

> As competent speakers we are aware of the many ways in which linguistic exchanges can express relations of power. We are sensitive to the variations in accent, intonation and vocabulary which reflect different positions in the social hierarchy. We are aware that individuals speak with differing degrees of authority, that words are loaded with unequal weights,

---

2 *Reginonis abbatis Prumiensis Chronicon cum continuatione Treverensi*, ed. Frederick Kurze, MGH SRG (Hannover: 1890), xx. The other two characteristics were origins and customs.

3 David Mellinkoff, *The Language of Law* (Boston: 1963); Bruce O'Brien, *Reversing Babel. Translation among the English during an Age of Conquests, c. 800 to c. 1200* (Newark, DE: 2011); Ditlev Tamm, *The History of Danish Law* (Copenhagen: 2011); Lawrence M. Solan and Peter M. Tiersma, eds., *The Oxford Handbook of Language and Law* (Oxford: 2012). Patrick J. Geary in the introduction to his *Language and Power in the Early Middle Ages* (Waltham, MA: 2013) has an interesting discussion on the particular problem of national scholarly traditions.

> depending on who utters them and how they are said, such that some words uttered in certain circumstances have a force and a conviction that they would not have elsewhere. We are experts in the innumerable and subtle strategies by which words can be used as instruments of coercion and constraint, as tools of intimidation and abuse, as signs of politeness, condescension and contempt.[4]

The power of legal language in the modern world resides in the fact that it is largely inaccessible to the average person: understanding, interpreting, and even using legal language well requires specialist training, whilst for the uninitiated, interactions with the language of law can be alienating and confusing, if not altogether incomprehensible. The most immediate manifestation of the power of legal language therefore is that it is inextricably connected to the distinctive identity of a professional caste of its purveyors and interpreters: the jurist, the lawyer, the judge, etc.[5] But its power runs deeper than this too. Because legal language in the modern world is the preserve of specialists, it has been easy to make ideological claims for the law's autonomy, nurtured and, to an extent, insulated by its professional caste of guardians: the different cadence and vocabulary of its language thus serve as important markers for the 'rule of law', a tag that on the one hand legitimates the legal institutions of the modern nation-state and, on the other, is legitimated by the unique characteristics of legal language itself. And it is here where one finds the fundamental power of legal language: as Lawrence Rosen puts it, 'the power of words is invariably part of the equation of power, and legal systems—however institutionalized, however separate from state control—are nothing if they are not forums for capturing the terms of discussion'.[6]

The corollary of power is legitimacy; if modern discussions (and critiques) of the power of legal language focus discussion on the legitimacy of state institutions, such as the judiciary, the police, etc., then for societies lacking the fully development institutions of state that characterize modern western governments, how scholars understand the interaction between power, legitimacy, and legal language must necessarily differ. It will not come as a surprise then that the underlying theme across this collection is precisely

4 John B. Thompson, 'Editor's Introduction', in Bourdieu, *Language and Symbolic Power*, 1.

5 Pierre Bourdieu, 'The Force of Law: Towards a Sociology of the Juridical Field', trans. Richard Nice. *The Hastings Law Journal* 38 (1987), 805–53.

6 Lawrence Rosen, *Law as Culture: An Invitation* (Princeton and Oxford: 2006), 166; see also the wide-ranging comments in Robert Gordon, 'Critical Legal Histories', *Stanford Law Review* vol. 36, no. 1/2 (1984), 57–125.

this interaction, and the essays explore the manifold ways in which legal language expresses and advances power or power relations, as well as the ways in which the language of law legitimates power. The wide geographical and chronological scope of this volume thus showcase the myriad ways in which power, legitimacy and language interact, moving discussion beyond the issues of identity or the formation and development of nation-states and their institutions. What emerges are different strategies reflective of the diverse and pluralistic political, legal, and cultural worlds of the Middle Ages.

Attention to strategy in the linguistic domain is underpinned by the methodological variety of approach adopted by the authors in this volume. As Lawrence Solan and Peter Tiersma have noted in their introduction to *The Oxford Handbook of Language and Law*, the interdisciplinarity of the study of law since the 1980s has helped revolutionize approaches to legal language.[7] A second underlying theme of this current volume is, therefore and unsurprisingly, its emphasis on interdisciplinarity when approaching the subjects of law and language. Analyses range from studies of translation, the interaction between multiple languages within legal communities, discourse analysis and attention to narrativity, to emphases on ritual and performativity. This volume takes us beyond, therefore, an approach to law and language that focuses on the professionalization of legal language and the underlying assumption that the language separates law from society in a manner that is essentially agonistic. The different methodological approaches adopted by the authors in this volume, however, showcase legal language from a variety of angles: if in some contexts and through some approaches, the power of such language was linked to domination and alienation of the uninitiated, in others the power of legal language helped conceptualize power and power relations in a discussable form which shaped and limited power. Paradoxically, therefore, legal language was not only an instrument of power, but also of empowerment.

The first part of this collection deals with the interpretation and translation of law. Bruce O'Brien poses fundamental questions concerning the motives behind translating legal texts in England over the period 800 to 1300. He offers three interwoven explanations: 'access', 'authority', and 'authenticity'. 'Access', he suggests, means 'providing access to readers from one language to a text in another' (p. 13); 'authority' refers to 'the quality of being official, or being perceived to have the qualities that make it look official' (p. 18); and 'authenticity' means that a legal text was 'perceived to be what it claimed to be, appropriate in form and contents to both time and place' (p. 22). O'Brien thus evocatively

7 Lawrence M. Solan and Peter M. Tiersma, 'Introduction', in *Oxford Handbook of Language and Law*, 1.

demonstrates how closely entwined were issues of textual translation and power, whilst at the same time illustrating that power was itself manifold and at times contradictory.

The importance of power also stands at the heart of Ada Kuskowski's paper, which examines the earliest French vernacular translations of Justinian's *Institutes*. By looking at how Roman legal concepts were translated into a language accessible and appropriate to the practical, cultural, and social needs of thirteenth-century France, she shows how law was a language of power that permeated all levels of society. Michael Gelting continues this notion by taking the Latin translation from *ca.*1300 of the Danish Law of Jutland (the *Leges Iutorum*) to revisit legal historians' methodological preoccupation with constructing a single *Ur*-text. Here, it is power in terms of authority of the language of law that has often driven the research of scholars. For Gelting, however, the *Leges Iutorum*, whose manuscript history and textual modifications over time are reconstructed in minute detail, was a 'living text', perhaps connected to the demands of learned audiences in ecclesiastical courts rather than to any authority of the language in which it was written.

In the final article in this section, Paul Russell deals with the tyranny of a construct, reminding us to approach that traditional relationship between law, language, and identity with great caution. By exploring the languages and registers of medieval Irish and Welsh law, he rejects any simplistic overarching label of 'Celtic law' to group these texts. His main points look at specific linguistic features, such as the apparent archaic language and alliterative functions of textual composition. These features, however, Russell suggests are not evidence of 'archaic' legal practice, but rather deliberate attempts to make the text appear archaic. He further stresses, importantly, that 'the mnemonic function of such sections of texts and phrasing would have been important not only in some context of oral performance … but also as a way for lawyers (and student lawyers) to learn the structure of the law' (p. 99).

The second section of papers all focus on a specific type of legal texts—charters—giving us a view across the medieval West; from Denmark in the north to Portugal in the south. At the heart of the documentary cultures that produced these texts sat language; as an important tool to establish authority but also to understand where it was located and why. This documentary culture shows both the commonalities and the diversity of the languages of legal practice, and the papers in this section consequently at times offer different solutions to the role and function of vernacular/Latin legal language than the papers in the previous section. The first article, from Anders Leegard Knudsen, offers a tour-de-force of Danish charters recording conveyances of land, from their origins in a Latin documentary culture in the thirteenth century, up to the transformations in the fifteenth century brought about by the turn to vernacular. He demonstrates the emergence of a Danish chancery style closely modelled off earlier Latin traditions of the *ars notaria*, both in terms of documentary form, and in the Latinization of Danish legal vocabulary. Interestingly, Knudsen's conclusion points not only to the power and authority of this particular style but also its remarkable endurance. Following up on authority through style, André Evangelista Marques examines roughly two hundred Portuguese dispute charters from before 1100. He is interested in the use of formulas representing judicial practice, especially oaths, and argues that formulaic language occupied an interstitial space between the language of formal legal texts on the one hand, and the amorphous aspects of actual legal practice on the other. Marques furthermore suggests that formulas were closely connected to the authority and legal value of charters in pre-1100 Portugal.

Moving from style to technical vocabulary, Dirk Heirbaut returns to the vexed problem of feudalism. Through an examination of vernacular terms in Latin charters from Flanders, from 1000 to *ca.*1300, he argues that Flanders was unique in that there was a clear distinction between feudal law and customary law, and he thereby problematizes the use of Latin charters written by ecclesiastical scribes when approaching the legal concepts of lay society. The final paper in this section is Matthew McHaffie's, exploring the formation of warranty clauses in western French charters from the eleventh to early thirteenth centuries. The issue he explores is how to locate the sources of legal language when charter-drafting did not utilize formal sources of written law when constructing legal language; he suggests that one source for the development of legal language was the institutional contexts of lordship, and that warranty clauses open a window into processes whereby charter-drafting was being orientated around seigneurial axes of legal authority.

The final section in the volume deals with the interactions between language, text, and legal practice. Here, the focus is specifically on vernacular language and law but examined in a context of their influences and manifestations, as well as through different approaches to the sources. Anette Kremer and Vincenz Schwab exemplify this by providing a methodological chapter, presenting the Leg-IT database which studies the vernacular language of the *leges barbarorum*. They outline the features of this methodological tool, and highlight the challenges in translating vernacular concepts of existing legal practice. In doing so, they give at least one example—*ploderaub*—that shows both changes over time, as seen in different legal manuscripts, and across space, through variations of the concept and the word across Germanic law texts.

In the second paper in this section, Werner Schäfke compares provisions over the dissolution of legal proceedings in the Icelandic text *Grágás* with narrative accounts of the same practice in the Sagas. He suggests that the authors of the Sagas understood the moral framework of voiding lawsuits very differently from how such issues were presented in formal legal texts. Ultimately, Schäfke argues, 'the Sagas of the Icelanders presented the act of influencing a court by use of force as a practical, legitimate practice, presenting it as a legal practice by expressing it through the language of legal discourse' (p. 284).

The final paper of this collection, returns to the thorny topic of the possible sources and influences of the earliest Anglo-Saxon law. Carole Hough examines the Kentish law of Æthelberht looking in particular at how the language may have been shaped by Biblical law. She concludes, perhaps provocatively, that 'potential analogues with Mosaic law may help to throw light on the interpretation of some problematic clauses in early Anglo-Saxon legislation' (p. 300). However, Hough's study is in some ways also a gentle reminder about the importance of comparisons and what these might or might not show. She highlights for instance that some legal ideas are commonplace in many ancient legal systems and that in order to show true influences or commonalities as opposed to coincidences, scholars require specific parallels and close reading of different texts, as well as the application of clear logic. Hough's cautionary tale of all may not be as it seems, is a fitting way to end the collection with a reminder that much work on law and language remains to be done.

In short then, *Law and Language in the Middle Ages* deals with the relationship between law and legal practice from the linguistic perspective. Together the papers show that medieval law was indeed as diverse and complex as medieval society itself. Europe in the period *ca.*600–*ca.*1500 was transforming linguistically and culturally, and as such, many of the essays raise, on the one hand, methodological questions about how historians can approach legal languages, and, on the other, theoretical questions about how to conceptualize the relationship between law and language within a Europe marked by multiple—sometimes conflicting, sometimes cooperating—legal systems.

This volume stems from a conference held in Copenhagen in September 2015. We wish to express our thanks to the Carlsberg Foundation for providing the funding for that conference and the Danish Academy for Science and Letters for hosting it; all of the participants at the conference, who contributed to the discussions and a convivial atmosphere; the authors of the supplementary essays we commissioned; the anonymous peer reviewers; and the staff at Brill for helping us bring this project to completion. We would also like to acknowledge the generous financial support from the Leverhulme Trust for the international network 'Voices of Law: Language, Text and Practice', which has aided the editorial process of the volume through workshops and meetings.

PART 1

Translation and Interpretation of Law

CHAPTER 1

Why Laws were Translated in Medieval England: Access, Authority, and Authenticity

Bruce O'Brien

Translators of laws, indeed all translators of any texts, do not choose to translate simply because they want to move a text from one language to another. Moving a text is what they do after they decide to translate. Another way of saying this is that the motivation for translating comes from somewhere other than the linguistic act translators perform. The motives originate in the culture of translators and patrons. They arise from ideas which make particular source texts important. What makes legal texts important per se is not particularly mysterious to any prospective medieval translator. Usually, but not always, the translator will know that the specific legislating king, and the date and location of the laws' promulgation, determine the text's importance. It also might matter that the content is perceived to be useful, according to the intended user. Is it expected to be consulted by lawyers and judges wanting to know the current law? Or will it be read mostly by chroniclers and the lay elite, who are more interested in the historical evidence for what kings had done?

In this paper I will explore the reasons translations of laws, legal treatises, royal edicts, and custumnals were made in England between the tenth and the thirteenth centuries, a period during which there was a significant amount of legal translation undertaken. In fact, more texts describing some sort of law were translated in England by more translators than happened anywhere else in Europe during this time. This large and diverse body of translations provide examples of the different reasons such translations were undertaken. They allow us to reach some conclusions about the main drivers of this translation activity. First, I will raise some important issues about translations and their interpretation as historical artifacts. Next I will discuss examples of the three principal motives behind these translations: access, authority, and authenticity. Last, I will consider how these, while distinguishable, are often complementary goals of individual translations.

Before considering the motivations behind translations of legal texts, I want to stress a few important methodological points that make it hard for us to discern motive behind medieval translations. First, the motive for translating texts is separate from the motive for composing texts, and yet we almost never

 | DOI 10.1163/9789004375765_003

see a clean demarcation of the two in any translator's prologue. Second, while explicit statements of motive are, for all their faults, more useful evidence than what implicit clues reveal, we almost never find such statements in prefaces to translations of legal texts. Usually, then, implicit evidence is all we have to go on to identify a motive. Clues about motive can be found in the kinds of manuscript contexts in which the translation survives. They can be found in the choice of language and dialect for the translation. Especially common are texts where editorial interventions (when we can know they are the translators' and not someone else's) are the only evidence we have to go on. The worry with this last kind of implicit evidence is that in almost every case, we cannot be sure what the actual source looked like. We will often not know, in the end, whether or not the omission in the translation was already in the version of the source the translator used; or whether the addition present in the translation had not already been added to the particular copy of the source being used by the translator.

Last, it is only a matter of methodological convenience that the motives of patron and translator are considered to be the same.[1] Given what we know about the composition of medieval texts, it is likely that a patron stood behind each of the translations we are studying. The translator responsible for the late eleventh- or early twelfth-century collection of English laws known as *Quadripartitus* writes that he has been asked to do the work by a patron, but that is all he reveals.[2] Any other disentangling of the motives of *Quadripartitus*' translator from the motives of his patron will have to be performed by scholars who build circumstantial arguments by assigning different weights to various claims made in *Quadripartitus*' two prologues. This is a task worth some effort, however frustrating it might turn out to be. In most cases, however, there is no possibility of such a separation of motives. We should always be aware that

1 Bruce R. O'Brien, *Reversing Babel: Translation among the English during an Age of Conquest, c. 800 to c. 1200* (Newark, DE: 2011), 127–8, 140–6.

2 Quadr, *Dedicatio* 2–4, in Felix Liebermann, *Quadripartitus, ein englisches Rechtsbuch von 1114* (Halle: 1892), 76; trans. Richard Sharpe, 'The Prefaces of "Quadripartitus"', in *Law and Government in Medieval England and Normandy: Essays in Honour of Sir James Holt*, ed. George Garnett and John Hudson (Cambridge: 1994), 151–2. Abbreviations for all codes are those used by Early English Laws: Cb Cn = *Colbertine Cnut*; Cons Cn = *Consiliatio Cnuti*; In Cn = *Instituta Cnuti*; ECf = *Leges Edwardi Confessoris* (versions 1–4); ECf Hk = *Holkham Leges Edwardi*; Leis Wl = *Leis Willelme*; Quadr = *Quadripartitus*. Citations will be to *Die Gesetze der Angelsachsen*, ed. Felix Liebermann, 3 vols. (Halle: 1903–1916) unless stated otherwise. New editions and translations for some as well as the standard edition of Liebermann for almost all are available at *Early English Laws*, at <http://www.earlyenglishlaws.ac.uk/laws/texts/>.

what we are divining as the motive for a translation has to be attributed not to the translator alone, but to patron and translator together.

Providing Access

Translation is understood as principally a means of providing access for readers of one language to a text in another. That at least is the task accomplished by translation. The reason why a translator would want to change the language of a legal text, however, speaks to more than mere access. Instead, a motive will explain why the access was needed. In the aftermath of 1066, it was the Francophones who needed the access and it is they who were responsible for almost all of the legal composition and translation surviving from the period. The nature of the need is revealed by both explicit statements as well as by the method of translation itself. One translator in the preface to his work worried about the propensity of human societies to foster crime, the general ignorance of the law, the corruption of lawyers and judges, and the need to have a punishment for every vice.[3] The translation method in his and other translators' texts shows that the contents of the law were still relevant. Some at that time still felt a need to learn the laws of England by studying older texts, and also acted to bring these older texts into line with recent developments in law. These are most simply explained as evidence of interest in law's present, rather than as antiquarian curiosity about law's past.[4]

The translation of texts to provide in a new language practical guidance to institutions and practices is not confined to laws and legal treatises. It can certainly be said to characterize the majority of translated charters, writs, and surveys produced in the century after 1066, just as it explains the general preservation and reorganization of records by episcopal households and monastic communities.[5] For all the complications arising from its terminology, construction, and evolving purpose, it is at least clear that Domesday Book represents the record of a grand inquest meant to record in a single language

3 Quadr, *Dedicatio*, 9–12, 24–8, 32–4, 38; *Argumentum*, 9–11, 26–7 (Liebermann, *Quadripartitus*, 77–8, 80–3, 84–5, 88–9).

4 Cf. John Hudson, *The Oxford History of the Laws of England Volume II: 871–1216* (Oxford: 2012), 869–71.

5 Michael T. Clanchy, *From Memory to Written Record: England 1066–1307*, 3rd edn. (Oxford: 2013), 35–8; See, e.g., translation activity at the Abbey of Abingdon, in *Historia Ecclesiae Abbendonensis*, ed. and trans. John Hudson, 2 vols. (Oxford: 2007), I, 198–201. See discussion in O'Brien, *Reversing Babel*, 134–6.

all of the rights, privileges, and claims of the king and his tenants which were at that time preserved orally or in writing in at least four or five languages. It was a particularly complex and useful product of countless acts of translation.[6] Nevertheless, the amount of technically adept translation in the legal field is noticeable.[7] This makes some sense, since the Normans were smart enough to recognize they needed a user's manual for the kingdom. Before 1066, most of these manuals would have been written in English.

A pragmatic desire for access explains a good deal of the legal translation. Support for this conclusion comes from the identity of those responsible for the translations. All of the post-conquest translations were produced by or for Francophones, rather than by nostalgic or nationalistic Englishmen as memoranda of their defeated culture.[8] This fact is revealed by occasional lapses into French, authorial perspective, and manuscript contexts, as well as by some direct allusions to differences between how the English say something and how the translator does. It is perhaps not far from the mark to say that the Normans did this translating because they came from a polity which had no written contemporary law. They did have books of law, but these were old and historical rather than current or recent.[9] A perusal of any of the libraries in Normandy, or in northwestern France in general, would turn up almost no law books that were not collections of sixth- to ninth-century Merovingian or Carolingian

6 Robin Fleming, *Domesday Book and the Law: Society and Legal Custom in Early Medieval England* (Cambridge: 1998), 11–17, 35.

7 Bruce O'Brien, 'Translating Technical Terms in Law-Codes from Alfred to the Angevins', in *Conceptualizing Multilingualism in England, c. 800–c. 1250*, ed. Elizabeth M. Tyler (Turnhout: 2011), 57–76.

8 Bruce O'Brien, *God's Peace and King's Peace: The Laws of Edward the Confessor* (Philadelphia: 1999), 133–4, responding to R. W. Southern, 'Aspects of the European Tradition of Historical Writing: The Sense of the Past', *Transactions of the Royal Historical Society* 23, fifth series (1973), 243–63.

9 Mark Hagger, 'Secular Law and Custom in Ducal Normandy, c. 1000–1144', *Speculum* 85 (2010), 831–7. While the issuance of capitularies in the Frankish kingdoms declines and ends in the tenth century, English kings produced a string of royal codes stretching from the seventh century to the eleventh. The reasons why are complex, but involve the background of the Gregorian mission as well as the nature of the relationship between the missionaries, King Æthelberht, and his Merovingian overlords; the development of a kingship growing out of this missionary crucible where law was a way to be imperial and Christian; the late ninth and tenth centuries' accidental creation of a single English Christian kingdom; and the strength of the vernacular written culture throughout the kingdom, especially evidenced in the tenth and eleventh centuries. The progress on the continent moves in the other direction, from a literate unified empire using its vernacular (represented by Latin) to a splintered set of unstable polities, none of which has any longer a vernacular in which to issue its laws.

leges and capitularies.[10] It is hard to understand why scribes and their masters, coming from such a desert of written texts of contemporary law, would translate laws unless they realized (or were told) that in England, written laws mattered.

The importance accorded to the laws as they were found is shown by the relative restraint translators of law codes exhibited when compared to the translators of other genres of pre-conquest English texts. Consider the treatment of the *Anglo-Saxon Chronicle* as a source by the generation of Anglo-Norman chroniclers at work in the first half of the twelfth century. The closest we have to a translation which attempts to preserve the shape of the source is the so-called F manuscript of the *Chronicle*. The translator, probably a member of Christ Church community in Canterbury, used a version of the *Chronicle* as his principal source, translating its passages from Old English into Latin mostly in the order in which they occur. This was only the start to what evolved into a very complex literary product. The F *Chronicle* is bilingual, recording both its Old English source and the Latin translation, but the translator has also added Latin chapters from other works or from his own knowledge, for which he generally provides English translations.[11] The final creation is something quite different in many respects from the text of its principal source. Much the same can be said of John of Worcester's *Chronicle*.[12] Several other Anglo-Norman historians writing in Latin and Anglo-French also used the Anglo-Saxon Chronicle as their principal source, but more as if it were a distrusted but occasionally useful informant than a text they wished to reproduce in another language.[13] Passages taken from the *Chronicle* constitute a substantial portion of these histories, but are much reworked. For instance, while by Diana Greenway's estimate forty percent of Henry of Huntingdon's *Historia* is derived from the Chronicle, it is rarely if ever a translation attempting to be merely the lexical equivalent of the source.[14]

10 See, e.g., Avranches, Bibliothèque Municipale, MS 145, described by Hubert Mordek, *Bibliotheca capitularium regum Francorum manuscripta: Überlieferung und Traditionszusammenhang der fränkischen Herrschererlasse*, MGH, Hilfsmittel 15 (Munich: 1995), 2–7.

11 *The Anglo-Saxon Chronicle: A Collaborative Edition, Volume 8: MS F*, ed. Peter S. Baker (Cambridge: 2000), lxix–lxxv.

12 John of Worcester, *Chronicle*, ed. R. R. Darlington and P. McGurk, trans. Jennifer Bray and P. McGurk, 3 vols. (Oxford: 1995–1998), II, xix.

13 E.g., Geoffrei Gaimar, *Estoire des Engleis*, ed. and trans. Ian Short (Oxford: 2009), 378 (notes to ll. 1806–1918), 380 (note to l. 1967), and 384 (note to line 2314).

14 Henry of Huntingdon, *Historia Anglorum*, ed. and trans. Diana Greenway (Oxford: 1996), lxxxv.

Translations of the laws, on the other hand, while showing sources adjusted or edited, rarely move the text very far from the shape and contents of the sources. It is as if the sagacious Normans saw that written law mattered to the English, and so decided that laws had to remain in something like their pre-conquest form. Such a situation provides the context for the Norman invention of the *laga Edwardi*. Even if crafted by William I's chancellor, as George Garnett argued, to help bolster the propaganda supporting the conquest, nevertheless, the phrase's quick popularity must have come from some pre-existing condition which disposed people to think it must be true.[15] Such a condition was the respect for written laws in England before 1066. The Normans picked Edward as their standard bearer not because he had good laws, or in fact any laws, but because he was portrayed as the king who chose William as his heir. However, it was Edward's laws that mattered to England's rulers, and so it mattered to those wanting to follow the royal lead to have access to the contents of this celebrated and reaffirmed *laga*. Many of those interested in the law recognized that the *laga Edwardi* was in reality the laws of Cnut (which Edward had sworn to uphold), and so for them, the response was to translate Cnut's laws.[16] Almost all of these translators adjusted to some degree the texts they found in their sources. At times, this amounted to a reordering of chapters or the removal of some chapters or portions of chapters, which left the source relatively intact and recognizable in its new skin.[17] In other cases, this adjusting resulted in the invention of new texts, created by combining many different texts into one new collection of laws; such a collection would, unless sources were laid out in a sequence, have had a different structure than the sources' due to the large amount of omission and reordering of chapters and the redistribution of individual chapters from each source throughout the new text.[18] Such a collection would also show the selective revision of the descriptions of individual laws. These new creations show thoughtful attention

15 George Garnett, *Conquered England: Kingship, Succession, and Tenure 1066–1166* (Oxford: 2007), 106; Bruce O'Brien, 'Pre-Conquest Laws and Legislators in the Twelfth Century', in *The Long Twelfth-Century View of the Anglo-Saxon Past*, ed. Martin Brett and David A. Woodman (Farnham: 2015), 233–40.

16 Quadr, *Argumentum*, 1, 9–11.

17 This is the case for the texts in *Quadripartitus*.

18 The translators responsible for the *Instituta Cnuti*, its revision in the *Colbertine Cnut*, and another revised text I call the *Holkham Leges Edwardi*, all show significant revisions: see Bruce O'Brien, 'The *Instituta Cnuti* and the Translation of English Law', *Anglo-Norman Studies* 25 (2003), 177–97; O'Brien, 'Pre-Conquest Laws', 246–65; and Bruce O'Brien, 'An English Book of Laws from the Time of *Glanvill*', in *Laws, Lawyers and Texts: Studies in Medieval Legal History in Honour of Paul Brand*, ed. Susanne Jenks, Jonathan Rose, and

to the substance of English law as well as an attempt to organize it in a more sensible or transparent way.[19]

After 1066 this attempt to comprehend and make accessible the evidence of the *laga Edwardi* was not happening in isolation just with translations of pre-conquest English legal texts. There seems to have been a general attempt by the Normans to comprehend what England possessed, what made it tick, and how it might best be controlled. This keen focus on domination and exploitation, so carefully described for Norman expansion in the British Isles in the work of Rees Davies, is seen in England in laws, charters, writs, estate surveys, administrative treatises, and is backed up by the stories of Norman behavior which fill the pages of the chroniclers.[20] That this control was not just raw exploitation, but was to a large extent sensitive to the rules of English life, is the story told by the massive borrowing of English legal and administrative vocabulary into the bureaucratic Latin used by the Normans for official records.[21] There would have been no reason for the Normans to have adopted so much from these registers unless the meaning of the words mattered. Echoes of this borrowing are heard, according to Michael Clanchy, in Richard fitz Nigel's reference to the 'common words' in which Domesday Book was written.[22] Fitz Nigel did not mean that the language was some sort

---

Christopher Whittick (Leiden: 2012), 51–67. My edition of the *Holkham Leges Edwardi* is available at <http://www.earlyenglishlaws.ac.uk/laws/texts/ECf2-Hk/>.

19 The very structure of the *Instituta Cnuti* shows an attempt to arrange laws for easier access to areas of interest. Consider the headings of the five books in which it first appears, in Textus Roffensis *ca.*1123:
Book 1: Incipiunt quędam instituta de legibus regum anglorum.
Book 2: Hęc est institutio secularis quam ego per consilium et consensum optimatum meorum seruare per totum regnum meum statui.
Book 3: [2 ½ blank lines in MS between end of book 2 and first chapter of book 3].
Book 4: Istę sunt consuetudines regum inter anglos.
Book 5: Hic intimatur quid Willelmus rex anglorum cum principibus suis constituit post conquisitionem anglię.

20 R. R. Davies, *Domination and Conquest: The Experience of Ireland, Scotland and Wales, 1100–1300* (Cambridge: 1990), 1–23.

21 Analogus to Old Norse loans (which themselves had been Anglicized and possibly begun the process of being Latinized before 1066): see Sara Pons-Sanz, *The Lexical Effects of Anglo-Scandinavian Linguistic Contact on Old English* (Turnhout: 2013), 156–92.

22 Richard wrote that 'totius terre descriptio diligens facta est … et uerbis communibus annotata in librum redacta est …' ('a careful survey of the whole country was made … and was set down in common language and drawn up into a book …'): Richard fitz Nigel, *Dialogus de Scaccario*, ed. and trans. Charles Johnson, F. E. L. Carter, and D. E. Greenway, 2nd edn. (Oxford: 1983), 63; Clanchy, *From Memory to Written Record*, 38.

of Latin administrative vulgate, but that these words, which gave almost all of Domesday Book's measures meaning, were the universally used English words of the pre-conquest kingdom.

All of these loans gave access to new Norman (and presumably Francophone) lords—especially ecclesiastical lords like bishops and abbots. Translation was the key to this access, but it was not for the most part indiscriminate, and did follow the lines laid down by the new rulers. Translation provided access to those portions of the English legal past which had been identified as important.

Maintaining Authority

For a medieval legal text, whether a collection of laws or an individual edict, authority is the quality of being official, or being perceived to have the qualities that make it look official. Unlike the authority of a modern code, the authority of a medieval legal text is not reflected in its enforceability or by its actual enforcement. Nor was a legal text with authority necessarily one whose laws were trusted to be accurate representations of the law, in the sense of an authorized edition. Medieval legal texts often possess two distinct qualities—one practical and the other ideological. In their practical guise, legal texts might reflect accurately current or recent law. Ideologically, they might also serve as demonstrations of royal power and legitimacy. I do not want to rehearse the details of the arguments about whether or not pre- or post-conquest laws were intended as statements of actual norms intended to be enforced, or whether they were ideological statements meant to make kings look kingly by signalling to readers and hearers some quality of the actual nature of royal power.[23] I want instead to consider authority in the broadest sense, encompassing both of these qualities of the term.

Translation could either add to or detract from a legal text's authority. Translation could help a text written in one language assume new authority in

---

23 Patrick Wormald, '*Lex scripta* and *verbum regis*: Legislation and Germanic Kingship from Euric to Cnut', in *Early Medieval Kingship*, ed. Peter H. Sawyer and Ian N. Woods (Leeds: 1977), 105–38; Simon Keynes, 'Royal Government and the Written Word in Late Anglo-Saxon England', in *The Uses of Literacy in Early Mediaeval Europe*, ed. Rosamond McKitterick (Cambridge: 1990), 226–57; David Pratt, 'Written Law and the Communication of Authority in Tenth-Century England', in *England and the Continent in the Tenth Century: Studies in Honour of Wilhelm Levison* (1876–1947), ed. David Rollason, Conrad Leyser, and Hannah Williams (Turnhout: 2010), 337–49; Alice Taylor, '*Lex Scripta* and the Problem of Enforcement: Anglo-Saxon, Welsh, and Scottish Law Compared', in *Legalism: Community and Justice*, ed. Fernanda Pirie and Judith Scheele (Oxford: 2014), 47–75.

another. The reason for this is simply that language mattered. Some languages were perceived to be the authoritative languages of law's publication, regardless of the language of the law's composition. King Alfred recognized this in the late ninth century while composing his laws. He was clearly aiming to join the authority of the Bible to the authority of his West Saxon laws by translating Mosaic laws from Exodus to serve as the first major section of his *Domboc*.[24] We should not be surprised. In Alfred's preface to his translation of Gregory I's *Pastoral Care*, he explained that

> I recalled how the Law was first composed in the Hebrew language, and thereafter, when the Greeks learned it, they translated it all into their own language.... And so too the Romans, after they had mastered them, translated them all through learned interpreters into their own language.[25]

Although the main thrust of Alfred's preface is his lament for the decline of knowledge of languages and of education in England in the ninth century, he is also acknowledging that all people translate important texts into their only language, and that the clearest and most important example of this is the translation of the laws received by Moses and recorded in the first five books of the Hebrew Bible. It is from these laws that the first portion of the *Domboc* was drawn.

With no prologue to explain the contents or the translation lying behind it, the selections from Exodus begin with the Decalogue: 'The Lord was saying these

---

24 David Pratt, *The Political Thought of King Alfred the Great* (Cambridge: 2007), 215–16, 222–3, 227–32; Patrick Wormald, *The Making of English Law: King Alfred to the Twelfth Century, volume 1: Legislation and Its Limits* (Oxford: 1999), 416–30. Wormald covers both Alfred's agenda as an English king and the deeper Roman, Irish, and Carolingian context behind other classical and early medieval treatments of Moses as a lawgiver. For one example, see Moses' appearance at the head of the *Law of the Bavarians*, where the language of the prologue listing lawmakers from Moses, the Egyptian pharoahs, Greek and Roman legislators is all cribbed from Isidore of Seville's seventh-century encyclopedia: *Lex Baiwariorum*, ed. E. de Schwind, MGH, Legum Sectio I, Legum nationum Germanicarum V.2 (Hannover: 1926), 198–200.

25 'Ða gemunde ic hu sio æ wæs ærest on Ebr[e]isc geðiode funden, & eft, ða hie Creacas geliornodon, ða wendon hie hie on hiora agen geðiode ealle, & eac ealle oðer bec. & eft Lædenware swæ same, siððan hie hie geliornodon, hie hie wendon eall[a] ðurh wise wealhstodas on hiora agen geðiode': Alfred, *King Alfred's West-Saxon Version of Gregory's 'Pastoral Care'*, ed. Henry Sweet, 2 vols., Early English Text Society, o.s., 45 and 50 (London: 1871), 4–7, and trans. by Simon Keynes and Michael Lapidge in *Alfred the Great: Asser's Life of King Alfred and Other Contemporary Sources* (Harmondsworth: 1983), 125–6.

words to Moses, and thus said I am the Lord your God; I led you out of the land of Egypt and your slavery'.[26] What follows are a selection of commandments and laws, some of which have been significantly edited, and which cover issues from idolatry and murder to widowhood and theft. This portion of the *Domboc* ends as abruptly as it began, with the *explicit*: 'These are the judgments which almighty God himself had spoken to Moses'.[27] Alfred's own contributions—the laws explicitly said to be his—are three times as long as the Mosaic section, while Ine's, which follow Alfred's laws in all of their manuscript witnesses, is twice as long. The length, however, matters less than the investment in time and thought that went into placing God's laws, spoken by Moses, at the head of a code of West Saxon law. It is also important to recognize that the laws included from Exodus cover many of the same areas of law as are covered by Alfred's and Ine's laws. The Mosaic laws are not simply a rhetorical flourish, but an attempt to imply the parity of the law-makers alongside the development of the law. They are of the same class, and shoulder the same responsibilities, even if God was said to have spoken to only one of them.

In England, despite the authority of the Latin Bible, law was always issued in English. This was true of the first written laws issued *ca.*600 by Æthelberht, the convert king of Kent, and continued to be the case until shortly after the Norman conquest. When Alfred wished to combine biblical laws from Exodus with his and his predecessor's laws, he translated the biblical extracts into English. If English was the language of authority before 1066—meaning it was the language in which all laws were promulgated—then movement of laws into that language was intended to make them not only accessible, but also authoritative. What makes this point much more strongly are the hints we have that laws might at times have been composed first in Latin, and then translated into English for promulgation. There is not much evidence outside of canon law and penitentials that normative texts in England started life in Latin and ended up in English for publication.[28] It may be, however, that the most prolific writer of laws before the conquest, Archbishop Wulfstan of York, composed in Latin, and then translated his work into English; he would likely have done this because it was the authoritative language of law.[29]

26 'Dryhten wæs sprecende ðas word to Moyse 7 þus cwæð: Ic eom dryhten ðin god. Ic ðe utgelaedde of Egipta londe 7 of hiora ðeowdome', Intro., prol., ed. Liebermann, *Gesetze*, I, 26.

27 'Þis sindan ða domas þe se ælmihtega god self sprecende wæs to Moyse 7 him bebead to healdanne', ed. Liebermann, *Gesetze*, I, 42.

28 Enid Raynes, 'MS Boulogne-sur-Mer 63 and Ælfric', *Medium Ævum* 26 (1957), 65–73.

29 Wormald, *Making of English Law*, 333–5.

After 1066 moving Old English laws into Latin was in part a response to the rising authority of Latin in the eleventh and twelfth century. Historians who study the impact of the conquest often explain this movement by reference to the low status of English because it was the language of the military losers. Occasional references to the barbaric sound of English seem to support this conclusion.[30] The choice to use Latin and avoid English, however, was not so much a judgement of English per se, but part of a devaluing of all vernaculars in comparison to the rising authority of Latin. We see this clearly in England because, unlike most western European kingdoms, it had a written vernacular tradition.

One legal translation seems to show this anti-vernacular bias. The translator who produced what is known as the *Consiliatio Cnuti* avoided using any English loans in his work.[31] If all we had were the *Consiliatio*, we would have to conclude that almost no English legal terms had been borrowed by Latin after 1066. However, what is just as striking as the avoidance of English by the *Consiliatio*'s translator is the peculiarly classical vocabulary which appears in its place.

The *Consiliatio*'s approach, however, is a minority position. Virtually all other legal texts moved in the opposite direction and made use of the Latinized forms of the Old English register of law. Instead of the heightened status of Latin in the twelfth-century Renaissance creating an impermeable barrier between it and lesser, 'barbaric' languages, in England at least Latin's rise drew a post-conquest invasion of English loans.[32] These loans were significant in many areas of life, but probably most of all in the register of law. Compared to the previous five centuries of contact between the English and Latin-speaking or Latin-using peoples or institutions, the loans from English to Latin in the century after 1066 constituted one of the most rapid and complete absorptions

30 E.g., William of Malmesbury, *Gesta regum Anglorum*, ed. R. A. B. Mynors, R. Thomson, and M. Winterbottom, 2 vols. (Oxford: 1998–1999), 1:14 (i.prol.4) and 70 (i.49.4); Gervase of Tilbury, *Otia Imperialia: Recreation for an Emperor*, ed. S. E. Banks and J. W. Binns (Oxford: 2002), 474–75 (ii.21). Most of these references are gathered and reviewed by P. V. D. Shelly, *English and French in England, 1066–1100* (Philadelphia: 1921), and in R. M. Wilson, 'English and French in England, 1100–1300', *History*, n.s., 28 (1943), 37–60.

31 Felix Liebermann, *Consiliatio Cnuti: Ein Übertragung Angelsächsischer Gesetze aus dem Zwölften Jahrhundert* (Halle: 1893), vi–viii.

32 R. E. Latham, D. R. Howlett, and R. K. Ashdowne, eds., *Dictionary of Medieval Latin from British Sources* (British Academy: 1975–2013), s.vv. (to cite a few examples) *ceapgildum, fyrdwita, grithbricha, hamsocna, hengewita, husbota, huscalrus, infangenetheofa, laga, lahceapum, lahslihta, wera, weralada,* and *wita*.

of any register from a vernacular into Latin.[33] One obvious conclusion is that this register had authority, and it was the preservation of this register in the Latin translations of law codes that gave them authority.

Ensuring Authenticity

A striving for authenticity is perhaps the hardest to see of all of these motives for translating law codes. This difficulty in finding notions of authenticity is not confined to the evidence of laws. It is an open question how strong a sense medieval people had of what made anything authentic. I am using authentic here in a narrower sense seen from the perspective of the medieval observer: to be thought of as authentic, a text, idea, or object would have to be perceived to be what it claimed to be, appropriate in form and contents to both time and place. I am not so much concerned with uncovering forgeries, where authenticity is the principle question to answer, as I am interested in medieval recognition of anachronism.

It might appear a fool's errand to hunt for medieval writers who are aware of and concerned with anachronism. The period as a whole is often portrayed as a time of rampant anachronisms in texts and in art. It seems unlikely that anyone was at all concerned when the Biblical pharaoh of Genesis appears in the guise of an eleventh-century English king.[34] The Hellenistic era leaders of the Maccabees become valiant twelfth-century knights.[35] Critiques of Alexander the Great transform the ancient world's reliance on philosophy and Fate into Christian motives and the actions of the Lord God.[36] A vernacular translation of the Aeneid produces a chivalric Aeneas who would fit comfortably in any

33 There are very few pre-conquest texts which exist in both Old English source and Latin translation with which to compare the post-conquest translations. One, King Edgar's *Whitbordesstan* code (IV Eg), does survive in one place with both source and a Latin translation. Except for what appears to be the scribe's or translator's aural slips, where he left a phrase in Old English though he changed its form to fit the Latin sentence, there are no Old English loans, let alone any from the legal register: see IV Eg 8.1, where 'ðam hundrodes ealdre' is translated as 'domino þæs hundredes' (Liebermann, *Gesetze*, I, 210, 212–13). Both phrases were written by the same scribe.

34 London, British Library, MS Cotton Claudius B.iv, fol. 59r.

35 Sylvain Gougenheim, 'Les Maccabées, modèles des guerriers chrétiens des origins au XIIe siècle', *Cahiers de civilisation médiévale* 54 (2011), 3–120.

36 George Cary, *The Medieval Alexander*, ed. D. J. A. Ross (Cambridge: 1956), 80.

twelfth-century court.[37] In a French Bible translation, the Philistines become the *gent Sarazine*, while the religion of the people of Canaan is *Mahomerie*.[38] Authenticity as we understand it seems not to be privileged or measured.

Nevertheless, there are hints that medieval writers or copyists at least had relative notions of time appropriateness and that this was relevant to a document's validity—thus a document's authenticity could be measured by considering the apparent date of its appearance (mostly). This was hardly more than a sense that something looked older than contemporary documents. We find such references here and there in western Europe during this period.

One such document that betrays some sense—albeit misconceived—of what an older document would look like is a letter said to have been discovered by the newly imported Cluniac monks who moved into the monastery of Much Wenlock.[39] The letter, discovered tucked away near the altar, or so the monks claimed, purported to identify where the remains of St Mildburg were buried. The account of the discovery of the letter tells us that the letter was written in English, which none of the monks knew. They found a translator, heard what the letter said, and then set off to excavate a sacred grave. We know the letter was a forgery. What is striking then is that it appears that the Francophone monks thought that this kind of letter from before the conquest would have been written in English, not Latin. Their fabricated letter was meant to appear authentic. They must have thought that a similar Latin letter would appear suspicious. The fact that we recognize that most such documents would have been written before 1066 in Latin rather than English just serves to emphasize the fact that the monks had made a judgement about which language was more authentic. They were thinking in terms of languages and texts appropriate in the past, but which were no longer in common use.

Such thinking about what was and was not an authentic legal text played no part in their production after 1066. All of the treatises purporting to be pre-conquest or from the reign of William I were composed in Latin and copied using Caroline script despite what must have been the overwhelming evidence that English was the language of pre-conquest laws and insular square minuscule

---

37 *Le Roman d'Eneas*, ed. Aimé Petit (Paris: 1997), 9; on this work's engagement with its time and place, see Laura Ashe, *Fiction and History in England, 1066–1200* (Cambridge: 2007), 124–46.

38 Pierre Nobel, ed., *Poème anglo-normande sur l'ancien testament*, 2 vols. (Paris: 1996), ll. 2599 and 9571.

39 Paul Antony Hayward, 'The *Miracula Inventionis beate Mylburge virginis* Attributed to "the Lord Ato, Cardinal Bishop of Ostia"', *English Historical Review* 114 (1999), 565–66 (c. 2).

almost unanimously their script.[40] Two of the three major translations of pre-conquest laws refer neither to their original language nor to the effort made to translate these sources.[41] It looks as though the people reading lawbooks after 1066 assumed that Latin was the language of authentic laws.[42] That at least is the first impression. It is likely that only a select group of people after *ca.*1100 would have actually seen any earlier laws in Old English. It would have been easy for the rest to conclude that all law in England was written and promulgated in Latin. The fact that this Latin was peppered with English loans does not alter this conclusion. The phrases which to our eyes betray a translation (e.g., '*quod Angli dicunt*') also appear in works that are in no way translations.[43]

During the twelfth century in England, Latin was the almost exclusive language for law. This was true for both new law, like Henry II's assizes, and what was labelled as old law, such as the so-called forest laws of Cnut or apocryphal treatise known as the *Leges Edwardi Confessoris*. The copying during the first half of the twelfth century of a few manuscripts of pre-conquest laws in English does not challenge this conclusion. Interestingly, the later twelfth-century Anglo-French translation of the *Leges Edwardi* reminds readers repeatedly that it is subordinate to its source, and not anything else.[44] The *Leis de Sant Eduard* begins almost every chapter with an introductory phrase announcing that 'the chapter says this' or 'the chapter shows that'. By the time this translation was undertaken, sometime in the late twelfth century, English had disappeared as a language used for legal texts of all kinds and no one was copying the older English-language legal manuscripts anymore. Instead, Latin had become the language of law, and French was only aspiring to be a useful way to access it.

40 Even as late as the middle of the twelfth century, lawbooks holding English-language legal texts were being produced. The three surviving examples are Strood, Kent, Medway Archive and Local Studies Centre, MS DRc/R1 (*Textus Roffensis*), Cambridge, Corpus Christi College MS 383, and London, British Library, MS Harley 55.

41 These two are the *Instituta Cnuti* and the *Consiliatio Cnuti*.

42 Ironically, English was the badge of authenticity before the conquest. Michael Clanchy observed that 'writing in English prose had originated as a way of expressing authenticity and directness in legal and administrative contexts': Clanchy, *From Memory to Written Record*, 35.

43 See, e.g., ECf1 6.2, 12, 20; Leis Wl 5. I am not including the two instance of this practice in Wl art (cc. 4, 6) because it is unclear whether all of this text derives ultimately from Old English originals (as is certainly the case for c. 6).

44 This text only survives in the fourteenth-century Cambridge, University Library, Ee.1.1, fos. 3v–8r, and has never been edited; an edition is now being prepared by Sara Harris for Early English Laws. The manuscript images for the whole text are available at <http://www.earlyenglishlaws.ac.uk/laws/manuscripts/cu/>.

Given these shifting language relationships, and given that only modest evidence at best attests to any sense of legal anachronism, the sense of what contemporaries deemed authentic in an English legal text is hard to find. In a copyist's selecting a script for legal texts, however, authenticity may have played a role. There is clear evidence that some in the eleventh and twelfth centuries had a notion that script changed with time, and that a document from an earlier time might best be written or rewritten using the script from that time.[45] This recognition is most obviously seen in a select group of forgeries where the forger has tried to imitate an earlier script.[46] The use of imitative script, however, is not limited to forgeries; some scribes who were merely copying older records seem to have felt that a new copy of an old document would do well to try to imitate the actual form of writing on that document. Since this imitation required effort and could end in failure, the decision to use an older script represents a choice and a commitment made by the scribe. The scribe would not then follow the easy path of copying works in his or her commonly used script. This association of script with previous times shows that some scribes had a sense of authenticity that was tied to the visual appearance of a text.

With one exception, there is no evidence for anything like this sense of authenticity in any of the copies of laws produced in England in the eleventh and twelfth centuries. There is one exception that might show an awareness of script as conveying authenticity to a copy, but because it is unique, it cannot tell us much about the ideas contemporaries generally had about the past. The manuscript I am speaking of is Paris, Bibliothèque nationale de France, MS Latin 4771, which has three Latin legal texts as well as a ducal and royal genealogy for the Normans, up to the time of Richard I. Someone responsible for the production of this book—patron, compiler, scribe—decided that some but not all of the Old English words in the otherwise Latin texts would not be written with the Pregothic minuscule used for the Latin and some of the Old English words. Instead, when an English term employed one of four special letters used for writing English—þ, ð, æ, and ƿ—the main scribe would not write the word but would leave a space, and the corrector of the volume would

45 Julia Crick, 'Historical Literacy in the Archive: Post-Conquest Imitative Copies of Pre-Conquest Charters and Some French Comparanda', in *The Long Twelfth-Century View of the Anglo-Saxon Past*, ed. Martin Brett and David A. Woodman (Burlington, VT: 2015), 159–90; Peter Stokes, 'The Problem of Grade in Post-Conquest Vernacular Minuscule', *New Medieval Literatures* 13 (2011), 23–47.

46 See, e.g., *Facsimiles of Anglo-Saxon Charters*, ed. Simon Keynes (Oxford: 1991), pp. 3 (no. 1), 4 (nos. 4, 6), and 11 (no. 11) are possibly all done in imitative script.

add the English word using insular script.[47] The script itself is not deliberately archaizing—it does not pretend to be older than the copy itself. It is simply a contemporary vernacular script written by a scribe who was not terribly well-practiced in its execution. The letters exhibit unevenness of form, inconsistent aspect, and error. The words are, nevertheless, immediately visible to the reader, and mark English legal terms, whether Latinized or not, as distinct from the rest of the words of the texts.[48] Given that the whole book looks like a collection arguing for royal legislative power, founded on precedents from the pre-conquest past, it is possible that the vernacular script was used to give some authenticity to the book.[49] The scribe copying the translation heightened the visibility of the English terms by tying them to the way law had been written in the past.

Final Observations

It should be clear by now that all three of the goals I have identified—access, authority, and authenticity—are in fact not isolated from one another in practice. For instance, the use of an authentic script gave a translation authority. The authority a translation was perceived to have contributed significantly to its choice as a means of access to English legal culture. From another direction, the English legal loan words in Latin can and did lend access, authority, and authenticity, depending on context. Figuring out which of the three these loan words were intended to convey is hard, since they can in fact do all three at the same time. A retention of the lexis of English law grants an access the writers and their readers likely wanted, an access to the actual technical vocabulary of the English. They provided access to what the law actually was. This tactic could also be said to give the text authority. A translation which retained English technical terms of law was using words of sufficient weight that they made the whole authoritative. As time went by and this practice became ubiquitous, especially after Domesday Book, the presence of this Latinized register signaled the 'official' quality of the record. Finally, this tactic can be thought to

47 O'Brien, 'Pre-Conquest Laws', 246–55 (and esp. figs 12.3 and 12.4).

48 Cf. Oxford, Bodleian Library, MS Auct. F.1.9, fol. 99v; see discussion by Charles Burnett, *The Introduction of Arabic Learning into England* (London: 1997), 39–46.

49 This goal would support the newly composed prologue of the codes, which voices imperial legal ambitions for England's new conqueror, Cnut: see the edition and translation of the prologue (Cb Cn prol.) at O'Brien, 'Pre-Conquest Laws', 269–72.

have lent authenticity to the record. It was what presumably at least one group of readers of law in the late twelfth century would have expected to find in a legal text, especially when the laws were attributed to the times of kings who had reigned in the distant past.

Bibliography

Manuscripts

Avranches, Bibliothèque Municipale, MS 145
Cambridge, Corpus Christi College, MS 383
Cambridge, University Library, Ee.1.1
London, British Library, MS Cotton Claudius B.iv
London, British Library, MS Harley 55
Oxford, Bodleian Library, MS Auct. F.1.9
Paris, Bibliothèque nationale de France, MS Latin 4771
Strood, Kent, Medway Archive and Local Studies Centre, MS DRc/R1 (*Textus Roffensis*)

Works Cited

Alfred. *King Alfred's West-Saxon Version of Gregory's 'Pastoral Care'*, edited by Henry Sweet, 2 vols., Early English Text Society, o.s., 45 and 50. London: 1871.

Ashe, Laura. *Fiction and History in England, 1066–1200*. Cambridge: 2007.

Burnett, Charles. *The Introduction of Arabic Learning into England*. London: 1997.

Cary, George. *The Medieval Alexander*, edited by D. J. A. Ross. Cambridge: 1956.

Clanchy, Michael T. *From Memory to Written Record: England 1066–1307*, 3rd edn. Oxford: 2013.

Crick, Julia. 'Historical Literacy in the Archive: Post-Conquest Imitative Copies of Pre-Conquest Charters and Some French Comparanda'. In *The Long Twelfth-Century View of the Anglo-Saxon Past*, edited by Martin Brett and David A. Woodman, 159–90. Farnham: 2015.

Davies, R. R. *Domination and Conquest: The Experience of Ireland, Scotland and Wales, 1100–1300*. Cambridge: 1990.

Early English Laws at <http://www.earlyenglishlaws.ac.uk/laws/texts/>.

Fleming, Robin. *Domesday Book and the Law: Society and Legal Custom in Early Medieval England*. Cambridge: 1998.

Garnett, George. *Conquered England: Kingship, Succession, and Tenure 1066–1166*. Oxford: 2007.

Geoffrei Gaimar. *Estoire des Engleis*, edited and translated by Ian Short. Oxford: 2009.

Gervase of Tilbury. *Otia Imperialia: Recreation for an Emperor*, edited by S. E. Banks and J. W. Binns. Oxford: 2002.

Gougenheim, Sylvain. 'Les Maccabées, modèles des guerriers chrétiens des origins au XIIe siècle'. *Cahiers de civilisation médiévale* 54 (2011): 3–120.

Hagger, Mark. 'Secular Law and Custom in Ducal Normandy, c. 1000–1144'. *Speculum* 85 (2010): 827–67.

Hayward, Paul Antony. 'The *Miracula Inventionis beate Mylburge virginis* Attributed to "the Lord Ato, Cardinal Bishop of Ostia"'. *English Historical Review* 114 (1999): 543–73.

Henry of Huntingdon. *Historia Anglorum*, edited and translated by Diana Greenway. Oxford: 1996.

Historia Ecclesiae Abbendonensis, edited and translated by John Hudson, 2 vols. Oxford: 2007.

Holkham Leges Edwardi, edited by Bruce O'Brien (Early English Laws, 2012) at <http://www.earlyenglishlaws.ac.uk/laws/texts/ECf2-Hk/>.

Hudson, John. *The Oxford History of the Laws of England, Volume II: 871–1216*. Oxford: 2012.

John of Worcester. *Chronicle*, edited by R. R. Darlington and P. McGurk, translated by Jennifer Bray and P. McGurk, 3 vols. Oxford: 1995–1998.

Keynes, Simon. 'Royal Government and the Written Word in Late Anglo-Saxon England'. In *The Uses of Literacy in Early Mediaeval Europe*, edited by Rosamond McKitterick, 226–57. Cambridge: 1990.

Keynes, Simon, editor. *Facsimiles of Anglo-Saxon Charters*. Oxford: 1991.

Keynes, Simon, and Michael Lapidge, editors. *Alfred the Great: Asser's Life of King Alfred and Other Contemporary Sources*. London: 1983.

Latham, R. E., D. R. Howlett, and R. K. Ashdowne, editors. *Dictionary of Medieval Latin from British Sources*. Oxford: 1975–2013.

Le Roman d'Eneas, edited by Aimé Petit. Paris: 1997.

Lex Baiwariorum, edited by E. de Schwind, MGH, Legum Sectio I, Legum nationum Germanicarum V.2. Hannover: 1926.

Liebermann, Felix, editor. *Quadripartitus, ein englisches Rechtsbuch von 1114*. Halle: 1892.

Liebermann, Felix, editor. *Consiliatio Cnuti: Ein Übertragung Angelsächsischer Gesetze aus dem Zwölften Jahrhundert*. Halle: 1893.

Liebermann, Felix, editor. *Die Gesetze der Angelsachsen*, 3 vols. Halle: 1903–1916.

Mordek, Hubert. *Bibliotheca capitularium regum Francorum manuscripta: Überlieferung und Traditionszusammenhang der fränkischen Herrschererlasse*, MGH, Hilfsmittel 15. Munich: 1995.

Nobel, Pierre, editor. *Poème anglo-normande sur l'ancien testament*, 2 vols. Paris: 1996.

O'Brien, Bruce. *God's Peace and King's Peace: The Laws of Edward the Confessor*. Philadelphia: 1999.

O'Brien, Bruce. 'The *Instituta Cnuti* and the Translation of English Law'. *Anglo-Norman Studies* 25 (2003): 177–97.

O'Brien, Bruce. *Reversing Babel: Translation among the English during an Age of Conquest, c. 800 to c. 1200*. Newark (DE): 2011.

O'Brien, Bruce. 'Translating Technical Terms in Law-Codes from Alfred to the Angevins'. In *Conceptualizing Multilingualism in England, c. 800–c. 1250*, edited by Elizabeth M. Tyler, 57–76. Turnhout: 2011.
O'Brien, Bruce. 'An English Book of Laws from the Time of *Glanvill*'. In *Laws, Lawyers and Texts: Studies in Medieval Legal History in Honour of Paul Brand*, edited by Susanne Jenks, Jonathan Rose, and Christopher Whittick, 51–67. Leiden: 2012.
O'Brien, Bruce. 'Pre-Conquest Laws and Legislators in the Twelfth Century'. In *The Long Twelfth-Century View of the Anglo-Saxon Past*, edited by Martin Brett and David A. Woodman, 229–72. Farnham: 2015.
Pons-Sanz, Sara. *The Lexical Effects of Anglo-Scandinavian Linguistic Contact on Old English*. Turnhout: 2013.
Pratt, David. *The Political Thought of King Alfred the Great*. Cambridge: 2007.
Pratt, David. 'Written Law and the Communication of Authority in Tenth-Century England'. In *England and the Continent in the Tenth Century: Studies in Honour of Wilhelm Levison* (1876–1947), edited by David Rollason, Conrad Leyser, and Hannah Williams, 331–50. Turnhout: 2010.
Raynes, Enid. 'MS Boulogne-sur-Mer 63 and Ælfric'. *Medium Ævum* 26 (1957): 65–73.
Richard fitz Nigel. *Dialogus de Scaccario*, edited and translated by Charles Johnson, F. E. L. Carter, and D. E. Greenway, 2nd edn. Oxford: 1983.
Sharpe, Richard. 'The Prefaces of "Quadripartitus"'. In *Law and Government in Medieval England and Normandy: Essays in Honour of Sir James Holt*, edited by George Garnett and John Hudson, 148–72. Cambridge: 1994.
Shelly, P. V. D. *English and French in England, 1066–1100*. Philadelphia: 1921.
Southern, R. W. 'Aspects of the European Tradition of Historical Writing: The Sense of the Past'. *Transactions of the Royal Historical Society* 23, fifth series (1973): 243–63.
Stokes, Peter. 'The Problem of Grade in Post-Conquest Vernacular Minuscule'. *New Medieval Literatures* 13 (2011): 23–47.
Taylor, Alice. '*Lex Scripta* and the Problem of Enforcement: Anglo-Saxon, Welsh, and Scottish Law Compared'. In *Legalism: Community and Justice*, edited by Fernanda Pirie and Judith Scheele, 47–75. Oxford: 2014.
The Anglo-Saxon Chronicle: A Collaborative Edition, Volume 8: MS F, edited by Peter S. Baker. Cambridge: 2000.
William of Malmesbury. *Gesta regum Anglorum*, edited and translated by R. A. B. Mynors, R. Thomson, and M. Winterbottom, 2 vols. Oxford: 1998–1999.
Wilson, R. M. 'English and French in England, 1100–1300'. *History* 28, n.s. (1943): 37–60.
Wormald, Patrick. '*Lex scripta* and *verbum regis*: Legislation and Germanic Kingship from Euric to Cnut'. In *Early Medieval Kingship*, edited by Peter H. Sawyer and Ian N. Woods, 105–38. Leeds: 1977.
Wormald, Patrick. *The Making of English Law: King Alfred to the Twelfth Century, Volume 1: Legislation and Its Limits*. Oxford: 1999.

CHAPTER 2

Translating Justinian: Transmitting and Transforming Roman Law in the Middle Ages

Ada Maria Kuskowski

The traditional relationship between languages of law in the secular courts of northern France began to change in the thirteenth century. Prior to that, the vernacular was generally the language of legal practice in the courts, which was informal in the sense of a low reliance on text—there was no manual to teach practice and records were piecemeal. Meanwhile, Latin was the language of record, written law, and communication between educated elites, the language of universities and erudition. The first revolution in legal language occurred in the eleventh and twelfth centuries—legal Latin became more conceptual, theoretical, and formal with the university study of Roman law and its beloved definitions, increasingly so with each layer of gloss. Then came another revolution in legal language when the vernacular developed as a language of writing and of law; Roman law was translated and texts of customary law developed as an original legal literature in the vernacular.

Despite the cultural and linguistic difference between vernacular and Latin, and between the secular court and university legal learning, it is well known that Roman law had a transformative effect on the concepts, language, procedure, and substantive law of the secular courts.[1] Pierre Legendre, for instance, aptly labelled Romano-canonical jurisprudence 'the other Bible of the West'.[2] While we know that change occurred, there is still much to learn about how exactly ideas moved from the world of Latinity inhabited by Romanists and canonists to the lay jurists who practiced customary law in secular courts—the *vulgo* and its vernacular.

1 The literature on this subject is enormous. For concise introductions, see Peter Stein, *Roman Law in European History* (Cambridge: 1999); Kenneth Pennington, 'Roman and Secular Law', *Medieval Latin: An Introduction and Bibliographical Guide*, ed. F. A. C. Mantello and A. G. Rigg (Washington, D.C.: 1996) 254–66; and Laurent Mayali, 'The Legacy of Roman Law', in *The Cambridge Companion to Roman Law*, ed. David Johnston (Cambridge: 2015) 374–95.

2 See Pierre Legendre, *L'autre bible de l'occident: Le monument romano-canonique. Étude sur l'architecture dogmatique des sociétés, Leçons IX* (Paris: 2009).

 | DOI 10.1163/9789004375765_004

This article will address one facet of this problem by examining translation, namely the movement of ideas between legal languages and legal cultures, in order to see how Roman, Latin-language, legal knowledge was 'vernacularized'. Because this subject is very broad, I will focus on the earliest Roman-law translation into *langue d'oïl*, the form of French spoken in northern France, which is a translation of the *Institutes* into French prose in the 1220s.

There is a vast amount of scholarship on medieval translation, modern legal translation, and law and language. This all makes it remarkable that, despite the importance of the *Corpus Iuris* in the medieval period and beyond, there is very little work on legal translation in the medieval period and, despite their importance, the translations of Roman Latin legal texts into the vernacular do not seem to have been systematically studied.[3] As Serge Lusignan noted, while the redaction of the *coutumiers* and the translation of great works of Roman law permitted the development of a legal register in the French language, this subject has received very little attention from historians of language or of law.[4] Scholarly discussion of the French legal translations boils down to pioneering articles by Willy van Hoecke, Hans van de Wouw, Claire-Hélène Lavigne, and Hélène Biu.[5]

---

3 For selected works on medieval translation, see Jeanette Beer, ed., *Medieval Translators and their Craft* (Kalamazoo: 1989); Rita Copeland, *Rhetoric, Hermeneutics, and Translation in the Middle Ages: Academic Traditions and Vernacular Texts* (Cambridge: 1991); Bruce O'Brien, *Reversing Babel. Translation among the English during an Age of Conquests, c. 800 to c. 1200* (Newark, DE: 2011); Karen L. Fresco and Charles D. Wright, eds., *Translating the Middle Ages* (Burlington, VT: 2012); Emma Campbell and Robert Mills, eds., *Rethinking Medieval Translation* (Rochester, NY: 2012). For selected works on law and language and legal translation, see David Mellinkoff, *The Language of Law* (Boston: 1963); Marshall Morris, ed., *Translation and the Law*, American Translators' Association Scholarly Monograph Series (Amsterdam: 1995); Peter M. Tiersma, *Legal Language* (Chicago: 1999); Harold Berman, *Law and Language: Effective Symbols of Community*, ed. John Witte Jr. (Cambridge: 2013); Lawrence Solan, *The Oxford Handbook of Language and Law* (Oxford: 2012); Le Cheng, King Kui Sin and Anne Wagner, eds., *The Ashgate Handbook of Legal Translation* (London: 2016). The historical portions in these treatments of law and language and legal translation are brief and ignore important medieval scholarship on the subject.

4 Serge Lusignan, *La langue de rois au Moyen Âge: Le français en France et en Angleterre* (Paris: 2004), 24.

5 Félix Olivier-Martin, *Les institutes de Justinien en français* (Paris: 1935); Willy van Hoecke, notably 'La "première réception" du droit romain et ses repercussions sur la structure lexicale des langues vernaculaires', *Medieval Antiquity* (1995) 197–217; Hans van de Wouw, 'Quelques remarques sur les versions françaises médiévales des textes de droit romain', in *El Dret Comú i Catalunya: ius proprium-ius commune a Europa*, ed. André Gouron and Aquilino Iglesia Ferreirós (Barcelona: 1993), 139–50; Claire-Hélène Lavigne, 'La traduction en vers des

These excellent articles mostly examined the methods medieval translators used to translate law. However, the wider impact and meaning of these legal translations has not been analysed in depth. At a very basic level, vernacular translations of Roman law provided a window into legal *Romanitas*—they opened the universities to those who did not understand Latin, giving them direct access to sophisticated legal ideas that otherwise they could not access. This was the direct effect of translation, to make available what was not previously available because of linguistic barrier.

Yet translation is not simply about replacing the words of one language with another, but also involves a cultural transfer, a transfer of ideas to a new culture where they may be more foreign or more familiar. Practically, this meant that there can be a tension between the original text and the lexical ability of the target language to render its concepts. Partially because of this, the original and translated versions of a text did not always offer access to the exact same ideas. Not only did each language have a special valence but it was also set in a cultural context that could not easily be translated. Beyond this, medieval translators were well known for a certain liberality in the way they transmitted knowledge, not only in their choice of words, but also for their habit of adding or removing text.

Law was no different. Vernacular translations of Roman law offered mediated, refracted versions of Latin Roman legal ideas. The translator's choice of words conditioned the translated version, as did those portions of text he excised from the original or that he added to the text. While the fact of translation is essential to understanding the transmission of Romanist legal ideas, the nature of the translation is essential to understanding what exactly was transmitted, to understanding what exactly was the difference between Roman law in a Latin and vernacular milieu. As this paper will show, the earliest translation of Roman law into *langue d'oïl* entailed a subtle transmutation of the original Latin, showing at once the desire to make Roman law accessible to a vernacular audience and how the Roman law was repackaged for its new audience and for the different preoccupations of vernacular culture.

Institutes de Justinien 1er: mythes, réalités et enterprise de versification', *Meta: Translator's Journal* 49, no. 3 (2004), 511–25; Hélène Biu 'La *Somme Acé*: prolégomènes à une étude de la traduction française de la "*Summa Azonis*" d'après le manuscrit Bibl. Vat., Reg. lat. 1063', *Bibliothèque de l'École des Chartes* 167, no. 2 (2009), 417–64.

Law and Language

To participate in the world of Latinity was to belong to an elite culture, one based on its own language, texts, and forms of thinking. This was especially true of legal Latin, replete with technical terms such as usufruct and emphyteusis, the latter adopted from Greek (both terms described different sorts of relationship with land). This sort of specialized legal jargon had developed out of ordinary language. However, though its purpose remained communication once jargonized, this language now had to be learned.[6] Students, from the Middle Ages to today, went to law school to study its particular language, phrases, and constructions and learn to 'talk like a lawyer'.[7] Law itself was also a form of language, or in the words of David Mellinkoff, a 'speech pattern with a separate identity'.[8] One might even call it a dialect, a particular form of a language used by a subgroup of society—a language that has to be learned to belong to a community of initiates.

Even within one language, as Jean-Marie Carbasse noted, the mastery of law implied a knowledge of its precise wording; from the beginning, practitioners had to pay attention to questions of vocabulary.[9] Indeed, definition and the dissecting of the meaning of words were central preoccupations for Roman as well as medieval jurists.[10] This was undoubtedly a sophisticated world of educated law that excluded the uninitiated, a world where not only language, but precise language, were quintessentially important. It thus must have excluded even the Latin-literate with no legal training, but must have especially excluded those who could not read or speak Latin at all.

The vast majority of those who ran the secular courts of northern France, participated in trials there, or watched them spoke only their own vernacular: they did not understand written language, let alone Latin, either spoken or written. At best, those who could not understand Latin had access to a refracted, mediated version of Roman law, and only if someone translated or explained it to them *viva voce*. This does not mean they did not understand law. Indeed, their immersion in the secular courts made them experts in the

6 For thoughts on the functional utility of legal language, see Lawrence M. Friedman, 'Law and Language', *George Washington Law Review* 33 (1964–1965), 563–79.

7 Tiersma, *Legal Language*, 51.

8 Mellinkoff, *The Language of Law*, 3–4. Legal language tends to use common words but gives them uncommon meanings, uses argot, formal language and terms of art (*ibid.*, 11).

9 Jean-Marie Carbasse, '*De verborum significatione*: Quelques jalons pour une histoire des vocabulaires juridiques', *Droits: Revue française de theorie juridique* 39 (2004), 3.

10 *Ibid.*, 5.

practice of law, in past precedent and current custom—all expressed orally and in the vernacular. This was in direct contrast to the Latin world of law that developed out of the 'rediscovery' of Roman law through the books of Justinian's *Institutes, Code, Digest*, and *Novels*, and the development of university legal studies around these texts.

The enthusiasm for the new Latin-language Justinianic legal studies was captured in a letter written around 1127 by a Benedictine monk to his abbot at Saint-Victor in Marseille, where he described the crowds of students flocking to Bologna to study law and noted the great benefit this knowledge could have for the monastery in its legal disputes.[11] Indeed, the popularity of Roman law in the south of France was institutionalized in 1140, when a statue of Justinian was erected in southern France in the Rouergue, inscribed with those first words of the *Institutes* that would ricochet in medieval legal texts, that imperial majesty ought be fortified not only with arms but also with laws.[12]

Legal translations show us that there was a swift and strong interest in Roman legal ideas outside of the university milieu. The desire for knowledge of Roman law outside the Latinate world is first attested in *Lo Codi*, written in Occitan (the French of southern France) in the mid-twelfth century. This was the earliest vernacular translation *qua* transmutation of Roman law. *Lo Codi* attested to the swift popularity of Roman law in the vernacular, and it was eventually translated into other vernacular languages as its influence extended into French regions such as Béarn, Anjou, Bourgogne, the Dauphiné, and beyond to Castile, Catalonia, Italy, and the Kingdom of Jerusalem.[13] The attraction of

---

11 Jean Dufour, Gérard Giordanengo and André Gouron, 'L'attrait des *leges*. Note sur la lettre d'un moine victorin (vers 1124/1127)', *Studia et documenta historiae et iuris* 45 (1979), 504–29. See generally James A. Brundage, *The Medieval Origins of the Legal Profession: Canonists, Civilians, and Courts* (Chicago: 2008), especially ch. 3.

12 Paul Ourliac, 'Une statue de Justinien en Rouergue vers 1140', in his *Les pays de Garonne vers l'an mil. La société et le droit, recueil d'études* (Toulouse: 1993), 167.

13 This early text manifested features that would also characterize thirteenth-century translations: as Johannes Kabatek has argued, this text was more than a simple translation and evinced the creative thinking so often found in medieval translation, and in medieval legal translation as well; see Johannes Kabatek, 'Lo Codi und die okzitanischen Texttraditionen im 12. und 13. Jahrhundert', in *Provenzalistik, Altokzitanistik und Okzitanistik. Geschichte und Auftrag einer europäischen Philologie (Akten der gleichnamigen Sektion des Deutschen Romanistentages in Osnabrück 1999)*, ed. Angelica Rieger (Frankfurt: 2000), 147–63. *Lo Codi* drew on Roman-law sources such as the *Summa trecensis* as well as on Occitan charters (*Ibid.*, 147). *Lo Codi* was translated into a multitude of languages including northern French *langue d'oïl*, Castilian, and even into Latin. The known manuscripts of the French translation, incipit *De summa trinitate ...*

the new knowledge, as well as the barriers to entry even for Latinists could be seen in the development of the legal lexicon, *libellus de verbis legalibus*, which appeared in southern France in *langue d'oc* as early as 1160–1170.[14]

The rise of the vernacular as a written language created the possibility of packaging conceptual, theoretical legal ideas in the vernacular. Outside of the British Isles, the European vernaculars began flourishing as written languages in the twelfth century.[15] The first real glimpse of a vernacular law in French, outside of the Oaths of Strasbourg in 842, came in the form of charters, which began appearing in the vernacular in the eleventh century and increased in frequency in the twelfth.[16] Outside of charters, written production in the French vernacular was generally in verse form throughout the twelfth century, the Song of Roland being the famous example. Prose only took off as a medium of writing in the thirteenth century with the first vernacular prose history in French written by Villehardouin around 1210 on the history of the Fourth Crusade.[17]

This set the groundwork for the translation movement that made Roman law into a form of vernacular knowledge, alongside the Latin one. The wave of translation of various Latin-language legal texts began, perhaps where it should, with Justinian's *Institutes*. This introductory 'textbook' of Roman law for students was translated sometime between 1220 and 1230.[18] This date

---

De totes les choses qui sont ou monde, are: Paris, BNF fr. 1933 (end thirteenth century), BNF fr. 1069 (1304), BNF fr. 1070 (fourteenth century). See 'CodiFr', 'Le Code de Justinien', in *Complément bibliographique du Dictionnaire Étymologique de l'Ancien Français*, ed. Frankwalt Möhren at <http://www.deaf-page.de/fr/bibl/bib99c.php>. (hereafter as DEAFBibl) (accessed May 26, 2016). See also André Gouron, 'Du Nouveau Sur Lo Codi', *Tijdschrift voor Rechtsgeschiedenis* 42, no. 2 (1975), 271–7.

14 Carbasse, '*De verbum significatione*', 9. Carbasse counts six lexicons from the mid-twelfth century.

15 The first texts in French appear in the late eighth century and, as Brian Stock noted, the development of this early written vernacular literary consciousness was a reaction to the reassertion of written Latin under Charlemagne: see Brian Stock, *The Implications of Literacy: Written Language and Models of Interpretation in the Eleventh and Twelfth Centuries* (Princeton: 1983), 24–6. However, there is no vast corpus left behind like in Ireland or Anglo-Saxon England.

16 See Thomas Brunner, 'Le passage aux langues vernaculaires dans les actes de la pratique en Occident', *Le Moyen Âge* 15 (2009), 29–72.

17 See Lusignan, *La langue de rois au Moyen Âge*, 21–3.

18 Claire-Hélène Lavigne puts the date at 1220 to 1230, in Claire-Hélène Lavigne, 'Consequences of Translation for Legal Terminology during the Middle Ages and Renaissance', in *Lexicography, Terminology, and Translation: Text-Based Studies in Honor of Ingrid Meyer* (Ottawa: 2006), 134. Institutes de Justinien, in French prose, first

is absolutely remarkable. To put it into perspective, the earliest date for the French translation of the Bible is potentially 1226 though it could be as late as 1250, the date of its earliest manuscript.[19] This means that the earliest French translation of the basic handbook to Roman law appeared at least at the same time and potentially quite a bit earlier than the French translation of the Bible. Translations of Roman law were clearly at the vanguard of what would become a general translation movement by the late thirteenth century. That these texts were coterminous affirms the place of Roman law in the hierarchy of lay desire for Latin knowledge.

Latin law continued to be translated in the 1230s and 1240s, with the French versions of the great texts of canon law, such as Tancred's *Ordo*, a procedural manual for the ecclesiastical courts, and Gratian's *Decretum*, the well-known *Concordance of Discordant Canons* that sought to harmonize the mass of conflicting canon law that preceded it.[20] The *Decretals of Gregory IX*, also known as *Liber Extra*, were translated in an abridged version between 1234 and 1245.[21]

French translations of the remainder of the *Corpus Iuris Civilis* appeared soon after. The earliest manuscript of the French prose translation of Justinian's *Code*, the part of the *Corpus* systematizing imperial legislation

---

composed around 1225 according to the *Dictionnaire Étymologique*, manuscripts: Paris, BNF ms. fr. 1064 (second half of thirteenth century), rubrics from BNF ms. fr. 1063 (second half of thirteenth century), BNF ms. fr. 498 (1342) fos. 1–47, BNF ms. fr. 1065 (second half of thirteenth century), BNF ms. fr. 1928 (end fourteenth century), BNF fr. 22970 (Paris beginning fourteenth century) fos. 2–70, Saint-Omer 439 (*ca.*1300), Montpellier Ec. de Méd. 316 (third quarter of thirteenth century), Montpellier Ec. de Méd. 373 (1296), Glasgow Hunter 63 (T.3.1) (fifteenth century), Bruxelles Bibl. roy. 10467 (*ca.*1475), Vatican, Vat. Reg. lat. 1927 (last quarter of thirteenth century), Orléans Bibl. mun. 393 (337) (last quarter of thirteenth century), London BL Roy. 20 D.IX (second half thirteenth century) only the table of contents (thirteenth century), and several versions in fragments. See 'InstJustO' in DEAFBibl.

19 Olivier-Martin, *Les institutes de Justinien en français*, xvi, n. 2.

20 *Li ordinaire de maistre Tancrez*, ms. fr. 1073, 1074, 25546, 1075 (see Paris, BNF, ms. fr. 1073 at <http://gallica.bnf.fr/ark:/12148/btv1b90596684>); for a late thirteenth-/early fourteenth-century manuscript, see Yale University, Beinecke Rare Book and Manuscript Library, New Haven Marston MS 228 (described at <http://brbl-net.library.yale.edu/pre1600ms/docs/pre1600.mars228.htm>); Leena Löfstedt. *Gratiani decretum: la traduction en ancien français du Décret de Gratien. Vol. II, Causae 1–14* (Helsinki: 1993). I would like to thank Ken Pennington for his helpful suggestions.

21 'Grégoire IX, Raymond de Peñafort, *Decretales Gregorii IX*, XIIIe s.', in *Translations médiévales: Cinq siècles de traductions en français au Moyen Âge (XIe–XVe siècles)*, ed. Claudio Galgerisi, vol. 2 (Turnhout: 2011), 506.

published in 534, dates to 1245.[22] The prose translation of Justinian's *Digest*, the collected wisdom of the jurists published in 533, probably dates to the third quarter of the thirteenth century.[23] The French prose version of the *Novels* or new laws, the fourth and last part of the *Corpus* composed between 534 and 565, also dated to the third quarter of the thirteenth century.[24] Azo's *Summa*, composed between 1208–1210, also found its vernacular form sometime in the thirteenth century.[25] Indeed, near the end of the thirteenth century, someone made a verse translation of the *Institutes*, for those who not only wanted to learn it in French but wanted to learn it by heart. Overall, then, this meant that between the 1220s and the end of the thirteenth century, the main, canonical, texts of Roman and canon law were available in the vernacular.[26]

It bears mentioning that much of this is contemporaneous with the writing of customary law in the vernacular. The customs of various areas of France were drawn up in French in texts known as the *coutumiers*. The earliest was the *Coutumes d'Anjou et du Maine* in 1246, so after the French *Institutes* of the 1220s but contemporaneous with other translations of Roman law. And we know that the translations are important for the dissemination of Roman law

22 Justinian's *Code* in French prose, incipit *Justinians dit: Nos avons proposé par l'aide de dieu le tout puissant, a metre en coumune remembrance les choses, manuscripts: Paris* BNF fr. 496 (thirteenth century) l. 1–9, BNF fr. 20119 (thirteenth century), BNF fr. 20119 (thirteenth century), BNF fr. 20120 (Orléans/Paris, *ca.*1245), BNF fr. 200 (thirteenth century), London BL Roy. 20 D.IX (second half of thirteenth century), BNF fr. 497 (fourteenth century) l. 1–9, BNF fr. 498 (1342) fos. 171–232 l. 10–12, BNF fr. 1934 (fourteenth century), BNF fr. 198 (fifteenth century), BNF fr. 20121 (fifteenth century). See 'CodeJust', 'Le Code de Justinien' in DEAFBibl.

23 *Le Digeste* (*Digesta* or *Pandectae*), incipit *Ulpians dit: il convient que tuit*, manuscripts: Montpellier Ec. de Méd. 47 (thirteenth century), Paris BNF fr. 495 (second half of the thirteenth century); BNF fr. 20118 (third quarter of the thirteenth century), BN fr. 197 (fourteenth century), Bruxelles Bibl. roy. 9234 (fourteenth century). See 'Digeste' in DEAFBibl.

24 *Novellae Constitutiones* or *Authentiques*, manuscripts: ms. London BL Roy. 20 D.IX (second half of the thirteenth century), Paris BNF fr. 498 (1342) fos. 48–170, BNF fr. 22970 (Paris, beginning fourteenth century) fos. 71–223, Bruxelles Bibl. roy. 10467 (*ca.*1475). See 'NovJust' in DEAFBibl.

25 'Azon, *Summa Azonis super Codicem*, XIIIe s.', in *Translations médiévales*, vol. 2, 327.

26 Latin, of course, continued to flourish and hundreds of manuscripts preserve the *Corpus Iuris* in Latin. It was only in 1539 with the Ordonnance of Villers-Cotterêts that French became the official language of royal legislation in France (*Ordonnance du 25 août 1539 sur le fait de la justice*, commonly referred to as the *Ordonnance de Villers-Cotteret*). In other words, this is not the story of an immediate or complete shift to the vernacular but of the dramatic expansion of the vernacular in conversation with and as a complement to Latin.

because those customary legal texts that do draw on some Roman law do not get their Roman law from the Latin originals, but from the translations. So we actually have direct proof that the translations were vehicles of transmission between Latin and vernacular, between university and secular court. And this all means that, by the end of the thirteenth century, there was a vast legal literature in the French vernacular comprised of both original composition and translation.

Translation

Modern translation theory and practice have often viewed legal translation as a case apart.[27] While medieval translation is quite different from the modern, it nonetheless remains the case that the technicality of legal language as well as the constitutive, constructive, and coercive force of legal ideas gives these ideas a special valence. Law imbues action with significance that is understood contextually, it 'is a resource in signification that enables us to submit, rejoice, struggle, pervert, mock, disgrace, humiliate, or dignify'.[28] Because of this, we have the problem of 'meaning in law', namely that 'no set of legal institutions or prescriptions exist apart from the narratives that locate it and give it meaning'.[29] The meaning of law is held together through the interpretive commitments of officials, the community, and others, who determine what law means and should be.[30]

The contextual and interpretative aspects of attributing meaning in law obviously create problems for translation. Indeed, some have even debated whether accurate legal translation is possible at all.[31] This is more of a problem for modern law, for instance in legal harmonization projects like those of the European Union. Nonetheless, it was a concern as well in the medieval world when texts like Magna Carta appear in Latin and in French, or Roman-law ideas pass from Latin to the vernacular. As Le Chang *et al.* have noted, it may be more helpful to think of 'legal translatability', or 'a space of possibilities, an autonomous realm of "cross-cultural events" within which the "system-bound" of legal concepts and notions deeply rooted in language, history and societal

27 Máirtin Mac Aodha, 'Legal Translation—An Impossible Task?', *Semiotica* 201 (2014), 207.

28 Robert Cover, 'Nomos and Narrative', in *Narrative, Violence, and the Law: The Essays of Robert Cover*, ed. Martha Minow, Michael Ryan, and Austin Sarat (Ann Arbor: 1995), 100.

29 *Ibid.*, 95–6.

30 *Ibid.*, 98–9.

31 For this debate, see Mac Aodha, 'Legal translation', 207ff.

evolution of one country are transformed and integrated into the language of another, and as a result, stratified over the course of time'.[32]

This focus on transformation and integration rather than accuracy is helpful for understanding medieval legal translation. Medieval translations were heterogeneous—there was no manual to consult, no specific modus operandi to follow.[33] Translation itself had a wider meaning than it does today. As Claudio Galgerisi noted, *translatio* was not merely a passive transfer of the values and knowledge of antiquity but a conjunction of culture and horizons of expectation, one that made the translator a *réécrivain*, a rewriter.[34] While translation could be literal, it seems more common that the medieval translator took liberties, reworking or recasting the original text. This is certainly something we can see in legal translation.

Divergences or changes between models and translations should not lead us to assume scribal stupidity or incompetence. In each case, we should consider whether the differences reflect, as Peter Dombrowski put it, an unwillingness to follow the original exactly and instead reveal a desire to recast and adapt according to their own particular needs.[35] When we open ourselves up to this, the question expands from whether or not the translator had a solid knowledge of the original language text or the content of the text, to how did the translator choose to recast and to adapt, and what needs were they fulfilling?

Roman Law in French: A New Framework for Justinian's *Institutes*

The prose translation of Justinian's *Institutes* from the 1220s can help us to begin answering this question. The *Institutes* provides a telling example of subtle recasting to fulfil new needs as a legal text transitioned from Latinate to vernacular culture. It was a handbook for students on introductory concepts of Roman law and provided a basic introduction to Roman law. It is our oldest translation of part of the *Corpus Iuris Civilis* in *langue d'oil*. It was translated twice in thirteenth-century France: first, an anonymous prose translation done

32 Anne Wagner, King Kui Sin and Le Cheng, 'Introduction: Legal Translatability Process as the "Third Space"—Insights into Theory and Practice', in *The Ashgate Handbook of Legal Translation*, ed. Le Cheng, King Kui Sin, and Anne Wagner (London: 2016), 1.

33 Jeanette Beer, 'Introduction', in *Medieval Translators and their Craft*, 1.

34 Claudio Galgerisi, 'Introduction: "La Belle captive" ou les âges du papier', in *Translations médiévales*, vol. 1, 29.

35 Peter F. Dembrowski, 'Two Old French Recastings/Translations of Andreas Capellanus's De Amore', in *Medieval Translators and their Craft*, 191.

between 1220 and 1230 and surviving in twenty-seven known manuscripts and, second, a verse translation attributed to Richard d'Annebaut completed in 1280 and surviving in only one manuscript.[36]

Generally, the early translator of the *Institutes* stuck very close to the original Latin text and was actually in the minority in terms of his approach. One of the more striking aspects of vernacular translation in the Middle Ages was the multiplicity of approaches that could be applied to the same source Latin text. As Hans van de Wouw noted, it was actually rather rare for translators to keep as closely as possible to their source to preserve its authority.[37] Instead, many translations came in the form of abridged versions of a text; other copies of this abridged version could reintroduce the omitted text as a gloss, while others seem more like collections of titles and paraphrases.[38]

Our translator of the *Institutes*, instead, was rather faithful and the changes he made were small. There was no large-scale textual change, in the sense of large sections excised, or full paragraphs added. However, the small changes reveal some important conceptual shifts between Latin and vernacular because here we have a conscientious translator who made a point of sticking closely to the text, which means that the small changes must have been deliberate, pointed, and purposeful. As we shall see, these deliberate changes were geared toward the new medium and the new audience of the text.

Each of these translation choices delivered a different idea of a shifting text, a different version of Roman law to the individual reader. Some of these small changes, in fact, were important changes in packaging that transformed the framework of the text. This is evident from the first words of the Latin and French versions of the *Institutes*. The incipit of the original Latin text is lathered in imperial triumphalism, it highlights Justinian's titles and conquests while also explaining the role of the text as a student handbook:

> In the name of our lord Jesus Christ, the Emperor Caesar Flavius Justinian, conqueror of the Alamanni, Goths, Franks, Germans, Antes, Alans, Vandals and Africans, and devout, fortunate, renowned, victorious and triumphant forever Augustus, to young enthusiasts of law.[39]

---

36 Lavigne, 'Consequences of Translation for Legal Terminology', 134.

37 van Hoecke, 'La "première réception" du droit romain et ses repercussions', 206.

38 See van de Wouw's comments on Azo's Summa and a paraphrase of the Code (Paris, BNF ms. fr. 497) in van de Wouw, 'Quelques remarques sur les versions françaises médiévales des textes de droit romain', 144–5.

39 'In nomine domini nostril Jhesu Christi, Imperator Caesar Flavius Justinianus Alamannicus Gothicus Francicus Germanicus Anticus Vandalicus Africanus, pius felix

The French translator chose to do away with nearly all of this. He excluded all the titles and conquests that dominate the original. In fact, he only really preserved the Christian inflection and the name of Justinian, simply stating: 'In the name of our lord Jesus Christ, here begin the Institutes of the Emperor Justinian' and then introduced the body of the text with 'the emperor Caesar Flavius Justinian says …'.[40] Unlike the original, the French *Institutes* nodded at the Christian context of the text and then presented it as the emperor's speech, passed from text to reader or listener, completely denuded of the imperial triumphalism of the Latin text.

The framework of the text was thus transformed in the vernacular version from imperial ideology and learning of law into the direct speech of an ancient emperor to the generalized contemporary audience.[41] The translation deliberately shifted the nature of authority in the text. While in the Latin text, Justinian's titles and conquests conferred authority and prestige upon him and thus his text, in the vernacular version it was the emperor himself: Justinian the law-giver backed by imperial authority.

This change of authority was paralleled by a change of authorship. In the Latin *Institutes*, the incipit to Book I dealt with the issue of authorship and credited the jurists who composed the text:

> The Institutes of our Lord Justinian, Perpetual Augustus, composed by Tribonian, Minister and former Chancellor of the Sacred Palace, eminent in rank, unmatched in legal knowledge; and the noble Theophilus,

---

inclitus victor ac triumphator semper augustus, cupidae legume iuventuti': see Justinian, *Justinian's Institutes*, ed. Paul Kruger, trans. Peter Birks and Grant McLeod (Ithaca: 1987), incipit.

40 'El non nostre saigneur Jhesu Crist. Ci commencent les Intitutes a l'empereeur Justinian. Li empereres Cesar, Flavius, Justinians dist …': see *Les Institutes de Jusitinien en français*, incipit. It was probably the translator's choice to change the incipit in this way, since Latin manuscripts generally preserve the original incipit (see for instance Paris, BNF ms. lat. 14343, BNF ms. lat. 4436).

41 This is not uniform across manuscripts or across time. One fourteenth-century manuscript, copied between 1300 and 1320, simply begins with 'Here begin the Institutes of the Saint emperor Justinian' (Paris, BNF ms. fr. 22970)—noteworthy because Justinian was not a saint in the West, but he was in the Eastern Orthodox Church, with a feast day on 14 November. Indeed, another manuscript copied in the 1340s offers no incipit, but begins with a beautiful illustration of Justinian handing the laws in a nicely bound codex complete with clasps to a large crowd of people (BNF ms. fr. 498).

> Jurist, and Professor of Law in this Capital City; and the Noble Dortheus, Minister, Jurist, and Professor of Law in the Splendid City.[42]

This was entirely excluded from the vernacular version. This meant that the authorship of Tribonian, Theophilus, and Dortheus was effaced and the text remained Justinian's word.[43]

We may ask why these changes to the framework. Was it to domesticate the text by removing the Byzantine titles? Was it to give the text greater immediacy, greater intimacy to the reader or listener? Or was it to present the text as ancient legal knowledge, where Justinian, like Solomon, was the font of law and justice? Was the vernacular reader more interested in the great legislator than in the great jurist? Perhaps it was all of these. One thing is certain: incipits provide a framework for their texts, and changes in framework entail changes in the substance of the texts they frame. Here, an imperial text authored by many jurists in Latin was transformed into the transmitted word of one emperor in the vernacular.

Within the actual text, there are moments when we can see a certain consciousness of historicity in the vernacular version. On one occasion, where the original Latin text referred to the jurist Gaius as 'our own Gaius' (*Gaius nostrii*), the vernacular translation reworked it as 'Gaius, our ancestor' (*Gaius, nostre ancesseur*).[44] The translator chose not to translate directly here but instead placed himself and his contemporaries in present time and the protagonists in the text in past time.

The translator did this again at another telling moment. A passage in the Latin original that referred to 'our law' (*nostrum ius*), was changed by the translator to refer to *li droit as Romains* (the law of the Romans).[45] The translator thus separated contemporary readers and listeners from the content of the text. He still claimed the past and the Roman law, but distanced it from the medieval present.

Unlike readers of the Latin original, the readers of the vernacular translation were made to understand that the text they were reading was not their own law, but the law of the Roman past. Reading a Latin and a vernacular version would thus provide a different connection to the content of the text—the Latin would provide an immediate and intimate link to the text and implied a

---

42 *Justinian's Institutes*, incipit Book I.

43 Emphasized by the explicit added in French version: 'Ci faillent les Institutez a l'empereur Justinian en françoiz' (*Les Institutes de Jusitinien en français*, explicit).

44 *Justinian's Institutes*, preface 6; *Les Institutes de Jusitinien en français*, preface 6.

45 *Justinian's Institutes*, 1.2.2; *Les Institutes de Jusitinien en français*, 1.2.2.

direct ownership of the material. Meanwhile, the vernacular version separated the reader from the past, from the Romans and their laws, and put them on the outside looking in.

Roman Law in French: The Domestication of Latin Concepts

Beyond recasting the framework of the *Institutes*, the translator made smaller translation choices that resulted in the domestication of text, making it less foreign and more familiar. The aim of the translation was less to convey a perfect imitation of the original, and more to convey something meaningful in the target language.

Even though the *Institutes* was an introductory text for students, it nonetheless contained considerable technical language. This would often lead a translator to create neologisms, new vernacular words created from the Latin to stick close to the original meaning.[46] However, the translator of the *Institutes* avoided new words. The *Institutes* contained terms like *res publica*, a form of government alien to thirteenth-century French readers (and a term that only appears in French in the fifteenth century). Instead of inventing a neologism that the readers would hopefully come to understand, the translator chose to translate that term as *empire*, a familiar term that meant not only empire, but also rule, governance, and authority.[47] In other words, the translator made lexical choices that privileged clarity in the target language over fidelity to the original meaning.[48]

The translator made other choices where he kept the translation consistent with contemporary understandings. In the translated version, *iuris prudentia*, or the philosophy and theory of law, shifted from the idea of a legal science

46 van Hoecke, 'La "première réception" du droit romain et ses repercussions', 207. van Hoecke was examining the creation of new words in Jean d'Antioche's translation of Cicero's Rhetoric. Jean, for instance, to translate *iudicatio*, the question or point at issue, Jean created the word *judicacion* (see *ibid.*). And for *translatio*, or transfer of jurisdiction, Jean created *translacion* (*ibid.*).

47 'Nostram rem publicam', see *Justinian's Institutes*, preface 7; 'nostre empires', see *Les Institutes de Jusitinien en français*, preface 7. He also translated *imperium* as *empire*, directly identifying form of government with the nature of power. For 'imperium' as 'empire', *Justinian's Institutes*, preface 1; *Les Institutes de Jusitinien en français*, preface 1.

48 Bruce O'Brien said this for the Latin translations of the Old English Laws, and our translator here proceeded in the same manner: see Bruce O'Brien, 'Translating Technical Terms in Law-Codes from Alfred to the Angevins', in *Conceptualizing Multilingualism in England, c. 800–c. 1250*, ed. Elizabeth M. Tyler (Turnhout: 2011), 61.

to *sens de droit* in French, which implied a more general understanding or knowledge of the meaning of law.[49] The translator then also adjusted the meaning of the term. The definition of jurisprudence that followed in Latin described it as the study of justice and injustice. The translator changed it to the affiliated but not coeval idea of the knowledge of right and wrong.[50] The text transitions here from legal terms of art to generalized terms, from a specialist audience to a generalized one.

The translator engaged in other acts of clarification, also adding interpretation that made sense of text in his context. We can see this is the section 'On Supervisors' (*de curatoribus*), which in the Latin original explained that 'from sexual maturity (*puberes*) to the age of twenty-five, young men and women have supervisors because, though grown-up, they are still not old enough to be able to look after their own affairs'.[51] The translator apparently found the age of sexual maturity to be too vague, replacing that part of the text with 'Males who have passed fourteen years of age and women who are able to endure the company of men receive supervisors until they are twenty-five years of age, since by this point their beards have begun to grow, nevertheless they are still of such age that they cannot conduct their own business'.[52] Here, the translator was inserting information somewhat consistent with Roman law. While normally the age of maturity for women was twelve, a male was indeed emancipated from their guardian at the age of fourteen, though remained under the supervision of a supervisor until the age of twenty-five. In the French version, however, the translator needs to explain why there is still supervision when the male in question has achieved manhood, as testified by his beard.

Claire Hélène Lavigne's work on the translations corroborates this. Lavigne compares one specific legal term for male blood relations, *adgnatorum*, to

49 'Iustitia est constans et perpetua voluntas ius suum cuique tribuere. *Iuris prudentia* est divinarum atque humanarum rerum notitia, *iusti atque iniusti* scientia', becomes 'Justice et volonté ferme et pardurable qui rant a chascun sa droiture, et *sens de droit* et conoissance des choses devines et humainez et esciences de *droit et de tort*': see *Justinian's Institutes*, 1.1.0–1.1.1; *Les Institutes de Jusitinien en* français, 1.1.0–1.1.1.

50 *Ibid.*

51 'Masculi puberes et feminae viripotentes usque ad vicesimum quintum annum completum curatores accipiunt: qui, licet puberes sint, adhuc tamen huius aetatis sunt, ut negotia sua tueri non possint': *Justinian's Institutes*, 1.23.0.

52 'Li masle qui ont passé .xiiij. ans et lez famez qui puent sosfrir conpaignie d'ome, recoivent procureurs tant que il aient aconpli .xxv. anz, car ja soit ce que la barbe lor commence a venir, non por quant il sunt ancore de tel aage que il ne puent paz procurer lor besongnes': *Les Institutes de Jusitinien en français*, 1.23.0.

see whether the translators successfully transferred the concept into French.[53] She found that both medieval translators 'try not to translate the legal term *adgnatorum* by using an equivalent, a calque, a synonymic binomial, or a circumlocution'.[54] The anonymous translator either dropped references to the term or used the umbrella term *parent*, while the verse translator used the non-technical term *cousins*—both translators, in other words, shifted the meaning because the Latin term refers specifically to the male line of the family.[55]

This is a brief account of one legal translation. It tells us that generally the translator conveyed the meaning of his text from one language into another in a way that privileged simplicity and clarity of ideas in the target language. He also added explicatory information, and on occasion made changes whose reasons are difficult to gage. This all tells us that while the translation conveyed the original Latin text for a new public, it was not transferred intact but with a modified intellectual and ideological underpinning.

Audience

The question of translation is connected to the question of audience. In fact, many of the deliberate changes our *Institutes* translator made are best understood through the lens of audience. Though the translators had to have a knowledge of both Latin and vernacular, their patrons were likely to be lay people who were investing in creating forms of vernacular knowledge. The vast majority give no clue as to the patron who commissioned the translation. At a time when mirrors of princes were encouraging secular rulers to take serious responsibility for justice and good governance, it seems plausible to look to lay lords as the patrons who were spurring these translation projects (incidentally, mirrors of princes were also being translated into French at this time).

On one preciously rare occasion, we have a hint as to why the legal translation: the verse translator of Justinian's *Institutes* explained that he created a French verse translation of the text to help those students preparing to study the same text in Latin.[56] The barrier to the study of law in Latin was

53 Lavigne, 'Consequences of Translation for Legal Terminology', 133.

54 *Ibid.*, 136.

55 *Ibid.*, 137–8.

56 'A commencier ceste besoigne/ Ne met ung enfant de gascogne/ Qui m'est baillie a introduyre/ Et a ensaigner et a duyre/ Et a tenir lay bien soubz pie./ Se il veult garder suvent/ Il y pourra asses aprendre/ Et plus legierement entendre/ Le Latin quant il le verra/ Et trouver ce qu'il querra' (ll. 21–32): Lavigne, 'La traduction en vers des *Institutes*

clearly a difficult one to surpass and some students relied on study aids such as verse translation. A student would find it useful to understand it in French, and even to memorize it—presumably the utility of putting it in verse—in order to then be able to learn and understand it in Latin. Hélène Biu noted a similar impetus for the translator of Azo's *Summa*, noting that he was a person who knew both Latin and the Roman civil law well, but used simple language in order to reach potential law students, practitioners with no Latin, or students preparing to study the texts in Latin.[57]

The audience for the Roman-law translations must otherwise be extrapolated from the texts themselves. These vernacular readers did not have to be legal professionals. Pierre Petot, for instance, argued that translations of Tancred's *Ordo* had a twofold audience; they were sometimes destined for people engaged in legal practice and teaching, but manuscripts in finer form were probably destined for great lords who were also men of letters.[58]

Translations could be grouped into two camps based on smaller clues within the manuscripts themselves. As Hans de Wouw noted, there were those that used Latin incipits to introduce each law or paragraph, and those without the Latin incipits; the former could be used by readers who were studying the manuscript with a gloss or Azo's *Summa* because their translations also retained the Latin incipits.[59] The translations with Latin incipits thus preserved the cues and equipment for a more specialized audience who would want to consult the Latin original. However, one could also read the text without a knowledge of Latin, just as the texts without Latin incipits.

Beyond this, we can trace the transmission of ideas by examining later texts which used the translations, and seeing how they used them. In fact, we do know of one group that used the *Institutes* translation. It actually circulated successfully amongst lay jurists who composed the customary laws of northern France and was used by the authors of three thirteenth-century *coutumiers*: Pierre de Fontaines' *Conseil à un ami*, the *Etablissments de Saint Louis*, and the *Livre de Jostice et de Plet*.[60]

de Justinien 1er', 515. This hints that even university-bound students did not have the best knowledge of Latin, and had to know the text before going off to university, preferably learning it by heart, as facilitated by this verse translation.

57 See generally Biu, 'La *Somme Acé*', 417ff.

58 Pierre Petot in van de Wouw, 'Quelques remarques sur les versions françaises médiévales des textes de droit romain', 139.

59 *Ibid.*, 140.

60 Olivier-Martin, *Les Institutes de Jusitinien en français*, xiv.

Conclusion

The rise of the vernacular changed the relationship between law, language, and power. It permitted the theoretical development of a sphere of 'vernacular legality', to borrow Bruce Holsinger's phrase for a slightly different use, where vernacular law, like its Latin counterpart, also acquired a body of literature, a corpus of texts, and a group of specialist scholars.[61] This was not an apolitical act, even when the relationship between the two languages was more convivial. As Pierre Bourdieu argued, language was not a neutral agent but a representation of symbolic power.[62] The political valence of language in the medieval period has been well shown by Patrick Geary in his examination of the jostling between Latin and vernacular for the role of transmitter of sacred and administrative text, and by Gabrielle Spiegel in her study of the production of ideology in French vernacular prose historiography.[63]

Because law was quintessentially a language of power, the choice to translate also had symbolic meaning that went beyond practical advantage. Piercing the veil meant challenging the monopoly of a small group of initiates on one of the key languages of power. By transforming Latin-language specialized legal ideas into French-language generalized ones, the translations permitted foreign concepts to be domesticated, tamed, and made familiar.[64] This, in turn, permitted ideas from Roman law to keep seeping into lay court and *coutumier*, and to shift slowly the language and structure of the secular legal culture that underpinned them.

61 'Vernacular legality' in Holsinger's article describes the process by which vernacular writers used official legal vocabularies for their own purposes, and in doing so infused their own writing with an authority usually reserved for the juridical sphere: see Bruce Holsinger, 'Vernacular Legality: The English Jurisdictions of The Owl and the Nightingale', in *The Letter of the Law: Legal Practice and Literary Production in Medieval England*, ed. by Emily Steiner and Candace Barrington (Ithaca: 2002) 154–84. In a sense this also works as a good description of the development of vernacular law itself.

62 See Pierre Bourdieu, *Language and Symbolic Power*, trans. Gino Raymond and Matthew Adamson (Cambridge, MA: 1991).

63 Patrick J. Geary, *Language and Power in the Early Middle Ages* (Waltham, MA: 2013); Gabrielle Spiegel, *Romancing the Past: The Rise of Vernacular Prose Historiography in Thirteenth-Century France* (Berkeley: 1993).

64 For the foreignization and domestication of concepts in translation, see Cheng, Sin and Wagner, 'Introduction: Legal Translatability Process as the "Third Space"—Insights into Theory and Practice', 1.

So, what, as Bruce O'Brien has asked, did translators like the one of the *Institutes* think they were doing when they were translating?[65] Looming behind all of this was, of course, the Tower of Babel, where human sin led to the loss of mutual understanding. The tower certainly loomed over the theory of language, but it was no guide to the translator. Instead, our legal translators fell more in the line of ancient and medieval thinking about the translator's method. Cicero, for instance, explained that he translated speeches from Greek to Latin

> not as a translator, but as an orator, using the same thoughts and manners … in fitting words according to our practice. I didn't think it necessary to render them word for word, but instead to preserve all the style and force of the words. For I didn't think I should count them out for the reader, but instead should weigh them.[66]

Our *Institutes* translator certainly did something similar—he chose words that were fitting according to the French vernacular and, like Cicero, he clearly weighed his words. The changes in the *Institutes* were clearly precise and deliberate: the deliberate choice to change the framing of the text, and so change the nature of authority as well as authorship, the deliberate choice to separate past and present, and the deliberate choice to convey Roman law in the existing French lexicon, rather than to stick closer to the original meaning by inventing neologisms.

Yet our translator also went beyond Cicero. As we have seen, it was not simply a matter of preservation of original meaning for him. The translation of the *Institutes* brought out something more or something different than what was in the Latin original. It was something that better fit the culture and language of its new lay, vernacular milieu. And here, he may have taken a cue from Isidore of Seville, who thought a good translation was not only literal and clear, but also, as he explained, it should express something 'truer' (*verior*).[67]

---

65 O'Brien, *Reversing Babel*, 14.

66 *Ibid.*, 44.

67 *Ibid.*, 43; Isidore of Seville, *The Etymologies of Isidore of Seville*, trans. by Stephen A. Barney, W. J. Lewis, J. A. Beach and Oliver Berghof (Cambridge: 2006), 6.4. This is how Isidore describes Jerome's translation of the Vulgate in a passage that appears in many but not all of the manuscripts.

Bibliography

Beer, Jeanette, editor. *Medieval Translators and their Craft*. Kalamazoo: 1989.
Berman, Harold. *Law and Language: Effective Symbols of Community*, edited by John Witte Jr. Cambridge: 2013.
Biu, Hélène. 'La *Somme Acé*: prolégomènes à une étude de la traduction française de la "*Summa Azonis*" d'après le manuscrit Bibl. Vat., Reg. lat. 1063'. *Bibliothèque de l'École des Chartes* 167, no. 2 (2009): 417–64.
Bourdieu, Pierre. *Language and Symbolic Power*, translated by Gino Raymond and Matthew Adamson Cambridge (MA): 1991.
Brundage, James A. *The Medieval Origins of the Legal Profession: Canonists, Civilians, and Courts*. Chicago: 2008.
Brunner, Thomas. 'Le passage aux langues vernaculaires dans les actes de la pratique en Occident'. *Le Moyen Âge* 15 (2009): 29–72.
Campbell, Emma and Robert Mills, editors. *Rethinking Medieval Translation*. Rochester, NY: 2012.
Carbasse, Jean-Marie. '*De verborum significatione*: Quelques jalons pour une histoire des vocabulaires juridiques'. *Droits: Revue française de theorie juridique* 39 (2004): 3–16.
Complément bibliographique du Dictionnaire Étymologique de l'Ancien Français, edited by Frankwalt Möhren, at <http://www.deaf-page.de/fr/bibl/bib99c.php>.
Copeland, Rita. *Rhetoric, Hermeneutics, and Translation in the Middle Ages: Academic Traditions and Vernacular Texts*. Cambridge: 1991.
Cover, Robert. 'Nomos and Narrative'. In *Narrative, Violence, and the Law: The Essays of Robert Cover*, edited by Martha Minow, Michael Ryan, and Austin Sarat. Ann Arbor: 1995.
Dufour, Jean, Gérard Giordanengo, and André Gouron. 'L'attrait des *leges*. Note sur la lettre d'un moine victorin (vers 1124/1127)'. *Studia et documenta historiae et iuris* 45 (1979): 504–29.
Fresco, Karen L. and Charles D. Wright, editors. *Translating the Middle Ages*. Burlington, VT: 2012.
Galgerisi, Claudio, editor. *Translations médiévales: Cinq siècles de traductions en français au Moyen Âge (XIe–XVe siècles)*, 2 vols. Turnhout: 2011.
Geary, Patrick J. *Language and Power in the Early Middle Ages*. Waltham, MA: 2013.
Gouron, André. 'Du nouveau sur Lo Codi'. *Tijdschrift voor Rechtsgeschiedenis* 42, no. 2 (1975): 271–7.
van Hoecke, Willy. 'La "première réception" du droit romain et ses repercussions sur la structure lexicale des langues vernaculaires'. *Medieval Antiquity* (1995): 197–217.
Holsinger, Bruce. 'Vernacular Legality: The English Jurisdictions of The Owl and the Nightingale'. In *The Letter of the Law: Legal Practice and Literary Production in*

Medieval England, edited by Emily Steiner and Candace Barrington, 154–84. Ithaca: 2002.

Isidore of Seville. *The Etymologies of Isidore of Seville*, translated by Stephen A. Barney *et al.* Cambridge: 2006.

Justinian. *Justinian's Institutes*, edited by Paul Kruger and translated by Peter Birks and Grant McLeod. Ithaca: 1987.

Kabatek, Johannes. 'Lo Codi und die okzitanischen Texttraditionen im 12. und 13. Jahrhundert'. In *Provenzalistik, Altokzitanistik und Okzitanistik. Geschichte und Auftrag einer europäischen Philologie (Akten der gleichnamigen Sektion des Deutschen Romanistentages in Osnabrück 1999)*, edited by Angelica Rieger, 147–63. Frankfurt: 2000.

Lavigne, Claire-Hélène. 'Consequences of Translation for Legal Terminology during the Middle Ages and Renaissance'. In *Lexicography, Terminology, and Translation: Text-Based Studies in Honor of Ingrid Meyer*, edited by Lynne Bowker, 133–44. Ottawa: 2006.

Lavigne, Claire-Hélène. 'La traduction en vers des *Institutes* de Justinien 1er: mythes, réalités et enterprise de versification'. *Meta: Translator's Journal* 49, no. 3 (2004): 511–25.

Lawrence, M. Friedman. 'Law and Language'. *George Washington Law Review* 33 (1964–1965): 563–79.

Le Cheng, King Kui Sin and Anne Wagner, editors. *The Ashgate Handbook of Legal Translation.* London: 2016.

Legendre, Pierre. *L'autre bible de l'occident: Le monument romano-canonique. Étude sur l'architecture dogmatique des sociétés, Leçons IX.* Paris: 2009.

Löfstedt, Leena. *Gratiani decretum: la traduction en ancien français du Décret de Gratien. Vol. II, Causae 1–14.* Helsinki: 1993.

Lusignan, Serge. *La langue de rois au Moyen Âge: Le français en France et en Angleterre.* Paris: 2004.

Mac Aodha, Máirtin. 'Legal Translation—an Impossible Task?'. *Semiotica* 201 (2014): 207–21.

Mayali, Laurent. 'The Legacy of Roman Law'. In *The Cambridge Companion to Roman Law*, edited by David Johnston, 374–95. Cambridge: 2015.

Mellinkoff, David. *The Language of Law.* Boston: 1963.

Morris, Marshall, editor. *Translation and the Law.* Amsterdam: 1995.

O'Brien, Bruce. *Reversing Babel. Translation among the English during an Age of Conquests, c. 800 to c. 1200.* Newark, DE: 2011.

O'Brien, Bruce. 'Translating Technical Terms in Law-Codes from Alfred to the Angevins'. In *Conceptualizing Multilingualism in England, c. 800–c. 1250*, edited by Elizabeth M. Tyler, 57–76. Turnhout: 2011.

Olivier-Martin, Félix, editor. *Les institutes de Justinien en français.* Paris: 1935.

Ourliac, Paul. *Les pays de Garonne vers l'an mil. La société et le droit, recueil d'études.* Toulouse: 1993.

Pennington, Kenneth. 'Roman and Secular Law'. *Medieval Latin: An Introduction and Bibliographical Guide*, edited by F. A. C. Mantello and A. G. Rigg, 254–66. Washington: 1996.

Solan, Lawrence M. and Peter M. Tiersma, editors. *The Oxford Handbook of Language and Law*. Oxford: 2012.

Spiegel, Gabrielle. *Romancing the Past: The Rise of Vernacular Prose Historiography in Thirteenth-century France*. Berkeley: 1993.

Stein, Peter. *Roman Law in European History*. Cambridge: 1999.

Stock, Brian. *The Implications of Literacy: Written Language and Models of Interpretation in the Eleventh and Twelfth Centuries*. Princeton: 1983.

Tiersma, Peter M. *Legal Language*. Chicago: 1999.

van de Wouw, Hans. 'Quelques remarques sur les versions françaises médiévales des textes de droit romain'. In *El Dret Comú i Catalunya: ius proprium-ius commune a Europa*, edited by André Gouron and Aquilino Iglesia Ferreirós, 139–50. Barcelona: 1993.

CHAPTER 3

Leges Iutorum: The Medieval Latin Translation of the Law of Jutland

Michael H. Gelting

It is probably not unfair to say that questions about origins and endeavours to determine the earliest state—the archetype, or *Urtext*—of any legal text have been in the forefront of research in medieval legal history for generations. The later vicissitudes of such texts have been comparatively neglected. Moreover, considering the importance of early legal texts in the vernacular for building national identities in the nineteenth century, it is hardly surprising that medieval translations into Latin of vernacular legal texts have been particularly disregarded in modern research. Yet, as I hope to show in the present article, such translations—and their subsequent manuscript transmission—were integral parts of an ongoing and collective (even if uncoordinated) effort at achieving the best text possible, in form as well as in substance. In choosing a medieval Danish law-book as my topic, I have the advantage of being able to refer to recent research by Professor Per Andersen, whose work has shifted the focus of attention from the study of 'canonised', critically edited texts to engaging with the continuous malleability of these texts, as witnessed by the critical apparatus of the scholarly editions.[1]

The Medieval Danish Law-Books and Their Latin Versions

As was the case in the other Nordic countries, the medieval Danish law-books were written and circulated in the vernacular. From the late thirteenth century onwards, they were each connected to one of the kingdom's legal regions:[2]

1 Especially Per Andersen, *Lærd ret og verdslig lovgivning: Retlig kommunikation og udvikling i middelalderens Danmark* (Copenhagen: 2006). On the Law of Jutland, see in particular *ibid.*, 271–2.

2 Two recent and convenient surveys of the medieval Danish law-books, based on the traditional view of their history, are the introductions to the English translations of these texts in *The Danish Medieval Laws: The Laws of Scania, Zealand and Jutland*, ed. and trans. Ditlev Tamm and Helle Vogt (London and New York: 2016); and Dieter Strauch, *Mittelalterliches nordisches*

 | DOI 10.1163/9789004375765_005

The Law of Scania (*Skånske Lov*) in the easternmost provinces, now Swedish except for the Baltic island of Bornholm;[3] the Laws of Zealand—two complementary texts, 'Valdemar's Law' (*Valdemars Sjællandske Lov*) and 'Erik's Law' (*Eriks Sjællandske Lov*)—in the island of Zealand (*Sjælland*) and adjacent islands;[4] and the Law of Jutland (*Jyske Lov*) in the western part of the kingdom.[5] The bulk of the law-books were created from the late twelfth to the mid-thirteenth century, and they remained in force until the new common law for the entire kingdom (*Danske Lov*) was promulgated in 1683. This means that a remarkable number of manuscripts of these texts have survived, as well as early printed editions, all providing a complicated and fascinating picture of how these laws developed over the centuries.

Only two of these vernacular law-books are known to have been rendered in Latin during the medieval period. One of these Latin versions is a rather particular case. The original text of the Law of Scania has been dated traditionally to between 1200/02 and 1216, but the present author has suggested more recently that it was compiled in the years immediately following the Fourth Lateran Council in order to assess the impact on Danish legal practice of the decisions of the Council, not least its prohibition of clerical participation in ordeals, which are shown by the original text of the Law of Scania to have been applied extensively in early Danish law.[6] The Law of Scania was subjected to extensive editing and learned commentary in Latin almost immediately after its completion, and there seems to be no reason for questioning the medieval tradition ascribing the authorship of this so-called Paraphrase[7] to

---

Recht bis 1500: Eine Quellenkunde. Ergänzungsbände zum Reallexikon der Germanischen Altertumskunde 73 (Berlin and New York: 2011), 283–7, 290–329.

3 DGL, vol. 1:1.

4 DGL, vols. 5–7. The southern islands of Lolland, Falster, and Møn were included in the legal province of Zealand by the royal ordinance of Nyborg 26 May 1284 in its version for the legal province of Zealand, ch. 16 (DRL, 143); apart from a privilege of King Valdemar (I or II?) specifically for the inhabitants of Lolland, which was maintained by the ordinance, nothing is known about the law of these islands before 1284.

5 DGL, vols. 2–4.

6 Michael H. Gelting, 'Skånske Lov og Jyske Lov: Danmarks første kommissionsbetænkning og Danmarks første retsplejelov', in *Jura & Historie: Festskrift til Inger Dübeck som forsker*, ed. Finn Taksøe-Jensen *et al.* (Copenhagen: 2003), 43–80, at 71–6. Per Andersen, *Legal Procedure and Practice in Medieval Denmark*, trans. by Frederik and Sarah Pedersen (Leiden and Boston: 2011), 74–7. The discussions triggered by this hypothesis are irrelevant to the topic of the present article, and the matter will not be pursued further here. See also n. 8 below.

7 'Paraphrase' is a modern title for the work, but consecrated by scholarly custom. The proper medieval title is *Liber legis Scaniae*; Strauch, *Mittelalterliches nordisches Recht*, 307–8.

Anders Sunesen, archbishop of Lund from 1201/02 to his resignation in 1222/23 (†1228). Due to the intrinsic interest of the commentary in the Paraphrase as well as its illustrious authorship, this text has been the subject of several modern studies.[8]

Much less attention has been devoted to the other medieval Latin translation of a vernacular Danish law. That was the Law of Jutland, which was promulgated in an assembly of the realm in 1241, just a few days before the death of the old King Valdemar II. It seems always to have enjoyed particular esteem, due both to its royal authorisation and to its clarity and legal sophistication, and there is a still ongoing debate as to whether it was originally intended as a national law-book and not just a 'provincial law' for Jutland.[9] It is not the purpose of the present article to go deeply into that debate,[10] but it might be suggestive

8 See Sten Ebbesen, 'Andreas Sunonis', in *Medieval Nordic Literature in Latin: A Website of Authors and Anonymous Works c. 1100–1530*, ed. Stephan Borgehammar, Karsten Friis-Jensen, Lars Boje Mortensen and Åslaug Ommundsen, at <https://wikihost.uib.no/medieval/index.php/Andreas_Sunonis> (accessed 11 May, 2018), with summary bibliography; Strauch, *Mittelalterliches nordisches Recht*, 307–13, with further references; Ditlev Tamm and Helle Vogt, 'Creating a Danish Legal Language: Legal Terminology in the Medieval Law of Scania', *Historical Research* 86 (2013), 505–14, cf. also Ditlev Tamm and Helle Vogt, 'Latino o volgare: la creazione del linguaggio giuridico nella Danimarca del Duecento', in *Honos alit artes: Studi per il settantesimo compleanno di Mario Ascheri*, vol. 4, *Il cammino delle idee dal medioevo all'antico regime: Diritto e cultura nell'esperienza europea*, ed. Paola Maffei & Gian Maria Varanini (Florence: 2014), 291–301.

9 Gelting, 'Skånske Lov og Jyske Lov', 43–52. This hypothesis has not won general acceptance; judicious discussions in Andersen, *Lærd ret og verdslig lovgivning*, 293–8, and Helle Vogt, *The Function of Kinship in Medieval Nordic Legislation* (Leiden and Boston: 2010), 65–8. Later contributions to the debate: Andersen, *Legal Procedure and Practice*, 82; Per Andersen, 'Biskop Gunner, Jyske Lov og den lærde ret', in *Liber Amicorum Ditlev Tamm: Law, History and Culture*, ed. Per Andersen, Pia Letto-Vanamo, Kjell Åke Modéer and Helle Vogt (Copenhagen: 2011), 23–33, at 25–6; Michael H. Gelting, 'The Law of Jylland, the Law of Skåne, and King Valdemar's Law for Sjælland: A Revision', in *Liber Amicorum Ditlev Tamm, edited by* Andersen *et al.*, 95–105; Helle Vogt, '"With Law the Land Shall be Built": Danish Legislation for the Realm in the Thirteenth Century', in *Legislation and State Formation: Norway and its neighbours in the Middle Ages*, ed. Steinar Imsen (Trondheim: 2013), 85–99; Helle Vogt, 'Regional or Central? Legislation and Law in Thirteenth-Century Denmark', in *Denmark and Europe in the Middle Ages, c. 1000–1525: Essays in Honour of Professor Michael H. Gelting*, ed. Kerstin Hundahl, Lars Kjær and Niels Lund (Farnham: 2014), 203–14. Cf. also Erland Kolding-Nielsen, 'Danske Lov 1241', *Skalk* (2013:3), 18–27, although Kolding-Nielsen's view that the 'Laws of King Valdemar' that were confirmed by King Erik V's great charter of 1282 referred only to the Law of Jutland is hardly tenable.

10 However, see further below for the titles given to the Latin translation in the medieval manuscripts.

that the Law of Jutland was the only Danish law-book to be translated literally into Latin, probably at the very end of the thirteenth century, and, moreover, that translation was the only Danish legal text to be provided with a learned gloss in Latin, in the fifteenth century. Even nowadays, the Law of Jutland has an almost iconic status as a national symbol,[11] and the opening words of its Prologue may be seen on several Danish court houses, amongst others the one in Copenhagen: *Med Lov skal Land bygges* ('The land must be founded in the law'). Indeed, the Prologue of the Law of Jutland has been hailed for centuries as a first masterpiece of Danish prose,[12] thereby frequently glossing over that it was actually stitched together from quotes and paraphrases from Gratian's *Decretum* and, to a lesser extent, from Roman law.[13]

The national prestige of the Danish text of the Law of Jutland has completely overshadowed its medieval translation into Latin, which has hardly been studied at all since J. E. Larsen in 1827 decisively demonstrated that the Latin text was a translation from the Danish one and not the original text of the Law.[14] Only in connection with the critical edition of the Latin text did a scholarly study by the editor appear, but both that article and a certain lack of care and exactitude in the preparation of the edition itself seem to indicate that the

11 The publication of a celebratory volume on the occasion of the seventh centenary of the law in 1941, during the German occupation of Denmark, is a case in point; *Med Lov skal Land bygges*, ed. Erik Reitzel-Nielsen (Copenhagen: 1941). The enduring prestige of the text was marked by the issuing of a second *Festschrift* for the Law's 750 years: *Jydske Lov 750 år*, ed. Ole Fenger and Chr. R. Jansen (Viborg: 1991).

12 Cf. Ole Fenger, 'Jydske lovs fortale: En sejr for kong Valdemar?', *Convivium: Årsskrift for humaniora, kunst og forskning* [1] (1976), 8–29, at 8–13.

13 As shown in greatest detail by Ludvig Holberg, *Dansk og fremmed Ret: Retshistoriske Afhandlinger* (Copenhagen: 1891), 37–65, and Niels Knud Andersen, 'Kanonisk Rets Indflydelse paa Jyske Lov', in *Med Lov skal Land bygges*, ed. Reitzel-Nielsen, 84–120, at 86–101. For a plausible model of the opening words of the Law's prologue in Dig. 1.2.2.4: *civitas fundaretur legibus*, see Knut Robberstad, *Frå gamal og ny rett*, (Oslo: 1950), 13; endorsed with perhaps excessively cautious reservations by Ditlev Tamm, 'Mæth logh scal land byggæs: Betrachtungen zur Rechtsauffassung des Mittelalters mit besonderem Hinblick auf nordische und spanische Rechtsquellen', in *Festschrift für Hans Thieme zu seinem 80. Geburtstag*, ed. Karl Kroeschell (Sigmaringen: 1986), 127–139, at 132; and Ditlev Tamm, 'Med lov skal land bygges eller om dansk og fremmed ret', in *Med lov skal land bygges og andre retshistoriske afhandlinger*, ed. Inger Dübeck and Ditlev Tamm (Copenhagen: 1989), 13–21, at 17 (originally published in *Ugeskrift for retsvæsen* [1988], 313–21); cf. Ditlev Tamm, *Dansk & Europæisk retshistorie: Studieudgave* (Copenhagen: 2001), 27, 379.

14 J. E. Larsen, 'Bidrag til de gamle danske Provindsiallovbøgers Historie', in J. E. Larsen, *Samlede Skrifter*, 1:1: *Retshistoriske Afhandlinger og Foredrag* (Copenhagen: 1861), 35–210, at 139–45 (originally published in *Juridisk Tidsskrift* 14:1, [1827]).

editor did not find the Latin text particularly interesting.[15] Yet in the context of the theme of *Law and Language in the Middle Ages*, it is certainly worth some reflection that a vernacular law-book was translated into Latin at a time when a majority of translations were made from Latin into the various European vernaculars, and to look at how the text developed. It is important to point out that this Danish specimen was not an isolated curiosity, but contemporary with other, similar initiatives; the most immediately relevant parallel is the several Latin translations of Eike von Repgow's *Sachsenspiegel*, of which the first was but slightly earlier than the Latin translation of the Law of Jutland.[16]

In the absence of any direct evidence of the reasons for translating the Law of Jutland into Latin, the almost contemporary Latin translation of the *Sachsenspiegel* provides an important clue: the *Versio Vratislaviensis* was commissioned by the Bishop of Wrocław (Breslau), and this would seem to indicate that the need for a Latin translation of vernacular law arose in the ecclesiastical courts, whose procedure was in Latin, but which frequently had to take account of the rules of local law. It is likely that the Latin translation of the Law of Jutland served the same purpose, even though the wholesale loss of the records of the ecclesiastical courts of medieval Denmark has deprived us of the evidence that might have supported this hypothesis.

The material for studying the development of the Latin text of the Law of Jutland is quite rich. We have eleven manuscripts and two early sixteenth-century printed editions of the Latin text,[17] which may be compared to some seventy-nine manuscripts and two early sixteenth-century printed editions of

15 Stig Iuul, 'Jyske Lov i Retslitteraturen før 1683', in *Med Lov skal Land bygges*, ed. Reitzel-Nielsen, 121–156. Iuul's introduction to his edition of the text in *DGL*, vol. 4 (1945), is largely a shortened version of this article. For problematic aspects of Iuul's edition, see Michael H. Gelting, 'Hvem var *opænbarligh gen guth* i Jyske Lovs fortale? Et studie i Lovbogens teksthistorie', *Fund og Forskning i Det Kongelige Biblioteks samlinger* 52 (2013), 9–54, at 36 n. 130.

16 The *Versio Vratislaviensis* was written sometime between 1272 and 1292 by Conrad of Oppeln for Bishop Thomas II of Wrocław (Breslau). Other medieval Latin translations of the *Sachsenspiegel* appeared during the fourteenth century, and a revised Latin translation was printed in Cracow in 1506. It seems that the jury is still out on the question of the status of the rhymed Latin *Auctor vetus de beneficiis*. According to its latest editor Karl August Eckhardt, it was based upon the original Latin text by Eike von Repgow, which he subsequently translated into German. See, e.g., Inge Bily, Wieland Carls and Katalin Gönczi, *Sächsisch-magdeburgisches Recht in Polen: Untersuchungen zur Geschichte des Rechts und seiner Sprache* (Berlin: 2011), 76–9.

17 *DGL*, vol. 4, II–IV.

the medieval versions of the Danish text.[18] Before going into details about the Latin *Leges Iutorum*,[19] a few words about the Danish text will be necessary.

The original Danish text of the Law is represented by only—and at best—four manuscripts, one of which is incomplete.[20] All four manuscripts have such wide divergences between them that it seems impossible to construct a hypothetical 'original text' from them. The largest group of manuscripts, dubbed AB by the editor, Peter Skautrup, originates from a conservative, even linguistically archaising revision that is likely to have taken place in the 1280s, after King Erik V had suffered defeat in his attempts to expand the powers of the king's justice, and had been forced to issue his great charter of 1282 confirming the permanent validity of the laws of King Valdemar—the king who in his last days had promulgated the Law of Jutland.[21] A second revision, this time modernising and clarifying, was probably carried out in court circles during the reign of Erik VI, who died in 1319; Skautrup termed this the I group. The I revision seems to have been intended as a new authoritative text, possibly elaborated around the time when Erik VI initiated the collection and enactment of a supplement to the Law of Jutland by an ordinance of 13 March 1304.[22] However, due to the

18 *DGL*, vol. 2, XV–XXXIII.

19 Cf. below for the medieval title of the text.

20 1) Stockholm, Royal Library, MS. C 37 (since 2011 on permanent loan to the Royal Library in Copenhagen), in Skautrup's edition designated as D_1 and dated *ca.*1350, currently dated *ca.*1280, but possibly even earlier (*DGL*, vol. 2, XXV; Thomas Riis, *Les institutions politiques centrales du Danemark, 1100–1332* (Odense: 1977), 60–5; Niels Skyum-Nielsen, review of Riis, *Les institutions politiques centrales*, (Danish) *Historisk Tidsskrift*, ser. 14, 1 (1980), 525–38, at 531; an even earlier date has been proposed in a preliminary publication by Kolding-Nielsen, 'Danske Lov 1241'. 2) A manuscript that belonged to the municipal council of Flensburg, roughly dated *ca.*1300, designated as E in Skautrup's edition (*DGL*, vol. 2, XXI–XXII); earlier scholars have considered the manuscript to be from the mid-thirteenth century (*Samling af gamle danske Love, udgivne med Indledninger og Anmærkninger og tildeels med Oversættelse*, ed. J. L. A. Kolderup-Rosenvinge, vol. 3, (Copenhagen: 1837), XII), which might be more likely, since its text shows no influence from the AB version. 3) University of Copenhagen, Arnamagnæan Collection, MS. AM 286 fol., originally belonging to the cathedral chapter of Ribe and dated *ca.*1320, which begins as a separate textual version, designated as F in Skautrup's edition, but whose scribe shifted his exemplar to a manuscript of the I group in the midst of book 2, chapter 21 (*DGL*, vol. 2, XV–XVI). 4) possibly Copenhagen, Royal Library, MS. GKS 3657, 8°, a slightly later manuscript (*ca.*1350), whose text seems to be based on the collating of an exemplar of the I group with an unknown and probably earlier textual version (*DGL*, vol. 2, XXII, LXXVIII–LXXIX; Andersen, *Lærd ret og verdslig lovgivning*, 210).

21 Andersen, *Lærd ret og verdslig lovgivning*, 200–16, esp. 215.

22 Gelting, 'Hvem var *opænbarligh gen guth*', 21–2.

collapse of Danish royal power in the second quarter of the fourteenth century, the I version was never able to supersede the AB text. Both continued to be copied, and soon they spawned a group of manuscripts with a mixed text, Skautrup's group C.[23] Finally, in the 1460s, Bishop Knud Mikkelsen of Viborg elaborated revised versions of both the Danish and the Latin text of the Law of Jutland, which became dominant after having been published in print in 1504.[24]

Leges Iutorum: A Text in Constant Development

The Latin translation of the Law of Jutland will here be called the *Leges Iutorum*.[25] In fact, there is some doubt as to the title that was originally given to the Latin text. The wording *Leges Iutorum* is derived from the colophon of one of the earliest manuscripts, Copenhagen, Royal Library, MS. Ledreborg 11, 4° (fourteenth century): *Expliciunt leges Iutorum secundum Woldemarum regem*.[26] Yet the same manuscript, as well as the closely related and approximately contemporary manuscript University of Copenhagen, Arnamagnæan Collection, MS. AM 11, 8°, carries an incipit describing the law as 'the Danish law that was given by King Valdemar' (*Primus prologus in legem Dacianam a rege Waldemaro editam*), and similar designations of the law simply as 'Danish' occur in two later manuscripts.[27] Furthermore, two fifteenth-century manuscripts call the text the 'constitutions' or the 'law-books' of King Valdemar, without any geographical reference.[28] It was not really until Bishop Knud Mikkelsen's revision of the Latin text was printed in 1504 that the designation of the law

23 *DGL*, vol. 2, LXX–LXXIV.

24 Gelting, 'Hvem var *opænbarligh gen guth*', 27–42.

25 In a recent article I have cited the Latin translation under the title *Lex Iutiae*; Gelting, 'Hvem var *opænbarligh gen guth*', 24. However, since that title is not supported by any medieval manuscript, I have now opted for one of the titles that do actually occur in the medieval manuscript transmission.

26 For this and the other colophons cited in the following, see *DGL*, vol. 4, 265. The incipits mentioned in the following are printed in *DGL*, vol. 4, 1.

27 Stockholm, Royal Library, MS. De la Gardie 61 (dated 1417: *Prologus regni Dacie* [sic!]); Copenhagen, Royal Library, MS. NKS 1312b, 4° (dated 1496: *Hic incipit primus liber legalis Danorum qui constituciones regis Woldemari latinice intitulatur*, echoed in the colophon: *Explicit liber tercius legum Danorum regis Waldemari*).

28 University of Copenhagen, Arnamagnæan Collection, MS. AM 37, 4° (first half of the fifteenth century: *Incipiunt constituciones Waldemari regis*); Stockholm, Royal Library, MS. C 60 (fifteenth century; colophon: *Expliciunt libri legales domini regis W.*).

as the Law of Jutland became firmly established.[29] One of the two earliest manuscripts of the Latin text thus clearly designates it as a law for Jutland, but the fact that both that manuscript and several others (also) call it a 'Danish law' or just royal constitutions in general might hark back to a not so far past, when the text was intended as a law-book for the entire kingdom.

The Latin translation of the Law of Jutland was made from a manuscript of the AB group.[30] This conclusion is supported by a comparison of the Latin text with the characteristic variants of each branch and sub-branch of the Danish text, as detailed in the introduction to the critical edition by Peter Skautrup.[31] A detailed exposition of this comparison would exceed the bounds of the present article, but a few general conclusions might be warranted. Evidently, many of the slighter variations between the manuscripts, interesting from the point of view of the historical development of the Danish language, have no bearing on the Latin translation. However, the critical edition shows that the number of substantial variants affecting the understanding of the law is quite large. Even such variants might not necessarily be reflected in translation, but many of them are. The result of the comparison at these points is that in every case where a sub-branch of the textual transmission has a significant variant compared to what I would call the mainstream, the Latin translation follows the mainstream. This suggests that the translation was made from a manuscript that was a close copy of the original manuscript of the AB version, if it was not simply the original itself. This, as well as a curious error in the two earliest manuscripts of the Latin text—to be mentioned shortly—are strong indications that the translation was made not long after the creation of the AB version, probably around the last decade of the thirteenth century.

None of the eleven manuscripts of the *Leges Iutorum* is the original manuscript of the translation, and none seems to be a direct copy of the original. Most of them were written by scribes whose own command of the Latin language was less than perfect. Grammatical errors, misspellings and misunderstandings abound, occasionally with involuntarily amusing effect. I am particularly fond of the early fifteenth-century manuscript Uppsala University

29 The earliest manuscripts of this group all call the law *leges Iucie* and *Iutorum legisterium*. However, it was not until the issuing of the first printed edition that this version of the text gained decisive influence on its transmission. Gelting, 'Hvem var *opænbarligh gen guth*', 42–9.

30 Cf. *DGL*, vol. 4, XII–XIV.

31 *DGL*, vol. 2, XLV–CXVIII.

Library, MS de la Gardie 61 and its error *compotauerat* (drank together) for *comparuerit* (appeared in court).[32]

One particular error seems to reveal rather too much learning in one of the copyists. The first words in the Latin Prologue are *Lex est asciscens honestum prohibens contrarium* ('The Law encourages what is honest and prohibits its opposite').[33] This was a widespread maxim among medieval authors, although of uncertain origin.[34] Yet the two earliest manuscripts of the Latin Law of Jutland both commit the egregious error of writing *accidens* for *asciscens* in the opening words of the Prologue.[35] It is a mistake that would hardly have

32 DGL, vol. 4, 66.

33 Significantly, the manuscripts have several variants for the word *asciscens*, which seems to have been unfamiliar to the scribes. The correct form of the maxim is found in Stockholm, Royal Library, MS C 60 (fifteenth century), and the manuscripts reproducing Bishop Knud Mikkelsen's revised text.

34 E.g., the *Summa* of Stephen of Tournai (*Stephan von Doornick* (*Étienne de Tournai, Stephanus Tornacensis*)*: Die Summa über das Decretum Gratiani*, ed. Johann Friedrich von Schulte (Giessen: 1891 [reprint Aalen: 1965]), 9); Huguccio's *Derivationes* (L 42; *Uguccione da Pisa: Derivationes*, ed. Enzo Cecchini *et al.*, vol. 2 (Florence: 2004), 658); William of Conches in his *Glosae super Boetium* (Bk. 1, ch. 4; *Guillelmi de Conchis Glosae super Boetium*, ed. Lodi Nauta [Opera omnia Guillelmi de Conchis, 2 = Corpus Christianorum, Continuatio mediaevalis, 158] (Turnhout: 1999), 86, 176, 271); the *Summa Lipsiensis* attributed to Rodoicus Modicipassus, where it was derived from the *Summa* of Johannes Faventinus (*Summa 'Omnis qui iuste iudicat' sive Lipsiensis*, ed. Rudolf Weigand, Peter Landau, Waltraud Kozur *et al.*, [Monumenta Iuris Canonici, ser. A: Corpus Glossatorum, 7] (Vatican City: 2007), 9); St Thomas Aquinas in his reporting of a course by St Albertus Magnus on the Nicomachean Ethics (Auguste Pelzer, 'Le cours inédit d'Albert le Grand sur la Morale à Nicomaque, recueilli et rédigé par S. Thomas d'Aquin (suite et fin)', *Revue néo-scolastique de philosophie* 24 [1922], 479–520, at 480–1); Alexander of Hales in his *Summa theologica* (*Doctoris irrefragabilis Alexandri de Hales Ordinis minorum Summa theologica*, edited by Bernardinus Klumper, vol. 3 (Quaracchi: 1924), 355). Considering the close relations between Denmark and Flanders in the thirteenth century, it might not be entirely coincidental that the maxim appears in the French king Philip IV's privilege for Bruges of 1296, approximately at the same time as the Latin translation of the Law of Jutland was made (*Les Olim, ou registres des arrêts rendus par la cour du roi sous les règnes de Saint Louis, de Philippe le Hardi, de Philippe le Bel, de Louis le Hutin et de Philippe le Long*, ed. Comte Beugnot, vol. 2 (Paris: 1842), 29). The origin of the maxim is discussed in Beryl Smalley, 'William of Auvergne, John of La Rochelle and St Thomas Aquinas on the Old Law', in Beryl Smalley, *Studies in Medieval Thought and Learning from Abelard to Wyclif* (London: 1981), 121–82, at 142 (originally published in *St Thomas Aquinas: Commemorative Studies*, ed. Armand A. Maurer (Toronto: 1974), 11–71).

35 DGL, vol. 4, 1. Since these two manuscripts are the earliest surviving text witnesses, the editor adopted their reading as 'authentic'.

occurred to a scribe who was not familiar with Aristotelian philosophy.[36] If, as seems likely, the *Leges Iutorum* was translated during the reign of King Erik VI (1286–1319), it might have come into existence during the period when the Aristotelian philosopher Martinus de Dacia served as that king's chancellor (*ca.*1287–*ca.*1299).[37] The error is too silly to have been committed by the chancellor himself, but it does suggest that the text was being copied by someone who had been listening to many an Aristotelian discussion, perhaps slightly beyond his comprehension. In itself, this evidence is insufficient to assign these two manuscripts to the Danish royal chancellery, but the possibility that the Latin translation was originally made there should not be ruled out.

Despite the numerous scribal errors, most of the manuscripts show signs of a certain amount of textual criticism on the part of their scribes (or the scribes of the exemplars from which they were copied). Even the exceptionally faulty manuscript Uppsala University Library, MS. de la Gardie 61 (dated 1417), has a substantial number of places where it has improved the Latin translation compared to the other branches of the transmission of the *Leges Iutorum*. Some examples: whereas all other early manuscripts of the Latin text have erroneously placed the last sentence of bk. 1 ch. 16 as the first sentence in the next chapter, de la Gardie 61 has it in its right place; in bk. 1 ch. 21, de la Gardie 61's *si legitimauerit et nichil scotauerit* is a more precise translation of the Danish text's *æn livs han thæt i kyn oc i koll oc scøtær ækki* ('but if he legitimates [the child] and does not transfer any property [to it]') than the other Latin manuscripts' *si legitimauerit et nichil dedit/dederit*;[38] in bk. 1 ch. 39 de la Gardie 61 brings the Latin *Uxor habens maritum* into accordance with the Danish text's *Hwsfrø thær bondæ hauær oc barn with* ('A wife who has a husband and a child by [him]') by adding *si habuerit puerum cum eo*;[39] etc. In a few cases it appears that de la Gardie 61 was collated with a Danish manuscript of the I recension; this is particularly clear in bk. 1 ch. 43, where the Latin text follows the majority of the manuscripts of the Danish AB recension (*oc ær hun vmannæth oc mæth brothær i fælagh* ['and if she is unmarried and in community with

36 I wish to thank Professor Mia Münster-Swendsen, Roskilde University, for useful discussions on this point.

37 Sten Ebbesen, *Dansk middelalderfilosofi ca.1170–1536* (Copenhagen: 2002), 63–5, 79–89; Sten Ebbesen, 'Martinus de Dacia', in *Medieval Nordic Literature in Latin: A Website of Authors and Anonymous Works c. 1100–1530*, ed. Stephan Borgehammar, Karsten Friis-Jensen, Lars Boje Mortensen and Åslaug Ommundsen, at <https://wikihost.uib.no/medieval/index.php/Martinus_de_Dacia> [2012] (accessed 11 May, 2018).

38 DGL, vol. 4, 33; cf. DGL, vol. 2, 57.

39 DGL, vol. 4, 56; cf. DGL, vol. 2, 92.

her brother']) by translating *et ipsa est non maritata et in communitate cum fratre*, whereas de la Gardie 61 has a variant text that corresponds to exactly the inverse case described in the Danish I recension (*of systær ær mannæth oc æi mæth brothær i fælagh* ['if a sister is married and not in community with her brother']): *et ipsa est maritata et non in communitate cum fratre.*[40] In bk. 1 ch. 25, the earlier manuscripts of the *Leges Iutorum* follow the majority of the Danish AB manuscripts in writing *non possunt esse tutores* ('they cannot be guardians'), while de la Gardie 61 accords with the Danish I text: *non possunt esse heredes* ('they cannot inherit').[41] At times, however, the desire in de la Gardie 61 to improve upon the Latin translation resulted in new errors; this affected particularly bk. 2 ch. 22, where its version of the rules for the payment of fines by the kinsmen of an outlawed killer has become utterly confused.[42] An additional characteristic of de la Gardie 61 is an augmentation of the number of Danish words and phrases, mostly by insertion, but sometimes by replacing the Latin translation with Danish text, as in bk. 2 ch. 21, where de la Gardie 61 has *fyrræ æn sworæth wrther vm* ('before they swear about it') instead of *hoc est uno placito priusquam iuratum fuerit de premissis* ('that is, in the court session before they swear about the aforementioned matters').[43] Curiously, in bk. 2 ch. 19 de la Gardie 61 does this by inserting a piece of Danish that does not correspond to any surviving manuscript of the Danish text: the *Leges Iutorum* has *quia non concepit puerum sine uoluntate sua*, which corresponds to the Danish *for thy at barn auældæs æi with hennæ vtæn hennæ egnæ willi* ('because she cannot be forced into pregnancy against her will'), but de la Gardie 61 reads *quia quod concepit puerum theth war bæggis thæræ wyli* ('because if she conceived a child it was according to their mutual decision').[44] A similar case is de la Gardie 61's *anthing meth fwl logh wæriæ hanum ælder fallæ* ('either they clear him with a full oath, or they fell him') in bk. 3 ch. 63, which again does not correspond to any extant manuscript of the Danish text.[45] Another Danish passage that is specific to de la Gardie 61 turns the legal rule upside down, saying that if a person who infringes the peace of God by drawing blood (*blothwidæ gorthæ*) is more than fourteen years old, he has to pay fines to the victim as well as to the king and the bishop, except in case of manslaughter (bk. 2 ch. 47); evidently the rule was that if such a culprit was less than fifteen years old,

40 DGL, vol. 4, 59; cf. DGL, vol. 2, 99.

41 DGL, vol. 4, 38; cf. DGL, vol. 2, 66–7.

42 DGL, vol. 4, 105–6.

43 DGL, vol. 4, 105.

44 DGL, vol. 4, 103; cf. DGL, vol. 2, 175.

45 DGL, vol. 4, 259; cf. DGL, vol. 2, 494 (bk 3, art. 64).

he was liable to pay a fine to the victim only and not to king or bishop, except in case of manslaughter: *Qui minor est XV annorum satisfaciat leso et nichil regi uel episcopo nisi pro solo homicidio.*[46]

Other manuscripts of the *Leges Iutorum* show similar corrections of the Latin text, based on collating with manuscripts of the Danish text, albeit less frequently. Thus University of Copenhagen, Arnamagnæan Collection, MS AM 443, 12° is the only one of the Latin manuscripts to add a passage corresponding to the Danish text in the rather free translation of the rules concerning the appointment of 'nominated men' (*nævninge*) in bk. 2 ch. 48: *tunc qui prius fuerat neffningus non potest adiudicari contra uoluntatem suam* ('then he who had previously been a "nominated man" cannot be assigned to it by the court against his will').[47] The scribe of this manuscript was also particularly prone to rephrasing the chapter titles.

A new phase in the development of the *Leges Iutorum* was reached in the third quarter of the fifteenth century, when a thoroughly revised version of the text was elaborated. The earliest witnesses of this recension are three sister manuscripts, which we may call the 'Bishop Knud' group, viz. Copenhagen, Royal Library, MSS GKS 3135, 4° and GKS 3136, 4°, and University of Copenhagen, Arnamagnaean Collection, MS AM 16, 8°. All three manuscripts contain a revised version of the Danish text of the Law of Jutland, the revised text of the *Leges Iutorum*, and the Latin glosses of Bishop Knud Mikkelsen of Viborg, and all three carry a colophon with the same date, 14 February 1488. There can be no doubt, however, that this revised Latin text had come into existence somewhat earlier, and that its author was Bishop Knud Mikkelsen. Bishop Knud's glosses are transmitted separately in the curious manuscript Copenhagen, Arnamagnæan Collection, MS AM 12, 8°, which may be earlier than the three '1488' manuscripts. They include references to otherwise lost judicial decisions and royal ordinances, the most recent of which is dated 1466. An investigation of the cue words in the glosses shows that with a few exceptions, most of which are cues referring to the Danish text of the Law of Jutland instead of the *Leges Iutorum*, the divergences between the cue words and the edited text of the *Leges Iutorum* are in accordance with all or some of the manuscripts of the 'Bishop Knud' group. This is particularly evident in some instances where the cue refers to passages of text that appear only in the latter group of manuscripts. It seems that before writing his glosses, Bishop Knud had established a new, critical text of the *Leges Iutorum*, apparently based on the collating of a considerable number of manuscripts. His gloss to the chapter

46 DGL, vol. 4, 126.

47 DGL, vol. 4, 128–9.

on sorcery, which occurs only in comparatively few and late manuscripts of the Danish text, is *Hoc c[apitulum] pauci libri continent* ('few books contain this chapter') which implies that he must have consulted a substantial number of manuscripts. The Bishop also based his revision of the Latin text on comparison with manuscripts of the Danish text of the Law of Jutland, occasionally resulting in an adjustment of the Latin text in conformity with the I recension of the Danish text (e.g. in bk. 1 ch. 1 the added passage *quod ita sunt eius inimici quod non potest eos habere secum in lege que dicitur logh*, corresponding to the I recension's *at the æræ swa hans uwinæ at han ma thæm æi hauæ i logh mæth sik* ['that they are so much his enemies that he cannot have them swear with him']; the latter reading was adopted also in the revised Danish text of the 'Bishop Knud' manuscripts). Although the revised Latin text improved upon the original translation on a number of points, it also introduced a few new errors.[48]

The Latin text presented by the three manuscripts is largely identical, but there are a number of variants, occasionally affecting even the substance of the law (notably in bk. 2 ch. 34, where GKS 3135, 4° gives the level of the fine as *tres marchas*, whereas the other two '1488' manuscripts follow the earlier manuscripts of the *Leges Iutorum* in reading *ix marchas*;[49] the same divergence is found in the Danish text of the Law of Jutland, where 9 marks is common in the earlier manuscripts, but especially the I recension reads 3 marks).[50] Possibly Knud Mikkelsen had left a rather untidy manuscript, reflecting his continuous work on the Latin text, and each scribe made different choices among the options offered by this exemplar.

However, if the 'Bishop Knud' manuscripts were intended to replace the earlier text versions that were circulating, that goal was not reached immediately. The earlier recensions of the Danish text continued to be copied after 1488, and not everybody appears to have been satisfied by Knud Mikkelsen's work on the Latin text. The manuscript Copenhagen, Royal Library, MS GKS 3137, 4°, a copy of the 'Bishop Knud' textual compound written in 1503 by Dr Johannes Martini, monk of the Cistercian abbey of Sorø (in Zealand, i.e. outside the legal region of Jutland), represents yet another stage of critical revision of the *Leges Iutorum*. As might be expected of a man with his academic title, Johannes Martini was a better Latinist than the scribes who produced the '1488' manuscripts, and he made numerous changes, most of

48 Knud Mikkelsen's revision of both the Danish and the Latin text of the Law of Jutland is discussed at length in Gelting, 'Hvem var *opænbarligh gen guth*', 27–39.

49 *DGL*, vol. 4, 117.

50 *DGL*, vol. 2, 203.

which improved on the text. He was also checking the Latin against the Danish text offered by the same manuscripts (thus in bk. 3 ch. 25, Johannes Martini corrected the '1488' manuscripts' *lytæ* ['damage']—which corresponds to the earlier manuscripts of the *Leges Iutorum*—into *lemmelest* ['maiming'], which must be based upon the revised Danish text of the '1488' manuscripts).[51] On the other hand, as he was living outside the legal region of Jutland, Johannes Martini was unfamiliar with the proper Latin terminology for rendering terms that were specific to the Law of Jutland. In bk. 2 ch. 39, he tried to explain the term *neffningi* by writing *ueridici id est neffninghi*; apparently he was unaware that *ueridici* was the *Leges Iutorum*'s technical term for the Law of Jutland's *sandemænd* ('truth-finders'), who were an entirely different board of jurors than the 'nominated men', *nævninge*.[52]

Whereas Dr Johannes Martini basically accepted Knud Mikkelsen's work while attempting to improve his text, another manuscript almost gives the impression of having been conceived in deliberate opposition to the bishop's recension of the Law of Jutland. Copenhagen, Royal Library, MS NKS 1312b, 4°, written in 1496 by an unnamed Dominican friar in Odense, contains both a Danish and a Latin text of the law. For the Latin text he seems to have relied upon the fifteenth-century manuscript Stockholm, Royal Library, MS C 60,[53] but being a much superior Latinist, he corrected most of the numerous and occasionally quite silly errors in his exemplar; the relationship between the manuscripts stands out most clearly in bk. 2 ch. 67, where most manuscripts of the *Leges Iutorum* read *quod putari possit* ('that it may be thought'); C 60 has the absurd misreading *quod purificari possit* ('that it may be cleansed'), which was corrected by the Odense Dominican friar into *quod purificari possit, tandem quia putari possit* ('that it may be cleansed, ultimately because it may be thought').[54] He also inserted Latin translations of passages that had previously been missing from the Latin text, e.g. in bk. 1 ch. 32 the provision concerning the payment of a fine to the king if a *fledføring*—a man who had given up his status as an independent householder because of infirmity or old age

51 *DGL*, vol. 4, 218; cf. *DGL*, vol. 3, 325.

52 Gelting, 'Hvem var *opænbarligh gen guth*', 43. On the various boards of jurors in the Law of Jutland, see Per Andersen, '"The Truth must always be Stronger": The Introduction and Development of *Næfnd* in the Danish Provincial Laws', in *New Approaches to Early Law in Scandinavia*, ed. Stefan Brink and Lisa Collinson (Turnhout: 2014), 7–36, at 21–7.

53 *DGL*, vol. 4, IX–X.

54 *DGL*, vol. 4, 146. The editor has preferred the reading *quod possit credi* ('that it may be believed'), unique to Copenhagen, Royal Library, MS Ledreborg 11, 4°, to *quod putari possit*.

and joined another household with his possessions—wounded the head of his new household; this passage is absent from all other manuscripts of the *Leges Iutorum* except Copenhagen, Royal Library, MS. Ledreborg 11, 4°, where it was added by a later hand.[55] As a good Latinist, the Dominican friar seems to have been averse to the numerous Danish words and phrases in the *Leges Iutorum*, eliminating many of them and providing others with a Latin explanation; one example is in bk. 2 ch. 48, on the procedure with 'nominated men' (*nævninge*), where the common text of the *Leges Iutorum* says that they should swear *quod uerius didicerint, utæn wild* ('what they found to be most true, without wilfulness'); to the last words in Danish, NKS 1312b, 4° adds the Latin explanation *id est sine fauore*.[56] The anonymous Dominican friar's Danish text of the Law of Jutland belongs to the B branch of the AB recension, but was collated with several other manuscripts.[57] There is no firm evidence that he was writing in conscious opposition to Knud Mikkelsen's texts, but he certainly did a serious piece of textual criticism, although even his text was not exempt from errors.

The manuscript transmission of the *Leges Iutorum* ended with the two printed editions of 1504 and 1508, which reproduced a manuscript of the 'Bishop Knud' recension. The prints also brought the manuscript transmission of the medieval recensions of the Danish text practically to a halt. The Brandis and Ghemen editions appear to have covered the needs of the market for the next forty years. When stocks of the Ghemen edition ran out, and production of manuscript copies of the Law of Jutland resumed in the mid-1540s, it was only the Danish text of the law that was copied.[58] Indirectly, this corroborates the explanation of the decision to have the Law of Jutland translated into Latin in the last years of the thirteenth century that was proposed above: the ecclesiastical courts needed not only canon law, but also a Latin version of local law in order to be able to pass judgement in the numerous cases where they had to take account of the rules of local secular law. By the 1540s, the Lutheran Reformation had been carried through (1536), eliminating the jurisdiction of the Catholic Church, and thereby also removing the practical need for the Latin text of the Law of Jutland.

55 *DGL*, vol. 4, 47.

56 *DGL*, vol. 4, 128.

57 *DGL*, vol. 2, LXX.

58 Gelting, 'Hvem var *opænbarligh gen guth*', 48.

The Interplay between Latin, Danish, and Low German

At some point in the fourteenth century, the *Leges Iutorum* served as the base for a translation of the Law of Jutland into Low German; close comparison of the texts shows that the Low German text is closer to the *Leges Iutorum* than to the Danish text of the law. The Low German text does not accord with any single branch of the manuscript transmission of the *Leges Iutorum*, and since occasionally it appears to be harmonising different variant readings in the Latin text, it was probably based upon collating several manuscripts of the latter.[59] The earliest surviving textual witness of the Low German translation was a now presumably lost manuscript from the manor of (Deutsch-)Lindau in the extreme south-eastern corner of the Duchy of Schleswig, palaeographically dated *ca.*1400.[60] Another early manuscript of the text (second half of the fifteenth century) belonged to the neighbouring parish of Gettorf at least by the sixteenth century.[61] Lindau and Gettorf are both located in the Dänischwohld, a forested border region that was settled by German-speaking immigrants between the eleventh and the thirteenth centuries. Yet the reason for translating the Law of Jutland into Low German was hardly a wish to provide a service to the as yet not very numerous German-speaking agrarian population of the duchy of Schleswig. Since the middle of the thirteenth century, continuous tensions and conflicts between the dukes of Schleswig and their cousins, the Danish kings, made the dukes increasingly dependent upon the financial and military resources of the neighbouring counts of Holstein and the wealthy nobility of Holstein. The result was a thorough Germanisation of the political leadership of the duchy, which also affected legal procedure. By 1400, the charters issued by the court-assemblies in the entire southern half of the duchy were consistently written in Low German. Although a large proportion of the population was probably bilingual, Low German was the dominant language, and this created a social and political need for a Low German translation of the law of the land.[62] There is no evidence as to where the Low German translation of the Law of Jutland was made, but the cathedral chapter of Schleswig might be a plausible guess; the choice of basing the translation on the Latin rather than the Danish version of the law-book indicates that the translation must

59 *DGL*, vol. 4, XXXIX–XLI.

60 *DGL*, vol. 4, XXXIV–XXXV, cf. XXIX. The manuscript was sold at an auction in the 1920s and has not resurfaced; photostatic copy in Copenhagen, Royal Library, MS. Phot. 8, 8°.

61 *DGL*, vol. 4, XXXIV.

62 Peter Skautrup, *Det danske sprogs historie*, vol. 2, *Fra Unionsbrevet til Danske Lov* (Copenhagen: 1947), 31–5.

have been made in a thoroughly Latinate environment. The Latin text of the *Leges Iutorum* was further used by a later copyist of the Low German text, who produced a thoroughly revised version of this text, probably in the early or mid-fifteenth century.[63]

Interestingly, the Latin text of the *Leges Iutorum* also had an impact on the transmission of the Danish text of the Law of Jutland. This is most evident in a few manuscripts which include snippets of Latin from the *Leges Iutorum* as explanations of or comments to the Danish text. This happens most extensively in the manuscript University of Copenhagen, Arnamagnæan Collection, MS. AM 9, 8°, written in 1490 by a certain Jens Nielsen (*Johannes Nicolai*) in Horsens who seems to have had a particularly prolific workshop producing copies of the Danish text of the Law of Jutland.[64] AM 9, 8° is the product of such an extensive critical collating of manuscripts of the Danish text that Peter Skautrup hesitated whether to count it as a representative of the AB or the I recension.[65] Its numerous loans from the Latin text have played a role in the discussion of the transmission of the text of the *Leges Iutorum*. In bk. 3 ch. 8, AM 9, 8° has a correct Latin rendering of a passage that is truncated in all other extant manuscripts of the *Leges Iutorum: id est fidelitatem non recipiant ab aliquibus extra proprios limites seu extra suam jurisdictionem* ('that is that they do not take fealty from anybody outside their own boundaries or outside their jurisdiction') against the *Leges Iutorum*'s *id est fidelitatem ab aliquibus* ('that is fealty from anybody' [!]).[66] The editor of the Latin text argued that this proves that Jens Nielsen drew upon a manuscript of the *Leges Iutorum* containing a better text than any of the eleven now extant manuscripts of the latter.[67] However, this conclusion is questionable. It seems to be based implicitly upon the fallacious assumption that the *Urtext* must necessarily have been perfect.[68] Yet there is no lack of erroneous or even nonsensical translations in the Latin text. Moreover, on another occasion Jens Nielsen proved himself capable of making an independent Latin translation from Danish. In bk. 3 ch. 21 of the Danish text, after the passage *for thy at aghæ waldæ mest gørsum*, he added *Quia tanta est offensa quantus est qui offenditur* ('because the offense is commensurate to

63 *DGL*, vol. 4, XLVII–XLIX.
64 *DGL*, vol. 2, LVIII–LX, LXV–LXVI.
65 *DGL*, vol. 2, LIX.
66 *DGL*, vol. 4, 202.
67 *DGL*, vol. 4, XIV.
68 Cf. Bernard Cerquiglini, *Éloge de la variante: Histoire critique de la philologie* (Paris: 1989), 90–1.

the offended person').[69] This translation is radically different from the *Leges Iutorum*'s *quia quilibet tantum offert in gørsum quantum timet de causa* (bk. 3 ch. 20: 'because each man offers as much in compensation as he fears the lawsuit').[70] It looks as if Jens Nielsen disagreed with the *Leges Iutorum*'s interpretation of the pithy and proverb-like—and slightly ambiguous—expression *aghæ waldæ mest gørsum* ('fear causes the greatest compensation') and coined his own Latin translation, which transferred the defendant's fear (or 'awe'?) from the sphere of feud and punishment to that of social hierarchy. If he was capable of this revision, there is no reason to ascribe his correct, complete Latin text in bk. 3 ch. 8 to a hypothetical lost manuscript of the *Leges Iutorum*. No doubt Jens Nielsen noticed the incomplete rendering of bk. 3 ch. 8 in the Latin text and improved it himself when inserting it into AM 9, 8°.

However, the influence from the *Leges Iutorum* was not limited to the very few Danish manuscripts that inserted Latin comments in the text. The practice of collating several manuscripts in order to improve the text was widespread also among the scribes of the Danish text. The Lachmannian concept of 'contamination' of the manuscript transmission is utterly misleading: we are dealing with rational, critical efforts to obtain the best text possible, even if the results were uneven. A case in point is the early fifteenth-century manuscript belonging to the city council of Ribe.[71] It is an AB manuscript, but no closer to the text of the *Leges Iutorum* than any other AB text. Yet its scribe was among the more critical and alert copyists of the Danish text,[72] and occasionally his work seems to be directly influenced by the Latin translation. Thus, in bk. 1 ch. 16, concerning the procedure to be followed if one sibling believes to have

69 DGL, vol. 2, 396.

70 DGL, vol. 4, 210.

71 DGL, vol. 2, XXV, where the manuscript is dated to *ca.*1450. Same dating in Lauritz Nielsen, *Danmarks middelalderlige Haandskrifter: En sammenfattende boghistorisk Oversigt* (Copenhagen: 1937), 131. However, besides the Law of Jutland, the manuscript also contains the borough statutes of Ribe of 1269, with later additions, and entirely ignores the new borough statutes issued for Ribe by King Christopher III in 1443. This suggests strongly that the manuscript is earlier than 1443; DGK, vol. 2, 19 (thus reverting to the early fifteenth-century dating of the manuscript by Kolderup-Rosenvinge, *Samling af gamle danske Love*, vol. 3, XIII); cf. Michael H. Gelting, 'Kong Svend, Slesvig Stadsret og arvekøbet i de jyske købstæder: Spor af Danmarks ældste købstadprivilegier', in *Svend Estridsen*, ed. Lasse C. A. Sonne and Sarah Croix (Odense: 2016), 195–216, at 212. The manuscript is now in the care of the Museum of Southwest Jutland, on permanent exhibition in the Old Town Hall in Ribe; I wish to thank Morten Søvsø of the Museum of Southwestern Jutland for information on the present whereabouts of the manuscript.

72 DGL, vol. 2, LXII–LXIII (ms. A^{15}).

been disadvantaged in the division of the inheritance from his or her parents, later scribes appear to have had difficulties understanding the meaning of the expression *of al lotæ vlivtæ æræ* ('if all the lots [of the inheritance] are intact'), resulting in a wide range of variants for the adjective *vlivtæ*. Faced with this difficulty and probably several more or less incomprehensible variants in the manuscripts, the scribe of the Ribe manuscript seems to have consulted the Latin text; having found there the easily intelligible rendering *indiuise*, he translated *udeelt* ('undivided'), a variant that is unique to this manuscript.[73] It is likely that quite a number of isolated variants in the manuscripts of the Danish text might be due to scribes consulting the *Leges Iutorum* in case of doubt.

The Translator's Practice

As will have become clear from the preceding discussion, the *Leges Iutorum* is interspersed with Danish words and sentences, sometimes to the point of being almost macaronic. The translator followed the Danish text closely, using a simple and straightforward Latin without any sign of literary ambition. Even the Prologue did not inspire him to demonstrate rhetorical skills, apart from flaunting his learning by inserting two Latin maxims. One of these was discussed above (*Lex est asciscens honestum prohibens contrarium*); apparently the translator despaired of finding a Latin rendering of the Prologue's Danish opening words *Med lov skal land bygges*. The other instance is an addition to the translation of the Danish Prologue's listing of the king's duties: *cum in hoc gratum deo offert seruicium, sicut scriptum est: Iudex dampnatur, cum reus absoluitur* ('because in this way he offers pleasing service to God, as it is written: the judge is condemned when a guilty man is cleared').[74] This maxim is a variant of one of the Sentences of Publilius Syrus († after 46 BC): *Iudex damnatur, ubi nocens absolvitur*.[75] In the Middle Ages, this collection was expanded by the addition of apophthegms by other authors, not least by Seneca, and it

73 DGL, vol. 2, 50; cf. DGL, vol. 4, 28–9. The inspiration for this variant could not have stemmed from the Low German translation, which has a different interpretation of this passage: that the brothers are living together without being in community of property (*an menschop*); DGL, vol. 4, 282.

74 DGL, vol. 4, 2.

75 *Die Sprüche des Publilius Syrus: Lateinisch—Deutsch*, ed. Hermann Beckby (Munich: 1969), 34.

sometimes circulated under the latter's name.[76] The translator may have cited it from memories of his schooldays.[77] Beyond that, he does not seem to have used any other models than the Danish text of the law. He seems to have been unaware that the Prologue was largely translating or paraphrasing passages from Gratian's *Decretum*. At least the relevant passages of the *Decretum* had no perceptible influence on the Latin version of the Prologue.[78]

Only in a few instances has the translator performed a superficial Latinisation of the Danish terms in the Law of Jutland. This was notably the case with the *nefningi*, the 'nominated men' (modern Danish: *nævninge*) who were competent to swear in cases of robbery and theft; the translator even created a derivative of this word designating the office of the *nefningi*: *nefningia*.[79] Mostly, however, there was no attempt to Latinise the Danish terms. The distribution of Danish expressions throughout the text is uneven. Out of 233 chapters in all, only thirty-seven do not contain any Danish terms, if we disregard the Latinised words *bondo* (the allodial householder with full legal rights) and *scotare* (the formal act of transferring land); by the late thirteenth century, both of these words had long been part and parcel of Danish legal Latin. Of the thirty-seven chapters without Danish terms, eighteen (out of fifty-six) are to be found in the law's first book, fifteen (out of 110) in the second book, and only four (out of sixty-seven) in the third book. Unsurprisingly, the concentration of Danish terms is at its highest in chapters dealing with agricultural law, but the translator also showed considerable reluctance to translating procedural terms. In many cases he would use both a Latin and a Danish term, but in such a way that the Danish term served as an explanation of the Latin, and not the other way around.

The translator's extensive use of Danish terms should not necessarily be seen as a sign of ignorance and poor Latinity. It more likely reflects a recognition that Danish legal procedures were so different from Romano-canonic law that

76 Franck Roumy, 'L'origine et la diffusion de l'adage canonique *Necessitas non habet legem*', in *Medieval Church Law and the Origins of the Western Legal Tradition: A Tribute to Kenneth Pennington*, ed. Wolfgang P. Müller and Mary E. Sommar (Washington: 2006), 301–19, at 304.

77 On the educational use of Publilius Syrus's Sentences in the Middle Ages, cf. Wilhelm Meyer, *Die Sammlungen der Spruchverse des Publilius Syrus* (Leipzig: 1877), 10–11; *Die Sprüche des Publilius Syrus*, ed. Beckby, 13.

78 Larsen, 'Bidrag til de gamle danske Provindsiallovbøgers Historie', 142. Incidentally, this observation lays to rest Stig Iuul's doubts as to whether the Latin text of the Prologue might actually be the original version; *DGL*, vol. 4, XII.

79 Bk. 2 ch. 51; *DGL*, vol. 4, 131.

the use of Romano-canonic legal terms would be misleading.[80] Occasionally the translator's familiarity with current Romano-canonic legal language shines through. In book 2, chapter 53, he apparently felt that the Latin technical term *exhibere iusticie complementum* was sufficiently close to the Danish expression for him to make the following translation:

> Nullus debet famulo suo exactionem suam committere exequendam, set debet eam committere alicui bondoni, qui potest de bonis suis satis dare, et qui in illo hæræth habitauerit, et qui possit cuilibet exhibere iusticie complementum.[81]

This renders book 2, chapter 55 in the Danish text:

> Ængi man thær lææn hauær scal thæt siin swæn sælæ at søkæ. num skal thæt sælæs annæn bondæ i hand thær thæt søkæ ma. oc i thæt læn boor. oc pænning hauær with at hætte. at gøræ thæm ræt. thær brytæs with.

> No man who has an office may entrust it to his servant to exercise it, but it shall be entrusted to another householder who is entitled to exercise it and who lives in the district of the office and has money as surety to do justice to those whom he may offend.[82]

The expression *exhibere* or *facere iusticie complementum* entered royal jurisprudence in France at the very end of the thirteenth century.[83] Assuming that the translator of the *Leges Iutorum* was writing in the 1290s, as has been argued here, his legal knowledge seems to have been quite up to date.

Hence the translator's decision not to translate numerous Danish legal terms is likely to have been determined by practical considerations of making the Latin text accessible to Danish lawyers even with mediocre Latinity. The result, however, was a text in which large parts must have been more or less incomprehensible to a Latinate reader who was not already familiar with Danish legal terms. The first part of book 2, chapter 9, may serve as an example:

80 Cf. Andersen, *Legal Procedure and Practice*, 112–18, 169–88.

81 DGL, vol. 4, 133.

82 DGL, vol. 2, 235–6. Translation by Tamm and Vogt, *The Danish Medieval Laws*, 267, with adjustments by the author. I wish to thank Helle Vogt for having given me access to their draft translation before publication.

83 Jean Hilaire, *La construction de l'État de droit dans les archives judiciaires de la Cour de France* (Paris: 2011), 201–16.

> *Si* laghlik mælæs æy æftær.
>
> *Si legaliter non fuerit prosequutum, id est*: af laghlik mælæs æi æftær oc liusæs æi sum logh ær, *et placitum, quod dicitur* laghthing, *preteriit, tunc nullus potest prosequi causam illam, que dicitur* æfter maal, *sine licencia regis. Et si rex non dederit licenciam prosequendi causam, que dicitur* æftær maal, *tunc nichil amplius potest extorqueri quam iusta emenda, hoc est xviii marchas ter, hoc est* thrinnæ attan mark pæning, *uel iuramentum, quod dicitur* kynsnænd, *si negauerit incausatus.* (etc.).[84]

The partly macaronic style of the Latin translation makes it less useful than might be expected for elucidating obscure or ambiguous passages in the Danish text. Nevertheless, there are occasions where it may fulfil such a role. A case in point is a much discussed passage in the Prologue, which says that the law that the king has given and the land has adopted, *then ma han oc ey skiftæ æth af takæ utæn landzæns wiliæ, utæn han ær opænbarlic gen guth*:[85] the king may not change or abrogate this law without the approval of the land—and then the subordinate clause poses the problem. Does it mean that if the king changes or abrogates the law without the consent of the land, he will be acting openly against God, or, on the contrary, that if the law is openly against God, the king may change or abrogate it even without the consent of the land? In this debate it has been pointed out that the *Leges Iutorum* comes out squarely in favour of the latter reading: *Nec potest eam rex reuocare uel mutare contra uoluntatem indigenarum, quorum consensu fuit imposita, nisi manifeste sit contra deum* ('Nor may the king revoke or change it against the will of men of the land, with whose consent it was imposed, unless it were manifestly contrary to God').[86] However, since the *Leges Iutorum* was based on a late thirteenth-century revision of the Danish text, this argument is incapable of resolving the question about the sense of the Prologue's original wording. I

---

84 DGL, vol. 4, 91–2. English translation: 'If no legal action is taken.—If no legal action is taken, and it is not made public according to the law, and the lawful assembly passes, then nobody may later take action without the king's permission. If the king does not give permission to take action later, then no more may be exacted than the lawful compensation, that is three times eighteen marks in money, or the oath that is called [oath by] nominated kinsmen, if the defendant denies'. Translation based on translation of the Danish text by Tamm and Vogt, *The Danish Medieval Laws*, 259, adjusted by the author.

85 DGL, vol. 2, 8–9.

86 DGL, vol. 4, 1; Anders Bjerrum, 'Utæn han ær opænbarlic gen guth', *Acta philologica Scandinavica* 22 (1954), 11–32, at 24; cf. Knud Mikkelsen's gloss to this passage, DGL, vol. 4, 6, and Iuul, 'Jyske Lov i Retslitteraturen', 139–40.

have argued elsewhere that the earliest manuscripts of the Danish text come out unequivocally in favour of the reading that the king could change the law if it was openly against God.[87] This was evidently also the interpretation of the translator of the *Leges Iutorum*.[88]

The evidence of the *Leges Iutorum* has greater weight in another discussion about the interpretation of the Danish text of the Law of Jutland. In bk. 2 ch. 50 the Danish text says that in order to qualify for serving as 'nominated' jurors (*nævninge*), the candidates had to own property worth at least three marks (i.e. to be *thriggi mark mæn*, 'men of three marks') and to be allodial householders (*athæl bøndær*) and neither stewards (*bryti*) nor tenants (*landbo*), adding: *num the thær vp haldæ for thæm full landz wærn*.[89] There have been divergent views as to the meaning of the archaic conjunction *num* introducing this last dependent clause: was it synonymous to the status of allodial householders that they were liable to full military service, or was this a further restrictive clause?[90] *Num* is absent from the possibly earliest surviving manuscript of the Danish text, Stockholm, Royal Library, MS C 37, and in several later manuscripts it was replaced by *men* ('but'). The Latin text is unambiguous at this point (bk. 2 ch. 48): the *nefningi* should be *homines trium marcharum, et qui sunt bondones, id est the thær up haldæ fult landwærn for them* ('men of three marks, and who are allodial householders, that is, such as are liable to do full military service'):[91] *num* is translated as *id est*, so that the qualification of full military service was synonymous to the qualification of being an allodial householder with property worth at least three marks.

These two examples show that the *Leges Iutorum* is an unduly neglected resource, which may have much more to offer for the interpretation of one of the foundational legal texts of medieval Denmark.

---

87 Gelting, 'Hvem var *opænbarligh gen guth*', 22–4, 51–3.

88 The translation by Tamm and Vogt, *The Danish Medieval Laws*, 242, 'That law which was given by the king and taken by the land, that law he may not change or abolish without the consent of the land, unless he is openly against God,' is a questionable reading of a possibly deliberately ambiguous passage that was introduced into the Prologue by the so-called AB text version, probably in the 1280s. It does not represent the original state of the text, but reflects the political conflict between the King and a powerful aristocratic faction in the early 1280s. See Gelting, 'Hvem var *opænbarligh gen guth*', 52.

89 *DGL*, vol. 2, 225.

90 Niels Lund, *Lið, Leding og Landeværn: Hær og samfund i Danmark i ældre middelalder* (Roskilde: 1996), 269–74, opting for the latter alternative.

91 *DGL*, vol. 4, 128.

Which Manuscript Has the 'Best' Text?

The history of the medieval reception of the *Leges Iutorum* illustrates the extent to which the Law of Jutland remained a living, dynamic text, whose development was shaped by the scribes' incessant struggle to achieve a reliable text by comparing not only various manuscripts of the text they were copying, whether Danish, Latin, or Low German, but also across the translations. Their difficulties were compounded by the fast changes that the Danish language was going through in the later Middle Ages, not least as a result of increasing influence from Low German.[92] Since the AB version of the Danish text was written in the late thirteenth century in a probably intentionally archaising language,[93] many words and turns of phrase in the law had become a challenge to the average scribe by the early fifteenth century. Some fifteenth-century manuscripts of the Danish text provided explanations in contemporary Danish for antiquated words that were no longer readily understood (notably University of Copenhagen, Arnamagnæan Collection, MS. AM 17, 8°, written in Aarhus in 1472), or they modernised the language tacitly (e.g. the previously mentioned manuscript of the municipal council of Ribe).[94] At the same time, out of reverence for 'King Valdemar's Law', few would dare to eliminate any of its chapters, even if they had become totally obsolete,[95] and many scribes were reluctant to change the wording of the Law, even though their errors show that they no longer understood the ancient words.[96]

As a result of the copyists' constant struggle with the text, if my reader should want to look for the 'best' text of the *Leges Iutorum*, it will be necessary to clarify what is meant by the 'best' text. If you want a text that approximates

---

92 Skautrup, *Det danske sprogs historie*, vol. 2, 28–119. See now also Niels Houlberg Hansen, 'The Transformation of the Danish Language in the Central Middle Ages: A Case of Europeanization?', in *Denmark and Europe in the Middle Ages*, ed. Hundahl *et al.*, 112–37, esp. 128–36.

93 Andersen, *Lærd ret og verdslig lovgivning*, 211.

94 Skautrup, *Det danske sprogs historie*, vol. 2, 11–12, 97–102.

95 Cf. the fifteenth-century glosses of Bishop Knud Mikkelsen to the *Leges Iutorum*, bk 3, ch. 1 and 2, listing the abrogated chapters in the law; *DGL*, vol. 4, 197–9. Despite their desuetude, these chapters were still being copied in all the branches of the manuscript transmission, whether in Danish, in Latin, or in Low German. In the I version of the Danish text, which is likely to represent an official revision in the early fourteenth century, one chapter in the Law's first book was eliminated because it had been superseded by rules that were added to the third book later in the thirteenth century. Gelting, 'Skånske Lov og Jyske Lov', 61–7.

96 Cf. Skautrup, *Det danske sprogs historie*, vol. 2, 11–12.

the original Latin translation, then you may use the critical edition in *Danmarks gamle Landskabslove*. But if you are looking for the most faithful rendering in Latin of the text of the Law of Jutland, I would suggest that you should use the 1496 manuscript of the Dominican friar from Odense.[97]

Concluding Reflections: The Origin, Context and Purpose of the *Leges Iutorum*

The principal focus of this article has been on the way the text of the *Law of Jutland* was rendered in Latin, not just by the original translator, but also—and not least—by a long succession of scribes and copyists from the end of the thirteenth century to the very first years of the sixteenth. It might be useful, by way of a conclusion, to sum up the results of this investigation with respect to the origin, context, and purpose of this Latin text.

This is far from easy, since neither the text itself nor any other sources contain the slightest hint of the origin of the translation. Much must remain hypothetical. It is unquestionable, however, that the translation was based on the so-called AB version of the Danish text of the *Law of Jutland*, which in all likelihood was created in the wake of the (provisional) end of the conflict over the king's jurisdiction between King Erik V and a substantial faction of the lay aristocracy, an accord that was sealed by that King's Great Charter of 1282. Sticking quite closely to what may be assumed to be the original state of the AB version, the translator was probably working very shortly after the creation of that version. This hypothesis is strengthened by the inadvertent and incorrect use of Aristotelian terminology in the two earliest manuscripts, suggesting that they were copied from an exemplar that had been copied in the royal chancellery during the tenure of the Aristotelian philosopher Martinus de Dacia, i.e. before *ca.*1299.

This does not necessarily imply that the translation was made in the royal chancellery, even though that possibility cannot be excluded. It might be tempting to surmise that the initiative to have the Law translated into Latin was triggered by the conflict between King Erik VI and the archbishop of Lund, Jens Grand. The conflict had been latent since Jens Grand's election and subsequent appointment by papal provision in 1289–90, but it broke out openly when the king arrested and imprisoned the archbishop in 1294, and,

97 It was no doubt for the same reason that Kolderup-Rosenvinge chose this late manuscript as the exemplar for his edition of the Latin text; *Samling af gamle danske Love*, ed. Kolderup-Rosenvinge, vol. 3, XV.

after his release the following year, when Jens Grand initiated a lawsuit against the king at the Papal Curia; the last years in office of Martinus de Dacia as the Danish King's chancellor were actually spent in procedures at the papal court. However, it does not seem particularly likely that the purpose of the *Leges Iutorum* was to support the pleading of either the royal or the archiepiscopal party in this lengthy process. Whereas a previous conflict between the Danish kings and Archbishop Jacob Erlandsen of Lund, in the third quarter of the thirteenth century, had in large part turned on the nature and extent of the archbishop's jurisdictional, military, and fiscal rights and obligations towards the crown, the main reason for the conflict between Erik VI and Jens Grand was the king's conviction that the archbishop was secretly abetting the king's enemies, the Norwegian king and the Danish magnates who had fled to Norway after the murder of King Erik V in 1286; several of these magnates were kinsmen of the archbishop.[98] Moreover, as has been argued in this article, the almost macaronic style of the Latin translation would have made it partly incomprehensible to anyone who was not already familiar with Danish law, and thus of scant value as an argument in the papal court.

The near-contemporary Latin translation of the *Sachsenspiegel* that was commissioned by Bishop Thomas II of Wrocław (Breslau) suggests a different setting for the *Leges Iutorum*. It is likely to have been elaborated in order to facilitate references to local secular law in procedures in the ecclesiastical courts of Denmark. This would suggest that the translation was made in an ecclesiastical milieu, and at an episcopal see rather than a monastic house. Which see is an open question. The most prominent intellectual centres in Denmark were connected to the cathedral chapters of Lund and Roskilde, but both of these were outside the legal province of Jutland. Perhaps the best educated guess would be the see of Ribe, which also had some intellectual prestige.[99]

On this hypothesis, the Latin translation of the Law of Jutland had a highly specialised purpose. While most translations and adaptations aimed to make texts accessible to readers without the necessary linguistic skills to read them in their original language, there is no reason to assume that the judges and canon

---

98 The legal aspects of the conflict with Jens Grand were analysed in particular detail by Niels Knud Andersen, *Ærkebiskop Jens Grand: En kirkeretshistorisk Undersøgelse*, 2 vols. (Copenhagen: 1943–44).

99 The cathedral school of Ribe was favoured by important donations and was clearly widely sought in the late thirteenth century; Victor Hermansen, 'Ribe Domkapitel', in *Ribe Bispesæde 948–1948: Festskrift i Tusindaaret*, ed. C. I. Scharling *et al.* (Copenhagen: 1948), 63–93, at 76–7.

lawyers operating in the ecclesiastical courts of medieval Denmark would have been unable to read the original Danish text of the *Law of Jutland*. What they gained by having a Latin translation at hand was that they were spared the effort of paraphrasing the Law in Latin every time they had to refer to it in court. German influence may have contributed to inspire the Latin translation, since translations from the vernacular into Latin seem to have been fairly common in the German cultural area.[100] Unfortunately, the loss of the records of the medieval Danish ecclesiastical courts makes it impossible to test this hypothesis about the purpose and intended audience of the *Leges Iutorum*, but the total interruption of the transmission of the Latin text after the Lutheran Reformation in 1536 does suggest that the text was closely connected to the judicial activities of the Catholic Church in medieval Denmark.

Of course the *Leges Iutorum* will always stand in the shadow of its famous Danish original. Yet it has considerable interest as a testimony of the legal culture of late medieval Denmark and of the remarkable efforts at textual criticism that were deployed by generations of scribes and copyists. It deserves much more attention than it has been afforded in the last couple of centuries.

Bibliography

Abbreviations

DGK, vol. 2: *Danmarks gamle købstadlovgivning*, vol. 2, *Nørrejylland*, edited by Erik Kroman. Copenhagen: 1952.

DGL: *Danmarks gamle landskabslove*, vol. 1:1 to vol. 8 + supplement to vol. 4, general direction Johs. Brøndum-Nielsen and Poul Johs. Jørgensen. Copenhagen: 1933–1961.

DRL: *Den danske rigslovgivning indtil 1400*, edited by Erik Kroman. Copenhagen: 1971.

Manuscripts

Copenhagen, Royal Library

GKS 3135, 4°
GKS 3136, 4°
GKS 3137, 4°
GKS 3657, 8°
Ledreborg 11, 4°
NKS 1312b, 4°
Phot. 8, 8° (Lindau manuscript)

100 N. Henkel in M.-A. Aris *et al.*, 'Übersetzer, Übersetzungen', in *Lexikon des Mittelalters*, vol. 8 (Stuttgart and Weimar: 1997), cols. 1148–63, at 1161.

Copenhagen, University of Copenhagen, Arnamagnæan Collection
AM 286, fol.
AM 37, 4°
AM 9, 8°
AM 11, 8°
AM 12, 8°
AM 16, 8°
AM 17, 8°
AM 443, 12°
Ribe, Museum of Southwest Jutland
Ribe manuscript of the Law of Jutland
Stockholm, Royal Library
C 37
C 60
Uppsala University Library
de la Gardie 61

Works Cited

Andersen, Niels Knud. *Ærkebiskop Jens Grand: En kirkeretshistorisk Undersøgelse*. 2 vols. Teologiske Studier 4 and 6. Copenhagen: 1943–4.

Andersen, Niels Knud. 'Kanonisk Rets Indflydelse paa Jyske Lov'. In *Med Lov skal Land bygges*, edited by Erik Reitzel-Nielsen, 84–120. Copenhagen: 1941.

Andersen, Per. *Lærd ret og verdslig lovgivning: Retlig kommunikation og udvikling i middelalderens Danmark*. Copenhagen: 2006.

Andersen, Per. 'Biskop Gunner, Jyske Lov og den lærde ret'. In *Liber Amicorum Ditlev Tamm: Law, History and Culture*, edited by Per Andersen, Pia Letto-Vanamo, Kjell Åke Modéer and Helle Vogt, 23–33. Copenhagen: 2011.

Andersen, Per. *Legal Procedure and Practice in Medieval Denmark*, translated by Frederik and Sarah Pedersen. Leiden and Boston: 2011.

Andersen, Per. '"The Truth Must Always be Stronger": The Introduction and Development of *Næfnd* in the Danish Provincial Laws'. In *New Approaches to Early Law in Scandinavia*, edited by Stefan Brink and Lisa Collinson, 7–36. Turnhout: 2014.

Aris M.-A., *et al.* 'Übersetzer, Übersetzungen'. In *Lexikon des Mittelalters*, vol. 8, cols. 1148–63.

Bily, Inge, Wieland Carls and Katalin Gönczi. *Sächsisch-magdeburgisches Recht in Polen: Untersuchungen zur Geschichte des Rechts und seiner Sprache*. Berlin: 2011.

Bjerrum, Anders. 'Utæn han ær opænbarlic gen guth'. *Acta philologica Scandinavica* 22 (1954): 11–32.

Cerquiglini, Bernard. *Éloge de la variante: Histoire critique de la philologie*. Paris: 1989.

Die Sprüche des Publilius Syrus: Lateinisch—Deutsch, edited by Hermann Beckby. Munich: 1969.

Doctoris irrefragabilis Alexandri de Hales Ordinis minorum Summa theologica, edited by Bernardinus Klumper, vol. 3. Quaracchi: 1924.

Ebbesen, Sten. *Dansk middelalderfilosofi ca.1170–1536*. Copenhagen: 2002.

Ebbesen, Sten. 'Andreas Sunonis'. In *Medieval Nordic Literature in Latin: A Website of Authors and Anonymous Works c. 1100–1530*, edited by Stephan Borgehammar, Karsten Friis-Jensen, Lars Boje Mortensen, and Åslaug Ommundsen, at <https://wikihost.uib.no/medieval/index.php/Andreas_Sunonis>. [2012]

Ebbesen, Sten. 'Martinus de Dacia'. In *Medieval Nordic Literature in Latin: A Website of Authors and Anonymous Works c. 1100–1530*, edited by Stephan Borgehammar, Karsten Friis-Jensen, Lars Boje Mortensen, and Åslaug Ommundsen, at <https://wikihost.uib.no/medieval/index.php/Martinus_de_Dacia>. [2012]

Fenger, Ole. 'Jydske lovs fortale: En sejr for kong Valdemar?'. *Convivium: Årsskrift for humaniora, kunst og forskning* [1] (1976): 8–29.

Gelting, Michael H. 'Skånske Lov og Jyske Lov: Danmarks første kommissionsbetænkning og Danmarks første retsplejelov'. In *Jura & Historie: Festskrift til Inger Dübeck som forsker*, edited by Finn Taksøe-Jensen, *et al.*, 43–80. Copenhagen: 2003.

Gelting, Michael H. 'The Law of Jylland, the Law of Skåne, and King Valdemar's Law for Sjælland: A Revision'. In *Liber Amicorum Ditlev Tamm: Law, History and Culture*, edited by Per Andersen, Pia Letto-Vanamo, Kjell Åke Modéer, and Helle Vogt, 95–105. Copenhagen: 2011.

Gelting, Michael H. 'Hvem var *opænbarligh gen guth* i Jyske Lovs fortale? Et studie i Lovbogens teksthistorie'. *Fund og Forskning i Det Kongelige Biblioteks samlinger*, 52 (2013): 9–54.

Gelting, Michael H. 'Kong Svend, Slesvig Stadsret og arvekøbet i de jyske købstæder: Spor af Danmarks ældste købstadprivilegier'. In *Svend Estridsen*, edited by Lasse C. A. Sonne and Sarah Croix, 195–216. Odense: 2016.

Guillelmi de Conchis Glosae super Boetium, edited by Lodi Nauta (Opera omnia Guillelmi de Conchis, 2 = Corpus Christianorum, Continuatio mediaevalis, 158). Turnhout: 1999.

Guillelmi de Conchis Glosae super Boetium, edited by Annaïg Penher at <http://hyperdonat.tge-adonis.fr/editions/html/GuilCons.html#notice_editoriale>. [2012]

Hansen, Niels Houlberg. 'The Transformation of the Danish Language in the Central Middle Ages: A Case of Europeanization?'. In *Denmark and Europe in the Middle Ages, c. 1000–1525: Essays in Honour of Professor Michael H. Gelting*, edited by Kerstin Hundahl, Lars Kjær, and Niels Lund, 112–37. Farnham and Burlington: 2014.

Hermansen, Victor. 'Ribe Domkapitel'. In *Ribe Bispesæde 948–1948: Festskrift i Tusindaaret*, edited by C. I. Scharling, *et al.*, 63–93. Copenhagen: 1948.

Hilaire, Jean. *La construction de l'État de droit dans les archives judiciaires de la Cour de France*. Paris: 2011.

Holberg, Ludvig. *Dansk og fremmed Ret: Retshistoriske Afhandlinger*. Copenhagen: 1891.

Iuul, Stig. 'Jyske Lov i Retslitteraturen før 1683'. In *Med Lov skal Land bygges*, edited by Erik Reitzel-Nielsen, 121–56. Copenhagen: 1941.

Jydske Lov 750 år, edited by Ole Fenger and Chr. R. Jansen. Viborg: 1991.

Kolding-Nielsen, Erland. 'Danske Lov 1241'. *Skalk* 3 (2013): 18–27.

Larsen, J. E. 'Bidrag til de gamle danske Provindsiallovbøgers Historie'. In J. E. Larsen, *Samlede Skrifter*, 1:1: *Retshistoriske Afhandlinger og Foredrag*, 35–210. Copenhagen: 1861 (originally published in *Juridisk Tidsskrift* 14:1, [1827]).

Les Olim, ou registres des arrêts rendus par la cour du roi sous les règnes de Saint Louis, de Philippe le Hardi, de Philippe le Bel, de Louis le Hutin et de Philippe le Long, edited by Comte Beugnot, vol. 2. Paris: 1842.

Lund, Niels. *Lið, Leding og Landeværn: Hær og samfund i Danmark i ældre middelalder*. Roskilde: 1996.

Med Lov skal Land bygges, edited by Erik Reitzel-Nielsen. Copenhagen: 1941.

Meyer, Wilhelm. *Die Sammlungen der Spruchverse des Publilius Syrus*. Leipzig: 1877.

Nielsen, Lauritz. *Danmarks middelalderlige Haandskrifter: En sammenfattende boghistorisk Oversigt*. Copenhagen: 1937.

Pelzer, Auguste. 'Le cours inédit d'Albert le Grand sur la Morale à Nicomaque, recueilli et rédigé par S. Thomas d'Aquin (suite et fin)'. *Revue néo-scolastique de philosophie* 24 (1922): 479–520.

Riis, Thomas. *Les institutions politiques centrales du Danemark, 1100–1332*. Odense: 1977.

Robberstad, Knut. *Frå gamal og ny rett*, 13. Oslo: 1950.

Roumy, Franck. 'L'origine et la diffusion de l'adage canonique *Necessitas non habet legem*'. In *Medieval Church Law and the Origins of the Western Legal Tradition: A Tribute to Kenneth Pennington*, edited by Wolfgang P. Müller and Mary E. Sommar, 301–19. Washington D.C.: 2006.

Samling af gamle danske Love, udgivne med Indledninger og Anmærkninger og tildeels med Oversættelse, edited by J. L. A. Kolderup-Rosenvinge, vol. 3. Copenhagen: 1837.

Skautrup, Peter. *Det danske sprogs historie*, vol. 2, *Fra Unionsbrevet til Danske Lov*. Copenhagen: 1947.

Skyum-Nielsen, Niels. Review of Riis, *Les institutions politiques centrales*, (Danish) *Historisk Tidsskrift* ser. 14 vol. 1 (1980): 525–38.

Smalley, Beryl. 'William of Auvergne, John of La Rochelle and St Thomas Aquinas on the Old Law'. In Beryl Smalley, *Studies in Medieval Thought and Learning from Abelard to Wyclif*, 121–82. London: 1981 (orig. 1974).

Stephan von Doornick (Étienne de Tournai, Stephanus Tornacensis): Die Summa über das Decretum Gratiani, edited by Johann Friedrich von Schulte. Giessen: 1891; reprint Aalen: 1965.

Strauch, Dieter. *Mittelalterliches nordisches Recht bis 1500: Eine Quellenkunde*. Berlin and New York: 2011.

Summa 'Omnis qui iuste iudicat' sive Lipsiensis, edited by Rudolf Weigand, Peter Landau, Waltraud Kozur *et al.* Vatican City: 2007.

Tamm, Ditlev. 'Mæth logh scal land byggæs: Betrachtungen zur Rechtsauffassung des Mittelalters mit besonderem Hinblick auf nordische und spanische Rechtsquellen'. In *Festschrift für Hans Thieme zu seinem 80. Geburtstag*, edited by Karl Kroeschell, 127–39. Sigmaringen: 1986.

Tamm, Ditlev. 'Med lov skal land bygges eller om dansk og fremmed ret'. In *Med lov skal land bygges og andre retshistoriske afhandlinger*, edited by Inger Dübeck and Ditlev Tamm, 13–21. Copenhagen: 1989 (orig. 1988).

Tamm, Ditlev. *Dansk & Europæisk retshistorie: Studieudgave*. Copenhagen: 2001.

Tamm, Ditlev, and Helle Vogt. 'Creating a Danish Legal Language: Legal Terminology in the Medieval Law of Scania'. *Historical Research* 86 (2013): 505–14.

Tamm, Ditlev, and Helle Vogt. 'Latino o volgare: la creazione del linguaggio giuridico nella Danimarca del Duecento'. In *Honos alit artes: Studi per il settantesimo compleanno di Mario Ascheri*, vol. 4, *Il cammino delle idee dal medioevo all'antico regime: Diritto e cultura nell'esperienza europea*, edited by Paola Maffei and Gian Maria Varanini, 291–301. Florence: 2014.

The Danish Medieval Laws: The Laws of Scania, Zealand and Jutland, edited and translated by Ditlev Tamm and Helle Vogt. London and New York: 2016.

Uguccione da Pisa: Derivationes, edited by Enzo Cecchini *et al.*, 2 vols. Florence: 2004.

Vogt, Helle. *The Function of Kinship in Medieval Nordic Legislation*. Leiden and Boston: 2010.

Vogt, Helle. '"With Law the Land Shall be Built": Danish Legislation for the Realm in the Thirteenth Century'. In *Legislation and State Formation: Norway and its Neighbours in the Middle Ages*, edited by Steinar Imsen, 85–99. Trondheim: 2013.

Vogt, Helle. 'Regional or Central? Legislation and Law in Thirteenth-Century Denmark'. In *Denmark and Europe in the Middle Ages, c. 1000–1525: Essays in Honour of Professor Michael H. Gelting*, edited by Kerstin Hundahl, Lars Kjær, and Niels Lund, 203–14. Farnham and Burlington: 2014.

CHAPTER 4

The Languages and Registers of Law in Medieval Ireland and Wales

Paul Russell

Introduction

The legal systems and languages considered in this chapter will be for most readers the least familiar of all the materials discussed in this volume; in fact, more generally, they are probably the least well known of the legal systems of medieval Europe. That is not to say that they are not well evidenced or well documented, but that the source material and the languages are not part of the standard curriculum of medieval or legal studies. In part this is because they have not had any effect on later legal developments but also because geographically and linguistically they have always, even within Britain and Ireland, remained marginal and very much in the shadow of the dominant legal discourse which took place in Latin, English, and French. In other words, these legal systems, which survive in numerous manuscripts from medieval Ireland and Wales, need to be introduced to a wider audience. This is one of the aims of this chapter.

The other aim is to attempt to dispel some of the confusions and myths which have grown up around the notion of 'Celtic law', and to act as an antidote to the brief and banal statements about it which preface many discussions of language and law (before they turn with a sigh of relief to the Anglo-Saxons); these tend to lump together the textual cultures of medieval Irish and medieval Welsh law (distinct in time and place and patterns of survival) and shroud it in a 'Celtic mist' of poets chanting an orally transmitted ancestral law.

We may begin with two quotations to exemplify the conventional, though outdated, approach, the first of which uses the term 'Celtic law':

> Although the British Isles have been inhabited for many thousands of years, the first people to have left historical traces are the Celts. Most of what we know about their legal system comes from Wales and Ireland.

 | DOI 10.1163/9789004375765_006

> Although Welsh and Gaelic are still spoken in the British Isles, Celtic law and its language have largely disappeared.[1]

The notion of 'Celtic law' is well established but problematic in the same way that the use of 'Celtic' in other fields has been questioned in recent years.[2] As a descriptive term, 'Celtic' has its starting point in comparative and historical linguistics as a term for a group of related languages which share a set of identifiable features and sub-groupings which distinguish them from the other Indo-European languages. This is possible to do because, since the mid-nineteenth century, the discipline has developed a series of methodological checks and balances which allows it to identify and classify language groupings; there may be debate over details but the broader framework is robust enough. Thus it is possible to reconstruct in outline some of the features of that Common Celtic language (sometimes called Proto-Celtic) on the basis of a principled comparison of its daughter languages, Irish, Manx, Scottish Gaelic, Welsh, Cornish, and Breton, and from an earlier period the remains of Celtic languages spoken in continental Europe. The difficulty is when the term is taken over to refer to features of the society and culture which spoke an apparently Celtic language, such as 'Celtic mythology' or 'Celtic law'. In both of these areas it might be possible to reconstruct the name of a god or goddess on the one hand, or the term for 'king' or 'fosterage' on the other, but it is much harder to reconstruct in any detail the structural features of a Common-Celtic religion or legal system; we simply lack the principled checks and balances (of the kinds we have for comparative linguistics) which allows us to decide that one inferred reconstruction is plausible and another not. Sims-Williams has also pointed out that this 'philological' model adopted by other fields has failed to keep up with developments in linguistics: 'At best the linguistics family-tree provides a metaphor for only one type of cultural relationship and needs to be offset by the very different linguistic models offered by the substratum theory and by linguistic typology'.[3] Transferred to other fields these other

1 Peter M. Tiersma, 'A History of the Languages of the Law', in *The Oxford Handbook of Language and Law*, ed. Lawrence M. Solan and Peter M. Tiersma (Oxford: 2012), 13–26, at 19.

2 Robin Chapman Stacey, 'Further musings on the "Celtic" in "Celtic law"', *Eolas* 9 (2016), 55–76, at 56–7; Patrick Sims-Williams, 'Celtomania and Celtoscepticism', *Cambrian Medieval Celtic Studies* 36 (1998), 1–36; Patrick Sims-Williams, 'Celtic Civilization: Continuity or Coincidence?' *Cambrian Medieval Celtic Studies* 64 (2012), 1–45; Patrick Sims-Williams, 'Post-Celtosceptisicm: a personal view', *in Saltair Saíochta, Sanasaíochta agus Seanchais: A Festschrift for Gearóid Mac Eoin*, ed. Dónall Ó Baoill, *et al.* (Dublin: 2013), 422–8.

3 Sims-Williams, 'Celtomania and Celtoscepticism', 34. It is characteristic of such transferred methodologies and frameworks that they tend to preserve a fossilized version while the

models would involve thinking about contacts and influences from adjacent and underlying or overlaid cultures, and about the possibility that apparently related characteristics might simply be typologically parallel, but unrelated.

Another approach, which is slightly less ambitious and can be more fruitful, has been to identify common features of the surviving legal materials from medieval Ireland and Wales, such as the patterns of inheritance within the kindred, the legalities of land-holding, or the enforcement of contracts by the use of a complex system of suretyship, etc., while at the same time recognizing how each of these legal systems might have changed and developed independently in reaction to local circumstances; the question then can be whether something that looks like a common feature is indeed such, or instead a later independent development in each system in response to similar needs. Fundamentally, the problem is that 'Celtic' (with a linguistic basis to its definition) is not a helpful way of talking about law, especially when what we mean about 'Celtic law' is itself only a reconstruction.[4] Better by far is it to consider medieval Irish and Welsh law each on its own terms, and not as a proxy for something else.

A second strand of assumptions about 'Celtic law' involve the supposed orality and poetical nature of the legal process:

> Like their language, the law of the British Celts has had little lasting impact on our legal system. We can, however, make some inferences about the legal language of the Britons, based on surviving manuscripts of Celtic law from Wales and Ireland. Like other Celts, the Britons seem to have expressed much of their law in legal sayings or maxims, which were in semi-poetic or rhetorical language often held together by alliteration. It may well have been that poets were guardians of this oral tradition and that they would 'sing out' these legal aphorisms when the need arose. Poets may also have acted as judges.[5]

---

methodology of the donating field moves on in the meantime; the effect is that to one familiar with both fields the borrowing field appears outmoded.

4 A further unhelpful (but probably now irresistible) use of 'Celtic' is its application as a regional term; thus, 'Celtic music' is music from the 'Celtic' countries (where 'Celtic' is itself a short-hand for countries where a Celtic language is spoken, was once spoken, or imagined to have been spoken).

5 Peter M. Tiersma, *Legal Language* (Chicago: 1999), 9; cf. also David Mellinkoff, *The Language of Law* (Boston: 1963), 36–7: 'We are told of Celtic lawyers, for centuries perpetuating a customary law in a "learned and archaic language"; the language of law was an unchanging ritual, with the slightest departure from the magic of word-for-word accuracy a violation of tribal taboo. Like prayer, the tradition is repetitive and oral'. To Mellinkoff we also owe

The apparently archaic nature of this activity (not helped by Julius Caesar's observations that druids in Gaul operated professionally without writing (*De Bello Gallico* VI.14)) has encouraged the notion that somehow 'Celtic law' (and therefore by implication Irish and Welsh law) was fundamentally an oral activity. As for 'Celtic law' we know nothing other than some broad outlines we can reconstruct, but it would be hardly surprising if a pre-literate society (as the Celtic-speaking world was until it came into contact with literacy, first via the Greeks in southern Gaul and subsequently in contact with Rome in all its manifestations) should conduct its legal business (and any other kind of business) orally. But what is clear, and will emerge from the following discussion, is that the legal process in medieval Ireland and Wales involved as much literacy as any other literate society. That said, in any culture certain aspects of the law are, and always have been, performative and involve public utterance which can often be couched in archaic and perhaps obscure language which may well involve mnemonic features such as alliteration, rhythm, and even rhyme.[6] But that would be the case in any culture and there is nothing specifically 'Celtic' about any of that; such evidence for the oral performance of law needs to put in context and such practices need not be thought of as 'archaic', but simply as part of what lawyers do.[7] Now it is certainly the case that there is evidence from medieval Ireland and Wales that poets operated in the same circles as lawyers and indeed sometimes came from the same families (cf. the late thirteenth-century Welsh poet Gruffudd ab yr Ynad Coch (lit.) 'Gruffudd, son of the Red Judge'), but this may simply be a function of how the broader society worked; they may have all belonged to the same learned class (and in Ireland probably literate from the seventh century onwards). Part of the problem may be that the modern world is used to the idea of a distinct group called 'lawyers', and that we need to think ourselves out of that anachronistic misconception.

One advantage of thinking in terms of a pure, unsullied 'Celtic law' back in the mists is that we are absolved from worrying about contact and influence from other legal systems. But when the discussion is re-calibrated and we start looking at language and register in the surviving law texts of medieval Ireland and Wales, we are forced to think about the influences at various periods of

---

the delightful suggestion that one of the three Celtic words which 'have established some connection with the law' is 'whisky' (37).

6 Robin Chapman Stacey, *Dark Speech. The Performance of Law in Early Ireland* (Philadelphia: 2007); note also that verbs based on the root **kan-* (lit.) 'sing' can also refer to other kinds of public utterance, both positive, e.g. 'teach', and negative, e.g. 'satirize'.

7 As will emerge below, it is also possible that the use of verse, or at least alliterating prose, can also be 'archaising' rather than (or as well as) being 'archaic'; see 91–2.

Roman law, ecclesiastical law, and Anglo-Norman law.[8] In other words, matters become much more complex and nuanced because we are dealing with real legal systems in real time, and not with some reconstructed abstract concept to which we can devote a nod and a passing mention before moving on the more important matters.[9]

After a brief introduction to each legal system, what follows focuses on the use of language and register.[10] The aim is to demonstrate that, first, these legal systems are worth thinking about and have something substantial to bring to the table and, secondly, that it is worth getting to grips with the languages and registers of these legal systems.

Law in Medieval Ireland

A very rich corpus of tracts survives from medieval Ireland. The core texts, which were originally composed in Old Irish, date from the seventh and eighth centuries, although they are preserved in manuscripts of the fourteenth to sixteenth centuries.[11] While much of the language was updated, there is sufficient evidence, in the form of confusions and mis-modernisations, to indicate when approximately a text was originally composed. In many cases the surviving texts do not preserve a simple text, but from the ninth century onwards many of them were glossed with interlinear and marginal comments and surrounded in extensive commentary as later lawyers tried to make

8 For Irish law, cf. Neil McLeod, 'External Influences on Medieval Irish Law: AD 600–1600', *Australian Celtic Journal* 11 (2013), 31–54; for a case study from Wales, see Meinir Harris, 'Compensation for Injury: A Point of Contact between Early Welsh and Germanic Law?' in *The Trial of Dic Penderyn and Other Essays*, ed. Thomas G. Watkin (Cardiff: 2002), 39–76.

9 It might be argued that all written forms of law are to some extent abstractions of reality, but the point here is that what survives of medieval Irish and Welsh law is no more or less real or abstract than what survives of, for example, Anglo-Saxon law.

10 The introductions to the two legal systems are in outline only; they are not intended to offer in-depth analysis but will be sufficient for the present purposes.

11 The texts are edited in Daniel A. Binchy, *Corpus Iuris Hibernici*, 6 vols. (Dublin: 1978); for discussion, see Fergus Kelly, *A Guide to Early Irish Law*, Early Irish Law Series 3 (Dublin: 1988 (2nd edn., 2005)); Thomas Charles-Edwards, 'Early Irish Law', in *A New History of Ireland*, vol. 1, ed. Dáibhí Ó Cróinín (Oxford: 2005), 331–70; Liam Breatnach, *A Companion to the* Corpus Iuris Hibernici, Early Irish Law Series 5 (Dublin: 2005); the older edition of the texts, Robert Atkinson, *et al.*, *The Ancient Laws of Ireland*, 7 vols. (Dublin: 1865–1901), is unreliable.

sense of the earlier core-texts.[12] Such is the encrustation of the later gloss and commentary that on occasions the original text is swamped and only a few words of the original text is wrapped around by a page or more of commentary. The early glossing of the texts can be especially helpful in understanding how particular words were being analysed; the glosses do different things, such as etymology (which was regarded as a way of accessing the basic sense of words), explanation, or indeed at times correction; sets of *glossae collectae* can also survive independently of a running text, and the text from which they derive may preserve better or older readings than any now surviving.[13] Not all of these core-texts are in plain prose; some texts are in verse and, occasionally and often at the beginning of a text, we find highly rhetorical alliterative prose and sometime even verse. But even though these sections have attracted considerable attention, they form a relatively small proportion of the whole corpus.[14]

The texts themselves fall into a number of groups. By far the largest collection is that know as the *Senchas Már* 'the great tradition'.[15] This collection, which seems to be have associated with the Uí Néill dynasty of the northern part of Ireland in the eighth and ninth centuries, contains texts which cover a wide range of topics including: clientship (*Cáin Aicillne* 'The Law of Base Clientship'); the proper conduct of society (*Córus Bésgnai* 'The Arrangements of Customary Behaviour'); marriage (*Cáin Lánamna* 'The Law of Couples'); neighbourly relations (*Bretha Comaithchesa* 'The Judgements of Neighbourhood'); sick-maintenance (*Bretha Crólige* 'The Judgements of Sick-maintenance'; *Bretha Déin Cécht* 'The Judgements of Dian Cécht'); laws on various animals (*Bechbretha* 'Bee-judgements', *Catṡlechta* 'Sections concerning cats', *Conṡlechta* 'Sections concerning dogs'), etc.[16] The prologue of the

12 Liam Breatnach, 'On the Glossing of Early Irish Law-texts, Fragmentary Texts, and Some Aspects of the Laws Relating to Dogs', in *Celtica Helsingiensia: Proceedings from a Symposium on Celtic Studies*, ed. Anders Ahlqvist (Helsinki: 1996), 11–20; Liam Breatnach, 'The Glossing of the Early Irish Law Tracts', in Grammatica, Gramadach, Gramadeg: *Vernacular Grammar and Grammarians in Medieval Ireland and Wales*, ed. Deborah Hayden and Paul Russell (Amsterdam: 2016), 113–32; for the later, often extensive, commentary, see Katherine Simms, 'The Contents of the Later Commentaries on the Brehon Law Tracts', *Ériu* 49 (1989), 23–40.

13 Breatnach, *Companion*, 338–53.

14 Calvert Watkins, 'Indo-European Metrics and Archaic Irish Verse', *Celtica* 6 (1966), 194–249.

15 Breatnach, *Companion*, 268–314.

16 Charles-Edwards, 'Early Irish Law', 337–47.

Senchas Már, which is somewhat later in date than the original compilation of texts, begins:

> Senchas fer n-Érenn cid conid·roīter? Comchuimne na[17] sen, ti[n]dnacul clūaise di araili, dīcetal filed, tormach o recht litre, nertad fri recht n-aicnid.
>
> What has preserved the tradition of the men of Ireland? The joint memory of the ancients, transmission from ear to ear, the chanting of poets, its augmentation by the law of Scripture, its being founded on the law of nature.[18]

We might note here the reference to oral transmission and to the joint-memory of the ancients, but at the same time there is an acknowledgement of the input from scripture. Several of the tracts of the *Senchas Már* also have narrative prefaces which set their composition at some distant (often mythological) period in the past. The point relates to claims about the antiquity of the law and tells us only about how they perceived their past, not about the reality of it.[19]

A second collection of texts, *Bretha Nemed* 'the judgements of privileged persons', probably derives from Munster in the south. The texts deal mainly with the rights and privileges of poets and, unsurprisingly given their content, tend to be presented in a highly alliterative form of verse called *rosc*(*ad*). Texts from the *Bretha Nemed* 'school' include: *Cáin Fhuithirbe* 'The Law of Fuithirbe' (written between 678 and 683); *Bretha Nemed Toísech* 'The First *Bretha Nemed*' (Breatnach 1989) and *Bretha Nemed Dédenach* 'The Last *Bretha Nemed*', both concerned with privileged persons.[20]

---

17 On reading *na* for *da* of the manuscript, see Rudolf Thurneysen, 'Aus dem irischen Recht IV', *Zeischrift für celtische Philologie* 16 (1927), 167–230, at 177–8.

18 Thurneysen, 'Aus dem irischen Recht IV', 175 (text), 177–8 (translation and notes); the main text of the manuscript is printed by Binchy, *Corpus*, II.344.24–352.7.

19 For other triads in the same context, see Proinsias Mac Cana, 'The Three Languages and the Three Laws', *Studia Celtica* 5 (1970): 62–78; Christophe Archan, '*Uraicecht becc* et les triades du droit. Les juges et leurs sources dans l'Irlande médiévale', in *Mélanges offerts en l'honneur de Pierre-Yves Lambert*, ed. Guillaume Oudaer, Gaël Hilly, and Hervé Le Bihan (Rennes: 2015), 359–75.

20 Liam Breatnach, 'The Ecclesiastical Element in the Old-Irish Legal Tract Cáin *Fhuithirbe*', *Peritia* 5 (1986), 36–52; Liam Breatnach, 'The First Third of the *Bretha Nemed Toísech*', *Ériu* 40 (1989), 1–40.

While the preceding groups consist of materials which look very much like texts for lawyers, full of explanation and discussion, there is a group of texts called *cána* 'regulations' (singular *cáin*), some of which seem to be closer to what one might think of as promulgated law, for example, *Cáin Adomnáin* 'The Law of Adomnán' (promulgated 697) on the status of non-combatants (especially that of women and children); *Cáin Iarraith* on the relationship between foster-parent and foster-child; *Cáin Sóerraith* on the relationship between lord and noble client.[21]

All the legal texts mentioned so far are written on Irish with gloss and commentary in later forms of the language, late Old Irish, Middle, and Early Modern Irish. But the ecclesiastical input in Latin should not be ignored, such as collections of canons, like the *Collectio Canonum Hibernensis*, and also penitentials.[22] In addition to these explicitly ecclesiastical texts, the subsequent transmission of these manuscripts in part at least through monastic *scriptoria* has left its mark; commentaries there contain numerous examples of Latin quotations (often in Irish orthography) throughout, many from the Bible or patristic texts and from decretals.[23]

21 Thomas Charles-Edwards, *The Medieval Gaelic Lawyer* (Cambridge: 1999).

22 Hermann Wasserschleben, ed., *Die irische Kanonensammlung* (Leipzig: 1885); Donnchadh Ó Corráin, 'Irish Law and Canon Law', in *Ireland and Europe: the Early Church*, ed. Próinséas Ní Chatháin and Michael Richter (Stuttgart: 1984), 157–166; Donnchadh Ó Corráin, 'Irish Vernacular Law and the Old Testament', in *Ireland and Christendom: the Bible and the Missions*, ed. Próinséas Ní Chatháin and Michael Richter (Stuttgart: 1987), 284–307; Liam Breatnach, 'Canon Law and Secular Law in Early Ireland: the Significance of *Bretha Nemed*', *Peritia* 3 (1984): 439–59; Ludwig Bieler, ed. and trans., *The Irish Penitentials*, Scriptores Latini Hiberniae 5 (Dublin: 1975).

23 See Donnchadh Ó Corráin, Liam Breatnach, and Aidan Breen, 'The Laws of the Irish', *Peritia* 3 (1984): 382–438; Damian Bracken, 'Latin Passages in Irish Vernacular Law: Notes on Sources', *Peritia* 9 (1995): 187–96; Fangzhe Qiu, 'Narratives in Early Irish Law: A Typological Study', in *Medieval Irish Law: Text and Context*, ed. Anders Ahlqvist and Pamela O'Neill (Sydney: 2013): 111–42 at 124, n. 26; McLeod, 'External Influences'. A particularly striking example is a passage of text printed by Binchy, *Corpus*, III.847.8–36, which consists of a series of Latin legal extracts from decretals and similar texts (not all of which have been identified); they are written in an Irish orthography and then translated into Irish; for example, *liseat excomuinecatus non potest agire potest tamen defeinndire oir da mbeth nabu eitir le nech conulbaite agra do denam fedaidh a ditin* 'although an excommunicated person cannot bring a dispute, nevertheless he can defend himself, for though an excommunicated person be unable to bring a case, he can defend himself' (Binchy, *Corpus* III.847.12; translated and briefly discussed in Daniel A. Binchy, '*Féchem, Fethem, Aigne*', *Celtica* 11 (1976): 18–33, at 31–2). I am grateful to Charlene Eska for discussing this passage with me. As will emerge below, the relative paucity of Latin in

Register and Language in the Medieval Irish Laws

In the brief overview of medieval Irish law above I have hinted at texts in different styles and also indicated that, while most of the material is in the vernacular there is a substantial element of ecclesiastical law in Latin. The Irish texts are mainly in prose, much (but not all) of which is surrounded in gloss and commentary. In addition, there are sections written in alliterative verse; these occur frequently at the beginning of a text which then continues in prose; for example, the text entitled *Din Techtugud*, which has to do with taking possession of disputed land, contains the following:

> bertai Sencha cétbrethach
> bantellach ar fertellach
> comdar ferba fulachta
> fora gruaidib iar cilbrethaib
>
> Sencha judged it in his first judgement,
> woman possession-taking as man possession-taking
> so that blisters were suffered
> on his cheeks after (having passed) wrong judgements.[24]

The metrical pattern in this *roscad* consists of two or three accented units in the line with a final trisyllabic word. While it is possible to see the difference between prose and verse as chronological (verse earlier, prose later), this is not a necessary formulation. There is some evidence that such passages of apparently 'archaic' verse should be regarded as 'archaising'; Breatnach has shown that some of the apparently 'archaic' verse is translating a section of the *Collectio Canonum Hibernensis* which was composed in the eighth century.[25] In other words, lawyers were able to compose apparently archaic verse rather

---

medieval Irish law may be contrasted with Welsh law where there are complete texts of medieval Welsh law preserved in Latin; see 94–5 below.

24 Watkins, 'Indo-European Metrics and Archaic Irish Verse', 227–8; text printed in Binchy, *Corpus*, I.209.12–13.

25 Breatnach, 'Canon Law and Secular Law'; id., 'Zur Frage der *Roscada* im Irischen', in *Metrik und Medienwechsel—Metrics and Media*, edited by Hildegard Tristram (Tübingen: 1991), 197–205; Johann Corthalls, 'Early Irish *Retoirics* and their Late Antique Background', *Cambrian Medieval Celtic Studies* 31 (1996): 17–36; Johann Corthalls, 'Zur Frage des mündlichen oder schriftlichen Ursprungs der Sagen*roscada*', in *Early Irish Literature—media and communication / Mündlichkeit und Schriftlichkeit in der frühen irischen Literatur*, ed. Stephen N. Tranter and Hildegard L. C. Tristram (Tübingen: 1989), 201–20.

later than had been thought, and it may well be that the choice of verse or prose has more to do with the context and form of the text than with chronology. Despite the fact that most medieval Irish law is written in Irish an implicit relationship between Latin and Irish in fact permeates Irish law; for example, the modes of analysis adopted in the commentaries are based on etymological techniques which are devoted to analysing in particular the titles of texts are based on those late-antique modes of analysis found in Isidore, Jerome, and the patristic commentators.[26]

The *literati* of medieval Ireland seem to have had a remarkably complex and nuanced view of the types and registers of language and, probably uniquely in the medieval world, legal language is identified as a distinct category of discourse, or in fact perhaps more than one category.[27] This is most explicitly set out in a section of *Auraicept na n-Éces* 'the Scholar's Primer' (a text which purports to present a grammar of early Irish), the core of which dates to the seventh or eighth century:[28]

> it é cóic gné bérla tóbaidi .i. bérla Féne ⁊ fasaige na filed ⁊ bérla etarscarta ⁊ bérla fortchide na filed tríasa n-agallit cach dib a chéle ⁊ íarmbérla
>
> there are five types of chosen language: the language of the Irish, the sayings of the poets, the separated language, the concealed language of the poets by which they speak to each other, and obscure (*or* unaccented) language.[29]

That these classificatory terms are not just 'one-off' inventions is indicated by the fact that some them also occur in other texts, notably *Sanas Cormaic* 'Cormac's Glossary' (a ninth-century quasi-encyclopaedic compilation of words listed in alpha-order with later additions).[30] A survey of early Irish learned texts produces the following list of terms for different types (perhaps

26 Breatnach, 'The Glossing of the Early Irish Law Tracts'.

27 Paul Russell, '"What Was Best of Every Language": The Early History of the Irish Language', in *A New History of Ireland*, vol. 1, ed. Ó Cróinín, 405–50, at 448–50.

28 Kim R. McCone, 'Zur Frage der Register im frühen Irischen', *Early Irish Literature*, ed. Tranter and Tristram, 57–97; for an overview, see Russell, '"What was Best of Every Language"'.

29 George Calder, ed., *Auraicept na n-Éces* (Edinburgh: 1917), 100–2 (ll. 1302–16) = 244–5 (ll. 4619–52).

30 For discussion of these, see Russell, '"What was Best of Every Language"', 448–50; for *Sanas Cormaic*, see Kuno Meyer, ed., '*Sanas Cormaic*', *Anecdota from Irish Manuscripts*, IV (Halle: 1912 (repr. Felinfach: 1994)), §§ 213, 755, 972.

registers) of Irish (*bérla* (Old Irish *bélrae*) 'language'): *bérla tóbaide* (also *téibide*) 'the selected (lit. "cut out") language, i.e. Irish'; *bérla Féne* 'the language of Irish law'; *bérla na filed* 'the language of the poets'; *bérla etarscarta* 'the language of separation' (i.e. Isidorean etymological analysis); *bérla fortchide na filed* 'obscure language of the poets'; *íarmbérla* 'obscure language', 'unaccented words'; *senbérla* 'archaic language'; *gnáthbérla* 'the usual language'; *bérla airberta* 'language of use (*or* legal procedure)'; *bélra bán biait* 'the white language of the *beati*' (i.e. Latin). There are clearly different parameters in use here and a single list risks creating all kinds of category errors; even so, there are some clear distinctions being made, chronological, functional (legal/poetical/etymological), deliberate obscurantism, etc. Calvert Watkins attempted to classify some of these terms:

gnáthbérla (ordinary)	:	senbérla (old)
bérla Féne (professional, legal)	:	bérla na filed (poetical)
bérla tóbaide (chosen)	:	bérla fortchide (obscure)[31]

But it is difficult to avoid a sense of artificiality on all of this; some of the distinctions may well be real and reflect some aspect of sociolinguistic reality, while others may have more to do with nit-picking professional distinctions which have nothing to do with the outside world. The use of *bérla Féne* to refer to legal language matches the traditional phrases which occur in the laws themselves, *la Féniu* (often abbreviated as *lā*) 'according to Irish law' and *amal ara-chain Fénechas* 'as the law states'. That said, verse, obscure language, and the use of etymological analysis also occur in the laws, and it is possible that in some contexts these categories might have been regarded as sub-categories of *bérla Féne*. It is possible that in some contexts some useful distinctions were being made; for example, *bérla Féne* might be used to refer to the core-text, while *bérla etarscarta* could be used more generally to refer to the language of analysis (i.e. the glosses and commentary).

It is clear that in medieval Ireland there was an unusually well-developed sense of the variation found in the language and how it might be described and explained. In the cases listed above, it can be associated with particular groups, e.g. lawyers or poets, or be distinguished by function.

---

31 Calvert Watkins, 'Language of Gods and Language of Men: Remarks on Some Indo-European Metalinguistic Traditions', in *Myth and Law among the Indo-Europeans in Comparative Indo-E*uropean Mythology, ed. Jaan Puhvel (Berkeley: 1970), 1–17; Calvert Watkins, *How to Kill a Dragon. Aspects of Indo-Europ*ean Poetics (Oxford: 1995), 179–93, especially 182–3.

Law in Medieval Wales

When we move eastwards across the Irish Sea matters are both similar and different. Generally medieval Welsh literature is attested much later than Irish, and with the arguable exception of some early Welsh verse, it is difficult to find texts with demonstrable composition dates much before *ca.*1100. Furthermore, no manuscript containing continuous medieval Welsh survives from before 1250, and the bulk of medieval Welsh manuscripts date from between 1250 and *ca.*1450. Until the Act of Union in 1536, Wales had its own legal system and legal manuscripts form a significant proportion of the surviving manuscript materials; some thirty or more manuscripts survive from this period and the copying of law manuscripts continued well into the later fifteenth and sixteenth centuries. The development of Welsh law, as it has come down to us, has traditionally been associated with Hywel Dda (†950) who is named in the prologues to the main law texts in most manuscripts;[32] however, there is some debate as to how much of the surviving tracts date to this period, and to what extent they contain, or are the product of, later legal developments. The presence of some Anglo-Saxon loanwords in the terminology of the officers of the king's court (*edling* 'heir-apparent' < Old English *æþeling, distain* 'butler' < Old English *disþegn*) suggest that some features may be attributed to the period of Hywel Dda. So while the profile of supposed composition dates in relation to the dates of surviving manuscripts is broadly similar to what we find in Ireland, the chronological framework as a whole is somewhat later.

Welsh law survives in texts in both Welsh and Latin. The Welsh ones fall into three redactions which originally seem to have been regionally differentiated.[33] In addition there are five surviving Latin redactions: the earliest manuscripts of

32 *Cyfraith Hywel website*, edited by Sara Elin Roberts, at <http://www.cyfraith-hywel.org.uk/en/index.php>. For an introductory overview, see Thomas Charles-Edwards, *The Welsh Laws* (Cardiff: 1989).

33 Versions of all of these redactions were originally edited and translated in Aneurin Owen, ed. and trans., *Ancient Laws and Institutes of Wales* (London: 1841) which is still very useful. More recent work on each of the redactions: Cyfnerth (Owen's 'Gwentian Code'; Arthur Wade-Evans, ed., *Welsh Medieval Law, Being a Text of the Laws of Howel the Good, Namely the British Museum Harleian MS. 4353 of the 13th Century* (Oxford: 1909)); Blegywryd (Owen's 'Demetian Code'; Melville Richards, ed., *Cyfreithiau Hywel Dda yn ôl Llawysgrif Coleg yr Iesu LVII Rhydychen*, 2nd edn. (Cardiff: 1990), translated in Melville Richards, trans., *The Laws of Hywel Dda (The Book of Blegywryd)* (Liverpool: 1954)); Iorwerth (Owen's 'Venedotian Code'; Aled Rhys Wiliam, ed., *Llyfr Iorwerth. A Critical Text of the Venedotian Code of Medieval Welsh Law, mainly from BM. Cotton MS. Titus D.ii*, Board of Celtic Studies, University of Wales, History and Law Series 18 (Cardiff: 1960) (translated in

three of the redactions (A, B, and C) date to *ca.*1250 and are thus contemporary with the earliest surviving manuscripts of the Welsh redactions; Latin redaction D is a little later (just before 1300) and redaction E is a sixteenth-century production.[34] The majority of these manuscripts contain versions of a broadly similar text (with variation from redaction to redaction) consisting of tractates on the king's court, women, country (land, value of buildings, animals, etc.), homicide, arson, theft, etc.[35] The structure is sufficiently similar that it is probable that they derive from an original model text; that said, it is not always easy to understand the textual relationships between the different versions, and it has often been argued that these texts are better treated as a series of tractates, each of which may have a different textual history. Within each redaction the textual relations between different copies is variable: for example, the representatives of the Iorwerth redaction are stemmatically very tightly related indicating a period of textual transmission by the close copying of texts; on the other hand, versions of each of the other redactions, Cyfnerth and Blegywryd, are much more loosely related to each other and they tend to say the same thing in many different ways.[36] This may perhaps be related to the distinction between professional *ynad* 'judge' in the north and the *brawdwr*, often a local dignitary, in the south; in the latter the law was not a verbally fixed entity in the way it was in the north. This may be one reason why the scribe of *Llyfr Colan*

Dafydd Jenkins, trans., *The Law of Hywel Dda: Law Texts from Medieval Wales* (Llandysul: 1986 (2nd edn. 1990))).

34 All five of the Latin redactions were edited by Hywel D. Emanuel, ed., *The Latin Texts of the Welsh Laws*, Board of Celtic Studies, University of Wales, History and Law Series 22 (Cardiff: 1967); the three earliest Latin redactions, Latin ABC, were also edited (but not translated) in (Owen, *Ancient Laws*); Latin A has been translated in Ian F. Fletcher, trans., *Latin Redaction A of the Law of Hywel*, Pamffledi Cyfraith Hywel (Aberystwyth: 1986); Latin C was recently re-edited by Paul Russell, ed. and trans., *Welsh Law in Medieval Anglesey. British Library, Harleian MS 1796 (Latin C)*, Texts and Studies in Medieval Welsh Law 2 (Cambridge: 2011).

35 In addition, there are other types of texts, such as triads, *damweiniau* (texts often framed as 'if X should happen, then …'), and *cynhawsedd* 'pleadings'; see respectively Sara Elin Roberts, ed. and trans., *The Legal Triads of Medieval Wales* (Cardiff: 2007); Dafydd Jenkins, ed., *Damweiniau Colan* (Aberystwyth: 1973); Thomas M. Charles-Edwards, '*Cynghawsedd*: Counting and Pleading in Medieval Welsh Law', *Bulletin of the Board of Celtic Studies* 33 (1986): 188–98.

36 On fixed and fluid transmission, see Thomas M. Charles-Edwards, 'The Textual Tradition of Medieval Welsh Prose Tales and the Problem of Dating', in *150 Jahre 'Mabinogion'—Deutsch-Walisische Kulturbeziehungen*, ed. Bernhard Maier and Stefan Zimmer, Buchreihe der *Zeitschrift für celtische Philologie* 19 (Tübingen: 2001), 23–39.

'the Book of Colan', a revision of the Iorwerth redaction advises resorting to a Latin version if there is any doubt about what the text says:

> Od amheuyr bot pob un o'r llessoet a ducpuyt uchot eu bot ykeureyth Hewel, edrecher e lleureu Lladyn ac eno y keffyr
>
> if there is any doubt that each one of the prohibitions mentioned above are in the law of Hywel, one should look in the Latin books and there it will be found.[37]

It might have been thought that the text preserved in Latin maintained a textual integrity which the Welsh versions did not. There is also a significant connection between the Latin and Welsh versions in that the Blegywryd redaction is a translation of a text close to Latin D;[38] Latin B is a composite text which later seems to have developed into an antiquarian compilation (both Latin A and E are tidier derivatives from it at different stages);[39] Latin C, on the other hand, is quite closely related to the Iorwerth redaction and may perhaps reflect an early version of that redaction.[40] It should also be pointed out that (apart from very specific glossing in Latin C)[41] none of these law texts is glossed nor do they display the kind of hierarchy of text (and in some case script) found in Irish; for example, there are no traces of a distinction between text and commentary.

Register and Language in Medieval Welsh Law

In striking contrast to Irish law, the language of Welsh law is generally not archaic; it of course contains technical, legal terminology, but the syntax and structure is not dissimilar to that of other non-legal prose texts. It is above all

---

37 Jenkins, *Llyfr Colan*, §565 (my translation).

38 Hywel D. Emanuel, 'Llyfr Blegywryd a Llawysgrif Rawlinson [C.]821', *Bulletin of the Board of Celtic Studies* 19 (1960–62): 23–28 (translated into English in *Celtic Law Papers Introductory to Welsh Medieval Law and Government*, ed. Dafydd Jenkins (Brussels: 1973), 161–70).

39 Paul Russell, 'The Arrangement and Development of the Three Columns Tractate', in Tair Colofn Cyfraith: *The Three Columns of Law in Medieval Wales, Homicide, Theft and Fire*, ed. Thomas Charles-Edwards and Paul Russell, The Welsh Legal History Society 5 (Bangor: 2007), 60–91.

40 Russell, *Welsh Law in Medieval Anglesey*.

41 *Ibid.*, xxvii–xxxiii.

else clear and functional. There is no verse as an integral part of the law, but there are some traces of alliterating and vivid phrases often introduced by phrases such as *y gyfreith honno a elwir* 'that law is called ...': in the context of oath-swearing, the phrases *telhitor gwedy halawc lw* 'payment is made after a dirty oath' (cf. *tal glan gwedy halauc lw* 'a clean payment after a dirty oath' and *llwyr dal wedi llwyr dwng* 'complete payment after a complete oath');[42] when a compensation payment for homicide has not been paid in full (down to the last penny), this is called *oergwymp galanas* 'the cold fall of (the fine for) homicide';[43] if a rightful claim in land law fails, then the claimant can utter a *diaspat uch annwn* 'a shriek above Annwfn' ('Annwfn' being the Welsh term for the underworld or hell).[44] While they might be suggestive of law as a more performance-related activity (perhaps at an earlier period), they tend to occur as descriptive headings for small sections of text and, as such, their mnemonic function need not in every case be a sign of antiquity so much as these are useful sections of text for a lawyer to know and so it is helpful if they have a mnemonic form.[45]

In the context of the present discussion, an important question concerns the relationship between the Welsh and Latin versions. In general terms, Welsh and Latin versions of the law seem relatively distinct, though there are cases such as Latin D which contains significant amounts of Welsh. We have noted that recourse to a Latin version was recommended in case of doubt, but a more general question is whether one can tell in which language a text was originally composed. It is clear that texts could be translated from Latin to Welsh; the case of Latin D and Blegywryd makes that clear, but is there evidence beyond that group for a similar process? This is not the place for a sustained discussion of possible instances because there is a bigger question lying behind this, namely, in which language were the laws of medieval Wales originally composed? The default assumption has always been that they were composed in Welsh, but it is at least worth considering whether some of them might have originally been in Latin. The problem is how we might be able to tell. Three examples can be briefly considered.

---

42 Cf., for example, Richards, *Cyfreithiau Hywel Dda*, 77.19 (Blegywryd redaction).

43 Cf., for example, *ibid.*, 26.5 (Blegywryd redaction); for discussion, see Sara Elin Roberts, '*Tri Dygyngoll Cenedl*: The Development of a Triad', *Studia Celtica* 37 (2003), 163–82.

44 Cf. for example, William, *Llyfr Iorwerth*, 56.3 (Iorwerth redaction); for discussion, see Jenkins, *The Law of Hywel Dda*, 263.

45 In linguistic terms only *telhitor* looks old; see Simon Rodway, *Dating Medieval Welsh Literature. Evidence from the Verbal System* (Aberystwyth: 2013), 90–1, 102–5.

First, in a section on the protection that the officers of the court can provide, the protection of the chief huntsman (i.e. his authority to provide safe-conduct) is described in terms of the distance over which his horn is audible: thus in Latin B *Refugium penkynyt est conducere hominem quo uox cornu eius auditur* 'The protection of the chief huntsman is to provide safe conduct to a man as far as the sound of his horn is heard';[46] this is also reflected in the Cyfnerth and Iorwerth redactions where *uox* is paralleled by *llef* 'voice'.[47] But in Latin A, C, and D the same sentence reads *uix* 'scarcely' for *uox*, and this is reflected in the Welsh translation in the Blegwyryd redaction as *y breid*.[48] The division between the texts clearly reflects an error made in a Latin text. That the error is embedded in more Latin texts than just Latin D suggests that it might offer a way of thinking about deeper textual relationships between the texts. On the other hand, the *uox*/*uix* error is relatively trivial and it is not impossible that it might have been made more than once. The second example has to do with Latin C (British Library, Harley 1796, *ca.*1240–50, copied in Anglesey), the Latin of which shows possible Welsh features, such as the use of Latin *debet* (rather than *debet habere*) to mean 'is entitled to receive' which parallels Welsh *dyly*.[49] While it might be possible to argue that the features reflect translation from Welsh into Latin, they may simply indicate that unsurprisingly the writer of this Latin text was a native-speaker of Welsh whose Latin was influenced by his first language. A third example does at least provide possible evidence for a legal text being translated into Welsh from Latin: fol. 63v of the Book of Llandaff (Aberystwyth, National Library of Wales, 17110E) contains an Old Welsh text known as *Breint Teilo* 'the privilege of Teilo' which sets out the privileges and obligations of the diocese of Llandaff; it is preceded by a Latin *Privilegium Teliaui*, and it has been argued that 'the Latin is a rendering of the Welsh version'.[50] However, closer reading suggests that it is probable that the

46 Emanuel, *Latin Texts* (Latin B), 195.11–12 (also Paul Russell, ed. and trans., 'The Laws of Court from Latin B', in *The Welsh King and His Court*, ed. T. M. Charles Edwards, Morfydd E. Owen, and Paul Russell (Cardiff: 2000), 478–526, at §1/6.6) = Emanuel, *Latin Texts*, 439.9 (Latin E).

47 Cyfnerth (Wade-Evans, *Welsh Medieval Law*) 5/8, Iorwerth (Wiliam, *Llyfr Iorwerth*) 15/23.

48 *Vix …*: Emanuel, *Latin Texts* (Latin A) 111.37–8; *ibid.* (Latin C) 278.25–6 (Russell, *Welsh Law in Medieval Anglesey*, §1.10/6); Emanuel, *Latin Texts* (Latin D) 319.25 (corresponding to Middle Welsh *y breid* 'hardly' in Richards, *Cyfreithiau Hywel Dda* (Blegywryd) 7.1–2).

49 For other examples and further discussion, see Paul Russell, '"Go and look in the Latin books": Latin and the Vernacular in Medieval Wales', in *Latin in Medieval Britain*, ed. Richard Ashdowne and Carolinne White, Proceedings of the British Academy (London: 2017), 213–46.

50 Wendy Davies, 'Braint Teilo', *Bulletin of the Board of Celtic Studies* 26 (1974–6), 123–37.

Welsh version is translated from an earlier Latin version, though not necessarily the Latin version adjacent to it.[51] This is important as these privileges, preserved in the Book of Llandaff, date from an earlier period (*ca.*1120s) than any of the law texts discussed above and so take us further back into the period when the law text might have been composed. The cumulative weight of these examples is indecisive, but at least gives us some sense of what we should be looking for to develop such an argument.

Some Conclusions

The aim of this contribution has been to introduce these texts to a wider audience, and to argue that they are significantly more interesting than thinking in vague terms about 'Celtic law'. In considering the linguistic issues these texts have to offer, it has only been possible to scratch the surface and touch briefly on what they have to offer. One of the more important themes considered involves the notion of archaism and the use of alliterative, verse-like forms of presentation; they are to be found in Irish and there are occasional phrases in Welsh. The point that emerges is that they need not be archaic, so much as archaising; it must also be recalled that the mnemonic function of such sections of texts and phrasing would have been important not only in some context of oral performance (which is not just some archaic practice but a necessary and regular part of all legal activity), but also as a way for lawyers (and student lawyers) to learn the structure of the law; no lawyer can look everything up. If nothing else, the linguistic aspects of these laws deserve to be incorporated into more general discussion of language and law in the legal systems of medieval Britain and Europe.

Bibliography

Archan, Christophe. '*Uraicecht becc* et les triades du droit. Les juges et leurs sources dans l'Irlande médiévale'. In *Mélanges offerts en l'honneur de Pierre-Yves Lambert*, edited by Guillaume Oudaer, Gaël Hilly, and Hervé Le Bihan, 359–75. Rennes: 2015.

Atkinson, Robert, *et al.*, editors. *The Ancient Laws of Ireland*, 7 vols. Dublin: 1865–1901.

Bieler, Ludwig, editor. *The Irish Penitentials*. Scriptores Latini Hiberniae 5. Dublin: 1975.

Binchy, Daniel A.. '*Féchem, Fethem, Aigne*'. *Celtica* 11 (1976): 18–33.

Binchy, Daniel A., editor. *Corpus Iuris Hibernici*, 6 vols. Dublin: 1978.

51 Paul Russell, '*Priuilegium Sancti Teliaui* and *Breint Teilo*', *Studia Celtica* 50 (2016), 41–68.

Bracken, Damian. 'Latin Passages in Irish Vernacular Law: Notes on Sources'. *Peritia* 9 (1995): 187–96.

Breatnach, Liam. 'Canon Law and Secular Law in Early Ireland: The Significance of *Bretha Nemed*'. *Peritia* 3 (1984): 439–59.

Breatnach, Liam. 'The Ecclesiastical Element in the Old-Irish Legal Tract Cáin *Fhuithirbe*'. *Peritia* 5 (1986): 36–52.

Breatnach, Liam. 'The First Third of the *Bretha Nemed Toísech*'. *Ériu* 40 (1989): 1–40.

Breatnach, Liam. 'Zur Frage der *Roscada* im Irischen'. In *Metrik und Medienwechsel—Metrics and Media*, edited by Hildegard Tristram, 197–205. Tübingen: 1991.

Breatnach, Liam. 'On the Glossing of Early Irish Law-texts, Fragmentary Texts, and Some Aspects of the Laws Relating to Dogs'. In *Celtica Helsingiensia: Proceedings from a Symposium on Celtic Studies*, edited by Anders Ahlqvist, 11–20. Helsinki: 1996.

Breatnach, Liam. *A Companion to the* Corpus Iuris Hibernici. Dublin: 2005.

Breatnach, Liam. 'The Glossing of the Early Irish Law Tracts'. In Grammatica, Gramadach, Gramadeg: *Vernacular Grammar and Grammarians in Medieval Ireland and Wales*, edited by Deborah Hayden and Paul Russell, 113–132. Amsterdam: 2016.

Calder, George, editor. *Auraicept na n-Éces*. Edinburgh: 1917.

Charles Edwards, Thomas M. '*Cynghawsedd*: Counting and Pleading in Medieval Welsh Law'. *Bulletin of the Board of Celtic Studies* 33 (1986): 188–98.

Charles Edwards, Thomas M. *The Welsh* Laws. Cardiff: 1989.

Charles Edwards, Thomas M. *The Medieval Gaelic Lawyer*. Cambridge: 1999.

Charles Edwards, Thomas M. 'The Textual Tradition of Medieval Welsh Prose Tales and the Problem of Dating'. In *150 Jahre "Mabinogion"—Deutsch-Walisische Kulturbeziehungen*, edited by Bernhard Maier and Stefan Zimmer, 23–39. Tübingen: 2001.

Charles Edwards, Thomas M. 'Early Irish Law'. In *A New History of Ireland*, vol. 1, edited by Dáibhí Ó Cróinín, 331–70. Oxford: 2005.

Corthals, Johann. 'Early Irish *Retoiric*s and their Late Antique Background'. *Cambrian Medieval Celtic Studies* 31 (1996): 17–36.

Corthals, Johann. 'Zur Frage des mündlichen oder schriftlichen Ursprungs der Sagen*roscada*'. In Tranter and Tristram, *Early Irish Literature*, 201–20.

Cyfraith Hywel website, edited by Sara Elin Roberts at <http://www.cyfraith-hywel.org.uk/en/index.php>.

Davies, Wendy. 'Braint Teilo'. *Bulletin of the Board of Celtic Studies* 26 (1974–1976): 123–137.

Emanuel, Hywel D., editor. *The Latin Texts of the Welsh Laws*. Cardiff: 1967.

Emanuel, Hywel D. 'Llyfr Blegywryd a Llawysgrif Rawlinson [C.]821'. *Bulletin of the Board of Celtic Studies* 19 (1960–1962), 23–8 [translated into English in *Celtic Law Papers Introductory to Welsh Medieval Law and Government*, edited by Dafydd Jenkins, 161–170. Brussels: 1973].

Fletcher, Ian F., trans. *Latin Redaction A of the Law of Hywel*, Pamffledi Cyfraith Hywel. Aberystwyth: 1986.
Harris, Meinir. 'Compensation for Injury: A Point of Contact between Early Welsh and Germanic Law?'. In *The Trial of Dic Penderyn and Other Essays*, edited by Thomas G. Watkin, 39–76. Cardiff: 2002.
Jenkins, Dafydd, editor. *Damweiniau Colan*. Aberyswyth: 1973.
Jenkins, Dafydd, translator. *The Law of Hywel Dda. Law Texts from Medieval Wales*. Llandysul: 1986.
Jenkins, Dafydd, editor. *Llyfr Colan*. Cardiff: 1963.
Kelly, Fergus. *A Guide to Early Irish Law*. Dublin: 1988 (2nd edn. 2005).
Mac Cana, Proinsias. 'The Three Languages and the Three Laws'. *Studia Celtica* 5 (1970): 62–78.
McCone, Kim R. 'Zur Frage der Register im frühen Irischen'. In Tranter and Tristram, *Early Irish Literature*, 57–97.
McLeod, Neil. 'External Influences on Medieval Irish Law: AD 600–1600'. *Australian Celtic Journal* 11 (2013): 31–54.
Mellinkoff, David. *The Language of Law*. Boston: 1963.
Meyer, Kuno, editor. '*Sanas Cormaic*'. *Anecdota from Irish Manuscripts*, IV. Halle: 1912 (repr. 1994).
Ó Corráin, Donnchadh. 'Irish Law and Canon Law'. In *Ireland and Europe: The Early Church*, edited by Próinséas Ní Chatháin and Michael Richter, 157–166. Stuttgart: 1984.
Ó Corráin, Donnchadh. 'Irish Vernacular Law and the Old Testament'. In *Ireland and Christendom: The Bible and the Missions*, edited by Próinséas Ní Chatháin and Michael Richter, 284–307. Stuttgart: 1987.
Ó Corráin, Donnchadh, Liam Breatnach, and Aidan Breen. 'The Laws of the Irish'. *Peritia* 3 (1984): 382–438.
Owen, Aneurin, editor. *Ancient Laws and Institutes of Wales*. London: 1841.
Qiu, Fangzhe. 'Narratives in Early Irish Law: A Typological Study'. In *Medieval Irish Law: Text and Context*, edited by Anders Ahlqvist and Pamela O'Neill, 111–42. Sydney: 2013.
Richards, Melville, translator. *The Laws of Hywel Dda (The Book of Blegywryd)*. Liverpool: 1954.
Richards, Melville, editor. *Cyfreithiau Hywel Dda yn ôl Llawysgrif Coleg yr Iesu LVII Rhydychen*, 2nd edn. Cardiff: 1990.
Roberts, Sara Elin. '*Tri Dygyngoll Cenedl*: The Development of a Triad'. *Studia Celtica* 37 (2003): 163–82.
Roberts, Sara Elin. *The Legal Triads of Medieval Wales*. Cardiff: 2007.
Rodway, Simon, *Dating Medieval Welsh Literature. Evidence from the Verbal System*. Aberystwyth: 2013.

Russell, Paul, editor. 'The Laws of Court from Latin B'. In *The Welsh King and His Court*, edited by T. M. Charles Edwards, Morfydd E. Owen, and Paul Russell, 478–526. Cardiff: 2000.

Russell, Paul. '"What Was Best of Every Language": The Early History of the Irish Language'. In *A New History of Ireland*, vol. 1, ed. Dáibhí Ó Cróinín, 405–50. Oxford: 2005.

Russell, Paul. 'The Arrangement and Development of the Three Columns Tractate'. In Tair Colofn Cyfraith: *The Three Columns of Law in Medieval Wales, Homicide, Theft and Fire*, edited by Thomas Charles-Edwards and Paul Russell, 60–91. Bangor: 2007.

Russell, Paul, editor. *Welsh Law in Medieval Anglesey. British Library, Harleian MS 1796 (Latin C)*. Cambridge: 2011.

Russell, Paul. '*Priuilegium Sancti Teliaui* and *Breint Teilo*'. *Studia Celtica* 50 (2016): 41–68.

Russell, Paul. '"Go and look in the Latin books": Latin and the Vernacular in Medieval Wales'. In *Latin in Medieval Britain*, edited by Richard Ashdowne and Carolinne White, 213–46. London: 2017.

Sims-Williams, Patrick. 'The Contents of the Later Commentaries on the Brehon Law Tracts'. *Ériu* 49 (1989): 23–40.

Sims-Williams, Patrick. 'Celtomania and Celtoscepticism'. *Cambrian Medieval Celtic Studies* 36 (1998): 1–36.

Sims-Williams, Patrick. 'Celtic Civilization: Continuity or Coincidence?'. *Cambrian Medieval Celtic Studies* 64 (2012): 1–45.

Sims-Williams, Patrick. 'Post-Celtosceptisicm: a Personal View'. *In Saltair Saíochta, Sanasaíochta agus Seanchais: a Festschrift for Gearóid Mac Eoin*, edited by Dónall Ó Baoill, Donncha Ó hAodha and Nollaig Ó Muraíle, 422–28. Dublin: 2013.

Stacey, Robin Chapman. 'Law and Literature in Medieval Ireland and Wales'. In *Medieval Celtic Literature and Society*, edited by Helen Fulton, 65–82. Dublin: 2005.

Stacey, Robin Chapman. *Dark Speech. The Performance of Law in Early Ireland*. Philadelphia: 2007.

Stacey, Robin Chapman. 'Further musings on the "Celtic" in "Celtic law"'. *Eolas* 9 (2016): 55–76.

Thurneysen, Rudolf. 'Aus dem irischen Recht IV'. *Zeischrift für celtische Philologie* 16 (1927): 167–230.

Tiersma, Peter M. *Legal Language*. Chicago: 1999.

Tiersma, Peter M. 'A History of the Languages of the Law'. In *The Oxford Handbook of Language and Law*, edited by Lawrence M. Solan and Peter M. Tiersma, 13–26. Oxford: 2015.

Tranter, Stephen N., and Hildegard L. C. Tristram, editors. *Early Irish Literature—Media and Communication / Mündlichkeit und Schriftlichkeit in der frühen irischen Literatur*. Tübingen: 1989.

Wade-Evans, Arthur, editor. *Welsh Medieval Law, Being a Text of the Laws of Howel the Good, Namely the British Museum Harleian MS. 4353 of the 13th Century*. Oxford: 1909.

Wasserschleben, Hermann. *Die irische Kanonensammlung*. Leipzig: 1885.

Watkins, Calvert. 'Indo-European Metrics and Archaic Irish Verse' *Celtica* 6 (1966): 194–249.

Watkins, Calvert. 'Language of Gods and Language of Men: Remarks on Some Indo-European Metalinguistic Traditions'. In *Myth and Law among the Indo-Europeans in Comparative Indo-European Mythology*, edited by Jaan Puhvel, 1–17. Berkeley: 1970.

Watkins, Calvert. *How to Kill a Dragon. Aspects of Indo-European Poetics*. Oxford: 1995.

Wiliam, Aled Rhys, editor. *Llyfr Iorwerth. A Critical Text of the* Venedotian Code *of Medieval Welsh Law, mainly from BM. Cotton MS. Titus D.ii.* Cardiff: 1960.

PART 2

The Languages of Legal Practice and Documentary Culture

CHAPTER 5

Latin and the Vernacular in Medieval Legal Documents: The Case of Denmark

Anders Leegaard Knudsen

When the Danish king, Harald 'Bluetooth', accepted Christianity as his new religion in the 960s, he got much more than just a new faith. He and his kingdom got a church with an organization centred in Rome. The church had an elaborate legal system governing not only the internal relations of the ecclesiastical hierarchy and its relations with the lay members of the church, but also relations amongst the laity itself. In this sense, the law of the church, canon law, is also an instrument for the propagation of Christianity: if one wanted to be a Christian, it was necessary to live like one. Hence, the determination of the church to influence the legal systems in newly converted kingdoms of Europe.[1] In recent years, Danish legal historians have shown that canon law influenced Danish law to a far greater extent than used to be believed just a generation ago. There can be little doubt that this influence meant an internationalisation and sophistication of Danish jurisprudence.[2]

The first documented attempt to influence the legal system in Denmark is from 1078 when the pope asked the Danish king to send young noblemen to Rome in order to be instructed in *sacris ac divinis legibus*, i.e. canon law.[3] We do

1 The literature on the Christianization of Denmark and the other Scandinavian countries is quite extensive. Among the recent contributions in English, see Sverre Bagge, *Cross and Scepter: The Rise of the Scandinavian Kingdoms from the Vikings to the Reformation* (Princeton and Oxford: 2014), 60–70. An older contribution in Danish has stood the test of time well: Inge Skovgaard-Petersen, 'Oldtid og vikingetid', in *Danmarks historie* ed. Aksel E. Christensen *et al.*, vol. 1, 2nd edn. (Copenhagen: 1978), 148–78. For the larger perspective, the conversion of all of Europe, including Denmark of course, see Richard Fletcher, *The Conversion of Europe: From Paganism to Christianity 371–1386 AD* (London: 1997), which should be read with the lucid review by R. I. Moore, 'A New Way of Doing Things: How Pagan Europe was Converted—and Upgraded', review of *The Conversion of Europe: From Paganism to Christianity 371–1386 AD*, by Richard Fletcher, *Times Literary Supplement*, February 6, 1998, 24.

2 To mention but a few of the contributions: Per Andersen, *Legal Procedure and Practice in Medieval Denmark* (Leiden and Boston: 2011); Helle Vogt, *The Function of Kinship in Medieval Nordic Legislation* (Leiden and Boston: 2010).

3 The text of the original papal letter is no longer extant, but its content is mentioned in a papal letter to king Olaf III (Kyrre) of Norway from 15 December, 1078, see *DD* 1.II.18. All

 | DOI 10.1163/9789004375765_007

not know whether the king heeded the suggestion, but once the organization of the Danish dioceses was underway around 1060, about a century after conversion, there must have been a need for legal expertise.[4]

In order to acquire this expertise, a solid grounding in Latin was needed. With the conversion to Christianity came the acceptance of a foreign language as liturgical language as well as the corporate language of the church. The benefits were obvious: it greatly eased international communication and, in addition, gave access to the knowledge transmitted from Antiquity, as well as the ever-growing body of new knowledge, taught in the schools and, eventually, the universities.

Denmark did not become a fully-fledged member of this Latin literary community overnight, however, and for a long time, Denmark was a receiver, rather than a contributor. This could hardly have been different, given the fact that Denmark joined Latin Europe, rather than *vice versa*. Leaving aside for the moment the use of charters and other legal documents and focusing on other types of text (i.e. neither charters nor legal texts), we see that the wide variety of texts for use by the church first came from Frankish Europe and later from other parts of Christendom.[5] Gradually, however, from the twelfth century onwards, Denmark had its own literature in Latin, mainly in history, theology, philosophy, and astronomy, though some of it was written abroad.[6] Danish students frequented the new centres of scholarship, the universities, and thus took part in the transmission of ancient learning as well as the international development of theology, law, medicine, and the arts. Danish students undoubtedly learned much and some of them were also able to make a scholarly contribution.[7] The training the law students received at the universities must

---

references to *Diplomatarium Danicum* are in the format most commonly used in Denmark, thus *DD* 1.II.18 refers to *Diplomatarium Danicum*, first series, vol. 2, no. 18.

4 On the organization of the Danish church in the mid-eleventh century, see Aksel E. Christensen, 'Tiden 1042–1241', in *Danmarks historie*, I, 226–33.

5 On libraries in medieval Denmark see Ellen Jørgensen, 'Studier over danske middelalderlige Bogsamlinger', *Historisk Tidsskrift*, eighth ser., 4 (1912–1913), 1–67.

6 The best introduction to Danish medieval literature in Latin is still found in Paul Lehmann, *Skandinaviens Anteil an der lateinischen Literatur und Wissenschaft des Mittelalters* 1 (Munich: 1936). For more up-to-date information about individual authors see Stephan Borgehammar *et al.*, eds., *Medieval Nordic Literature in Latin: A Website of Authors and Anonymous Works ca.1100–1530*, last modified December 30, 2012, at <https://wikihost.uib.no/medieval/index.php/Medieval_Nordic_Literature_in_Latin>.

7 On the subject of Scandinavian students at European universities in the Middle Ages see Sverre Bagge, 'Nordic Students at Foreign Universities', *Scandinavian Journal of History* 9, no. 1 (1984), 1–29. The fundamental Danish contributions remain Ellen Jørgensen, 'Nordiske

have been crucial to the development of Danish law. However, one need not be a writer in order to be a member of a literary community: one can be a reader or listener as well. This more passive approach is difficult to demonstrate, but the production of manuscripts is surely evidence of a demand for texts, whatever the genre.

The production of manuscripts in Denmark was nearly as slow in getting started as the writing of new texts, but the earliest extant manuscript produced in Denmark is the so-called Dalby Book, a bible from the eleventh century, written in Dalby in Scania.[8] With the growing number of ecclesiastical institutions (chapters, monasteries, and churches) came a growing demand for the books needed for the running of these institutions. As the chapters and later on also the monasteries kept schools open also to lay people, the number of literate people (in the medieval sense of the term: people with a knowledge of Latin) began to grow, further enlarging the literary community.[9] This must be kept in mind when surveying the rather small body of evidence, i.e. the medieval manuscripts produced in Danish *scriptoria* or kept in Danish libraries during the Middle Ages, as well as those no longer extant manuscripts whose existence is otherwise attested: they are only the tip of an iceberg.[10] After the Reformation, many of the ecclesiastical texts were considered useless at best—and possibly even harmful—and the parchment was used to bind books or put to other uses.[11] Fires and other depredations in the early modern period also took their toll, but enough has remained that book historians agree that throughout the Middle Ages, the church was by far the largest producer in

Studierejser i Middelalderen', *Historisk Tidsskrift* 5, eighth series (1915), 331–82, and Ellen Jørgensen, 'Nogle Bemærkninger om danske Studerende ved Tysklands Universiteter i Middelalderen', *Historisk Tidsskrift* 6, eighth series (1916), 197–214.

8 Merete Geert Andersen, 'The Dalby Book', in *Living Words and Luminous Pictures: Medieval Book Culture in Denmark. Essays*, ed. Erik Petersen (Aarhus: 1999), 63–6.

9 The famous article, which everyone builds on, is Herbert Grundmann, 'Litteratus–Illitteratus: Der Wandel einer Bildungsnorm vom Altertum zum Mittelalter', *Archiv für Kulturgeschichte* 40 (1958), 1–65. See also Michael Clanchy, *From Memory to Written Record: England 1066–1307*, 2nd edn. (Oxford: 1993), 224–52.

10 The standard work on Danish medieval manuscripts is Lauritz Nielsen, *Danmarks middelalderlige Haandskrifter: En sammenfattende boghistorisk Oversigt* (Copenhagen: 1937); but see also Thorkil Damsgaard Olsen, 'De ældste bøger', 'Skriften i administrationen', 'Analfabeternes oprør', and 'Dansk som skriftsprog', in *Dansk litteraturhistorie*, ed. Søren Kaspersen *et al.*, vol. 1 (Copenhagen: 1984), 130–56, 381–403; as well as the contributions in Erik Petersen, ed., *Living Words and Luminous Pictures*.

11 On the transmission of Denmark's medieval manuscripts, see Nielsen, *Danmarks middelalderlige Haandskrifter*, 163–81.

Denmark of Latin manuscripts. Even the few Danish manuscripts were most likely produced in ecclesiastical institutions, at least until the fifteenth century. The provincial law codes and church laws as well as a few medicinal tracts were in Danish—a remarkable feat in the twelfth and thirteenth centuries.[12] For a long time Danish was not used for any other genres. Manuscript production in Danish was very small, however, and remained so until the fifteenth century.

The production of charters had a slow start, too. Once again, the extant material is only the tip of the iceberg: inventories made in the sixteenth and seventeenth centuries of then still extant medieval ecclesiastical archives show that the subsequent loss of legal documents has been massive, and to this must be added the number of documents which are lost without a trace. How great a number that is remains anyone's guess. Counting the extant originals and the copies, as well as the terse items in archive inventories, the following figures emerge: from the eleventh century only three are known; from the entire twelfth century *ca.*250; from the entire thirteenth century *ca.*1,500; from the first half of the fourteenth century *ca.*2,300; from the second half of that century *ca.*3,800; and from the first half of the fifteenth century *ca.*6,650. All together there are *ca.*14,500 legal documents whose existence is known to us.[13]

Until *ca.*1400, almost all of these documents were in Latin, with a small number of Danish documents appearing in the last decade of the fourteenth century. In the fifteenth century, Danish rapidly gained ground, however, and after *ca.*1425, the use of Latin became rare, except for international or internal ecclesiastical matters. The number of legal documents increased greatly in the course of the fifteenth century and most of them were in Danish.

The crown and the church were the first to adopt the use of legal documents in Denmark. The church because it was inherent in the organization, the crown partly because there was a demand for privileges, immunities, statutes, etc. from the church as well as from lay people, and partly because it was such a useful instrument of communication with every corner and every level of society. In addition, this was also the way the papacy communicated with the Christian kingdoms and communication between the popes and the Danish kings intensified during the Middle Ages. The crown used clerical personnel to

12 Britta Olrik Frederiksen, 'Medieval Books in Danish—in Plain and Less Plain Figures', in *Living Words and Luminous Pictures*, 154–62; Ditlev Tamm and Helle Vogt, 'Creating a Danish Legal Language: Legal Terminology in the Medieval Law of Scania', *Historical Research* 86 (2013), 505–14.

13 Kr. Erslev, William Christensen, and Anna Hude, eds., *Repertorium Diplomaticum Regni Danici Mediævalis, Fortegnelse over Danmarks Breve Fra Middelalderen med Udtog af de hidtil utrykte* 4 (Copenhagen: 1912), 4.

a large degree and the chancery was staffed by clerics.[14] It is difficult to ascertain when this practice was adopted because so much has been lost but *ca.*1100 is an educated guess. What came before was probably drafted by the recipients, i.e. what the Germans call 'Empfängerausfertigungen'.[15] In fact, most of the documentation for private conveyance of land before the fourteenth century was probably drafted by the ecclesiastical recipients. This picture is possibly skewed by the one-sided transmission of documents—almost all of them owe their survival to the archives of the church.[16]

In the following, I shall limit myself to legal documents dealing with conveyance of land. Since 2008, I have worked at the editorial project *Diplomatarium Danicum* at the Society for Danish Language and Literature, funded by the Carlsberg Foundation. My job has been to edit the surviving documents from the years 1413 to 1450 concerning conveyance of land as well as the documents from the royal and ecclesiastical law courts.[17]

Danish law focused on oral testimony to an almost excessive degree, which is surely one of the reasons for the low number of legal documents from the twelfth and thirteenth centuries. As pointed out by Michael Gelting, the fact that Innocent III accepted the peculiar Danish form of land conveyance known as *scotacio*, and that his acceptance was included in *Liber Extra* in 1234, greatly contributed to the conservatism of the laws of land conveyance in medieval Denmark.[18]

---

14 See Niels Skyum-Nielsen, 'Den danske konges kancelli i 1250'erne', in *Festskrift til Astrid Friis på halvfjerdsårsdagen den 1. august 1963*, ed. Svend Ellehøj, Svend Gissel, and Knud Vohn (Copenhagen: 1963), 225–45; Niels Skyum-Nielsen, 'Kanslere og skrivere i Danmark 1250–1282', in *Middelalderstudier tilegnede Aksel E. Christensen på tresårsdagen 11. september 1966*, ed. Tage E. Christiansen, Svend Ellehøj, and Erling Ladewig-Petersen (Copenhagen: 1966), 141–84.

15 The closest thing to an English term is 'documents produced outside the chancery', which is less precise. See Maria Milagros Cárcel Ortí, ed., *Vocabulaire international de la diplomatique*, Commission internationale de diplomatique. Comité international des sciences historiques, 2nd edn. (València: 1997), 69 § 267.

16 There is no manual of Danish Diplomatics, but see Michael Gelting, 'Circumstantial Evidence: Danish Charters of the Thirteenth Century', in *Medieval Legal Process: Physical, Spoken and Written Performance in the Middle Ages*, ed. Marco Mostert and P. S. Barnwell (Turnhout: 2011), 157–95, which discusses Danish documents of the twelfth and thirteenth centuries.

17 *Diplomatarium Danicum* is now exclusively an online edition: *Diplomatarium Danicum: Kilder til Danmarks historie 789–1450—på originalsprog og oversat til dansk*, published by The Society for Danish Language and Literature at <http://diplomatarium.dk/>.

18 Gelting, 'Circumstantial Evidence', 162–6, 167 n. 35, and 189.

It was primarily the ecclesiastical institutions that wanted written legal documents—probably because they needed them for use in the ecclesiastical courts—and the number of such documents rose steadily during the thirteenth century. These documents were issued by donors and sellers, but normally drawn up by the recipients. This meant that the great institutions, such as the monasteries, each had their own way of doing things, their own models or formularies. The rather long and artful legal documents of the twelfth century did, however, tend to become shorter and more business-like during the thirteenth century, particularly from the mid-century.[19]

Private charters in the proper sense, i.e. charters issued by private persons appeared rather late. Throughout the twelfth and thirteenth centuries, all known recipients were clerics or ecclesiastical institutions; the first documented transaction between private parties does not appear until 1317.[20]

What effect did this have on the Latinity of the legal documents? Gelting noticed a shift from a more artful form in the twelfth century to a more business-like form in the thirteenth, especially from the mid-century. This is indeed due to a shift from a model based on *ars dictaminis* to a model based on *ars notaria*. Letter writing was probably always taught at school, being part of rhetoric and thus belonging to the *trivium*. The *ars dictaminis* was a medieval genre, however. It developed in Italy in the late eleventh century but soon spread to the rest of Latin Christendom where it had an enormous influence on letter writing.[21]

In his groundbreaking book on rhetoric in the Middle Ages, James Murphy characterized what he called the dictational movement, as 'essentially an attempt to apply Ciceronian rhetoric to a specific compositional problem—that of writing letters'.[22] By this, he meant that the *ars dictaminis* established the

19 See Gelting, 'Circumstantial Evidence', 169–80 on the practices of the Cistercian house of Esrom and the Augustinian house of Æbelholt, both on Zealand. For the long and artful letters of the twelfth century, see *ibid.*, 162.

20 Herluf Nielsen, 'Über die dänische Privaturkunde bis zum 14. Jahrhundert mit einem Schlusswort über das Notariat', in *Notariado público y documento privado: de los orígenes al siglo XIV*. Actas del VII Congreso Internacional de Diplomática, Valencia 1986, 2 (València: 1989), 951–9.

21 See James J. Murphy, *Rhetoric in the Middle Ages: A History of the Rhetorical Theory from Saint Augustine to the Renaissance* (Tempe, Ariz: 2001 (orig. 1974)), 194–268. While accepting that the *ars dictaminis* was a medieval genre, Carol Lanham called attention to the fact that letter writing was always on the school curriculum; see Carol Dana Lanham, 'Freshman Composition in the Early Middle Ages: Epistolography and Rhetoric before the Ars Dictaminis', *Viator* 23 (1992), 115–34.

22 Murphy, *Rhetoric in the Middle Ages*, 266.

norm of five formal letter parts: *salutatio, captatio benevolentiae, narratio, petitio*, and *conclusio*. The stylistic feature most characteristic of the movement was prose rhythm, or *cursus*. Manuals continued to be written for centuries to come, but by the end of the thirteenth century, there was no longer any movement, and no innovation either.

The principal aim of the *ars dictaminis* was elegance, hence the attention to *cursus*. Much energy was also devoted to choosing the right form of address. Within the tradition of the *ars dictaminis*, focus was on the recipient, and his or her status—relative to the issuer—determined the form of the letter. It was not ideally suited for legal purposes, therefore, and fell out of use when a more specific solution became available in the form of the *ars notaria*.[23] The *ars dictaminis* did have certain lasting effects on the legal documents all over Europe. The very common use of address and greeting in legal documents is an epistolary feature.[24] The tradition of careful attention to social status is another feature, which the legal documents borrowed from the epistolary genre.

Within the tradition of the *ars notaria*, the content determined the form of the letter. The type of legal document most often associated with the *ars notaria* was the notarial instrument or *instrumentum publicum*.[25] The form of the notarial instrument was determined partly by law and partly by custom. Justinian's *Code* and *Novels* set out the basic, legal requirements.[26] As regards custom, the great manuals of Rainerius of Perugia (fl. 1220), Salathiel of Bologna (†1280) and Rolandinus Passagerii (†1300) set the standard.[27]

In addition to the part dealing with the business at hand, it was to have certain formal parts, often called *solemnitates*. These were as follows: a verbal invocation; an elaborate dating, referring to the date of the transaction,

23 *Ibid.*, 244, 263–6.

24 See Olivier Guyotjeannin, Jacques Pycke and Benoît-Michel Tock, *Diplomatique médiévale*, 3rd edn. (Turnhout: 2006), 75–6, 104–5.

25 Knut Wolfgang Nörr, *Romanisch-kanonisches Prozessrecht: Erkenntnisverfahren erster Instanz in civilibus*, (Heidelberg, Dordrecht, London, and New York: 2012), 154–60, Enzyklopädie der Rechts- und Staatswissenschaft, Abteilung Rechtswissenschaft; Peter-Johannes Schuler, *Geschichte des südwestdeutschen Notariats: Von seinen Anfängen bis zur Reichsnotariatsordnung von 1512*. (Bühl (Baden): 1976).

26 C.J. 4.21 (Theodor Mommsen *et al.*, *Corpus Iuris Civilis*, 3 vols. (Berlin: 1872–1877), II, 160–4) and Nov. 44 and 73 (Mommsen *et al.*, *Corpus Iuris Civilis*, III, 273–7, 363–70).

27 See the short, succinct biographies of all three: Peter Weimar, 'Rainerius Perusinus', in *Lexikon des Mittelalters* 7 (Stutttgart and Weimar: 1999), 420–1; Peter Weimar, 'Rolandinus Passagerii', in *ibid.*, 959; and Peter Weimar, 'Salathiel', in *ibid.*, 1286.

consisting of the date in the year of the Lord; the indiction;[28] the year of the reigning emperor or pope;[29] the month, day, and time of day; the place; a list of the witnesses, each clearly identified; the subscription (*eschatocol*) of the notary, which functions as the authenticating clause, and his official mark, his *signum*.[30]

The business part of the notarial instrument should state the presence of the clearly identified parties. It was incumbent upon the notary to make sure that they were acting voluntarily, had a legal personality, and were trustworthy, or *fide digni* in Latin—a qualification also necessary for the witnesses. In addition to the record of the transaction, it was essential to have a clause of rogation—stating that the notary was asked by one or more of the parties to witness the transaction and draw up the notarial instrument, as this was the very reason for his issuing the document.

In notarial practice, the *solemnitates* were divided between the *protocol* and the *eschatocol* of the document, thus framing the business part. The issuer of the document was the notary who was also the chief witness.

The *instrumentum publicum* was meant not only to describe the transaction in question, but also to show that the proper procedure had been followed. This dual purpose set the limitations for the form of the document.

The *ars notaria* was of immediate use in the areas of Europe that used Roman law, but also gradually came to be used in large parts of Europe that had never been part of the ancient Roman Empire.[31] In 1215, in an attempt to modernize and streamline the workings of the ecclesiastical courts, canon 38 of Lateran IV decreed the use of a notary (if one could be had) or two people skilled in the notarial art for the making and keeping of records.[32] The rule

---

28 C. R. Cheney, *A Handbook of Dates: For Students of British history*, new ed., rev. by Michael Jones (Cambridge: 2000), 2–4.

29 Cheney and Jones, *A Handbook of Dates*, 4.

30 Schuler, *Geschichte des südwestdeutschen Notariats*, 262–89, in particular 262–4.

31 The literature on the notariate and the *ars notaria* is very large. A good place to start is the published acts of the seventh conference of the Commission internationale de diplomatique: *Notariado público y documento privado: de los orígenes al siglo XIV.*, which give an overview of Europe and the very different conditions in the individual regions and countries. In addition, there are several more localized studies, see, *inter alia*, Andreas Meyer, *Felix et inclitus notarius: Studien zum italienischen Notariat vom 7. bis zum 13. Jahrhundert* (Tübingen: 2000); Schuler, *Geschichte des südwestdeutschen Notariats*; and James M. Murray, *Notarial Instruments in Flanders between 1280 and 1452* (Brussels: 1995).

32 Antonius García y García, ed., *Constitutiones Concilii quarti Lateranensis una cum Commentariis glossatorum*. Monumenta Iuris Canonici. Series A: Corpus Glossatorum 2 (Vatican City: 1981), 80–1.

was included in the *Liber Extra* via *Compilatio quarta*.[33] From then on, every bishop, *qua* judge, would need a notary. But getting one might be difficult, though the pope could authorize a bishop to appoint a number of capable men as notaries—like the emperors, the popes had assumed the right to appoint notaries public—and the number of such men must have grown steadily.[34]

Still, the notarial art did not make itself felt in Denmark until the middle or second half of the thirteenth century and the delay was most likely due to a lack of trained personnel. Eventually, the *ars notaria* influenced the form of legal documents in Denmark, hence the shift noticed by Gelting. The more business-like form is simply due to the notarial influence.

However, there is more to the *ars notaria* than just a rigid scheme. In a study of the Latinity of the notarial instruments of Genoa from 1150 to 1250, John McGovern characterized the two guiding principles as clarity and unity.[35] Clarity was achieved with the clear expressions of time, the careful description

---

33 X 2.19.11 (Emil Friedberg, *Corpus Iuris Canonici* 2 (Graz: 1959), 313–14) and 4 Comp. 2.6.3.

34 A total of five authorizations for two Danish archbishops of Lund and two bishops of Roskilde are known from the period 1290–1304. On the day of his appointment, archbishop Jens Grand received papal permission to appoint three notaries from his archdiocese, 15 March, 1290, *DD*, 2.III.395. The notaries would swear the same oath of obedience to the pope as other notaries by apostolic authority, but there is no doubt that the permission to appoint these notaries was a valuable means of patronage. He received another permission on 31 May, 1298, after a long and serious struggle with the Danish king during which he had been incarcerated for a year-and-a-half, and had been living in exile in Rome for a couple of years. It is evident from the sources that he did not have the full backing of his clergy and it is tempting to assume that he needed to recruit new and trustworthy notaries for his own use. The second permission seems to have been part of an attempt at a general solution of the struggle by the pope, and the archbishop would dearly need trustworthy helpers on his return to Denmark. We know the identity of only one of these notaries, Kjeld Jensen from Slagelse, who assisted the archbishop in 1299, see *DD*, 2.V.47, 67, 72–3, 75–6. Likewise, the successor to Jens Grand, Isarn, former papal legate, who was transferred from the archdiocese of Riga to the archdiocese of Lund on 11 April, 1302, was authorized to appoint three notaries on 27 November, 1303, on his own application, *DD*, 2.V.277. Jens Krag, bishop of Roskilde 1290–1300, received papal authorization to appoint two notaries on 25 December, 1291, *DD* 2. IV.48. Oluf, his successor, likewise received papal authorization to appoint two notaries on 10 March, 1304, *DD*, 2.V.305.

35 John F. McGovern, 'The Documentary Language of Medieval Business, AD 1150–1250', *The Classical Journal* 67 (1972), 229. McGovern argued that these principles were peculiar to the Genoese notaries and were due to the demands of their business clients and the special nature of their affairs, rather than to any influence from the theorists and teachers of the *ars notaria*. McGovern's view is wrong, as the features which he describes are found in documents from other parts of Europe as well, and not just in documents dealing with the affairs of merchants.

and identification of persons and places, the clarification of special terminology, and the avoidance of vernacular expressions. The aim was to avoid any misinterpreting or misconstruing, whether intentional or not. Textual unity was achieved by an extensive use of identifiers and 'reidentifiers', as McGovern called them, as well as conjunctions, adverbials, and participials. The effect was to make each segment of the text grammatically inseparable from the rest.

How does this relate to conditions in Denmark? The influence from the *ars notaria* went beyond the notarial instruments. Around the 1290s, a specific type of document—the *testimonium placiti*—was developed in Denmark along the lines of the notarial instrument. This type of document—while in many ways very different from the *instrumentum publicum*—suited Danish law as well as the notarial instrument fitted Roman law.[36]

The influence of the *ars notaria* extended beyond the *testimonium placiti*. Even the ordinary letter patent—if there is such a thing—was influenced by the notarial art. Indeed, the letters often come in pairs, a letter patent and a *testimonium placiti*, both documenting the same transaction and showing obvious similarities, one using first person verbs, the other third person verbs.[37]

---

36 Anders Leegaard Knudsen, 'Testimonia Placiti—Private Charters as Public Instruments: A Study in Medieval Danish Diplomatics', *Archiv für Diplomatik, Schriftgeschichte, Siegel- und Wappenkunde* 57 (2011), 147–80.

37 See, e.g., Mogens Madsen's sale of his estate in Malmö to Bent Unge in 1402, DD 1402 11 September, <http://diplomatarium.dk/dokument/14020911001> and <http://diplomatarium.dk/dokument/14020911002>; Knud Andersen's sale of some of his land to Ingvar Andersen in 1415, DD 1415 13 July <http://diplomatarium.dk/dokument/14150713002> and <http://diplomatarium.dk/dokument/14150713001>; as well as Christine Esgedatter's conveyance by *scotacio* of her lands to Dueholm Priory of 1422 10 May, and her donation of October 1 of the same year to Dueholm Priory in return for board and lodging for the rest of her life, as well as an annual requiem mass after her death, <http://diplomatarium.dk/dokument/14220510001> and <http://diplomatarium.dk/dokument/14221001001>. All six of these documents are in Latin, but the pattern is the same in Danish documents, see e.g., Anders Prep's and Jens Grim's sale of their inheritance in the district of Harjager to Niels Svendsen of Ellinge in 1402, DD 1402 16 December, <http://diplomatarium.dk/dokument/14021216001> and <http://diplomatarium.dk/dokument/14021216002>; and Peder Sommer's, Peder Gedsted's and Thomas Gedsted's sale and conveyance by *scotacio* of their paternal inheritance in the parish of Gedsted to queen Margaret in 1408, DD 1408 11 August and 1 September, <http://diplomatarium.dk/dokument/14080811001> and <http://diplomatarium.dk/dokument/14080901001>; as well as Christine's surrender of her right of inheritance after her brother to queen Philippa in 1424, DD 1424 8 March, <http://diplomatarium.dk/dokument/14240308001> and <http://diplomatarium.dk/dokument/14240308002>. For examples from the cartulary from Aarhus and the registers from

Danish law in the Middle Ages never defined the form of the Danish *testimonia*. Theoretically, the *testimonia* could have taken any number of forms. The laws merely specified the proper venue for conveyance of land, the proper time, and the necessary attendance. Conveyance was to take place at the local court or assembly, at one of its ordinary sessions, in the presence of at least seven witnesses.[38] Incidentally, when the legislators determined that conveyance of land was to take place at the local court–cum–public assembly, they were not only aiming at publication before the local residents. They were also, in effect, prescribing a process known as *confessio in iure* on the basis of the Roman law principle 'those who confess in court are held to be convicted' (*confessi pro iudicatis habentur*).[39] These specifications came to determine the form of the *testimonium placiti*. The seven or more clearly identified witnesses of the transaction are also the issuers of the *testimonium*. They promulgate their presence at a specific court of law at a specific time. At this occasion, a clearly identified party who was present (*constitutus*) conveyed some land to another party, who was also present. All this was witnessed by the issuers and other trustworthy men—*fidedigni*—who corroborated the document and authenticated it by appending their seals to it.

Several of the formulas and clauses, which make up the elements of the *testimonia placiti*, are also found in the notarial instruments. Witnesses are *fidedigni*. The transaction takes place *in presencia nostra* ('in our presence') or *coram nobis* ('before us'). The parties are *constitutus* ('present'), *personaliter constitutus* ('personally present') or even *propter hoc personaliter constitutus* ('personally present because of this matter'). The final section, or *eschatocol*, typically contains a short dating clause *datum anno, die et loco supradictis* ('given in the above-mentioned year, day, and place'), corresponding to the

Sorø Abbey and Skovkloster Abbey, see Chr. Kjer, *Om Overdragelse af Eiendomsret over faste Eiendomme for Tiden indtil Chr. V.' Lov: Et Bidrag til dansk Retshistorie* (Aarhus: 1889), 64–5.

38 On the peculiar Danish form of conveyance of land called 'skøtning' ('skødning' in modern Danish), or *scotacio* in Latin, see Kjer, *Om Overdragelse af Eiendomsret*, 36–59; Gelting, 'Circumstantial Evidence', 162–6, and Knudsen, 'Testimonia Placiti', 148–9. The Danish text of the crucial Law of Jutland ('Jyske Lov') is found in *Danmarks gamle Landskabslove* 2, ed. Peter Skautrup (Copenhagen: 1933), 89–91; a fourteenth century Latin translation is edited in *Danmarks gamle Landskabslove* 4, ed. by Stig Iuul and Peter Jørgensen (Copenhagen: 1945), 53–4. For an English translation, see *The Danish Medieval Laws: The Laws of Scania, Zealand and Jutland*, ed. and trans. Ditlev Tamm and Helle Vogt (London and New York: 2016), 252.

39 Dig. 42.2.3 (Theodor Mommsen *et al.*, *Corpus Iuris Civilis*, I, 669); C.J. 7.59.1 21 (Theodor Mommsen *et al.*, *Corpus Iuris Civilis*, II, 320).

clause *acta sunt hec quibus supra* ('this was enacted on the date and place mentioned above') of the notarial instruments.

There are differences, though. First of all, the *testimonium* is authenticated by the seals of the issuers, not by a subscription plus *signum*. No *testimonium* ever mentions the notary; the very elaborate dating system of the notarial instruments is never found in the *testimonia*, which always use the liturgical calendar; the witnesses are mentioned only once in the *testimonia* rather than twice as in the notarial instruments; etc.

There is no denying the differences between the two types of document, but the similarities outweigh the differences. The common approach of the two types of document is the most important common feature. Both place the witnesses and the parties at the same venue at the same time. The witnesses make public the transaction they witnessed. The date given is the date of the transaction, which is also the document's official date of issue.

The two types of documents also share the same stylistic principles. Both of them aim for clarity and textual unity and they use the same devices to achieve this, i.e. clear expressions of time, careful description and identification of persons and places, clarification of special terminology, and an extensive use of identifiers as well as conjunctions, adverbials, and participials.

This is a skilful way of adapting a model, based on Roman law, to Danish conditions. It shows a sophisticated adaptation of the *ars notaria* for Danish law. People skilled in the notarial art must have drawn up the *testimonia placiti*, which became increasingly common throughout the fourteenth century. There was nothing mechanical about the way they applied the *ars notaria* to Danish documents. In all likelihood, they were employed in the royal chancery, which at that time was staffed by clerics, chaplains, or even canons 'on loan', so to speak, from the cathedral chapters. It should not surprise us that these men were skilled in the *ars notaria*.

Among the concepts they borrowed, we find the following examples.[40] In Roman law, the verb *alienare* means to transfer property through a transaction, such as a sale or a donation. It is known all over Europe in this sense and often found in the Danish *testimonia* and then always in connection with a sale or a donation in which the buyer or donee acquires full and lasting possession.[41] Two other verbs with a similar legal content are regularly found in charters

40 See Knudsen, 'Testimonia Placiti'.

41 *Lexicon Mediae Latinitatis Danicae*, ed. Franz Blatt *et al.* (Aarhus: 1987–2014), 29, s.v. *alieno* (hereafter as LMLD).

from Latin Europe: *appropriare*, meaning, 'to grant',[42] and *assignare*, meaning, 'to confer'. Like *alienare*, they are common in Danish legal documents.[43] The medieval neologism *disbrigare* was borrowed as well. According to the standard dictionaries of Medieval Latin this term is the Latinisation of an Italian word meaning 'to free of obligation', 'to clear of debt', etc.[44]

Whenever we hear of a sale in the Danish *testimonia*, we also find the seller's recognition of having been paid in full, or to his or her satisfaction. This touches on more than just the well-known canonical theory of the just price. In Roman law 'there can be no sale without a price' or *nulla emptio sine pretio esse potest* in Latin.[45] The payment of the price constitutes proof of the nature of this transaction.

But not all Danish legal concepts could be expressed in the vocabulary of Roman Law. Danish lawyers found it necessary to coin a few new words of their own, such as *scotare* and *bondo*. *Scotare* is a Latinization of the Danish verb 'skøte', meaning to place a piece of turf in the fold of a cloak—the ceremony accompanying a conveyance of land. The corresponding noun is *scotacio*.[46]

Bondo is a Latinization of the Danish noun 'bonde', originally the personally free, landowning peasant who is the legal person of the Danish laws in the Middle Ages. With the declining number of free landowning peasants in the later Middle Ages, the term seems to have acquired the more general meaning of 'householder'. It was still a more specific term than 'country-dweller' or 'agriculturist' for which there were several classical Latin words to choose from. These Danicisms represent a successful attempt to create precise technical terms for specific Danish institutions.[47]

Another solution was the use of technical terms in Danish as a sort of 'linear gloss' on the Latin text. This practice was quite common. This phenomenon was studied by Jonathan Adams, who concluded that the glosses would normally add a more specific meaning to the more generic description given

---

42 LMDL, 48, s.v. *approprio*. Strictly speaking, *approprio* does not seem to have been a legal term in Classical Latin. Both Lewis and Short, *A New Latin Dictionary* (Oxford: 1984), 144; and *Der Neue Georges. Ausführliches Lateinisch-Deutsches Handwörterbuch* 1, ed. Thomas Baier and Tobias Dänzer (Darmstadt: 2013), 400 have only one witness: the fifth-century Caelius Aurelianus' *Tardae* or *Chronicae passiones*. Whether this makes *appropriare* a medicinal, rather than a legal expression is doubtful, however. In medieval legal documents it is used with the sense 'to grant'.

43 LMDL, 58–9, s.v. *assigno*.

44 LMDL, 226, s.v. *disbrigo*.

45 Inst. 3.23 (Mommsen *et al.*, *Corpus Iuris Civilis*, 1, 39).

46 LMLD, 665–6, s.vv. *scotatio, scoto*.

47 LMLD, s.v. *bondo*, 79.

in Latin.[48] In this sense, it is equivalent to a prominent feature in the notarial instruments.

Characteristic of the *ars notaria* is the extensive use of doublets, triplets, and even quadruplets—a feature that is also found in Danish legal instruments—such as:

1) *uendidit alienauit scotauit et ad manus assignauit iure perpetuo possidenda*.... ('sold, alienated, deeded and assigned in the hands to possess with everlasting right ...'), 1405, 15 September.[49]
2) *scotauit alienauit et in manus libere et legaliter assignauit iure perpetuo possidendam*.... ('deeded, alienated and freely and lawfully assigned in the hands to possess with everlasting right ...'), 1405, 17 December.[50]
3) *appropriauit alienauit et in sinum scotauit iure perpetuo possidenda*.... ('appropriated, alienated and deeded in the fold to possess with everlasting right ...'), 1406, 10 May.[51]

In the cases just mentioned, we see that the donor, seller, mortgagor, etc. first relinquishes the property, then deeds it to the recipient, buyer, mortgagee, etc., and finally conveys it to that person or institution in perpetuity.

Another very prominent feature is the extensive use of so-called 'pro-forms' (what McGovern calls identifiers and reidentifiers) to modify the noun and clarify to whom or what the document refers, such as various forms of 'said', 'aforesaid', 'above-mentioned', 'below-mentioned', or 'oft-mentioned': *dictus* / *predictus* / *antedictus* / *supradictus* / *infradictus* / *sepedictus* + noun; or 'mentioned', 'aforementioned': *memoratus* / *antememoratus* + noun; 'the same': *idem* + noun; 'he himself': *ipse* + noun; 'below-written', or 'above-written': *infrascriptus* / *suprascriptus* + noun.

The use of standardized phrases is common: *constitutus in presencia nostra* / *coram nobis et aliis pluribus fidedignis; scotare* (or *assignare*) *in sinum alicuius; assignare* (or *resignare*) *in manus* (or *ad manus*) *alicuius iure perpetuo possidenda.*

A characteristic of the legal documents not just in Denmark but also all over Europe is the close attention to rank. Issuers and witnesses are ordered in strict accordance with their station in society: royalty first, members of the

48 Jonathan Adams, 'In Danico Dicitur: Glossing in Danish Manuscripts', *Scandinavian Studies* 82, no. 2 (2010), 117–58, in particular 133–52.

49 *DD*, <http://diplomatarium.dk/dokument/14050915001>.

50 *DD*, <http://diplomatarium.dk/dokument/14051217001>.

51 *DD*, <http://diplomatarium.dk/dokument/14060510001>.

clergy—in hierarchical order—then lay people, knights, squires, burgesses—mayors and town councillors first, in that order—and finally peasants, with those holding any kind of official post first. It seems that nobility outranked gender, as high-ranking women preceded lower ranking men. In this aspect, legal usage seems to have much in common with the *ars dictaminis*, which was excessively preoccupied with the correct form of address. The parallel is also seen in the use of adjectives to qualify the various ranks: rulers were referred to as '(most) illustrious', or '(most) serene': *illustrissimus* (or *illustris*) *rex* or *princeps, serenissimus* (or *serenus*) *rex* or *princeps*. Bishops and prelates (and not infrequently all clergy) were 'venerable' or 'honourable' (*venerabilis* or *honorabilis*). Nobles were 'noble lord' and 'noble lady' (*nobilis dominus* or *vir*, and *nobilis domina* or *femina*). In the later Middle Ages, knights were often *strenui milites* (roughly 'bold knights'). Burgesses and occasionally peasants were 'prudent' (*discretus vir*) and women were 'honest' (*honesta matrona, femina*, or *vidua*).

It seems quite clear, then, that the legal documents in Latin from medieval Denmark were not simply translations from Danish. Rather, they were legal documents expressed in Latin. Moreover, not just any Latin, but an international legal language modelled on the notarial art. As regards aim and style, there is nothing specifically Danish about them—they share most of these features with legal documents from all over Latin Europe. Much of the terminology is borrowed from Roman law, but in a very deliberate way. Expressing Danish law in Latin was the norm for the people who drew up the legal documents. What does that tell us? It is an old and well-known dictum that law schools do not teach students the law; they teach them to think like lawyers. If this dictum holds true, then Latin was part of Danish jurisprudence: Danish lawyers were, to a degree, thinking in Latin.

For a long time the *testimonia* were written exclusively in Latin. The earliest surviving *testimonium* written in Danish dates from 1388, but it is not until *ca.*1425 that Latin ceased to be used. For reasons no one has been able to explain, Denmark was among the last countries in Europe to abandon Latin in favour of the vernacular.[52] This must raise the question whether the interested parties understood what was going on. In the case of ecclesiastical institutions,

52 The choice of the vernacular over Latin was part of a general European trend of 'vernacularisation', see Thomas Brunner, 'Le passage aux langues vernaculaires dans les actes de la pratique en Occident', *Le Moyen Âge* 115 (2009), 29–72; on the situation in Denmark, see Knudsen, 'Testimonia Placiti'. The uneven pace of 'vernacularisation' of the various countries and regions may mean that the process is not one passage, but several, each *sui generis*.

the crown, or the town magistrates and burgesses the answer is probably yes. If not, easy access to people—often clerics—who would be able to understand and explain the content was at hand. The linguistic barrier was thin in these cases. However, what about the laity at large: the knights, the esquires, or even the peasants?

There can be no doubt that the attendants at the local courts transacted their affairs in Danish, or Middle Low German in parts of Southern Jutland. Yet the attendants were no strangers to Latin. In the fourteenth and fifteenth centuries, they issued an increasing number of authenticated copies of legal documents, itself a type of legal document known as a *vidisse* in Denmark or a *vidimus* in England. A large number of documents only exist today in the form of such authenticated copies. Prior to authenticating the copy by the application of their seals, the attendants would examine both the original and the copy. The original had to appear unsuspicious in every way, as well as still valid; the copy was checked to see if it was properly and faithfully done. Thus, seeing and hearing a Latin document was familiar to the frequent attendants of the local or regional courts. The lesson drawn from this was straightforward—documents mattered. One had to be able to trust documents, but fortunately, there were criteria by which they could be judged, a sort of proto-diplomatics, so to speak.

However, that still does not tell us if the great silent majority of the lay population understood the contents of the Latin letters. It does seem unlikely, though, that knowledge of Latin should have been widespread among lay Danes in the tenth to fifteenth centuries, or indeed later. They were certainly familiar with hearing it in church and anywhere else the priest performed his duties.[53] However, on average, the priests do not seem to have been very highly educated, even if exceptions to the rule can be found.[54] Besides, as any modern-day solicitor will tell us, it is an everyday experience that there is more to understanding a legal document than merely being able to read the text. The implications of an agreement between two parties may not be immediately clear to the uninitiated reader of the text of that agreement. The important

53 On the difficult subject of the laity's proficiency in Latin, see Clanchy, *From Memory to Written Record*, 206–11, 220–3, and in particular 234–40; and Thomas Frenz, 'Vocavit nos pius: "Öffentlichkeitsarbeit" durch päpstliche Urkunden im späten Mittelalter und der frühen Neuzeit', in *La langue des actes* (Troyes: 2003), online at <http://elec.enc.sorbonne.fr/CID2003/frenz>.

54 For a fairly dim view of the level of education of the parish priests in medieval Denmark, see Troels Dahlerup, 'Prästutbildning: Danmark', in *Kulturhistorisk Leksikon for Nordisk Middelalder fra vikingetid til reformationstid*, ed. John Danstrup, 21 vols., plus index, 2nd edn. (Rosenkilde and Bagger: 1981), XIII, 570–1.

thing was trust in the document: that it was valid under the law and that the text faithfully rendered the terms agreed upon by all interested parties.[55]

What happened when Danish supplanted Latin as the legal language? I would like to quote professor Bent Jørgensen, who once—speaking on the subject of Danish letters of the fifteenth century—called them 'Latin letters written in Danish'! A remarkable statement, but true.[56] The striving for clarity and unity is the same, even if Danish does not offer the same opportunities as Latin. Word order, for instance, is far more important in Danish than in Latin. Within the syntactical limitations, though, the Danish letters are clearly modelled on the Latin ones.[57]

The characteristic use of doublets, triplets and quadruplets also appears in the Danish letters:

1) *'wnt oc giwit oc skøøt oc affhent ... til ewerdelich eghe ...'* ('granted and given and deeded and alienated ... in everlasting possession ...'), 1393, 6 July.[58]
2) *'wpladet schøøt affhent oc antwordhet ... wgencalleleghe til ewerdelegh eye ...'* ('conveyed, deeded, alienated and delivered ... irrevocably in everlasting possession ...'), 1400, 15 June.[59]
3) *'saalt skøt oc affhænt hauer ... til ewerdeleghe æye....'* ('have sold, deeded and alienated ... in everlasting possession ...'), 1406, 5 October.[60]

Danish letters also extensively use identifiers, but almost exclusively *fornævnd*, i.e. 'the previously mentioned', the Danish equivalent of *predictus* and *antedictus* in Latin.

As regards the vocabulary, the Danish letters often uses words borrowed from Middle Low German when there were no suitable Danish terms. Occasionally, we know that there was, in fact, a Danish word, but it was still supplanted by a loan word.[61]

55 See Clanchy, *From Memory to Written Record*, 294–327.
56 The characterization was given in the course of a presentation of a new edition of the medieval cartulary from Æbelholt Abbey, Bent Jørgensen, Gorm Tortzen, and Bent Christensen, 'Æbelholtbogen—Om at udgive en middelalderlig klosterbrevbog' (presented at Center for Europæiske Middelalderstudier, KUA, March 12, 2012).
57 See § 41 C in Peter Skautrup, *Det danske Sprogs Historie* 2 (Copenhagen: 1947), 69–73.
58 *DD*, 4.V.54.
59 *DD*, 4.VII.316.
60 *DD*, <http://diplomatarium.dk/dokument/14061005001>.
61 See the important contribution by Birgit Christensen, 'Die mittelniederdeutschen Lehnwörter in dänischen Urkunden aus dem Zeitraum 1378–1435', *Kopenhagener Beiträge zur Germanistischen Linguistik* 20 (1982), 40–1.

Latin usage, firmly grounded in the *ars notaria*, became the model for Danish usage in the fifteenth century. This legal-administrative sublanguage became the norm of the bureaucracy; it is known in Danish as 'kancellistil' or 'kancellisprog' (chancery style or chancery language).[62] These days, it is being deliberately phased out of use, but certain features proved very tenacious: even in the 1980s, Danish deeds still contained the phrase 'sælger, skøder og endeligt overdrager' ('sell, deed, and irrevocably convey'), resonant of *vendo, scoto, et alieno*. More than half a millennium after Danish supplanted Latin in legal documents one could still hear a faint Latin echo.

Bibliography

Adams, Jonathan. 'In Danico Dicitur: Glossing in Danish Manuscripts'. *Scandinavian Studies* 82, no. 2 (2010): 117–58.

Andersen, Merete Geert. 'The Dalby Book'. In *Living Words & Luminous Pictures: Medieval book culture in Denmark. Essays*, edited by Erik Petersen, 63–6. Aarhus: 1999.

Andersen, Per. *Legal Procedure and Practice in Medieval Denmark*. Boston and Leiden: 2011.

Bagge, Sverre. 'Nordic Students at Foreign Universities'. *Scandinavian Journal of History* 9, no. 1 (1984): 1–29.

Bagge, Sverre. *Cross and Scepter: The Rise of the Scandinavian Kingdoms from the Vikings to the Reformation*. Princeton and Oxford: 2014.

Borgehammar, Stephan, Karsten Friis-Jensen, Lars Boje Mortensen and Åslaug Ommundsen, eds. *Medieval Nordic Literature in Latin: A Website of Authors and Anonymous Works ca. 1100–1530*, last modified December 30, 2012 at: <https://wikihost.uib.no/medieval/index.php/Medieval_Nordic_Literature_in_Latin>.

Brunner, Thomas. 'Le passage aux langues vernaculaires dans les actes de la pratique en Occident'. *Le Moyen Âge* 115 (2009): 29–72.

62 Skautrup has shown how in the Middle Ages, the 'Kancellistil' developed from the style of the legal documents, see Skautrup, *Det danske Sprogs Historie*, II, 71–2; on the later development of this sublanguage, see § 72 B in Skautrup, *Det danske Sprogs Historie*, III, 260–3; and § 85 B in Skautrup, *Det danske Sprogs Historie*, IV, 175–7. See also the fine exposition of the 'Kancellistil' by a professor in jurisprudence at the University of Copenhagen: W. E. von Eyben, 'Juridisk stil og sprogbrug', in *Juridisk grundbog: Affattelse af love, domme, forvaltningsakter og kontrakter*, ed. W. E. von Eyben, (Copenhagen: 1962), 480–517.

Cárcel Ortí, and Maria Milagros, eds. *Vocabulaire international de la diplomatique*. 2nd edn. València: 1997.

Cheney, C. R. *A Handbook of Dates: For students of British history*, new edn., revised by Michael Jones. Cambridge and New York: 2000.

Christensen, Aksel E. 'Tiden 1042–1241'. In *Danmarks historie* 1, edited by Aksel E. Christensen *et al.*, 211–399. Copenhagen: 1978.

Christensen, Birgit. 'Die mittelniederdeutschen Lehnwörter in dänischen Urkunden aus dem Zeitraum 1378–1435'. *Kopenhagener Beiträge zur Germanistischen Linguistik* 20 (1982): 1–66.

Clanchy, Michael T. *From Memory to Written Record: England 1066–1307*, 2nd edn. Oxford and Cambridge, MA: 1993.

Dahlerup, Troels. 'Prästutbildning: Danmark'. In *Kulturhistorisk Leksikon for Nordisk Middelalder fra vikingetid til reformationstid*, vol. 13, 570–1. Copenhagen: 1968.

Danmarks historie, vol. 1. edited by Aksel E. Christensen, *et al.* Copenhagen: 1978.

Danmarks Riges Breve. Published by The Society for Danish Language and Literature. 35 vols. in four series. Copenhagen: 1938–2000.

Danstrup, John, editor. *Kulturhistorisk Leksikon for Nordisk Middelalder fra vikingetid til reformationstid*, 21 vols. Kopenhagen: 1981.

Diplomatarium Danicum. Published by The Society for Danish Language and Literature. 35 vols., in four series. Copenhagen: 1938–2000.

Diplomatarium Danicum: Kilder til Danmarks historie 789–1450—på originalsprog og oversat til dansk. Published by The Society for Danish Language and Literature at <http://diplomatarium.dk/>.

Erslev, Kr., William Christensen, and Anna Hude, editors. *Repertorium Diplomaticum Regni Danici Mediævalis, Fortegnelse over Danmarks Breve Fra Middelalderen med Udtog af de hidtil utrykte*, 4 vols. Copenhagen: 1894–1912.

von Eyben, W. E. 'Juridisk stil og sprogbrug'. In *Juridisk grundbog: Affattelse af love, domme, forvaltningsakter og kontrakter*, edited by W. E. von Eyben, 480–517. Copenhagen: 1962.

Fletcher, Richard. *The Conversion of Europe: From Paganism to Christianity 371–1386 AD*. London: 1997.

Frederiksen, Britta Olrik. 'Medieval Books in Danish—in Plain and Less Plain Figures'. In *Living Words and Luminous Pictures: Medieval Book Culture in Denmark. Essays*, edited by Erik Petersen, 154–62. Aarhus: 1999.

Frenz, Thomas. '"Vocavit nos pius": Öffentlichkeitsarbeit' durch päpstliche Urkunden im späten Mittelalter und der frühen Neuzeit'. In *La langue des actes. Actes du XIe Congrès international de diplomatique* (*Troyes, jeudi 11–samedi 13 septembre 2003*), at <http://elec.enc.sorbonne.fr/CID2003/frenz>.

Friedberg, Emil, editor. *Corpus Iuris Canonici*, 2 vols. Graz: 1959 (orig. 1879).

García y García, Antonius, editor. *Constitutiones Concilii quarti Lateranensis una cum Commentariis glossatorum*. Monumenta Iuris Canonici. Series A: Corpus Glossatorum 2. Vatican City: 1981.

Gelting, Michael. 'Circumstantial Evidence: Danish Charters of the Thirteenth Century'. In *Medieval Legal Process: Physical, Spoken and Written Performance in the Middle Ages*, edited by Marco Mostert and P. S. Barnwell, 157–95. Turnhout: 2011.

Grundmann, Herbert. 'Litteratus–Illitteratus: Der Wandel einer Bildungsnorm vom Altertum zum Mittelalter'. *Archiv für Kulturgeschichte* 40 (1958): 1–65.

Guyotjeannin, Olivier, Jacques Pycke and Benoît-Michel Tock. *Diplomatique médiévale*, 3rd edn. Turnhout: 2006.

Jørgensen, Ellen. 'Studier over danske middelalderlige Bogsamlinger'. *Historisk Tidsskrift*, eighth ser., 4 (1912–1913): 1–67.

Jørgensen, Ellen. 'Nordiske Studierejser i Middelalderen'. *Historisk Tidsskrift* 5, eighth series (1915): 331–82.

Jørgensen, Ellen. 'Nogle Bemærkninger om danske Studerende ved Tysklands Universiteter i Middelalderen'. *Historisk Tidsskrift* 6, eighth series (1916): 197–214.

Knudsen, Anders Leegaard. 'Testimonia Placiti—Private Charters as Public Instruments: A Study in Medieval Danish Diplomatics'. *Archiv für Diplomatik, Schriftgeschichte, Siegel- und Wappenkunde* 57 (2011): 147–80.

Lanham, Carol Dana. 'Freshman Composition in the Early Middle Ages: Epistolography and Rhetoric before the Ars Dictaminis'. *Viator* 23 (1992): 115–34.

McGovern, John F. 'The Documentary Language of Mediaeval Business, AD 1150–1250'. *The Classical Journal* 67, no. 3 (1972): 227–39.

Meyer, Andreas. *Felix et inclitus notarius: Studien zum italienischen Notariat vom 7. bis zum 13. Jahrhundert*. Tübingen: 2000.

Mommsen, Theodor, *et al.*, editors. *Corpus Iuris Civilis*, 3 vols. Berlin: 1954–1959 (orig. 1872–1895).

Moore, R. I. 'A New Way of Doing Things: How Pagan Europe was Converted—and Upgraded'. Review of *The Conversion of Europe: From Paganism to Christianity 371–1386 AD*, by Richard Fletcher. *Times Literary Supplement*, February 6, 1998, 24.

Mostert, Marco and Paul Barnwell, editors. *Medieval Legal Process, Physical, Spoken and Written Performances in the Middle Ages*. Turnhout: 2011.

Murphy, James Jerome. *Rhetoric in the Middle Ages: A History of the Rhetorical Theory from Saint Augustine to the Renaissance*. Tempe (AZ): 2001 (orig. Berkeley: 1974).

Nielsen, Herluf. 'Über die dänische Privaturkunde bis zum 14. Jahrhundert mit einem Schlusswort über das Notariat'. In *Notariado público y documento privado: de los orígenes al siglo XIV*, Actas de VII Congresso Internacional de Diplomática, vol. 2, 951–9. València: 1989.

Nielsen, Lauritz. *Danmarks middelalderlige Haandskrifter: En sammenfattende boghistorisk Oversigt*. Copenhagen: 1937.

Nörr, Knut Wolfgang. *Romanisch-kanonisches Prozessrecht: Erkenntnisverfahren erster Instanz in civilibus*. Heidelberg, etc.: 2012.

Notariado público y documento privado: de los orígenes al siglo XIV, Actas de VII Congresso Internacional de Diplomática, 2 vols. València: 1989.

Olsen, Thorkil Damsgaard. 'De ældste bøger', 'Skriften i administrationen', 'Analfabeternes oprør', and 'Dansk som skriftsprog'. In *Dansk litteraturhistorie*, vol. 1, edited by Søren Kaspersen *et al.*, 130–56 and 381–403. Copenhagen: 1984.

Petersen, Erik, editor. *Living Words and Luminous Pictures: Medieval Book Culture in Denmark. Essays*. Aarhus: 1999.

Schuler, Peter-Johannes. *Geschichte des südwestdeutschen Notariats: Von seinen Anfängen bis zur Reichsnotariatsordnung von 1512*. Bühl (Baden): 1976.

Skautrup, Peter. *Det danske Sprogs Historie*, 4 vols. Copenhagen: 1944–1970.

Skovgaard-Petersen, Inge. 'Oldtid og vikingetid'. In *Danmarks historie*, vol. 1., edited by Aksel E. Christensen *et al.*, 15–209. Copenhagen: 1978.

Skyum-Nielsen, Niels. 'Den danske konges kancelli i 1250'erne'. In *Festskrift til Astrid Friis på halvfjerdsårsdagen den 1. august 1963*, edited by Svend Ellehøj, Svend Gissel, and Knud Vohn, 225–45. Copenhagen: 1963.

Skyum-Nielsen, Niels. 'Kanslere og skrivere i Danmark 1250–1282'. In *Middelalderstudier tilegnede Aksel E. Christensen på tresårsdagen 11. september 1966*, edited by Tage E. Christiansen, Svend Ellehøj, and Erling Ladewig-Petersen, 141–84. Copenhagen: 1966.

Tamm, Ditlev and Helle Vogt. 'Creating a Danish Legal Language: Legal Terminology in the Medieval Law of Scania'. *Historical Research* 86 (2013): 505–14.

The Danish Medieval Laws: The Laws of Scania, Zealand and Jutland, edited and trans. Ditlev Tamm and Helle Vogt. London and New York: 2016.

Vogt, Helle. *The Function of Kinship in Medieval Nordic Legislation*. Leiden and Boston: 2010.

CHAPTER 6

Between the Language of Law and the Language of Justice: The Use of Formulas in Portuguese Dispute Texts (Tenth and Eleventh Centuries)

André Evangelista Marques

Introduction

While commenting on the 'divorce' between the 'ideological aspiration' and the 'practical application' of written law in north-western Europe, Patrick Wormald has stressed the absence of a notarial tradition that would work as a transmission chain between royal legislation and social order.[1] He suggested, on the contrary, that such was to be the role performed by the notarial tradition that kept 'the basics' of Roman legal practice in southern Europe during the early Middle Ages.[2] This proposition deserves qualification, as 'southern Europe' is too large and diverse an area to be taken as a whole. But there is no doubt that a diplomatic tradition was in place in Visigothic Iberia and

---

1 This paper is indebted to the PRJ research project, funded by the Spanish government (HUM2007–61233; HAR2011–26685). I am grateful to Isabel Alfonso (PI) and José Andrade for their continuous advice and support. Special thanks are due to Professor Alfonso for permission to reproduce the map printed here. I also wish to thank Wendy Davies for allowing me to read the manuscript of her recent book on justice in northern Iberia before 1000, which deeply influenced this paper. Professors Alfonso and Davies have both read an earlier version of this text and made invaluable comments, as have the editors of the volume and the anonymous reader for Brill, to whom I am also grateful. I alone am responsible for any shortcomings that remain. Charters are referred to by the abbreviation of the edition, number in the edition, and year in brackets, e.g. *DC* 13 (906).

2 Patrick Wormald, *Legal Culture in the Early Medieval West: Law as Text, Image and Experience* (London: 1999), xii–xiv: 'Yet in northern Europe there was no notarial apparatus to convert legislative steam into empowered law. Social order at local level therefore continued to be preserved by traditional means' (at p. xiii); for a lengthier treatment see Patrick Wormald, *The Making of English Law: King Alfred to the Twelfth Century, Volume I: Legislation and its Limits* (Oxford: 1999), 70–92.

 | DOI 10.1163/9789004375765_008

that it remained as the general framework of documentary practice until the twelfth century.[3]

One cannot equate this tradition with the formal lay notarial tradition found in Italy or its offshoots in some other parts of the Carolingian Empire. The professional notariate was already declining in the seventh century;[4] and it seems to have disappeared in post-Visigothic Iberia, largely replaced by scribes writing on behalf of charter beneficiaries.[5] However, a steadily growing number of monasteries and cathedrals assured the continuity of late antique scribal practices in northern (Christian) areas. They were responsible for keeping and transmitting a significant number of early medieval records written by both clerical and lay scribes who shared a 'common culture of documentary practice'.[6]

This practice is mostly documented in records of transactions (gifts, sales, exchanges, etc.), which represent the bulk of the extant charter material. But records of disputes, and especially those related to judicial cases, also reveal some standard features in terms of structure, materiality, formulas, and

3 Roger Collins, 'Literacy and the Laity in Early Mediaeval Spain', in *The Uses of Literacy in Early Mediaeval Europe*, ed. Rosamond McKitterick (Cambridge: 1990), 109–33; Nicholas Everett, 'Lay Documents and Archives in Early Medieval Spain and Italy, c. 400–700', in *Documentary Culture and the Laity in the Early Middle Ages*, ed. Warren Brown *et al.* (Cambridge: 2012), 63–94; Michel Zimmermann, *Écrire et lire en Catalogne (IX*e*–XII*e *siècle)*, 2 vols. (Madrid: 2003); José Antonio Fernández Flórez, *La elaboración de los documentos en los reinos hispánicos occidentales (ss. VI–XIII)* (Burgos: 2002), 62ff; Miguel Calleja Puerta, 'Ecos de las *Fórmulas* visigóticas en la documentación altomedieval astur-leonesa', in *Les formulaires. Compilation et circulation des modèles d'actes dans l'Europe médiévale et moderne: XIII*e *congrès de la Commission internationale de diplomatique (Paris, 3–4 septembre 2012)*, ed. Olivier Guyotjeannin, Laurent Morelle, and Silio P. Scalfati (Paris: 2016), at <http://elec.enc.sorbonne.fr/cid2012/part4> (accessed 25 August, 2017). I thank Dr Calleja for kindly allowing me to read this paper in advance of its publication.

4 Public notaries (*notarii publici*) are mentioned in the *Liber iudiciorum: Leges Visigothorum*, ed. Karl Zeumer, MGH LL nat. Germ. I, 1 (Hannover: 1902), 7.5.9 (pp. 308–9). But the fact that a document was drawn up by one of these notaries 'had no effect on the document's legal validity' already in the seventh century (Everett, 'Lay Documents and Archives', 70, 85).

5 Collins, 'Literacy and the Laity', 118, 124; correcting his former suggestion that 'legal records were made publicly by court notaries, perhaps as part of the proceedings', in Roger Collins, '"Sicut lex Gothorum continet": Law and Charters in Ninth- and Tenth-century León and Catalonia', *The English Historical Review* 100, no. 396 (1985), 489–512, at 506. See also Wendy Davies, *Windows on Justice in Northern Iberia, 800–1000* (Abingdon: 2016), 234.

6 Adam J. Kosto, '*Sicut mos esse solet*: Documentary Practices in Christian Iberia, c. 700–1000', in *Documentary Culture and the Laity*, 259–82, at 260.

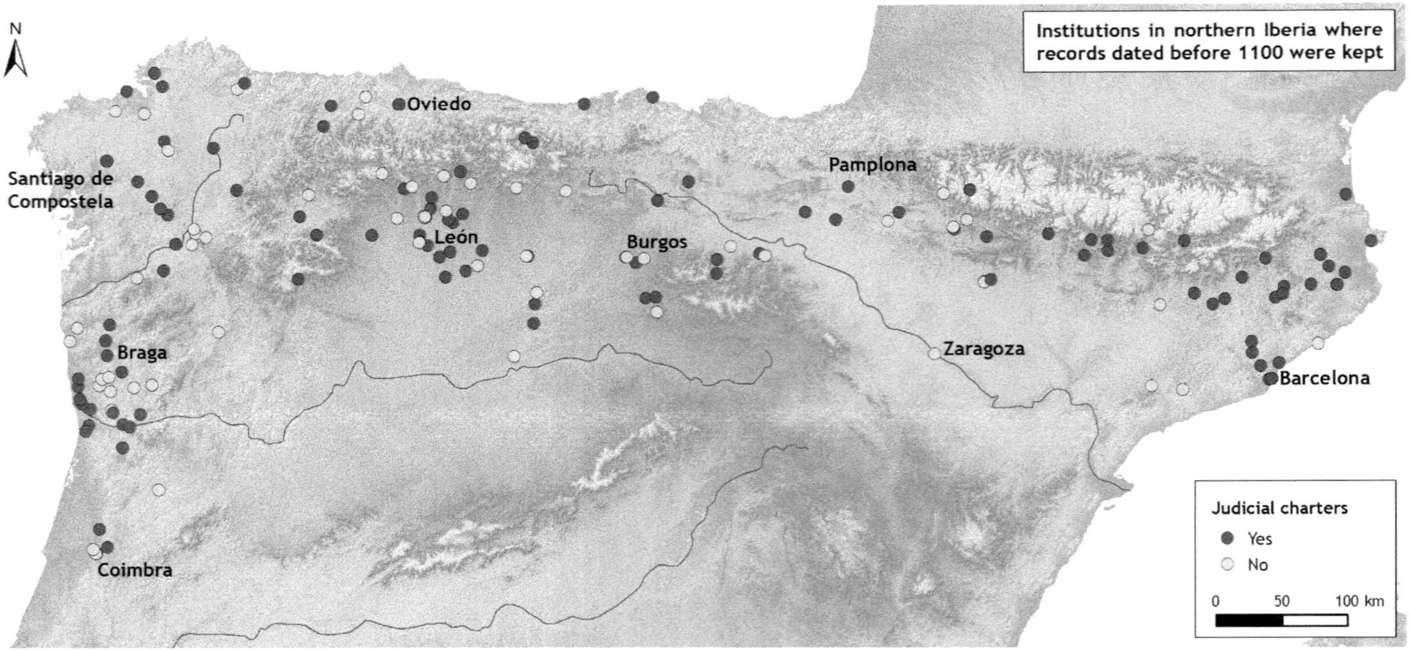

MAP 6.1 *Northern-Iberian institutions where records dated before 1100 were kept.*
MAP DRAWN BY ANTONIO URIARTE (LABORATORIO DE ARQUEOLOGÍA DEL PAISAJE Y TELEDETECCIÓN. CSIC-INSTITUTO DE HISTORIA. MADRID). REPRODUCED WITH THE PERMISSION OF PRJ PROJECT, CSIC (PI: ISABEL ALFONSO).

language, which led Wendy Davies to speak of a 'common recording tradition' across the Asturian-Leonese kingdom in the ninth and tenth centuries.[7] The consistent use of certain formulas in dispute texts, especially formulas reflecting specific procedures and the utterance of ritual words in court, displays less variation when compared with some gift and sale formulas.[8] And despite the absence of a comprehensive analysis of the eleventh-century material, judicial records dated after 1000 seem to have kept that same diplomatic tradition, whether they were written in monastic *scriptoria* or in royal circles.[9]

Furthermore, as Davies has clearly shown, a 'long-established judicial system', defined by some standard procedures and a common legal framework, was also in place across the Asturian-Leonese kingdom already in the ninth and tenth centuries;[10] and no major changes seem to occur in the first decades of the eleventh century, according to some micro-regional analyses.[11] Some of those procedures and legal practices, namely the frequent references to written (Visigothic) law in charters, look distinctive when compared against other European regions, where law texts are sometimes reflected in charters, but explicit citations are rare (as in some Carolingian areas north of the Alps) or non-existent (as in England).[12] Legal historians have actually suggested that the Visigothic legal tradition, transmitted by the *Liber iudiciorum* as well as by

7 Davies, *Windows on Justice*, 234, and throughout chs. 2–5. The Asturian-Leonese kingdom encompassed the whole of north-western Iberia: Castile, León, Asturias, Galicia and Portugal. Despite some differences, the same recording tradition can be traced in Catalonia (the best documented area in north-eastern Iberia): Jonathan Jarrett, 'Comparing the Earliest Documentary Culture in Carolingian Catalonia', in *Problems and Possibilities of Early Medieval Charters*, ed. Jonathan Jarrett and Allan Scott McKinley (Turnhout: 2013), 89–126, esp. 105–14.

8 Davies, *Windows on Justice*, 148.

9 Isabel Alfonso, 'El formato de la información judicial en la Alta Edad Media peninsular', in *Chartes et cartulaires comme instruments de pouvoir: Espagne et Occident chrétien (VIIIe–XIIe siècles)*, ed. Julio Escalona and Hélène Sirantoine (Toulouse: 2013), 209.

10 Davies, *Windows on Justice*, 202–3, 245–6 (quotation at 256); Wendy Davies, 'Judges and Judging: Truth and Justice in Northern Iberia on the Eve of the Millennium', *Journal of Medieval History* 36, no. 3 (2010), 202; Wendy Davies, 'Summary Justice and Seigneurial Justice in Northern Iberia on the Eve of the Millennium', *Haskins Society Journal* 22 (2010), 47–9, 54–7.

11 See, e.g., Pascual Martínez Sopena, 'La justicia en la época asturleonesa: entre el liber y los mediadores sociales', in *El lugar del campesino. En torno a la obra de Reyna Pastor*, ed. Ana Rodríguez (València: 2007), 239–60, at 241.

12 Davies, *Windows on Justice*, 232–54, esp. 236–37; Davies, 'Judges and Judging', 197; Davies, 'Summary Justice and Seigneurial Justice', 47. Other distinctive features are the high number of criminal cases and the office of *saio*.

'custom, memory or even formulas', dominated judicial procedure in ninth to twelfth century northern Iberia.[13]

It comes as no surprise that such a judicial system relied on diplomatic—as much as on legal and procedural—norms. One might even ask whether diplomatic norms are partially responsible for conveying the image of a judicial system as such.[14] But what should be stressed here, to go back to Wormald's argument, is the existence of some sort of recording system that brought law (or at least legal legitimacy) and legal practice together. Formulas were instrumental in fulfilling this role. This is true of the more elaborate (charter-length) 'legal formulae' compiled in formularies, as Alice Rio remarked.[15] But the same point can also be made about the shorter (phrase-length) formulas found in actual charters.[16] These formulas are seldom direct citations of legislation or other types of legal texts (which they often paraphrase), but are somehow inspired by these texts and share their 'prescriptive style'.[17] Formulas thus embody a

13 Agustín Prieto Morera, 'El proceso en el reino de León a la luz de los diplomas', in *El reino de León en la Alta Edad Media, II: Ordenamiento jurídico del reino*, 381–518 (León: 1992), 517. On the influence of the *Liber iudiciorum* in Visigothic court documents, see Everett, 'Lay Documents and Archives', 88–9; for its uses in the ninth to eleventh centuries, see Collins, '"Sicut lex Gothorum continet"'; Roger Collins, 'Visigothic Law and Regional Custom in Disputes in Early Medieval Spain', in *The Settlement of Disputes in Early Medieval Europe*, ed. Wendy Davies and Paul Fouracre, (Cambridge: 1986), 85–104; Zimmermann, *Écrire et lire*, 922–49; Pascual Martínez Sopena, 'El uso de la Ley Gótica en el reino de León', in *Remploi, citation, plagiat. Conduites et pratiques médiévales (Xe–XIIe siècle)*, ed. Pierre Toubert and Pierre Moret, (Madrid: 2009), 97–114; Amancio Isla Frez, 'La pervivencia de la tradición legal visigótica en el reino asturleonés', *Mélanges de la Casa de Velázquez* 41, no. 2 (2011), 75–86; Davies, *Windows on Justice*, 26–7, 235–7.

14 This raises the question of whether the idiosyncrasies of other types of court (less formal and undocumented) are downplayed by the 'correct' way of recording judicial proceedings used in the extant charter material.

15 Alice Rio, *Legal Practice and the Written Word in the Early Middle Ages: Frankish Formulae, c. 500–1000* (Cambridge: 2009), 202–11, 240.

16 See Rémi Oulion, *Scribes et notaires face à la norme dans la Toscane du Haut Moyen Âge (VIIe–XIe siècles)* (S.l.: 2013). The word 'formula' is used hereafter to refer to standard phrases and expressions employed in different parts of charters; not to 'legal formulae', as Rio defines them: 'documents prepared by scribes for their own use and organised into collections (formularies), to serve as an inspiration in drawing up future documents' (Rio, *Legal Practice*, 20; see also 43–5.) Both meanings are associated with the word 'formula' in the *Vocabulaire international de la diplomatique*, ed. María Milagros Cárcel Ortí, 2nd edn. (València: 1997), nos. 83, 183, and 314.

17 An expression used by Davies, *Windows on Justice*, 26. 'L'obsession de la légalité est, avec la célébration de la mémoire écrite, la caractéristique principale de la pratique notariale', as remarked by Zimmermann, *Écrire et lire*, 922.

normative and stereotyped discourse that is, however, used to frame charters stemming from specific transactions, disputes, etc., in which non-formulaic parts are also to be found.

If, on the one hand, formulas invest charters with legal legitimacy (when not an intended political and ideological charge), on the other hand, they are an important device at the scribe's disposal to fulfil the practical and context-bound functions of this kind of record.[18] In charters that record judicial cases, formulas play an intermediate role between the 'language of law' (that of a body of normative texts) and the 'language of justice' (that of records describing and legitimizing judicial practice).[19] Isabel Alfonso has rightly stressed that the 'topoi of the formulation of legal narrative' and the 'judicial rhetoric' deployed in eleventh- and twelfth-century records of lawsuits brought before the king were a major source of 'political legitimation' in northern Iberia.[20] It seems to have been no different down the political and social scale. As I shall argue in this paper, there are good grounds for believing that simple diplomatic formulas would also perform a legitimizing function in less elaborate (and less ideologically driven) records.

Moreover, some formulas take their intermediate role between law and legal practice beyond the written record, and become an important feature of judicial performance. Bearing in mind Robin Chapman Stacey's remarks on the overlapping of legal performance with speech and language, redefined by the very performative act, one feels inclined to think of formulas recorded in dispute texts as part and parcel of judicial practice, and not just as an erudite and rhetorical resource deployed by scribes to construct standardized (and later) accounts of such practice.[21] Davies has indeed argued for a strong link

---

18 On formulaic writing, see Davies, *Windows on Justice*, chs. 4–5, and Sébastien Barret, 'Les actes écrits comme instruments de pouvoir: la contribution des formulaires', in Julio Escalona and Hélène Sirantoine, eds., *Chartes et cartulaires comme instruments de pouvoir*, 87–99; on the political and ideological charge of formulas, see, e.g., Jarrett, 'Comparing the Earliest Documentary Culture'; on legal formulae, law, and charters, see Rio, *Legal Practice*.

19 'Law' and 'justice' are used here as analytical concepts, whose distinction was by no means evident, nor necessary, to early medieval minds: Zimmermann, *Écrire et lire*, 924–5; cf. Davies, *Windows on Justice*, 255–60.

20 Isabel Alfonso, 'Judicial Rhetoric and Political Legitimation in Medieval León-Castile', in *Building Legitimacy: Political Discourses and Forms of Legitimacy in Medieval Societies*, ed. Isabel Alfonso, Hugh Kennedy, and Julio Escalona, (Leiden: 2004), 53.

21 Robin Chapman Stacey, *Dark Speech: the Performance of Law in Early Ireland* (Philadelphia: 2007), 4. This might help explain the growing influence of 'Romance' over Latin formulas, as will be seen below.

between 'court procedure' and 'performance' (or 'staging') in northern Iberia before 1000, and has highlighted some specific procedures, such as confessions and oaths, which relied on ritual words that were uttered in court and carefully recorded by scribes.[22]

This paper is an attempt to assess the place of formulas in dispute texts, in an effort to understand, first, how these texts were constructed in order to become authoritative records and, secondly, how they relate to a judicial practice that shaped formulas just as much as formulas shaped judicial practice itself.[23] I will examine formulas and language in tenth- and eleventh-century Portuguese dispute texts, considering not only judicial records but also charters with indirect references to disputes. The broad notion of 'dispute text' used here includes all sorts of texts related to 'public' mechanisms of dispute resolution, even if these are not judicial mechanisms strictly speaking.[24]

Traditionally seen as 'records of practice', with a strong narrative character, dispute texts defy straightforward diplomatic categories, as they encompass different forms, formulas, and language that derive both from legal practice and from legal erudition. This means that dispute texts also lend themselves to the sort of detailed textual analysis that until recently was conducted mostly on laws, without acknowledging that both types of texts share some common features in form and function. In an attempt to broaden the way we look at dispute texts, I will start with some considerations about their form, which is often linked to the judicial procedures they stem from and to the contexts in which they were written. I shall then look at formulas and their usage, bearing in mind that different types of texts imply (and are defined by) different sets of formulas and different modes of assembling them. Finally, I will briefly consider the language of formulas, namely those legal words that reveal notions of law, justice, and procedure, as well as the dynamics by which this vocabulary was updated and kept changing.

---

22 Davies, 'Judges and Judging', 203; Davies, *Windows on Justice*, 247–9. On ritual words, see Davies, *Windows on Justice*, 121–49.

23 The first approach is suggested by Davies, *Windows on Justice*, 121, 143.

24 I follow the broad definition proposed by Davies, *Windows on Justice*, 35–6; and Alfonso, 'El formato'. On the 'public' nature of local and supra-local judges in Portugal before the twelfth century, see José Mattoso, 'Portugal no reino asturiano-leonês', in *História de Portugal*, ed. José Mattoso, vol. 1: Antes de Portugal (Lisbon: 1992), 467–70.

Form

The corpus of pre-1100 Portuguese dispute texts comprises 212 documents, that is, roughly sixteen per cent of the 1,364 charters identified so far in Portuguese archives for this period.[25] The bulk (180) date from the eleventh century, thirty from the tenth and only two from the last quarter of the ninth century, which makes variation difficult to trace across time, particularly before the mid-tenth century.[26] Nearly half of these texts (109) were transmitted in cartulary copies, whereas originals (eighty-nine) and a few single-sheet or antiquarian copies (fourteen) fill the other half.[27] They were all kept by ecclesiastical institutions, although many are concerned with disputes involving lay persons, and were incorporated into monastic or diocesan archives only at a later stage, mostly as title deeds for property these institutions came to acquire.[28]

Several types of dispute texts can be identified, according to the criteria one adopts: form and structure, materiality and transmission, moments in which records were written vis-à-vis the original procedures they record (whether in court or at a later stage), the persons or institutions responsible for writing these texts, etc.[29] Unable as I am to go into much detail here about documentary types, I shall just address some major distinctions.

---

25 Some will remain unnoticed. On the overall corpus, see André Evangelista Marques, 'Para um inventário da documentação diplomática anterior a 1101 conservada em arquivos portugueses', in *Mundos medievales: espacios, sociedades y poder: homenaje al profesor José Ángel García de Cortázar y Ruiz de Aguirre*, ed. Beatriz Arízaga Bolumburo, *et al.*, vol. 2 (Santander: 2012), 705–18.

26 The corpus of pre-1100 Portuguese dispute records, as well as those of all other regions in northern Iberia, are now available online at <http://prj.csic.es/> (accessed 25 August, 2017). Search tools can be used to perform relational queries by region, archive ('institution'), date, and type of transmission (original or copy).

27 'Cartularization' raises important issues concerning the editing of texts and especially of their formulaic sections: Calleja Puerta, 'Ecos de las *Fórmulas* visigóticas', section IV; André Evangelista Marques, *Da representação documental à materialidade do espaço: território da diocese de Braga (séculos IX–XI)* (Porto: 2014), 176; on judicial records specifically, see Alfonso, 'El formato', 214–16; Davies, *Windows on Justice*, 83–4. We still know very little of Portuguese cartularies in this respect.

28 A good example is the monastery of Moreira da Maia (in the vicinity of Porto). More generally, see Warren Brown, *et al.*, eds., *Documentary Culture and the Laity*, especially the contribution of Kosto on Spain. Out of thirty-three Portuguese institutions that kept records of any kind dated up to 1100, nineteen preserved dispute texts (see Map above).

29 These criteria were all explored by Davies, *Windows on Justice*, chs. 2–5. The author came up with a classification system that advances the discussion launched by Alfonso, 'El formato', 195–6. Aiming at an avowed 'operative' system to classify the rich documentation

The first is the distinction between judicial records and charters with indirect references to disputes.[30] The former are texts written with the specific purpose of recording some kind of judicial procedure or outcome. The latter are documents primarily concerned with recording transactions that may or may not directly relate to disputes, but nevertheless provide some information about them. Transactions that explicitly aimed at compensation or the payment of judicial fines lie somewhere in between, since they are related to court procedure (or at least determined by it), but share the formal characteristics of every other transaction. For this reason, I will consider them amongst the charters with indirect references. These charters represent around sixty per cent of all Portuguese dispute texts before 1100 (125 out of 212), a high percentage even by Iberian standards; although it should be noted that most (eighty) are indeed fines and compensations. The remaining forty per cent are judicial records (eighty-seven).

There are clear differences between both types of record when it comes to the stock of formulas scribes might have used and the way records were framed. Whether they are records of gift, sale or exchange, property inventories, or other, charters with indirect references to disputes are no different from other charters and follow the same formulaic structure. Moreover, as Davies has remarked, 'the form of reference to the dispute is haphazard and does not conform to any standard template'.[31] This means that the existence of dispute elements does not alter standard formulaic habits, although this kind of charter occasionally features short formulas and words characteristically used in judicial records.[32] Sometimes they will even display lengthy narratives of a given process, usually included as the *narratio* anticipating (and contextualizing)

---

kept by the monastery of Sahagún (León), Alfonso payed special attention to the contents and function of records, rather than their form; see also the broader remarks included among the explanatory material of the PRJ project, which has acknowledged the diversity of dispute records and attempted to challenge the traditional diplomatic approach: <http://prj.csic.es/criterios.php?m=5&c=6&s=4> (accessed 25 August, 2017). Cf. the less detailed classifications suggested by Prieto Morera, 'El proceso en el reino de León', 386–94; and Adam J. Kosto, *Making Agreements in Medieval Catalonia: Power, Order, and the Written Word, 1000–1200* (Cambridge: 2001), 43–52.

30 Cf. Davies, *Windows on Justice*, 35–55, 145.

31 Davies, *Windows on Justice*, 40; see also 121, 139–45.

32 Davies, *Windows on Justice*, 139–41. The author notes that some sale and gift records use formulas and language characteristic of '"pure" dispute records', when these refer to the commitment of one of the parties: *agnoui/cognoui in ueritate; deuenimus ad iudicium; adsignaui, compromittimus*. Some Portuguese examples: *LF* 36 (1031), *DC* 364 (1048), *DC* 115 (976).

TABLE 6.1 *Chronological distribution of Portuguese dispute texts (850–1100)*

	850–900	901–1000	1001–1100	Total
Charters with indirect references to disputes	1	17	107	125 (59%)
Judicial records	1	13	73	87 (41%)
Total	2	30	180	212

the charter's *dispositio*.[33] But more often than not, drawing up charters with indirect references to disputes would involve little more than using standard formulas and filling in the details of particular transactions.

Judicial records were framed in a different manner and often seem to have required more from their redactors. They deploy a vast array of textual strategies, ranging from free narrative accounts of disputes to quasi-verbatim transcriptions of what was said in court, not to mention the use of conventional formulas for recording specific procedures. Widespread as these formulas were over northern Iberia in the ninth and tenth centuries, they must have been old in origin, particularly those that reflected classical technical legal language. All of this means that producing judicial records would demand specialized knowledge that might not be attainable to ordinary local scribes. It would rather be the work of legal experts (though not necessarily professionals), like judges, legal officers (*saiones*), and skilled scribes attached to monasteries, episcopal sees, or aristocratic households, as Davies has suggested.[34] Some of these men would even teach law, such as the *iudices que* (*sic*) *legem docebant* mentioned in an eleventh-century document of Guimarães, a major monastery in the Portuguese area.[35] Indeed, some scribes did use (and occasionally cite) legal texts in Portugal just as elsewhere in northern Iberia.[36]

---

33 For example, DC 53 (943), LP 134 (1019), DC 340 (1045). See Prieto Morera, 'El proceso en el reino de León', 393; Alfonso, 'El formato', 199–200.

34 Davies, *Windows on Justice*, 141–3; cf. Collins, 'Visigothic Law', 86. A gift made by Garcia Moniz and his wife Elvira to King Garcia II of Galicia, which some historians regard as a concealed confiscation, seems to have been penned by a judge: DC 451 (1066).

35 DC 225 (1014); see also DC 425 (1060).

36 This might include verbatim citations of Visigothic law, providing full references to *liber*, *titulus*, and *sententia*: e.g. LF 22 (1025), LP 528 (1039), DC 386a (1053?), LF 63 (1062), DC 904

Nevertheless, judicial records encompass some very different types of record, with their own distinctive formulas—although these are seldom confined to any single type. This reminds us of the limits of strict typologies, which rely on modern diplomatic categories and tend to forget that form, language, and function frequently overlap.[37] Different types of record might perform similar functions, whereas one single judicial procedure, for instance, might be recorded in different types of record. Language, furthermore, adds some complexity to this picture, since words could mean different things in different formal and functional contexts, and different *scriptoria* and different individual scribes might use them idiosyncratically.

Still, an important distinction can be made amongst judicial records between procedural and narrative texts.[38] The former are associated with specific aspects of court proceedings that might be written at some point *in medias res* of judicial process, namely oaths, confessions/acknowledgements, agreements, and formal commitments (to appear in court, to accept judgment, to relinquish a claim, to hand over property, etc.). These records seem to have been drafted according to some well-defined templates, which included several first-person and present-tense formulas that responded to the declarative nature of such records. On the contrary, narrative *notitiae* and other types of retrospective account, framed as past-tense, third-person texts, seem to have a less clear-cut formulaic structure, in spite of some distinctive formulas and language. Their 'freestyle', so to speak, is the result of their narrative nature, but it might also suggest that scribes composed them at a later stage, drawing on miscellaneous previous materials, including procedural records.[39]

The distinction between procedural and narrative records should not overshadow the close correlation between both types, though.[40] This is particularly true in the Portuguese case. On the one hand, many procedural records include narrative bits that provide some context on the dispute

---

(1099); although the reference provided is occasionally wrong: e.g. DC 376 (1050). But, in most cases, scribes only included generic references to the *lex, lex gotica, liber iudicum, liber gotorum*, etc.: e.g. DC 210 (1009), DC 330 (1043), DC 183 (999), DC 523 (1075). On verbatim citations, see José Mattoso, 'Les Wisigoths dans le Portugal médiéval: état actuel de la question', in *L'Europe héritière de l'Espagne wisigothique: colloque international du C.N.R.S. tenu à la Fondation Singer-Polignac (Paris, 14–16 mai 1990): actes*, ed. Jacques Fontaine and Christine Pellistrandi (Madrid: 1992), 333–4.

37 Kosto, *Making agreements*, 32–64, esp. 43–4; Alfonso, 'El formato', 193–5.

38 Cf. Davies, *Windows on Justice*, 147–9.

39 Davies, *Windows on Justice*, 121. This is also apparent in Sahagún material: Alfonso, 'El formato', 198.

40 Alfonso, 'El formato', 198.

and briefly describe the court proceedings leading to the exact procedure recorded.[41] On the other hand, most narrative records are of a composite nature: they open with an account (either long or short) of the dispute and the proceedings, and close with an *agnitio* and/or *placitum* recording the final procedure and featuring the essential clauses of an independent charter, whose issuer is usually the loser.[42] In the end, records comprising a narrative text only are rare, and most were designed not so much to give an overview of the proceedings as to formally record and justify the outcome of a case.[43] This seems to happen elsewhere in the Asturian-Leonese kingdom, where many narrative accounts of disputes and court proceedings are actually formalized as *placiti*, or less frequently as *manifesta/agnitiones*, especially after 1000.[44] But perhaps 'pure' narrative accounts are even rarer in Portugal than in other regions.

The fact that the Portuguese material is overwhelmingly dated after 1000 (and especially between 1050 and 1100) is not sufficient to explain this prevalence of composite records. Maybe the key explanation lies in the confirmatory nature of the long, elaborate and visually imposing narrative records,

41 For example, *Arouca* V (1094–1096) (confession + quitclaim); LP 353 (1032) (agreement); DC 280 (1033) (agreement + compensation); LP 210 (1075) (formal commitment), DC 387 (1053) (quitclaim). No dedicated records of confession could be found.

42 The most common are records combining narrative + *agnitio/placitum* (=formal commitment): e.g. LP 202 (1016), DC 823 (1095). But single combinations also occur: (i) narrative + *placitum* (=agreement): e.g. DC 13 (906); (ii) narrative + *placitum* (=formal commitment): e.g. DC 183 (999). No records of narrative + *agnitio* only could be found. Nearly all composite records are from the eleventh century.

43 Among the thirty-nine narrative records identified in Portugal (dated between 936–1100), only twelve are 'pure' narrative texts: e.g. LP 212 (1004), LP 119 (1086–1091), LTL 71 (1064–1086?); although six are explicitly framed as court decrees: e.g. CDMM 84 (972), DC 304 (1038), LP 115=140 (1040).

44 Alfonso, 'El formato', 203–5, 207; Gonzalo Martínez Díez, 'Terminología jurídica en la documentación del reino de León. Siglos IX–XI', in *Orígenes de las Lenguas Romances en el Reino de León: siglos IX–XII*, vol. 1 (León: 2004), 252; Prieto Morera, 'El proceso en el reino de León', 386, n. 17, 390, 399–400. This author notes that the word *placitum* is particularly linked in Portuguese records to the notion of 'commitment' towards different actions: to abide by someone's authority, to sell or donate property, etc. On agnitiones/*manifesta* and their Catalan equivalent (*professiones, exvacuationes*), see Collins, '"Sicut lex Gothorum continet"', 494; Kosto, *Making Agreements*, 44–5 (stressing the relevance of combination *notitia* + *exvacuatio*). In Portugal the word *manifestum* is rare, unlike *agnitio*, used with different meanings (see below).

frequently brought before the king or another powerful authority.[45] They might have been somehow less needed, or less known, in the Portuguese area: the king was far away and there were no powerful bishops (before 1070–1080) or abbots (apart from Guimarães), nor many lay lords, who could play the role of influential authorities whose confirmation would be required; and there were few *scriptoria* able to draw up such elaborate records.[46]

Be that as it may, it is sometimes difficult to decide whether one is looking at a 'procedural' record with strong narrative features, intended at constructing some rhetorical effect and stressing a particular version of the case, or at a 'narrative' text whose redactor has deliberately kept a procedural tone (or even whole chunks of text), in order to legitimate his narrative composition. Moreover, there is a common stock of formulas scribes employed in composing judicial records. While some formulas are mostly associated with specific types of records, others are used across different types. In any case, formulas were an important element of dispute texts and played a key role in shaping the standard way of framing judicial matters.

Formulas

Oaths

Let us first consider some of the formulas associated with specific types of record, starting with those classified as 'procedural'. Oaths, in the first place, might either originate in dedicated records (which are rare in north-western Iberia) or be referred to in both procedural and narrative records that describe court proceedings.[47] Primary oath records do not survive from Portugal before 1100, but some examples remain of either short or detailed summaries of oaths in other types of record, mostly narrative accounts but also agreements, formal commitments, and judicial transactions.[48] Some long accounts of court

---

45 Alfonso, 'Judicial Rhetoric', 54; Davies, *Windows on Justice*, 39, 93–4, 148; an idea already hinted at by Collins, '"Sicut lex Gothorum continet"', 501. Royal confirmation seems to be particularly relevant in the case of Sahagún's lawsuits in the second half of the eleventh century: Alfonso, 'El formato', 206, 208, n. 63, 209.

46 For general context, see Mattoso, 'Portugal no reino asturiano-leonês'; Maria João Branco, 'Portugal no Reino de León. Etapas de uma relação (866–1179)', in *El Reino de León en la Alta Edad Media, IV: La Monarquía (1109–1230)* (León: 1993), 533–625.

47 Collins, '"Sicut lex Gothorum continet"', 493; Prieto Morera, 'El proceso en el reino de León', 392; Davies, *Windows on Justice*, 49–50.

48 Short references: Azevedo 1 (1003–1008?), *LP* 353 (1032), *LTL* 71 (1064–1086?); detailed: *DC* 225 (1014), *LF* 621 (1073), *LP* 108 (1099).

cases might even include full transcriptions of oaths, probably taken from an earlier document drafted in court or soon after. There is one single example in Portugal, not surprisingly in a long account of two subsequent disputes over the properties donated to Guimarães by several kings, which ends with the confirmation—and acknowledgement (*agnitio*)—by King Alfonso V of the monastery's rightful claim to these properties. Following a third-person account of the proceedings, the redactor introduces abruptly the first-person oath taken by the abbot and his monks:

> nos adunati iuraturi sumus per as conditiones sacramentorum et per deum patrem omnipotentem ... et per IIII^or euangelia ... et per XII^m prophetas et per XII^m apostolos quia ipsos testamentos quod fecit Rex domno Ranemiro et Rex domno Ordonio et confirmauit Rex domno Veremudo in eius diebus sunt uerificos. Et si mentiti sumus et nomem domini in falsum nominauimus descendat super nos iram domini sicut descendit super datan et abiron quia propter scelera eorum terra illa uiuos obsorbuit.[49]

This is an exceptional record, whose final *agnitio* by Alfonso V was written in León by an unidentified scribe who probably worked for the king. But the overall construction of the narrative, as well as some tiny partisan comments on the part of the redactor, show that the full record must have been composed in Guimarães, at least in its final shape. Besides, it is more likely than not that its redactor drew upon earlier records written in Portugal, since the proceedings (including the oath) took place there. This shows that at least some *scriptoria* in the Portuguese area had access to the common template used elsewhere in northern Iberia to frame oath records. Such template is introduced by the technical term *conditiones sacramentorum* and includes: (i) the invocation of God and (sometimes many) holy persons, (ii) a formula confirming that those taking the oath had proper knowledge of what they were swearing, (iii) and sometimes, as is the case here, a sanction against false declarations. The consistency

49 DC 223 (1014): 'We the assembled are about to swear by the terms of the oaths and by God the Almighty Father ... and by the four Gospels ... and by the twelve prophets and by the twelve disciples, that the documents issued by King Ramiro and King Ordoño, which were confirmed by King Vermudo afterwards, are authentic. Should we perjure and falsely call on God's name, may His wrath come upon us, as it came upon Dathan and Abiron, who were swallowed up alive by the ground because of their sins'.

in structure and style shown by oath records across northern Iberia before 1000 has led Davies to suggest that they reflected ritual words uttered in court.[50]

A single document is not enough to suggest the widespread usage of this template in Portugal. But if one bears in mind the references to oaths in narrative records, and the fact that they were regularly performed in churches and followed highly ritualized procedures, then it becomes very likely that Portugal was no different from other regions in the Asturian-Leonese kingdom. Formulas must have also played an important role there in framing both the written record and the oral performance of oaths.

Confessions

Dedicated records of confession/acknowledgement are also virtually absent from the Portuguese corpus, although the procedure is frequently mentioned in narrative records.[51] In some cases, scribes include only a brief reference to the *agnitio* that ended a case—thus closing the account of the dispute—and which was immediately followed by final clauses.[52] More often, however, references to *agnitiones* occur in composite records that feature an initial third-person account of the dispute and then a first-person record whereby the loser might recognise his guilt or the other party's claim and, at the same

50 Davies, *Windows on Justice*, 124–5. On the Visigothic origin of oath formulas and procedures, see Ángel Canellas López, *Diplomática hispano-visigoda* (Zaragoza: 1979), 57–8; Collins, '"Sicut lex Gothorum continet"', 495–6. Gil's edition of the *Formulae Visigothicae* provides some examples of tenth-century Asturian-Leonese charters whose scribes used some variation of formula 39 (*Conditiones Sacramentorum*): 'Formulae Wisigothicae', in *Miscellanea Wisigothica*, ed. Juan Gil (Seville: 1972), 106–8; cf. José Antonio Fernández Flórez, 'La génesis documental: Desde las pizarras visigodas y la *Lex Romana Wisigothorum* al siglo X', in *VIII Jornadas Científicas sobre Documentación de la Hispania altomedieval (siglos VI–X)*, ed. Nicolás Ávila Seoane, Manuel Joaquín Salamanca López, and Leonor Zozaya Montes (Madrid: 2009), 112–15; and Calleja Puerta, 'Ecos de las *Fórmulas* visigóticas', section V.1. Zeumer provides other examples from Catalonia and Septimania: 'Formulae Visigothicae', in *Formulae Merowingici et Karolini Aevi*, ed. Karl Zeumer, MGH Legum Sectio V: Formulae (Hannover: 1886), 592. A similar formula (*Columnellum*) appears in a tenth-century formulary from the Catalan monastery of Ripoll: Michel Zimmermann, 'Un formulaire du Xème siècle conservé à Ripoll', *Faventia* 4, no. 2 (1982), 81–2.

51 Dedicated records are also rare among the Sahagún material: Alfonso, 'El formato', 201. References to this procedure are common in Catalan 'records of judgment': Kosto, *Making Agreements*, 43.

52 For example, DC 163 (991), Azevedo 1 (1003–1008?), DC 216 (1011). Similar references occur in judicial transactions as well: e.g. DC 870 (1098). On confession as a key procedure in conflict resolution, see Alfonso, 'El formato', 203.

time, commit himself to relinquish his own claim, abide by the court's decision or the agreement reached between the parties, pay compensation, etc. Unsurprisingly, these first-person records are usually labelled as both *agnitio vel/et placitum*.[53] This might echo the practice of writing confessions and agreements together in (or immediately after) court sessions.[54] But it also suggests the different meanings covered by the word *agnitio*, which is used to name several types of record and procedures in addition to confessions.[55]

Without excluding other possibilities, *agnitiones* encompass three main actions in the Portuguese corpus:

(i) a recognition of wrong on the part of the loser, who on occasion would accept as true or false a statement made in court; or a simple acknowledgement of the other party's rights.[56]
(ii) a public acknowledgement of a court decision, which might be issued either by one of the parties or by the tribunal itself;[57] it does not take a big a leap to see why court decrees, or perhaps the records whereby these were publicly communicated, were also sometimes termed *agnitiones*.[58]
(iii) and finally a quitclaim, often issued before the proceedings were over.[59]

There is, however, a stock formula that clearly expresses more than one of these notions at a time: *agnovere/agnosco* (or *cognoscere/cognosco*) *se/ego in veritate*:

53 For example, LP 202 (1016), LF 22 (1025), LF 23 (1062), DC 746 (1091), *Junqueira* 47 (1100). There remain only two *agnitiones vel/et placita* that are not associated with long narrative accounts; and they were both preserved (if not written) in the same monastery: *Arouca* V (1094–1096), DC 941 (1100).

54 Davies, *Windows on Justice*, 55.

55 Davies, *Windows on Justice*, 127. On the different meanings of *agnitio* (and *manifestum*), see Prieto Morera, 'El proceso en el reino de León', 395–7.

56 For example, DC 870 (1098), DC 225 (1014); DC 183 (999), LP 202 (1016).

57 For example, DC 163 (991) (issued by the loser), DC 216 (1011) (issued by the victor), DC 304 (1038) (subscribed by four out of six members of a tribunal presided over by the abbot of Guimarães; in this case the *agnitio* seems to have been written precisely because the losing party had abandoned the trial).

58 LP 115=140 (1040), DC 384 (1053).

59 Additional to other examples given above: LP 212 (1004). Quitclaims are usually implied in first-person records that ensure compliance with court decisions and respect for the other party's rights; but only sometimes are they explicitly stated: e.g. LF 621 (1073), LP, 53=75 (1082), *Junqueira* 47 (1100).

> orta fuit intentio inter Eirigo et Honorigo … et iudicavit Menendo Pelaiz que iurasset Eirigo cum suo testimonio illa karta et post hoc venerunt ad iuramento et agnovit se Honorigo quia erat veritas de Eirigo et conrogavit illum et dedit in rogo illum agrum de Pumares.[60]

This is how confessions/acknowledgements are usually referred to in narrative records, both in Portugal and in other parts of northern Iberia. Even if this is not one of the ritual formulas uttered in court that Davies could identify in 'raw' confession records, it certainly hints at a standard and correct manner of recording this procedure.[61] Legal historians have emphasized two meanings for this formula: renunciation of a claim and acknowledgement of the other party's claim.[62] However, it also encompasses the loser's recognition of wrong and his acceptance of the court's decision.[63] Tellingly, such a procedure is often mentioned as taking place immediately before the final oath, ordered by the tribunal to corroborate its own decision as to which party presented better claims and/or proofs. That the loser abandons his claim, or is rather unable to pursue it, is certainly relevant from a procedural perspective, but the rhetorical effect intended by this type of narrative account seems to underscore not only the act of recognition of one's wrong and the opponent's right, but also the general acceptance of the whole process and the public acknowledgement of the court's authority. A well-known standard formula whose meaning was considerably wide-ranging came in handy to achieve that effect.

---

60 LF 91 (1057): 'A dispute arose between Eirigo and Honorigo … Menendo Pelaiz decided that Eirigo should swear to the value of the document [he had presented] and so he did [or was about to do?], leading Honorigo to acknowledge that Eirigo said the truth. Honorigo then begged him to accept recompense and gave him a field planted with fruit trees'. Other examples cited above: DC 183 (999), LP 212 (1004), DC 225 (1014), LP 202 (1016). Many more can be found: Azevedo 1 (1003–1008?), LF 22 (1025), LP 53=75 (1082), etc.

61 Davies, *Windows on Justice*, 127–8; Alfonso, 'El formato', 201–3.

62 Paulo Merêa, cit. in Rui Pinto de Azevedo, 'A expedição de Almançor a Santiago de Compostela em 997, e a de piratas normandos à Galiza em 1015–1016 (Dois testemunhos inéditos das depredações a que então esteve sujeito o Território Portugalense entre Douro e Ave)', *Revista Portuguesa de História* 14 (1974), 90, n. 8; Prieto Morera, 'El proceso en el reino de León', 395–6; Martínez Díez, 'Terminología jurídica', 258–9.

63 It comes close to the formula *veritatem accipere*, found in different types of record: e.g. DC 144 (985), DC 304 (1038). On the equivalence between the concepts of *iustitia* and *veritas* and the 'process whereby the truth was effectively objectified in the judicial arenas', see Alfonso, 'Judicial Rhetoric', 78–85.

Agreements

Agreements are more complex and constitute a mixed type of record, not easily defined in terms of structure and formulaic writing.[64] Different circumstances could lead to an agreement, meaning that agreements could take different forms, such as bilateral agreements reached at the end of a dispute, formal commitments whereby one or both parties agreed to abide by court decisions (either interlocutory or final decisions), or commitments to hold fast to a compromise reached during the proceedings. Formal commitments often imply a mutual agreement between both contending parties, despite being usually issued by one party only.[65] These texts show remarkable formal resemblances to 'pure' agreements.

We have seen that formal commitments (usually framed as an *agnitio vel/et placitum*) often form the concluding section of composite records. But dedicated records of such commitments (usually classified as *placita* only) are more numerous. These are also texts written in the first person and present tense, whose author is almost always the losing party. But they lack any long narrative account of the dispute, since they were drafted with the purpose of recording a commitment to perform an action, either during proceedings, or at their end. This might coincide, as it often did, with the final outcome of the process, but the focus of these records is not so much on the general acknowledgement of the whole process and the decision reached in court, but rather on its consequences. This is why scribes hardly ever term them *placita vel/et agnitiones*, as they do with the formal commitments included in composite records.[66] Moreover, it should be noted that some agreements and formal commitments did not arise from judicial contexts, but from other modes of conflict resolution leading either to an agreement between the parties or some imposition on one of them. This partly explains why dedicated *placita* records feature so prominently amongst extant dispute texts in Portugal.[67]

Some excerpted quotations can best illustrate the main differences amongst records of agreement and formal commitment, both with respect to their content (function) and their form (formulas). Seven main types can be singled out, although there is clear overlapping and many *placita* conflate several types of commitment:

64 Davies, *Windows on Justice*, 130–6.

65 Formal commitments issued by both parties: DC 386b (1053), DC 440 (1064).

66 Only two exceptions: *Arouca* V (1094–1096), DC 941 (1100).

67 Forty-three records, representing twenty per cent of the 212 dispute texts identified.

(i) agreements reached by both parties upon a judicial or extra-judicial resolution of a dispute.[68] These texts are mostly framed as unilateral formal commitments, although the other party may explicitly voice approval, in addition to subscribing the record:

> Pelagio Menendiz et coniugia eius Lovilli pactum simul et plazum facimus tibi Eirigo Eitaz per scriptura firmitatis ... pro parte de illas hereditates ... et habuimus iudicium et assessiones super eas usque hodie et devindicavi ego Eirigo illas hereditates de Pelagio Menendiz et de sua muliere et de illis qui illas voces impulsant et proinde roboramus nos tibi isto plazo ... ut des odie die non sedeamus ausatum ut te calumniare pro illis hereditatibus ... [a sanction follows] Pelagio et Leovilli hoc plazum manibus nostris roboramus ... Pro testes: ... Eirigu.[69]

But they can also be framed as pure bilateral agreements:

> Alvitus, abbas, una cum subrino meo, Izila Sabariguizi, et Tudeildus, abbas, et domna Unisco, placitum facimus inter nos unus ad alius, pro scriptura firmitatis ... pro illa intencio que inter nos fui pro villa Sunillaner ... et devenimus inde ibi ad compagina, que parciant ipsos abbas ambobus ipsam nominatus ipsa medietate....[70]

(ii) formal commitments to appear in court, give oath-helpers and/or sureties, and accept judgment:

---

68 Sometimes the dispute is mentioned, sometimes it is only implied: e.g. *LP* 360 (867–912), *LP* 160 (1091).

69 *LF* 96 (1084): 'I Pelayo Menéndez, and my wife Lovilli, make a pact and agreement by charter with you, Eirigo Eitaz ... about those properties ... which we disputed in court. I Eirigo [successfully] claimed them from Pelayo Menéndez, his wife and those who supported them and we [Pelayo and his wife] hence confirm this agreement ... and we shall not dare to dispute these properties hereafter ... We Pelayo and Leovili confirm this agreement by our own hands ... As witnesses: ... Eirigo'. Other examples: *DC* 280 (1033), *LP* 150=138 (1045).

70 *LP* 353 (1032): 'I Abbot Alvito, together with my relative Izila Sabariguiz, and we Abbot Tudeildo and *domna* Unisco, we all make an agreement by charter between ourselves ... following the dispute that arose between us over the *villa* of Sevilhães ... We then arrived at an agreement, and so the aforementioned abbots shall divide between themselves the [disputed] half [of the *villa*]'.

> Pelagio sagatiz in uoce de vimaranes ... et domna ileuba cognomento maior gunsaluiz et filiis suis tibi sagioni nostro citi saluatoriz per hunc nostrum plazum tibi conpromittimus ... Vt de ego pelagio sagatiz istos dominos superius nominatos pro ad iuramento hodie ... et domna ileuba et filiis suis que suscipiant ipso die et ipsa domna et filiis suis dent fiadores ad illa trebuna ut post iuramento que compleant que lex ordinauerit per manu de ipse sagioni citi saluadoriz ... [a sanction follows].[71]

(iii) formal commitments to abide by the decision reached in court, as well as to avoid any further litigation. Since court decrees and agreements were frequently not written up, formal commitments seem to replace them somehow on several occasions:

> Didago tructesindiz et odoiro sarraziniz placitum simul et dimissione facimus uobis guttierre tructesindiz ... pro parte de illa intemtio que inter nos fuit ... et ipsa sententia de illo iudicio unde abuimus iudicio in presentia menendo guntsalbez et per sagioni ermerigo et deuenimus inde ad conpagina per manus de ipsos dominos et de ipse sagio ... uertimus totas alimas de ipso iudicio in terra. Ita ut de odie die et tempore non calumniemus uos pro ipsa intemtio ... [a sanction follows].[72]

(iv) formal commitments to relinquish a claim, which are sometimes associated with the former type, as the example cited above shows. These commitments, usually termed *placitum (sicut/et) dimissione*, often imply not only

71 DC 386b (1053): 'I Pelayo Sagatiz, acting as the representative of the monastery of Guimarães, on the one hand, and *domna* Eleuva, dubbed Maior González, and her offspring, on the other, we all commit ourselves to you Cid Salvatoriz, our *saio*, by this agreement ... I Pelayo Sagatiz commit myself to give the aforementioned [abbot and monks of Guimarães] as oath-helpers, who shall take their oath today ... and *domna* Eileuva and her offspring commit themselves to accept what shall happen today and to appoint sureties that guarantee [their] compliance with the court's orders, through the aforementioned *saio*, Cid Salvatoriz'. Other examples: *LP* 193 (1009), *LF* 134 (1080).

72 DC 387 (1053): 'We Diego Tructesindiz and Odorio Sarraziniz make a commitment and a quitclaim to you Guterre Tructesindiz ... on account of the dispute that arose between us ... and of that judicial decree, given that we went to court before Menendo González, assisted by *saio* Ermerigo, and reached an agreement through those lords and this *saio* ... We drop all the obligations that we have sustained against each other in court. And we shall not dare to bring this dispute back to court again'. Other examples: DC 144 (985), DC 380 (1052), *LP* 210 (1075), *CDMM* 74 (1095).

the renunciation of claim but also the payment/reception of compensation, or the restitution/receipt of disputed property:

> Olidi naustiz placitum simul et dimisione facio ad tiui godina … ut sedeas liuer et persoluta de illa intentio de illa uaca et pro quamtas alimas te inquiadaba in presentia gutierre tructesimdiz et louesimdo suariz ic in acisteiro de moraria. et proinde acepimus de te in rogo IIas obelias … et per tali actio uertimur illas alimas totas in terra quantas contra te abuimus … [a sanction follows].[73]

(v) formal commitments to hand over disputed property, make compensation, and pay the *iudicatum* due to whomever was judging the case. Although these commitments are very close to the former type, the focus here is placed on the transaction, often performed before the *saio*:

> Ego Salamirus presbitero uobis domna Uiuili Truitesendiz pactum simul et plazum facio uobis et heredibus uestris per scripture firmitatis pro parte de ip[s]a ecclesia uocabulo Sancti Mametis … unde intencio inter nos fuit … et uobis damus ipsa ecclesia ante sagion et sanabit uos et uestros heredes … [a sanction follows].[74]

(vi) formal commitments to avoid any future litigation following a transaction or an agreement, which in several cases are the result of some past litigation:

> Garcia tructesindizi placito facio uobis domno gundisaluo gutierrizi … pro parte de ipsa ereditate que mici destes de gemundi quomodo in hanc kartula resona que non facia proinde nulla suposita mala ad uobis non

73 *DC* 362 (1048): 'I Olidi Naustiz make a commitment and a quitclaim to you Godina … so that you become free, with my consent, of that charge over a cow and of all the obligations that I demanded from you before Guterre Tructesindiz and Lovesendo Suariz, here in the monastery of Moreira. Likewise, I accept two sheep from you as recompense … And through this action I drop all the obligations that I have sustained against you in court'. Renunciations of claim only: e.g. *DC* 439 (1064), *Arouca* V (1094–1096).

74 *LTPS* 142 (1015): 'I Salamirus, priest, make a pact and agreement by charter with you Vivili Tructesendiz and your offspring, concerning the church of St Mamede … over which we went to court … and I give you this church before a *saio*, thus settling the case with you and your offspring'.

> per potestate non per saion non per nuloque generis homo ... [a sanction follows].[75]

(vii) finally, there are some texts recording commitments and provisions of guarantees (sometimes by sureties) in case of default of either court decisions or transactions that might or might not result in judicial proceedings;[76] and there are also some commitments aimed at guaranteeing third parties' interests over disputed property.[77]

Apart from obvious idiosyncrasies in form and content, these different types of agreements and formal commitments share a common structure and some common formulas and language, also widespread across the kingdom of Asturias-León before 1000.[78] Scribes systematically describe these texts using the word *placitum*, sometimes intensified as *placitum vel pactum*; which shows how blurred the distinction between commitment and agreement might be.[79] These two words, and especially *compagina* and *consensum*,[80] occur frequently to name an agreement between the parties, reached through the intervention of the tribunal, of some legal officer in charge of the proceedings, or of *boni homines*. A standard formula, *devenire ad compagina*, occurs sometimes (and not only in this type of text) in relation to agreements reached in court.[81]

Furthermore, the notion (and indeed the very act) of commitment is sometimes expressed through the technical classical Latin legal term

---

75 DC 710 (1088): 'I Garcia Tructesindiz make an agreement with you Gonzalo Gutiérrez ... concerning that property in Gemunde which you have leased out to me by charter, and I shall not raise any bad assumptions against you, resorting to neither a lord (*potestas*) nor a *saio* nor any other kind of man'. Many other examples: LTL 35 (966–985), DC 440 (1064), DC 513b (1074), DC 554b (1078), DC 584b (1080), CDMM 61 (1092), CDMM 77 (1096), DC 904 (1099), DC 941 (1100).

76 Court decisions: DC 167b (993–995), LP 415 (1092–1098); transactions: LF 79 (1044), DC 766 (1091), 916 (1099).

77 DC 314 (1041), DC 426 (1060).

78 Davies, *Windows on Justice*, 130–6.

79 Alfonso, 'El formato', 203–5; Prieto Morera, 'El proceso en el reino de León', 399–400. In the seventh century, Isidore of Seville was still able to contrast the two meanings: Isidore of Seville, *The Etymologies of Isidore of Seville*, trans. Stephen A. Barney, *et al.* (Cambridge: 2006), 120: V.xxiv.19.

80 But not *atiba*, as in other areas of northern Iberia.

81 Several examples, some of which have been cited already: LP 353 (1032) (agreement), LF 184 (1052) and DC 502 (1072) (judicial transactions); DC 387 (1053) and CDMM 74 (1095) (formal commitments); DC 663 (1086?) (composite record).

(*com*)*promittere*. As Davies remarked, the widespread use of this notion across the Asturian-Leonese kingdom 'must reflect a standard way of recording a commitment, of some antiquity, indeed perhaps even a standard way of declaring an agreement'.[82] The set formula *compromitto/compromittimus ut* is used to express a commitment made either to the other party, or to the *saio* or another officer. Scribes seem to have favoured this formula—particularly in the *scriptorium* of Guimarães—to describe commitments to appear in court and give oath-helpers,[83] or to hand over disputed property, in which case the verb *assignare* or *consignare* came next.[84]

Finally, different types of commitment (as well as transactions) include standard formulas preventing further litigation, sometimes explicitly stating the prohibition of going before any authority.[85] Ensuring that the parties involved in a dispute would comply with the decision reached in court seemed to be a vital concern for those who drew up these records. It comes as no surprise, then, that a final common feature of virtually every agreement or commitment is the presence of sanction clauses aimed at enforcing compliance, and of witness lists.

What is striking about different types of agreement and commitment is that, despite dissimilarities in form and function, they were all framed in quite a similar manner and shared a common language, which must have been regarded as the standard—and correct—manner of recording not only agreements but all actions (and transactions) that followed the resolution of a dispute in court. Although the main purpose of these texts was to record the outcome of a case, or occasionally an intermediate commitment, some provide a summary of the proceedings, especially when they are not used as the concluding section of a composite record whose initial narrative account would fulfil that role.[86] Albeit briefer and less elaborate, such summaries are similar, in form and wording, to the long accounts of disputes and court proceedings that we have classified as narrative records.

---

82 Davies, *Windows on Justice*, 131.

83 For example, DC, 386b (1053) (cited above).

84 For example, LTL 35 (966–985) (formal commitment), DC 183 (999), DC 225 (1014) (composite records).

85 For example, DC 380 (1052), DC 412 (1058), DC 420 (1059). See also the charters cited above §vi.

86 E.g. LTPS 142 (1015); DC 387 (1053); LF 96 (1084) (all cited above).

Narrative Records

Nearly all the formulas that we have seen so far are traceable in narrative judicial records whose redactors often relied on simple records of oaths, confessions, agreements, formal commitments, etc.[87] Simple procedural records might be copied almost verbatim, or, conversely, referred to or quoted (and thus edited) in different ways, depending on the scribe's aims and skills. Some narrative records (composite records included) are very long and elaborate texts, drawn up by erudite scribes, mostly monastic, who tried to convey a 'correct' version of the case, usually according to the victor's views.[88] Others are rather simpler, even if they might have the same goal, and do little more than assemble a short account of the court proceedings at the beginning (including often a reference to a confession) and then the text of the confession and/or agreement or commitment that had brought the case to an end.

Not many 'pure' accounts of judicial processes survive in the Portuguese corpus, since most records seem to fit into the account + confession/agreement/commitment type, as we have seen. But what is striking about narrative accounts in general is that scribes drew them up using a common structure, as well as standard language and formulas.[89] All of this might somehow echo procedure and ritual words uttered in court, but it owes as much to the written conventions and the legal rhetoric used by scribes in the vast array of documents that might be written up in the course of and after a judicial process. Due to their miscellaneous and narrative nature, these accounts take in many formulas originally used in procedural records. There is no need to come back to these here. However, the idiosyncrasy of accounts seems to lie in their narrative structure, which scribes constructed using a couple of short formulas.

First, most texts (whether long or short) start with a universal notification drawing everyone's attention to the 'truth' of what is being recorded. This notification stands alone sometimes, but more often than not scribes conflated it with one of two similar formulas used to introduce the description of the case:

87 Collins, '"Sicut lex Gothorum continet"', 501–2. See the detailed discussion by Davies, *Windows on Justice*, chs. 2–5.

88 Davies, *Windows on Justice*, 27–9, 147–8; Alfonso, 'Judicial Rhetoric', 53–54. In the late eleventh century, under Alfonso VI, scribes working for the royal 'chancery' were already copying the 'narrative structure' used by monastic scriptoria to draft accounts of judicial processes (Alfonso, 'El formato', 208–9).

89 Alfonso, 'El formato', 206–9; Davies, *Windows on Justice*, 37–9, 121–4.

orta fuit/est intentio/contentio or *X habuit intentionem cum Y*.[90] To quote but two examples:

> Non est enim dubium sed plerisque cognitum eo quod orta fuit contemptio inter partem domni Nausti colimbriensis sedis episcopi et domni Sisnandi hiriensis sedis episcopi pro eclesia et uilla uocabulo Sancta Eulalia….[91]

> Dumuium quidem non est set multis mane pleuis acque nodisimu eo quod ego abuit intenzio sagulfu presbiter cum gontigio presbiter pro eglesia uogauolum sancto martinum….[92]

These formulas must have been regarded as the standard way of starting narrative accounts of disputes settled in court, regardless of the judicial authority before which these were brought (kings, counts, lords, bishops, abbots, *boni homines*, etc.). Moreover, by addressing a general audience to whom the 'truth' found in court should be communicated, scribes intended to underline the public nature of judicial process, even though it had arisen from a private grievance brought to court by one of the contending parties, as is clearly stated in the first-person variants of the *intentio/contentio* formula (like in the example just cited).

Although these are narrative records, there seems to be an attempt on the part of their redactors to shroud them in the sort of legal rhetoric that we have detected in other types of judicial record. This is particularly striking in the Portuguese corpus, given the high number of narrative records that include procedural documents copied *in extenso* at the end, with their own final

90 Amongst the thirty-nine narrative records identified, the notification formula is used in twenty-nine (seventy-four per cent), whereas the *intentio/contentio* formulas are used in twenty-five (sixty-four per cent); seventeen records (forty-four per cent) feature both, whereas twelve feature only the former and eight the latter; two feature none. Most records (twenty-two) use the word *intentio*, rather than *contentio* (three). Both had wide currency in northern Iberia: Davies, *Windows on Justice*, 37. The word *intentio* also features prominently in Sahagún material: Alfonso, 'El formato', 205.

91 DC 13 (906): 'There can be no doubt, as it is known to many, that there arose a dispute between *domnus* Nausto, bishop of Coimbra, and *domnus* Sisnando, bishop of Iria[-Santiago de Compostela], over the *villa* called St Eulalia'. Some variants: DC 572 (1079), DC 823 (1095). A shorter variant of the notification formula only: *Junqueira* 47 (1100).

92 DC 163 (991): 'There can be no doubt, as it is known to many, that I presbyter Sagulfo started a dispute against presbyter Gontigio over the church of St Martin …'. A variant: CDMM 84 (972).

clauses (sanctions, witness lists, etc.). But most 'pure' narrative records also feature such clauses.[93] Following Alfonso's remarks, we can argue that there is an 'argumentative logic' underlying the combination of an initial narrative of the dispute, using the past tense and indirect speech, with a final declarative text, using the present tense and direct speech, whereby one or both parties commit themselves to the decision reached at the end of the process.[94]

Sewing both sections together demanded an articulating element, which scribes found, again, in a set formula that is widespread across the Asturian-Leonese kingdom: *Obinde ego/nos….*[95] This formula is commonplace in composite records but can also be traced in other types of dispute texts, mostly transactions (both judicial and non-judicial) which feature a narrative bit, often introduced by the same notification formula found in narrative records.[96] Both formulas seem thus to indicate the judicial origin of such transactions, or perhaps just the fact that scribes copied these formulas from the preceding judicial records that they were drawing on.

Other Formulas Used across Several Types of Record

Formulaic writing in judicial records is not limited, however, to formulas mainly associated with specific types of record. Some other formulas show a widespread use across several types of record. Such is the case of a couple of phrases referring to one or both parties' appearance in court, before a judge or an officer. The most frequent is *deuenimus/abuimus inde ad iuditio/concilio*, usually followed by *ante/in presentia N.*[97] Other procedures are also referred to in the same formulaic manner. When describing petitions addressed by the parties to court holders, judges, and other legal officers, or sometimes addressed by the loser to the victor, scribes tend to use the verbs *petire* and *rogare* (or often *rogo*, the noun), and to qualify such action with words denoting

93 For example, LTL 36 (936), LP 212 (1004), DC 163 (991), DC 384 (1053). Some lack any final clause though: LTL 71 (1064–1086?), LP 119 (1086–1091).

94 Alfonso, 'El formato', 208.

95 For example, LP 203 (1005), LF 176 (1027), DC 376 (1050), LTPS 109 (1085), DC 823 (1095). This formula can also be found among Sahagún records: Alfonso, 'El formato', 208.

96 *Obinde* only: e.g. DC 200 (1008), DC 470 (1068), DC 888 (1098); notification + *obinde*: e.g. DC 53 (943); Azevedo 2 (1018); DC 425 (1060).

97 For example, LF 22 (1025; composite: narrative + *agnito/placitum*): 'Causatus fuit ipse Tardenatus in voce Sancte Marie in presentia principis domni Adefonsi et suorum iudicum' ('Tardenatus, speaking for St Mary [See of Lugo], was called before King Alfonso [v] and his judges'). Other examples: LP 193 (1009; formal commitment to appear in court), DC 387 (1053) (formal commitment to abide by the decision reached, cited above §iii); LF 63 (1072) (transaction).

the petitioner's subordination and the other party's mercy.[98] References to decisions of court-holders, judges, and legal officers often use the phrase *ordinare ut* (sometimes replaced by *mandare*).[99]

Language

By revealing how formulaic writing worked in practice, the texts quoted thus far show that some keywords were just as relevant as formulas when composing judicial records. Words were actually part and parcel of formulas, but scribes also used them independently. This means that words carried their own meaning, which might then be modelled according to the formulaic contexts in which they were used. A detailed analysis of the language deployed in Portuguese dispute texts is not feasible here, but it is worth listing some of the most frequent words, grouped according to some major legal and procedural categories.[100]

Two points can be raised by browsing this list and collating it with the texts quoted above. The first is that many words were used in several types of judicial record across the two centuries considered here, only with minor variation

98 For example, DC 183 (999) (composite: narrative + *placitum*): 'sciente domno eigica quod erat ipsa hereditate de ipso plazo fecit inde petitione ad ipsos dominos et ad caritate et ad benequerentia fecerunt ei donationis de ipsa hereditate' ('knowing that the property belonged by charter [to the monastery of Guimarães], *domnus* Égica petitioned the monks and they gave him the property out of charity and goodwill'). Other examples: DC 362 (1048) (formal commitment to relinquish a claim, cited above §4); DC 330 (1043) (transaction).

99 For example, LP 367 (1037; transaction): 'Et habuimus ipsa baralia in presencia ante Diagu Donnanizi; in ipso concilio, ordinarunt nos judices et lex, ut vindigase omnia cuncta quod michi dederat ipsius pater meus, quia ego erat filio primogenito' ('We brought this dispute before Diego Donnanizi; and I was ordered by the judges and the law in that court/assembly to retain all the property my father had given me, as his eldest son'). Other examples: CDMM 84 (972; narrative account), LF 22 (1025) (composite: narrative + *agnito/placitum*), LF 134 (1080) (formal commitment to appear in court).

100 The following considerations (and table) are based on a sample analysis that includes the dispute texts kept by the monasteries of Moreira da Maia (thirty-nine) and Guimarães (twenty-nine), forming the largest and third-largest collections of dispute texts extant in Portugal. They are especially interesting because nearly all of Moreira texts survive in single sheets, whereas those from Guimarães were copied in a cartulary, the so-called *Livro de Mumadona*.

TABLE 6.2 *Judicial vocabulary identified in dispute records kept by the monasteries of Moreira da Maia and Guimarães*

Semantic fields	Keywords
Grievance/ violence	*adulterium, calumniare/calumnia, captivare/captivitas, crimen, disturbatio, exire (placitum, fituria), fillare, fugare, furtare, homicidium, inrumpere, levare, maliare/malefactoria/mal (facere), occidere, praesumere, predare, prendere, raptum, rauso, sacare, scelus, superbia, usurpare*
Litigation	*actio, alimas, altercare/altercatio, baraliare/baralia, calumniare/ calumnia, causa/causatus, contemptio, (de)vindicare, exire calumniosus, inimicus, inquietare, intentio, potestas, praesumere, querelare, querimonia, soposida/subposita/suposita mala, surgere(contra), vindicare (per veritatem)*
Process	*adimplere, adprehendere, adserere/asserere, adverare, affirmare, agnitio, assignare (saio), attestare, complere, conditione(s) (sacramentorum), constringere, crepantare/crepare, custodia, defendere, diem actum, dilatio, discussio, eligere iudicem, examinare (pro pena), (per)exquirere (veritatem), firmare/firmamentum, invalidus, invenire, iurare/iuramento (sacrosancto), mandare, manifestum, ordinare, per manus, plazum, praesentare, prendere, prospicere, religere, respondere/responsum, roborare, sacare, saionitium, suscipere, testificare/testimonias/testimonium, tradere, troucire/traucire, (in a) vice, vox*
Judgement	*censura (lex), concilium, congregatio, definitio, intelligere, iudicare (veritatem)/iudicium, concilium, mallus, sententia (legis), trebuna, veritas (accipere, facere, habere)*
Conviction	*culpa, reatus*
Penalties	*carescare, caecare, cedare, componere, iudicatum, multare, (dare in) offretione, (a)pariare/pario, peitare/peito/pecto, pena (placiti)*
Petition/mercy	*complacentia, dimittere/dimissio, intercessor, petire/petitio, rogare/ rogo/rogatores, subjectio/sugessio*
Agreement/ commitment	*auctorizare/auctorgare, colmellus (diuisionis), compagina, (com-) promittere, conligatio/conligatus, consensum, habere verbum, pactum, placitum/plazum, persolta/persolutio/persolutus, verbum alligatum*
Guarantees	*affirmare, certificare, fidiare/fiare, fidiator/fiator, recabito*
Justice	*ius, iussio, iustitia, (ire pro ad) lex, veritas*

between different *scriptoria* (and local scribes) producing dispute texts.[101] They are part of a technical legal vocabulary that is richer and more erudite than historians are sometimes willing to acknowledge outside the sphere of law texts and for the period before 1100. Most of these words have an origin in classical or late Latin legal language and many indeed feature in the Visigothic laws.[102] But some other words (*alima, baralia, peitare, rauso, traucire, trebuna,* etc.) will sound odd to non-hispanists. As stressed by Alfonso, judicial records before 1100 responded to the audiences they were addressing, and not only to the Visigothic legal tradition.[103]

This introduces a second remark. Albeit technical and tradition-bound, this language was not static, which applies as much to the words as to the formulas containing them. I could not trace significant variation in Portuguese dispute texts over the tenth and eleventh centuries, although further research needs to be done in this respect. But, in the long run, language was certainly changing in early medieval Iberia, as elsewhere.[104] The texts cited thus far do not use classical or late Latin, but rather Ibero-romance, which slowly emerged from Late Antiquity onwards. As Roger Wright has rightly shown, this was the language of charters before the late eleventh century, when reformed Latin was adopted by the main ecclesiastical *scriptoria*.[105]

At the same time, scribes made a creative use of diplomatic formulas before the twelfth century. Viewed as authoritative rhetorical sources, rather than textual models that had to be copied verbatim, formulas were modified, abridged (occasionally extended), paraphrased, combined, etc., so as to suit new semantic and pragmatic contexts.[106] Interestingly, the two Iberian formularies dated before the twelfth century that are known to us (the *Formulae Visigothicae* and the tenth-century formulary of Ripoll) present a marked rhetorical character,

101 Moreira and Guimarães provide a stark example. Despite using common documentary forms, the erudite language and formulas deployed by Guimarães scribes clearly surpass the widespread use of Ibero-Romance and plainer formulas in the records kept in Moreira.

102 See Martínez Díez, 'Terminología jurídica', 271–2; Davies, *Windows on Justice*, 26–7, 95–145.

103 Alfonso, 'El formato', 209.

104 A good general summary in Rio, *Legal Practice*, 15–18, 21–2, noting that this change can be traced in surviving charters and legal formulae (formularies) alike.

105 Roger Wright, *Late Latin and Early Romance in Spain and Carolingian France* (Liverpool: 1982); Roger Wright, *A Sociophilological Study of Late Latin* (Turnhout: 2002). On Portugal, see António Henrique de Albuquerque Emiliano, *Latim e Romance na segunda metade do século XI. Análise scripto-linguística de documentos notariais do "Liber Fidei" de Braga de 1050 a 1110* (Lisboa: 2003).

106 Rio, *Legal Practice*, 31–3; Zimmermann, *Écrire et lire*, 246–84, 1269–70; Calleja Puerta, 'Ecos de las *Fórmulas* visigóticas'.

as they include mostly literary clauses. This implies that they would be used as scholarly models, rather than diplomatic manuals. Skilled scribes must have been able both to paraphrase such formulas and to draw up less elaborate clauses themselves, when composing actual—and effective—charters.[107]

Be that as it may, charters were clearly moulded by what Francesco Sabatini called 'realism demands', in a classic paper where he noted that the first manifestations of Romance languages in different areas of southern Europe can be found (before 1000) in 'legal texts', and particularly in the 'free' parts of charters associated with verbal declarations, inventories, and boundary clauses.[108] Sabatini suggested a marked distinction between the language used in 'free' and 'formulaic' parts of charters, which is not tenable in the light of more recent scholarship.[109] However, his basic hypothesis—that there is a strong link between the practical functions of some texts and the language they adopt—still stands. This was obviously the case with judicial records in northern Iberia. And not only those recording verbal declarations in court, but all records concerned with court proceedings, including those just aimed at keeping some memory of a dispute and its outcome.

These records have a strong narrative character and are designed to capture (if not construct) the detail of specific cases and actions, which prevents the scribe from copying fixed formulas and encourages his own 'free' wording, and thus the use of his own language.[110] But there is more than form and content to the use of Ibero-Romance in these texts. Their function is also part of the explanation. Be they 'procedural' or 'narrative' records, nearly all extant dispute texts had some claim to make, which is why they were kept in the end. Making such claims—usually about property rights and the wider social and political implications they entail—could not be done without deploying the language contemporaries used, even in what may seem formulaic (but never meaningless) chunks of text to us.[111] Since that language kept changing,

107 Jarrett, 'Comparing the Earliest Documentary Culture', 99, 102; Calleja Puerta, 'Ecos de las *Fórmulas* visigóticas', sections I–II; cf. Rio, *Legal Practice*, 187–97.

108 Francesco Sabatini, 'Esigenze di realismo e dislocazione morfologica in testi preromanzi', *Rivista di Cultura classica e medioevale* 7 (Studi in onore di A. Schiaffini) (1965), 972–98.

109 Wright, *Late Latin*, 61–6; cf. María del Pilar Álvarez Maurín, 'El formulismo en la lengua de los documentos notariales altomedievales', *Helmantica. Revista de Filología Clásica y Hebrea* 46, no. 139–141 (1995), 430–1; Maurilio Pérez González, 'El latín medieval diplomático', *Archivum Latinitatis Medii Aevi (Bulletin Du Cange)* 66 (2008), 96–8.

110 Fernández Flórez, *La Elaboración de los Documentos*, 67.

111 Alfonso, 'El formato', 193–4, 209, 217; Isabel Alfonso, 'Litigios por la tierra y "malfetrías" entre la nobleza medieval castellano-leonesa', *Hispania* 197 (Desarrollo legal, prácticas judiciales y acción política en la Europa medieval, ed. Isabel Alfonso) (1997), 917–55.

so did the legal words and formulas used in charters, and especially in dispute records.[112]

Conclusion

Portuguese dispute texts display a whole set of standard features that parallel drafting practices used elsewhere in northern Iberia during the ninth to eleventh centuries. Such practices are characterized by well-defined documentary types, stock formulas (some of which correlate to specific types of record), and a technical legal language of ancient stock, although not fixed. It goes beyond the 'broad similarities in wording which, given the generally high level of standardisation in the language of documents during this period, could be due as much to coincidence as to an actual textual link'.[113] In fact, dispute texts embody particularly well the tension between the respect for widespread late Latin formulas and words, on the one hand, and the need to meet more localized Ibero-Romance developments. Scribes were thus divided between two different modes of legitimation: old authoritative legal models versus contemporary audiences (whether readers or listeners).

The formal features of judicial records seem to be part and parcel of their intrinsic legal value. If no official lay notarial tradition was in place in Iberia to bind law and legal practice together, a diplomatic tradition was. This recording system was actually the counterpart, rather than a simple mirror, of the 'judicial system' identified by Davies across the Asturian-Leonese kingdom before 1000, which certainly evolved but did not disappear in the course of the eleventh century. As law represented a theoretical framework whose invocation alone would bind any court and judicial decision to a broader system of authority, so did the documentary forms, formulas and language scribes used to construct an enduring memory of each case. As I have tried to show in this article, this recording system seems to have played a key role—along with law and procedure—in legitimating both the process whereby disputes were settled and their outcomes, thus reinforcing the very public nature of dispute resolution in court.

On such implications, see Matthew Innes, 'Practices of Property in the Carolingian Empire', in *The Long Morning of Medieval Europe. New Directions in Early Medieval Studies*, ed. Jennifer R. Davis and Michael McCormick (Aldershot: 2008), 247–66.

112 Emiliano, *Latim e Romance*, 23.

113 Rio, *Legal Practice*, 29.

Law, procedure, and recording system did not, however, always interact in the same way everywhere. Portugal was a peripheral area within the kingdom of Asturias-León, where kings were occasionally present but power remained mostly in the hands of regional and local aristocracies, where few high-ranking courts (and none above the comital level) seem to have been operating on a regular basis, and where sophisticated *scriptoria* were to be found only in a few major monasteries (Guimarães, Lorvão, Vacariça, and Leça). Yet, there was a strong link between judicial practice in this area and the broader procedures and practices that characterize courts more widely across northern Iberia.

Law, that is written Visigothic law, was certainly known, used, and occasionally cited in Portuguese texts, as elsewhere, mostly regarding procedural rather than substantive issues.[114] But it was essentially a framework within which a given case might unfold, when (and only to the extent that) the judicial authorities and the relevant parties deemed it convenient.[115] Legal texts need not be at the core of judicial practice, especially outside the high-ranking monastic, comital, and a few other aristocratic courts—and this is perhaps more evident in Portugal than in the core areas of the Asturian-Leonese kingdom.[116] Formulas, on the contrary, played a central role in judicial process, no matter what type of court: as a set of ritual words to be uttered in different moments of the proceedings, and above all in the written record, when an authoritative memory of such proceedings was to be constructed. Partly because they were inspired by legal texts and concepts, but mostly because

114 Collins, '"Sicut lex Gothorum continet"', 494. Outside the procedural sphere, citations of Visigothic law seem to have no bearing other than on property and its conveyance: Isla Frez, 'La pervivencia de la tradición legal', 80, n. 22.

115 Martínez Sopena, 'La justicia en la época asturleonesa', 247, 258; Martínez Sopena, 'El Uso de la Ley Gótica', 110; Isla Frez, 'La pervivencia de la tradición legal', 76, 83–5; Davies, *Windows on Justice*, 246–7, stressing how the 'normative' and 'processual' characteristics of early medieval judicial process both apply, rather than being alternatives, in northern Iberia. See the similar remarks about the Frankish world by Rio, *Legal Practice*, 206–10.

116 A non-exhaustive survey has allowed José Mattoso to identify roughly thirty explicit citations of Visigothic law in Portuguese documents dated up to the late twelfth century, all produced (some perhaps only preserved) in a small group of monastic scriptoria that enjoyed direct access to royal and episcopal circles. This has led him to conclude that 'la diffusion du droit écrit wisigothique ... se restreint étroitement aux cercles qui furent en rapport avec les représentants du roi de León' (Mattoso, 'Les Wisigoths', 333–4). The author has underestimated, though, all the briefer, but rather more numerous, references to the *lex* (generally named) or to some passage in the *Liber iudiciorum*, and this is not to mention implicit citations to it, which testify to a much more extended knowledge and use of Visigothic law than has been admitted.

their very usage made them normative, formulas were widely accepted as the right way to write about (or even perform) judicial actions.

One might ask at this point whether the importance of formulas was inversely proportional to that of written law—that is to say, whether formulas played a bigger role in peripheral regions, like Portugal, where the remoteness from central power might imply a lesser use (and a weaker enforcement) of royal legislation.[117] Formulas would thus work not so much as a transmission chain between law and social order, as suggested by Wormald, but rather as a simulacrum of the law itself.[118] Answering this question demands further research on the relationship between legal texts and formulas, and a comparative analysis of their uses in both peripheral and core areas of the realm. For now, one can only say that by bringing legal legitimacy and judicial practice together, formulas somehow lay in between the language of law and the language of justice in early medieval Portugal.

Bibliography

Abbreviations

Arouca: Coelho, Maria Helena da Cruz. *O Mosteiro de Arouca: do século X ao século XIII*, 2nd edn. Arouca: 1988.

Azevedo: Azevedo, Rui Pinto de. 'A expedição de Almançor a Santiago de Compostela em 997, e a de piratas normandos à Galiza em 1015–1016 (Dois testemunhos inéditos das depredações a que então esteve sujeito o Território Portugalense entre Douro e Ave)'. *Revista Portuguesa de História* 14 (1974): 73–93.

CDMM: *Cartulário de D. Maior Martins: século XIII*, edited by Filomeno Amaro Soares da Silva. Arouca: 2001.

117 For the period considered here, this means basically the *Liber iudiciorum*. No original legislative production took place in the Asturian-Leonese kingdom before the twelfth-century, barring some short and very specific texts, such as the so-called *Fuero de León* (1017), the canons of the Council of Coyanza (1055) and several charters of privileges (*fueros*) dated from 974 onwards. See Prieto Morera, 'El proceso en el reino de León', 384–85. The author doesn't list eight Portuguese *fueros* dated before 1100: *Portugaliae Monumenta Historica a saeculo octavo post Christum usque ad quintumdecimum. Leges et consuetudines*, vol. 1 (Lisbon: 1856–1873), 343–53.

118 Cf. Oulion, *Scribes et notaires*, 21–4, 402–4: 'Par la sélection des règles et formes à appliquer, en rapport avec des facteurs culturels et contextuels spécifiques, le notariat haut-médiéval constitue un véritable foyer normatif, spécialement lorsque la source législative se tarit' (at 22–3).

DC: *Portugaliae Monumenta Historica: a saeculo octavo post Christum usque ad quintumdecimum. Diplomata et chartae*, vol. 1. Lisbon: 1867–1873.

Junqueira: Lira, Sérgio. *O Mosteiro de S. Simão da Junqueira*, vol. 2: Colecção Documental. Vila do Conde: 2002.

LF: *Liber fidei sanctae bracarensis ecclesiae*, edited by Avelino de Jesus da Costa, 3 vols. Braga: 1965–1990.

LP: *Livro Preto: Cartulário da Sé de Coimbra*, edited by Manuel Augusto Rodrigues and Avelino de Jesus da Costa. Coimbra: 1999.

LTL: *Liber testamentorum ceonobii laurbanensis*, edited by José Fernández Catón and Aires A. Nascimento, 2 vols. León: 2008.

LTPS: 'Livro dos testamentos do mosteiro de Paço de Sousa', edited by Maria Teresa Monteiro and J. J. Rigaud de Sousa. *Bracara Augusta* 24 (57–58), no. 69–70 (1970): 138–283.

Works Cited

Alfonso, Isabel. 'Litigios por la tierra y "malfetrías" entre la nobleza medieval castellano-leonesa'. *Hispania* 197 (Desarrollo legal, prácticas judiciales y acción política en la Europa medieval, edited by Isabel Alfonso) (1997): 917–55.

Alfonso, Isabel. 'Judicial rhetoric and political legitimation in medieval León-Castile'. In *Building Legitimacy: Political Discourses and Forms of Legitimacy in Medieval Societies*, edited by Isabel Alfonso, Hugh Kennedy and Julio Escalona, 51–88. Leiden: 2004.

Alfonso, Isabel. 'El formato de la información judicial en la Alta Edad Media peninsular'. In *Chartes et cartulaires comme instruments de pouvoir: Espagne et Occident chrétien (VIIIe–XIIe siècles)*, edited by Julio Escalona and Hélène Sirantoine, 191–218. Toulouse: 2013.

Álvarez Maurín, María del Pilar. 'El formulismo en la lengua de los documentos notariales altomedievales'. *Helmantica. Revista de Filología Clásica y Hebrea* 46, no. 139–141 (1995): 419–31.

Barret, Sébastien. 'Les actes écrits comme instruments de pouvoir: la contribution des formulaires'. In *Chartes et cartulaires comme instruments de pouvoir. Espagne et Occident chrétien (VIIIe–XIIe siècles)*, edited by Julio Escalona and Hélène Sirantoine, 87–99. Toulouse: 2013.

Branco, Maria João. 'Portugal no Reino de León. Etapas de uma relação (866–1179)'. In *El Reino de León en la Alta Edad Media, IV: La Monarquía (1109–1230)*, 533–625. León: 1993.

Brown, Warren, *et al.*, editors. *Documentary Culture and the Laity in the Early Middle Ages*. Cambridge: 2012.

Calleja Puerta, Miguel. 'Ecos de las *Fórmulas* visigóticas en la documentación altomedieval astur-leonesa'. In *Les formulaires. Compilation et circulation des modèles d'actes dans l'Europe médiévale et moderne: XIIIe congrès de la Commission internationale de diplomatique (Paris, 3–4 septembre 2012)*, edited by Olivier Guyotjeannin, Laurent Morelle and Silio P. Scalfati. Paris: 2016, at <http://elec.enc.sorbonne.fr/cid2012/part4>.

Canellas López, Ángel. *Diplomática hispano-visigoda*. Zaragoza: 1979.

Cárcel Ortí, Mariá Milagros, editor. *Vocabulaire international de la diplomatique*, 2nd edn. Valencia: 1997.

Collins, Roger. '"Sicut lex Gothorum continet": Law and Charters in Ninth- and Tenth-Century León and Catalonia'. *The English Historical Review* 100, no. 396 (1985): 489–512.

Collins, Roger. 'Visigothic law and regional custom in disputes in early medieval Spain'. In *The Settlement of Disputes in Early Medieval Europe*, edited by Wendy Davies and Paul Fouracre, 85–104. Cambridge: 1986.

Collins, Roger. 'Literacy and the Laity in Early Mediaeval Spain'. In *The Uses of Literacy in Early Mediaeval Europe*, edited by Rosamond McKitterick, 109–33. Cambridge: 1990.

Davies, Wendy. 'Judges and Judging: Truth and Justice in Northern Iberia on the Eve of the Millennium'. *Journal of Medieval History* 36, no. 3 (2010): 193–203.

Davies, Wendy. 'Summary Justice and Seigneurial Justice in Northern Iberia on the Eve of the Millennium'. *Haskins Society Journal* 22 (2012): 43–58.

Davies, Wendy. *Windows on Justice in Northern Iberia, 800–1000*. Abingdon: 2016.

Emiliano, António Henrique de Albuquerque. *Latim e Romance na segunda metade do século XI. Análise scripto-linguística de documentos notariais do "Liber Fidei" de Braga de 1050 a 1110*. Lisbon: 2003.

Everett, Nicholas. 'Lay Documents and Archives in Early Medieval Spain and Italy, c. 400–700'. In *Documentary Culture and the Laity in the Early Middle Ages*, edited by Warren Brown, *et al.*, 63–94. Cambridge: 2012.

Fernández Flórez, José Antonio. *La elaboración de los documentos en los reinos hispánicos occidentales (SS. VI–XIII)*. Burgos: 2002.

Fernández Flórez, José Antonio. 'La génesis documental: Desde las pizarras visigodas y la *Lex Romana Wisigothorum* al siglo X'. In *VIII Jornadas Científicas sobre Documentación de la Hispania altomedieval (siglos VI–X)*, edited by Nicolás Ávila Seoane, Manuel Joaquín Salamanca López, and Leonor Zozaya Montes, 89–117. Madrid: 2009.

'Formulae Visigothicae'. In *Formulae Merowingici et Karolini Aevi*, edited by Karl Zeumer, MGH Legum Sectio V: Formulae 572–95. Hannover: 1886.

'Formulae Wisigothicae'. In *Miscellanea Wisigothica*, edited by Juan Gil, 69–112. Seville: 1972.

Innes, Matthew. 'Practices of Property in the Carolingian Empire'. In *The Long Morning of Medieval Europe. New Directions in Early Medieval Studies*, edited by Jennifer R. Davis and Michael McCormick, 247–66. Aldershot: 2008.

Isidore of Seville. *The Etymologies of Isidore of Seville*, translated by Stephen A. Barney, *et al.* Cambridge: 2006.

Isla Frez, Amancio. 'La pervivencia de la tradición legal visigótica en el reino asturleonés'. *Mélanges de la Casa de Velázquez* 41, no. 2 (2011): 75–86.

Jarrett, Jonathan. 'Comparing the Earliest Documentary Culture in Carolingian Catalonia'. In *Problems and Possibilities of Early Medieval Charters*, edited by Jonathan Jarrett and Allan Scott McKinley, 89–126. Turnhout: 2013.

Kosto, Adam J. *Making Agreements in Medieval Catalonia: Power, Order, and the Written Word, 1000–1200*. Cambridge: 2001.

Kosto, Adam J. '*Sicut mos esse solet*: Documentary Practices in Christian Iberia, c. 700–1000'. In *Documentary Culture and the Laity in the Early Middle Ages*, edited by Warren Brown, *et al.*, 259–82. Cambridge: 2012.

Leges Visigothorum, edited by Karl Zeumer, MGH LL nat. Germ. 1, 1. Hannover: 1902.

Marques, André Evangelista. 'Para um inventário da documentação diplomática anterior a 1101 conservada em arquivos portugueses'. In *Mundos medievales: espacios, sociedades y poder: homenaje al profesor José Ángel García de Cortázar y Ruiz de Aguirre*, edited by Beatriz Arízaga Bolumburo, *et al.*, vol. 2, 705–18. Santander: 2012.

Marques, André Evangelista. *Da representação documental à materialidade do espaço: território da diocese de Braga (séculos IX–XI)*. Porto: 2014.

Martínez Díez, Gonzalo. 'Terminología jurídica en la documentación del reino de León. Siglos IX–XI'. In *Orígenes de las Lenguas Romances en el Reino de León: siglos IX–XII*, vol. 1, 229–72. León: 2004.

Martínez Sopena, Pascual. 'El uso de la Ley Gótica en el reino de León'. In *Remploi, citation, plagiat. Conduites et pratiques médiévales (Xe–XIIe siècle)*, edited by Pierre Toubert and Pierre Moret, 97–114. Madrid: 2009.

Martínez Sopena, Pascual. 'La justicia en la época asturleonesa: entre el liber y los mediadores sociales'. In *El lugar del campesino. En torno a la obra de Reyna Pastor*, edited by Ana Rodríguez, 239–60. València: 2007.

Mattoso, José. 'Portugal no reino asturiano-leonês'. In *História de Portugal*, vol. 1: Antes de Portugal, edited by José Mattoso, 438–565. Lisbon: 1992.

Mattoso, José. 'Les Wisigoths dans le Portugal médiéval: état actuel de la question'. In *L'Europe héritière de l'Espagne wisigothique: colloque international du C.N.R.S. tenu à la Fondation Singer-Polignac (Paris, 14–16 mai 1990): actes*, edited by Jacques Fontaine and Christine Pellistrandi, 325–39. Madrid: 1992.

Oulion, Rémi. *Scribes et notaires face à la norme dans la Toscane du Haut Moyen Âge (VIIe–XIe siècles)*. S.l.: 2013.

Pérez González, Maurilio. 'El latín medieval diplomático'. *Archivum Latinitatis Medii Aevi (Bulletin Du Cange)* 66 (2008): 47–101.

Portugaliae Monumenta Historica a saeculo octavo post Christum usque ad quintum-decimum. Leges et consuetudines, vol. 1. Lisbon: 1856–1873.

Prieto Morera, Agustín. 'El proceso en el reino de León a la luz de los diplomas'. In *El reino de León en la Alta Edad Media, II: Ordenamiento jurídico del reino*, 381–518. León: 1992.

Rio, Alice. *Legal Practice and the Written Word in the Early Middle Ages: Frankish Formulae, c. 500–1000*. Cambridge: 2009.

Sabatini, Francesco. 'Esigenze di realismo e dislocazione morfologica in testi preromanzi'. *Rivista di Cultura classica e medioevale* 7 (Studi in onore di A. Schiaffini) (1965): 972–98.

Stacey, Robin Chapman. *Dark Speech: the Performance of Law in Early Ireland.* Philadelphia: 2007.

Wormald, Patrick. *Legal Culture in the Early Medieval West: Law as Text, Image and Experience*. London: 1999.

Wormald, Patrick. *The Making of English Law: King Alfred to the Twelfth Century, Volume. I: Legislation and its Limits*. Oxford: 1999.

Wright, Roger. *Late Latin and Early Romance in Spain and Carolingian France*. Liverpool: 1982.

Wright, Roger. *A Sociophilological Study of Late Latin*. Turnhout: 2002.

Zimmermann, Michel. 'Un formulaire du Xème siècle conservé à Ripoll'. *Faventia* 4, no. 2 (1982): 25–86.

Zimmermann, Michel. *Écrire et lire en Catalogne (IXe–XIIe siècle)*, 2 vols. Madrid: 2003.

CHAPTER 7

The Dangers of Using Latin Texts for the Study of Customary Law: The Example of Flemish Feudal Law during the High Middle Ages

Dirk Heirbaut

The Particularities and Languages of Flemish Feudalism during the High Middle Ages

Leaving aside regions like the British Isles or the North of Europe, texts of customary law in the vernacular appeared quite late in the Middle Ages.[1] Even an early text, like the German *Saxon Mirror*, only saw the light in the first half of the thirteenth century.[2] The inevitable consequence for legal historians is that they have no choice but to consult documents in Latin, with all the dangers that entails. Rather than studying the problems of using Latin texts in general, this article will focus on the specific pitfalls in one case, namely Flemish feudal law during the period from around 1000 until the early fourteenth century. For the purposes of this article, feudal law is the law dealing with lords, fiefs, and vassals. There are many reasons why feudal law in Flanders, thus understood, is an interesting case study. First of all, there is the feudal angle. Previous generations of historians assumed that feudalism was already widespread in the Frankish empire, so that the High Middle Ages (1000–1300) were the classic age of feudalism. Research of the last decades has shown this view as too

1 The author would like to thank the editors of this volume for their remarks and Gerard Sinnaeve, Stefan Huygebaert, Maarten Vankeersbilck, and Amélie Verfaillie for checking his text for errors. This article was written thanks to the project 'Legal History Meets Lexical Semantics: Feudal Legal Terminology in Flanders and England of the 13th and 14th Centuries', funded by the FWO (Flemish research fund). Unless stated differently, etymological references in this article are taken from <http://www.etymologiebank.nl>, based on: Marlies Philippa *et al.*, *Etymologisch woordenboek van het Nederlands*, 4 vols. (Amsterdam: 2003–2009) for Dutch and from http://www.cnrtl.fr/etymologie based on *Le trésor de la langue française: dictionnaire de la langue du XIXe et du XXe siècle* (1789–1960), 16 vols. (Paris: 1971–1994), and *Dictionnaire du Moyen Français*, version 2015 (DMF 2015). ATILF—CNRS and Université de Lorraine, at <http://www.atilf.fr/dmf> for French.

2 See Heiner Lück, *Über den Sachsenspiegel: Entstehung, Inhalt und Wirkung des Rechtsbuches* (Dössel: 2013).

 | DOI 10.1163/9789004375765_009

optimistic. Feudalism came later than had earlier been assumed and, in some regions, only became important after 1300.[3] Interestingly, Flemish sources of the High Middle Ages have played a crucial role in misunderstanding the chronology of feudalism. Unlike most other regions, Flanders already experienced a break-through of feudalism around the year 1000. The mistake of earlier historians was to extrapolate Flemish data to the rest of Western Europe, neglecting that Flanders was well ahead of the pack and that, for a study of feudal terminology, Flanders is more interesting than other regions.[4] Flemings could not just copy well-tried terminology and legal rules from elsewhere, they had to develop their own without a vast array of examples from which they could learn

An example is the term 'liege', which arose in the context of multiple vassalage. Like so many other aspects of feudalism, multiple vassalage arrived later than earlier generations of historians had thought.[5] It created a serious problem for the man with two lords: whom should he serve if they came into conflict? The solution was to award one lord priority over the others. The typical term for this was liege[6] (L: *ligius*[7] or *legius*).[8] In Flemish charters, the word only appeared for the first time in 1111,[9] but the terminology predated this. Describing events in 1051, a text from neighbouring Cambrai described John of Arras as a liege knight (*ligius miles*) of the count of Flanders.[10] As this

3 An excellent introduction to the research is: Steffen Patzold, *Das Lehnswesen* (Munich: 2012). See also Dirk Heirbaut, 'Feudal law', in *Oxford Legal History of Europe* (Oxford: forthcoming).

4 Even within the Low Countries, Flanders was well ahead of other principalities: see Dirk Heirbaut, 'Feudalism in the twelfth century charters of the Low Countries', in *Das Lehnswesen im Hochmittelalter. Forschungskonstrukte-Quellenbefunde-Deutungsrelevanz*, ed. Jürgen Dendorfer and Roman Deutinger (Ostfildern: 2010), 217–53.

5 Roman Deutinger, 'Seit wann gibt es Mehrfachvasallität?', *Zeitschrift der Savigny-Stiftung für Rechtsgeschichte, Germanistische Abteilung* 119 (2002), 78–105. For reasons which I hope to explore in another article I do not completely agree with Deutinger.

6 *Ligius* < Germanic **liþiga* (free, unhindered).

7 Thérèse de Hemptinne and Adriaan Verhulst, *De oorkonden der graven van Vlaanderen (juli 1128–1191)* (Brussels: 1988–2009), vol. 2/1, no. 164 (1142) (pp. 108–9). *Ligius* < Germanic *ledig* (free, unhindered).

8 de Hemptinne and Verhulst, *Oorkonden*, vol. 2/1, no. 111, pp. 179–82 (1148).

9 Fernand Vercauteren, *Actes des comtes de Flandre (1071–1128)* (Brussels: 1938), no. 52 (pp. 130–3).

10 'Gesta episcoporum Cameracensium continuatio. Gesta Lietberti episcopi', ed. Ludwig Bethmann in *Monumenta Germaniae historica, Scriptores in folio*, vol. 7 (Hannover: 1846), ch. 9, 493.

part of the Cambrai text was written between 1051 and 1054,[11] it may even be a quarter of a century older than the first use of the word in the Vendômois.[12] As we will see below, the first use of a technical term of customary law does not indicate how long it had already been in use, as scribes may have been late in picking up the right terminology, using other terms, like *contra omnes* (against all), to express the idea of a liege relationship.[13]

Flanders is an interesting case study, not only because of its pioneering role but also because of its extreme character. In Flanders the lines between feudal law and the rest of customary law seem to have been much sharper than in many other parts of Europe. Two principles determined Flemish feudalism: the count monopolized service by the vassals, and the feudal inheritance had to remain with the heads of aristocratic families as much as possible. These principles were rather ruthlessly applied in Flemish feudal law, which set it apart from the rest of customary law in Flanders.[14] Flemish feudalism is more ordered and structured than usual.[15] That makes it easier to use for a study of terminology.

Another interesting element is the specific linguistic situation. Flemish-speaking Flanders,[16] i.e. the territories between the river Lys and the North Sea, spoke Middle Dutch. The much smaller Walloon Flanders on the other side of the river Lys spoke Old French. The name Walloon Flanders is somewhat confusing as the dialect of Walloon Flanders, was not Walloon, but Picard French.[17] Flemish-speaking Flanders was larger than Walloon Flanders,

11 The part of the source which interests us here was written between 1051 and 1054; for this date, see Erik Van Mingroot, 'Kritisch onderzoek omtrent de datering van de Gesta episcoporum Cameracensium', *Belgisch tijdschrift voor filologie en geschiedenis* 53 (1975), 331–2.

12 It seems very likely that a copyist added the word *ligius* in 1076 to a text that was thirty years older; see Deutinger, 'Mehrfachvasallität', 100.

13 Galbert of Bruges, *De multro, traditione, et occisione gloriosi Karoli comitis Flandriarum*, ed. Jeff Rider (Turnhout: 1994), ch. 56, 105–6 (1127).

14 For more details, see Dirk Heirbaut, 'Zentral im Lehnswesen nach Ganshof: das flämische Lehnsrecht, ca.1000–1305', *Zeitschrift der Savigny-Stiftung für Rechtsgeschichte. Germanistische Abteilung* 118 (2011), 301–48.

15 Cf. Patzold, *Lehnswesen*, 120–21.

16 For the names of all the different parts of Flanders, see Antoon Viaene, *Veelnamig Vlaanderen. Een historiografisch overzicht van de samenstellingen tot 1800* (Bruges: 1973).

17 See Serge Lusignan, 'Langue et société dans le Nord de la France: le picard comme langue des administrations publiques (XIIIe–XIVe s.)', *Comptes rendus des séances de l'Académie des Inscriptions et Belles-Lettres* 15 (2007), 1275–95; Reine Mantou, *Actes originaux rédigés en français dans la partie flamingante du comté de Flandre (1250–1350). Étude linguistique* (Liège: 1972).

so most of the population of the county spoke Middle Dutch. However, the situation was different in a feudal context, as the court[18] and the nobility preferred French.[19] Thus charters on feudal affairs in Dutch are less common,[20] even in cases where most participants were Dutch-speaking.[21] Dutch-speaking nobles even sent their sons to French-speaking abbeys to learn the language.[22] Consequently, a charter in Old French may suddenly refer to a term in Dutch, which was more familiar to its audience. For example: '*franc akaat … qu'on dit en flamenc vrikoop*'[23] (*franc akaat*[24] is called *vrikoop*[25] in Dutch; *vrikoop, franc akaat* = free purchase).[26] Thus, the number of charters in Dutch is quite limited, at least compared to the overall number of charters for Flanders. Maurits Gysseling published some 2,000 pre-1300 charters in Dutch, which have been preserved in the original,[27] and most of these charters come from the county of Flanders. To put this in perspective, until fire destroyed them during the First World War, the city archives of Ypres, a Dutch-speaking city, preserved more than 7,000 chirographs in French from the second half of the thirteenth century.[28] Moreover, the first charters in Old French appeared around 1200[29] whereas those in Middle Dutch appeared only about half a

18 Cf. Thérèse de Hemptinne, 'De doorbraak van de volkstaal als geschreven taal in de documentaire bronnen. Op zoek naar verklaringen in de context van de graafschappen Vlaanderen en Henegouwen in de dertiende eeuw', in *Handelingen van het colloquium georganiseerd door de Koninklijke Zuid-Nederlandse maatschappij voor Taal- en Letterkunde en Geschiedenis* 53 (1999), 10, 20.

19 Mantou, *Actes*, 36, 86–7, 92–6.

20 Cf. Maurits Gysseling, 'Die Einführung des Niederländischen als amtliche Sprache im 13. Jahrhundert', in *Neerlandica manuscripta. Essays presented to G. I. Lieftinck*, ed. J. P. Gumbert and M. J. M. de Haan, vol. 3 (Amsterdam: 1976), 12.

21 Cf. Namur, State archives, Charters of the counts of Namur, no. 173 (1284).

22 Lille, Archives départementales du Nord, 12 H, 2, fo. 99v, no. 132/CXX (1271).

23 Namur, State archives, Charters of the counts of Namur, no. 173 (1284).

24 *Franc* < Germanic **frank* (free); *akaat*: cf. the current French verb *acheter* < Latin *accaptare* (to take, to obtain).

25 *Vri*: current Dutch *vrij*, < germanic *frija* (unbound, free). *Koop*: substantive from the verb *kopen* (buy) derived very early in germanic from Latin *caupo* (small merchant).

26 Namur, State archives, Charters of the counts of Namur, no. 173 (1284).

27 Maurits Gysseling, *Corpus van Middelnederlandse teksten (tot en met het jaar 1300)*, vol. 1 (The Hague: 1977).

28 Carlos Wyffels, *Analyses de reconnaissances de dettes passées devant les échevins d'Ypres (1249–1291) éditées selon le manuscrit de (†) Guillaume Des Marez* (Brussels: 1991).

29 Maurits Gysseling, 'Les plus anciens textes français non littéraires en Belgique et dans le nord de la France', *Scriptorium* 3 (1949), 190–210.

century later.[30] Even though only a few thousand charters in Middle Dutch before 1300 were consulted for this article, whereas tens of thousands in Old French and Latin were read, this number is still considerable. In many ways, the situation in Flanders was comparable to the one of post conquest England: Latin, as the learned language, competed with a Germanic vernacular and the French of the elite.[31] The word French is misleading here, as the French spoken in Flanders was different from the French in England.[32] In Flanders linguistic choices were not linked to political affiliations. For example, during the Franco-Flemish wars around 1300 the lords of Gistel sided with the French occupiers of Flanders,[33] but the Gistel family was nevertheless one of the few aristocratic families issuing charters in Middle Dutch.[34] Given that in Flanders vernacular texts did not appear before the twelfth century, this present article will mostly focus on the thirteenth century, when one can find both Latin and the earliest vernacular texts.

Flemish feudal law during the High Middle Ages was to a large extent indigenous due to its early appearance. Influence from foreign customary legal systems came rather late. Roman and canon law had only a limited impact. Charters already contained references to learned law in the first, rather than in the second half of the thirteenth century, as previous research indicated. Nevertheless, this does not really make a difference for the topic studied in this article. Whether in the first or the second half of the thirteenth century, references to learned law in Flemish charters on feudal affairs mainly consisted

30 Ute Boonen, *Die mittelniederländische Urkundensprache in Privaturkunden des 13. und 14. Jahrhunderts* (Münster: 2010), 29–30; Armand Berteloot, 'Das Mittelniederländische als Urkundensprache im 13. Jahrhundert', in *Beiträge zum Sprachkontakt und zu den Urkundensprachen zwischen Maas und Rhein*, ed. Kurt Gärtner and Günter Holtus (Trier: 1995), 174–7. For the reasons for switching to the vernacular, see Emily Kadens, 'De invoering van de volkstaal in ambtelijke teksten in Vlaanderen: een status quaestionis', *Millennium, tijdschrift voor middeleeuwse studies* 14 (2000), 22–41.

31 Paul Brand, 'The Languages of the Law in Later Medieval England', in *Multilingualism in Later Medieval Britain*, ed. David Trotter (Cambridge: 2000), 63–76. See also for the French used in the law courts: Caroline Laske, 'Losing Touch with the Common Tongues—The Story of Law French', *International Journal of Legal Discourse* 1 (2016), 169–192.

32 Serge Lusignan, 'A chacun son français: la communication entre l'Angleterre et les régions picardes et flamandes (XIIIe–XIVe siècles)', in *Approches techniques, littéraires et historiques: IIe journée d'études anglo-normandes organisée par l'Académie des Inscriptions et Belles-Lettres*, ed. André Crépin and Jean Leclant (Paris: 2012), 117–33.

33 Cf. Louis Gilliodts-Van Severen, *Coutumes des petites villes et seigneuries enclavées* (Brussels: 1890–1893), vol. 5, no. 3 (pp. 35–6) (1303).

34 Gysseling, *Corpus*, vol. 1/1, no. 455 (pp. 696–7) (1282).

of renunciations rejecting rather than embracing Roman and canon law.[35] It is telling that the first real use of a Roman legal term only occurred in a charter from 1303.[36] For the loss of a fief the French word *commettre*[37] was used. The term, in this case, was derived from the Roman law on *emphyteusis* (a very long term lease in Roman law).[38] The 1303 charter, however, remains exceptional and its use of the Roman law term can be explained by its author. Philip, the senior member of the house of Flanders who was not in a French prison at that time, acted as regent over Flanders; since he had previously been count of Chieti and Loreto in Italy by marriage,[39] he must have taken his inspiration from there.

A problem of early Flemish feudalism is that, unlike feudalism that developed later and elsewhere, it was not bureaucratic.[40] Flemish feudalism was largely a personal affair, even though from the mid-twelfth century onwards the count had to use others to represent him. Nevertheless, the idea remained that a parchment could not take the place of a person. One major exception is the renunciation of the homage made to one's lord. Vassals who did so, because they rebelled against their lord, preferred to send a letter,[41] but that was just common sense. In the circumstances, appearing in person before the lord would have been a folly. Since people still met one another personally, Flemish feudalism was, to a large extent, based on rituals[42] which brings us to the problem of the gap between the written source the historian has to rely on and the spoken words and meaningful gestures of the rituals.

35 Dirk Heirbaut, 'Afstand van Romeinsrechtelijke excepties in Vlaanderen: vroeger dan gedacht', *Ius romanum—ius commune—ius hodiernum. Studies in honour of Eltjo J. H. Schrage*, ed. Harry Dondorp *et al.* (Amsterdam and Aalen: 2010), 177–85.

36 Gilliodts-Van Severen, *Coutumes des petites villes*, vol. 5, no. 3 (pp. 35–6) (1303).

37 < Latin *committere* (to commit).

38 Cf. Laure Verdon, 'La paix du prince. Droit savant et pratiques féodales dans la construction de l'état en Provence (1250–1309)', *Revue historique* 678 (2010), 311–16.

39 On the role of Philip and the house of Flanders in the Anjou kingdom of Sicily, see Jean Dunbabin, *The French in the kingdom of Sicily, 1266–1305* (Cambridge: 2011), 124–32.

40 Dirk Heirbaut, 'Finding the Sources of a Non-Bureaucratic Feudalism: the Case of Flanders during the High Middle Ages', *Le vassal, le fief et l'écrit. Pratiques d'écriture et enjeux documentaires dans le champ de la féodalité* (*XI*^{e}*–XV*^{e} *siècles*), ed. Jean-François Nieus (Louvain-la-Neuve: 2007), 97–122.

41 E.g., Lille, Archives départementales du Nord, B, 498/3898 (1297).

42 Dirk Heirbaut, 'Rituale und Rechtsgewohnheiten im flämischen Lehnrecht des hohen Mittelalters', *Frühmittelalterliche Studien* 41 (2007), 351–61.

As there is extensive literature on this subject,[43] this article will only mention some elements typical for the Flemish sources used, without any claims to validity in other situations. The rituals left their impact on the terminology. The charters preferred verbs over nouns,[44] as the former brought to life activities, i.e. rituals, whereas the latter were more apt for expressing concepts. One should not overestimate the role of the rituals. Later witnesses did not have to remember each and every ritual in all of its smallest details. The feudal court declared in a final judgment that all demands of the law had been met.[45] Any irregularities were thus covered and could no longer invalidate the legal act.[46] Moreover, it was not very difficult to get a judgment, as in most cases a lord or his representative as president needed only two vassals in order to have a court.[47] Given the importance of rituals compared to charters, Flemish lords did not develop a feudal administration. Systematic record-keeping only became a practice in the fourteenth century. Even by the end of the thirteenth century, one does not find more than simple lists of vassals and/or fiefs.[48] Thus, clerics were responsible for producing and preserving the bulk of our sources. As we will see, in many cases they offered only a cracked mirror of the past, because they were outsiders to the events they described, as will be explained in the next paragraph.[49] Some clerics were aware that it was sufficient to state

43 See, e.g., Marco Mostert, ed., *New Approaches to Medieval Communication* (Turnhout: 1999); Marco Mostert and Paul Barnwell, eds., *Medieval Legal Process: Physical, Spoken and Written Performance in the Middle Ages* (Turnhout: 2011). Very valuable, but unfortunately not available in English are: Christa Bertelsmeier-Kierst, *Kommunikation und Herrschaft. Zum Verschriftlichungsprozeß des Rechts im 13. Jahrhundert* (Stuttgart: 2008); Martin Pilch, *Der Rahmen der Rechtsgewohnheiten. Kritik des Normensystemdenkens entwickelt am Rechtsbegriff der mittelalterlichen Rechtsgeschichte* (Cologne: 2009).

44 See below, for several examples.

45 E.g., Charles Carton and Ferdinand Van de Putte, *Chronique et cartulaire de l'abbaye de Hemelsdaele* (Bruges: 1858), no. 39 (pp. 73–4) (1257).

46 Theo Luykx, *Johanna van Constantinopel, gravin van Vlaanderen en Henegouwen. Haar leven (1199/1200–1244). Haar regering (1205–1244), vooral in Vlaanderen* (Brussels: 1946), no. 52 (pp. 579–80) (1238).

47 Lille, Archives départementales du Nord, B, 1250/2197 (1281); Ferdinand Van de Putte, *Chronique et cartulaire de l'abbaye de Groeninghe à Courtrai* (Bruges: 1872), 27–9 (1285).

48 Michel Vandermaesen, 'Het ontstaan van enkele "Cartularia van Vlaanderen" in 1336. De grafelijke kanselarij aan het werk', in *Actief in archief. Huldeboek Hilda Coppejans-Desmedt* (Antwerpen: 1989), 147–53.

49 One can of course make the same remarks for some poets; cf. Ursula Peters, 'Das Forschungsproblem der Vasallitätsterminologie in der romanischen und deutschen Liebespoesie des Mittelalters', *Beiträge zur Geschichte der deutschen Sprache und Literatur* 137 (2015), 623–59.

that all requirements had been met[50] and one even expressly declared that it was not necessary to give a detailed account of the proceedings.[51] Others did not and thus wrote down a lot of information which was irrelevant according to contemporary law, but very helpful for the historian,[52] at least to the extent that such scribes only recorded those parts of the proceedings which they deemed important. If this is not taken into account today, it may easily appear that chaos reigned in documentary production.

A hard question to answer is how truthful the scribes were in their accounts of proceedings. Normally in Flanders a report by two members of the court later sufficed as proof,[53] so a charter was not strictly necessary. However, only a charter ensured that the memory of a legal act would live on.[54] It could, therefore, happen that years after the event participants reported upon it, and a charter at that later occasion might be drawn up.[55] Moreover, members of the court later never had problems testifying that everything had gone smoothly, but they did not always remember the details. For example, in one case the person reporting knew exactly how much had been paid, but not what the currency had been.[56] Therefore, many disputes were settled by charters, inspected by the members of the feudal court, and read out before them.[57] This may have made some scribes writing in Latin so nervous that they tried to cover every possibility or, exceptionally, used the word in the vernacular which had actually been used in court.[58] This may also have come in handy for the person who had to translate the charter into the language of the members of the court,[59] though from the point of view of the lords and vassals themselves the best option was a charter in their own language.[60]

---

50 E.g., Charles Mussely and Emile Molitor, *Cartulaire de l'ancienne église collégiale de Notre-Dame de Courtrai* (Ghent: 1880), no. 132 (pp. 145–6) (1270).

51 Felix-Henri D'Hoop, *Recueil des chartes du prieuré de Saint-Bertin à Poperinghe, et de ses dépendances à Bas-Warneston et à Couckelaere* (Bruges: 1870), no. 85 (pp. 89–91) (1249).

52 For example, to reconstruct the procedure for transferring a fief: see Dirk Heirbaut, 'De procedure tot overdracht van onroerende goederen in het oud-Vlaamse recht: enkele voorbeelden uit de dertiende eeuw', *Handelingen van de Maatschappij voor Geschiedenis en Oudheidkunde van Gent* 51 (1997), 37–59.

53 E.g., Lille, Archives départementales du Nord, 12 H, 2, fos. 65r–66r, no. LVIII/67 (1287).

54 Cf. Piot, *Cartulaire*, no. 113 (p. 93) (1212).

55 Lille, Archives départementales du Nord, B 1101/2828 (1287 on events from 1275).

56 *Ibid.*, B 1250 (1281).

57 E.g., D'Hoop, *Recueil*, no. 89 (p. 99) (1250).

58 For examples, see below.

59 Namur, State archives, Charters of the counts of Namur, no. 173 (1284).

60 Cf. for Luxemburg: Winfried Reichert, '"In lingua Guallica sive Romana pro commoditate domini": Beobachtungen zur Aufkommen volkssprachiger Urkunden in der Grafschaft

Normally we do not know who really made customary law. In Flanders, feudal law was a creation of feudal courts. The lord or his representative acted as chair and the vassals sat as judges. The president of the court asked questions and its members answered. These answers were their judgments. This mechanism of collective judgements was common in customary law courts in Western Europe during the High Middle Ages. The problem is that we may know who sat on the court, but not the actual contribution of every single member to its judgments. Susan Reynolds suggested that there was a group of semi-professionals, but she was unable to identify these persons further.[61] However, in Flemish sources we can actually do so. For complicated questions the members of the court retired to deliberate amongst themselves, the person who would then carry the discussion thereafter acted as spokesman of the court, with the other members following his opinion. Flemish charters, at least from the early twelfth century on, will award the spokesman the first place in the list of the members of the court,[62] a practice which seems to have been unique to Flanders and some neighbouring regions.[63] Unfortunately, clerics were not spokesmen or members of the feudal court and they were barred from witnessing its deliberations.[64] Notes from the spokesmen themselves have only been preserved from the 1260s on.[65] Nevertheless, it is clear that thanks to the spokesmen Flemish feudal law had its own experts.

Typical Feudal Terminology (Relatively) Unknown in Flemish Feudalism

Some terms, considered by handbooks as belonging to the standard stock of feudalism,[66] were either absent or not very popular in Flanders. Flemish

Luxemburg', in *Urkundensprachen im germanisch-romanischen Grenzgebiet*, ed. Kurt Gärtner and Günter Holtus (Trier: 1997), 369–489.

61 Susan Reynolds, 'The Emergence of Professional Law in the Long Twelfth Century', *Law and History Review* 21 (2003), 347–66.

62 Dirk Heirbaut, 'The Spokesmen in Medieval Courts: The Unknown Leading Judges of the Customary Law and Makers of the First Continental Law Reports', in *Judges and Judging in the History of the Common Law and Civil Law: from Antiquity to Modern Times*, ed. Paul Brand and Joshua Getzler (Cambridge: 2012), 192–208.

63 See, for Hainaut, Frédéric De Reiffenberg, *Monuments pour servir à l'histoire des provinces de Namur, de Hainaut et de Luxembourg*, vol. 1 (Brussels, 1844), no. 45 (pp. 372–3) (1281).

64 Vercauteren, *Actes*, no. 108 (pp. 247–51) (1122).

65 Heirbaut, 'Spokesmen', 201–7.

66 A useful book for that is still F.-L. Ganshof, *Feudalism*, trans. Philip Grierson, 3rd edn. (Toronto: 1996), even though Ganshof's generalisations and chronology can no longer be

feudal law did not know the word felony[67] (L. *felonia*; F. *felonie*) for a breach of the contract between a lord and his man.[68] Other words like investiture (L. *investitura*;[69] F. *investiture*)[70] or seisin[71] (L. *saisina*,[72] *saisinia*;[73] F. *saisine*)[74] occur only a few times in the sources and a Dutch equivalent is not recorded in the period studied.[75] Tenure[76] (L. *tenura*;[77] F. *tenure*)[78] is another of these

---

followed. For an in-depth study of feudal terminology, see Kenneth James Hollyman, *Le développement du vocabulaire féodal en France pendant le haut moyen âge (étude sémantique)* (Geneva: 1957).

67 Cf. current French *félon* < Germanic **fillo* (vilain).

68 On the term *felonia*/*felonie*/*felony* in feudalism, see Elizabeth Kamali, '*Felonia felonice facta*: Felony and Intentionality in Medieval England', *Criminal Law and Philosophy* 9 (2015), 400–3.

69 Galbert of Bruges, *De multro*, ch. 56 (pp. 105–6), but a verb (*investire*) is more likely: see Edouard Hautcoeur, *Cartulaire de l'*église collégiale de Saint-Pierre de Lille (Lille: 1894), vol. 1, no. 332 (pp. 285–7) (1243).

70 Once again in the form of verbs: *envestir*. See, e.g., Theo Luykx, *De grafelijke financiële bestuursinstellingen en het grafelijk patrimonium in Vlaanderen tijdens de regering van Margareta van Constantinopel (1244–1278)* (Brussels: 1961), no. 31 (pp. 351–2) (1264); for *ravestir*, see Hautcoeur, *Église*, I, no. 564 (p. 399) (1264).

71 < Germanic **sazjan* (to occupy).

72 Walter Prevenier, *De oorkonden der graven van Vlaanderen (1191–aanvang 1206)*, vol. 2 (Brussels: 1964), no. 97 (pp. 212–14) (1199).

73 Leopold Warnkönig and Albert Gheldolf, *Histoire de la Flandre et des ses institutions civiles et politiques jusqu'à l'année 1305*, vol. 4 (Brussels: 1835–1864), no. 47 (pp. 415–17) (1226).

74 Raymond Monier, *Les lois, enquêtes et jugements des pairs du castel de Lille. Recueil des coutumes, conseils et jugements du tribunal de la Salle de Lille, 1283–1406* (Lille: 1937), 37–8 (1291).

75 For investiture an explanation is that the charters pay less attention to the transfer of possession than to the acquisition of a heritable right by the acquirer, an idea expressed by the terminology *adhereditare* (Armand d'Herbomez, *Chartes de l'abbaye de Saint-Martin de Tournai*, vol. 2 (Brussels: 1898–1901), no. 680 (pp. 126–7) (1256)); for *inhaeredare* see Joseph-Jean De Smet, 'Codex diplomaticus abbatiae Ninoviensis', in *Recueil des chroniques de Flandre*, vol. 2 (Brussels: 1841), no. 262 (p. 952) (1286); for L. *heredare* see Joseph-Jean De Smet, *Cartulaire de l'abbaye de Cambron*, vol. 1 (Brussels: 1869), no. 32 (p. 447) (1267); for F. *ayreter* see Charles Piot, *Cartulaire de l'abbaye d'Eename* (Bruges: 1881), no. 317 (pp. 290–2) (1278); for D. *erven* see Gysseling, *Corpus*, vol. 1/1, no. 35 (pp. 88–9) (1266).

76 Cf. French *tenir* < Latin *tenire* (to hold).

77 Leopold August Warnkönig, *Flandrische Staats- und Rechtsgeschichte bis zum Jahr 1305*, vol. 3 (Tübingen: 1842), no. 36 (pp. 43–4) (1212).

78 Eusèbe Feys and Aloïs Nelis, *Les cartulaires de la prévôté ou abbaye de Saint-Martin à Ypres (1102–1543)*, vol. 2 (Bruges: 1880–1887), no. 253 (pp. 170–1) (1269).

words which was known, but lacked popularity. The expression 'aid and counsel' could be feudal,[79] but was rather general in Flanders.[80] Its component terms can be found separately,[81] with aid (L. *auxilium*,[82] F. *ayde*,[83] D. *helpe*),[84] also having the specific technical meaning of the testimony by one's peers before the feudal court.[85]

Sometimes contemporaries did not develop specific terminology because they failed to realise that they were dealing with a new situation. For example, the count's court[86] (L. *curia Flandriae*;[87] F. *court de Flandres*)[88] was held from the start in two forms, a general and open meeting, and a more restricted consultation with trusted confidants.[89] Only from 1237 was the latter called the council (L. *consilium*;[90] F. *consel*;[91] D. *raet*),[92] although it already existed in the eleventh century.[93] In some cases, contemporaries never saw the need, during the period studied, to distinguish a certain situation from others by giving it a special name. For example, the term fief-rente, which entitled its

79 Hautcoeur, *Église*, vol. 1, no. 556 (pp. 392–3) (1262).

80 See, e.g., Ghent, State archives, Charters of the counts of Flanders, Chronological supplement, 198 (1282).

81 See, e.g., Lille, Archives départementales du Nord, B, 498/4213 (1233).

82 Warnkönig and Gheldolf, *Histoire*, vol. 4, no. 47 (pp. 415–17) (1226).

83 Monier, *Lois*, no. 1 (p. 19) (1286). *Aide*, cf. current French *aider* < Latin *adjutare* (to help).

84 Gysseling, *Corpus*, vol. 1/3, no. 1365 (pp. 2125–7) (1297). Cf. English *help*, Dutch *helpen* < Germanic **helpan* (to help).

85 Cf. Egied Strubbe, *Egidius van Breedene (11..–1270). Grafelijk ambtenaar en stichter van de abdij Spermalie. Bijdrage tot de geschiedenis van het grafelijk bestuur en van de Cisterciënser orde in het dertiendeeuwsche Vlaanderen* (Bruges: 1942), no. 3 (pp. 274–5) (1228).

86 < late Latin *curtis* < classic Latin *cohors*.

87 Lille, Archives départementales du Nord, 12 H, 2, fos. 114v–115r, no. CXLII/153 (1220).

88 Brussels, National archives of Belgium, Court of accounts, Charters of Flanders, series 2, 2013 (1274).

89 Dirk Heirbaut, *Over heren, vazallen en graven. Het persoonlijk leenrecht in Vlaanderen, ca.1000–1305* (Brussels: 1997), 154–64.

90 Louis Gilliodts-Van Severen, *Coutume de la Prévôté de Bruges*, vol. 2 (Brussels: 1887), no. 25 (pp. 49–50).

91 Charles Duvivier, *La querelle des d'Avesnes et des Dampierres jusqu'à la mort de Jean d'Avesnes (1257)*, vol. 2, *Preuves (1200–1310)* (Brussels: 1894), no. 48 (p. 72) (1237). Remark that the first recorded use is in French, not in Latin.

92 Gysseling, *Corpus*, vol. 1/2, no. 783 (pp. 1281–5) (1288). Raet, cf. current Dutch *raad* < Germanic **reda* (deliberation).

93 Cf. 'Miracula Sancti Ursmari in itinere per Flandriam facta', ed. Oswald Holder-Egger, MGH SS, vol. 15, 2 (Hannover: 1888), 840.

holder to an income, but awarded him no rights over its source, is only a later creation. Contemporaries saw no need for a special word in this case, because they treated fiefs-rentes just like other fiefs. In this case, a distinct terminology would not have been of any use, and research has shown that, at least in Flanders, it did not matter whether a fief was a fief-rente or an ordinary fief.[94] For Flemings this was so evident that only charters for foreigners mention that the common rules of feudal law were applicable.[95] In other cases, a specific term would have been useful. One may think here of what learned literature misleadingly called a *feudum oblatum* (offered fief),[96] as it was actually an allod a person surrendered to another, whereupon the latter awarded it to him as a fief. One can easily imagine that fiefholders in this case may have had some bargaining power to obtain better conditions. However, a distinct terminology is lacking, even though the sources offer all kinds of descriptions of the cession and retrocession involved in the creation of a fief this way.[97] Once again, the lack of a distinct terminology is revealing. As soon as the man had received his former allod as a fief, it was no different from other Flemish fiefs.[98] The example of the fief-rente and the *feudum oblatum* should warn historians not simply to copy terminology from other regions or later periods when studying a particular territory, because to do so may easily lead to wrong conclusions.

Terminology in Three Languages: Latin Confusion versus Vernacular Precision

If Flemish feudal law during the High Middle Ages used technical terms, the most common situation was that these can be found in the three languages. Several examples can be given:

94 Dirk Heirbaut, 'The Fief-Rente: a New Evaluation Based on Flemish Sources (1000–1305)', *Tijdschrift voor rechtsgeschiedenis* 67 (1999), 1–37.

95 Ghent, State archives, Charters of the counts of Flanders, Collection Saint-Genois, 681 (1293).

96 Thomas Brückner, *Lehnsauftragung* (Frankfurt: 2011).

97 See, e.g., Lille, Archives départementales du Nord, B, 1561, fo. 12RV, no. 445 (1293).

98 With the exception of the fiefs of the peers of Flanders, who enjoyed a special status; cf. Lambert of Ardres, 'Historia comitum Ghisnensium', ed. Johannes Heller, in MGH SS, vol. 24 (Hannover: 1879), ch. 119 (p. 619) (*ca.*1200; reporting on events in 1086–1091).

- to disinherit oneself, i.e. to divest oneself (of a fief): L. *exheredare*,[99] F. *desyreter*,[100] D. *onteerven*.[101]
- for the benefit of: L. *ad opus*,[102] F. *a oes*,[103] D. *ter boef*.[104]
- full feudal relief:[105] L. *plenum relevium*,[106] F. *plein relief*,[107] D. *volle cope*.[108]

Needless to say, some of these terms were more generic technical terms of customary law and were only feudal by their application to fiefs, and in some cases the common term is nothing more than a common tariff, as in tenth penny:[109] L. *decimus denarius*,[110] F. *disime denier*,[111] D. *tienden peneghe*.[112]

The common technical terms sometimes go back to the Germanic vernacular, as for example:

99 De Smet, *Cambron*, vol. 2/1, no. 32 (p. 447) (1267).

100 Piot, *Cartulaire*, no. 317 (pp. 290–2) (1278). < Latin *dishereditare*.

101 Gysseling, *Corpus*, I/3, no. 1252 (pp. 1913–15) (1293). Cf. current Dutch *onterven*, consisting of the negative *ont* + *erven* < Germanic **arbjan* (inherit).

102 Hautcoeur, *Église*, vol. 1, no. 332 (pp. 285–7) (1243).

103 Piot, *Cartulaire*, no. 317 (290–2) (1278). It is well-known that in England this terminology would develop into 'use' (< *a oes* < Latin *ad opus*), the name for the predecessor of the trust. However, the continental feudal terminology still needs to be studied in detail.

104 Gysseling, *Corpus*, vol. 1/3, no. 1080 (pp. 1672–3) (1291). *Ter boef*: cf. current Dutch *ten behoeve van*. *Behoeven* < Germanic **bihōb* (to behove).

105 The feudal relief was the succession tax to be paid by the heir of a fief to the lord. In Flanders, it consisted of the revenue of the fief during one year, with a maximum of 10 pounds. Hence, the full relief was 10 pounds: see Heirbaut, *Over lenen en families*, 105–14.

106 Ghent, State archives, abbey of St. Bavo, R 31 quire 1, fos. 9r, 28r, 29r (1280). < *relevare* (to relieve).

107 Rik Opsommer, 'Splitsing van de heerlijkheid Hemsrode (Anzegem) anno 1284: leenrechtelijke bemerkingen', *Jaarboek van de geschied- en heemkundige kring 'De Gaverstreke'* 15 (1987), 79–80 (1284).

108 Gysseling, *Corpus*, vol. 1/4, no. 1567, 2354–6 (1297).

109 The tax to be paid in the case of transfers of fiefs. It is first documented in the mid thirteenth century and cannot have been much older: see Heirbaut, *Over lenen en families*, 150.

110 Carlos Wijffels, 'Getuigenverhoor betreffende de machtsmisbruiken van de baljuw van de heerlijkheid Waasten (1250)', *Handelingen van de koninklijke commissie voor de uitgave der oude wetten en verordeningen van België* 20 (1962), no. 36 (p. 337).

111 Brussels, National archives of Belgium, Court of accounts, Accounts in roles, 1000 (1305).

112 Gysseling, *Corpus*, vol. 1/3, no. 1270 (pp. 1937–9) (1293).

- to warrant:[113] L. *warandire*/[114]*garandire*,[115] F. *warandir*/[116]*garandir*,[117] D. *waranderen*.[118]
- to abandon: L. *werpire*/[119]*guerpire*,[120] F. *werpir*/[121]*guerpir*,[122] D. *werpen*.[123]

In these cases, it may happen that a scribe writing in Latin is not familiar with the Germanic loan word and betrays his unease when using it in Latin. For example, one charter uses both the words *grandizare* and *garandizare*.[124]

If the three languages have one word, all terms could be equal; but it could also be the case that the vernacular terminology was more precise. Take, for example, the word *primogenitus* (firstborn son),[125] which was actually not very accurate. One or more sons could die and it was not uncommon for a second, third, or other further son to succeed his deceased brother through

---

113 < Germanic *_warjan_ (to warrant). In this context, not the warranty of a seller towards a buyer, but tenurial warranty, the duty of the lord to protect his man's rights in the fief and also his obligation to compensate his man if the latter loses the fief: see Heirbaut, *Over lenen en families*, 30–4. For tenurial warranty, see Paul Hyams, 'Warranty and Good Lordship in Twelfth Century England', *Law and History Review* 5 (1987), 437–503. See also David Postles, 'Seeking the Language of Warranty of Land in Twelfth-Century England', *Journal of the Society of Archivists* 20 (1999), 209–22.

114 Lille, Archives départementales du Nord, B, 1292/445 (1227).

115 Cyriel Vleeschouwers, *De oorkonden van de Sint-Baafsabdij te Gent*, vol. 2 (Brussels: 1990), no. 321 (pp. 347–8). There are also the variations *warantizare*: Auguste Van Lokeren, *Chartes et documents de l'abbaye de Saint Pierre au Mont-Blandin à Gand* (Ghent: 1868–1871), I, no. 464 (pp. 245–6) (1221); and *garantizare*, for which see Joseph Kervyn de Lettenhove, *Codex Dunensis sive diplomatum et chartarum medii aevi amplissima collectio* (Brussels: 1875), no. 41 (pp. 53–4) (thirteenth century).

116 Lille, Archives départementales du Nord, B, 1561, fo. 84r, no. 282 (1284).

117 Feys and Nelis, *Cartulaires*, vol. 2, no. 320 (pp. 230–2) (1284).

118 Warnkönig and Gheldolf, *Histoire*, vol. 4, no. 7 (pp. 234–9) (1269).

119 Vleeschouwers, *Oorkonden*, vol. 2, no. 397 (pp. 428–9) (1262). < Germanic *_werpan_ (to throw).

120 Mussely and Molitor, *Cartulaire*, no. 125 (pp. 133–4) (1267).

121 Reine Mantou, *Chartes en langue française antérieures à 1271 conservées dans les provinces de la Flandre orientale et de Flandre occidentale* (Paris: 1987), no. 9, (pp. 10–11) (1248).

122 Piot, *Cartulaire*, no. 317 (pp. 290–2) (1278).

123 Gysseling, *Corpus*, vol. 1/3, no. 1104 (pp. 1702–3) (1292).

124 Kervyn de Lettenhove, *Codex*, no. 41 (pp. 53–4) (thirteenth century).

125 D'Hoop, *Recueil*, no. 116 (pp. 128–9) (1280). Also, *maior natu*: Ghent State archives, St. Peter's abbey, 659 (1258).

primogeniture.[126] The terminology in the vernacular, eldest son (F. *aisnei fil*,[127] D. *oudsten sone*),[128] better indicated that, in order to inherit, it was less important to be born firstborn than it was actually to be the eldest when at the point of succession.

In many cases the precision in the vernacular stands in sharp contrast to the bewildering variety of terms in Latin. Of course, there is no problem when the Latin text only has a small number of variants, as in the following case: L. *defestucare*,[129] *effestucare*,[130] *festucare*,[131] (F. *enfestukier*,[132] D. *halmen*)[133] to renounce the fief by throwing away a straw. One can even, with some indulgence, make allowance for the Latin terminology for homage:[134] *homagium*,[135] *hominagium*,[136] *hominium*[137] (F. *houmage*,[138] D. *manscepe*).[139] Confusion reigns, however, for the verb to hand over (the fief to the lord):

126 André du Chesne, *Histoire généalogique des maisons de Guines, d'Ardres, de Gand et de Coucy. Preuves* (Paris: 1631), 546–7 (1262).

127 Ignace de Coussemaker, *Documents relatifs à la ville de Bailleul en Flandre* (Lille: 1877–1878), I, no. 31, (pp. 32–4) (1288). Note that for masculine Old French words I generally use the oblique form (= accusative) in this article, because this is the form which survives in current French and may thus be more familiar to the reader. In this case, however, modern French uses the nominative, *fils*.

128 Cf. Robert Fruin, *De keuren van Zeeland* (The Hague: 1920), no. B, art. 9 (p. 74) (1290), which is a charter by the count of Holland, but based on Laurent Van den Bergh, *Oorkondenboek van Holland en Zeeland tot het einde van het Hollandsche huis* (The Hague: 1866–1873), II, no. 668 (p. 295) (1290), by the count of Flanders.

129 Prevenier, *Oorkonden*, vol. 2, no. 280 (pp. 612–15) (1205). This and the following words derived from classical Latin (cf. *festuca*, 'stalk').

130 Vleeschouwers, *Oorkonden*, vol. 2, no. 397 (pp. 428–9) (1262).

131 Aalst, City archives, Hospital of our Lady, Charters, 2 (1241).

132 Mantou, *Chartes*, no. 9 (pp. 10–11) (1248).

133 Gysseling, *Corpus*, vol. 1/2, no. 855 (p. 1371) (1289). Cf. current Dutch *halm* (stalk) < Germanic **halma* (stalk).

134 All three languages composed their word for man with a suffix.

135 Hautcoeur, *Église*, vol. 1, no. 264 (pp. 228–9) (1235).

136 Lille, Archives départementales du Nord, B, 1570, fo. 47v, no. 88bis (*ca.*1226).

137 Piot, *Cartulaire*, no. 193 (pp. 161–2) (1231). One manuscript of Galbert of Bruges has *omnia* instead of *hominia*. The latest edition by Rider has *hominia* (Galbert of Bruges, *De multro*, ch. 20, 48–49), but the older edition still had *omnia* (ed. Henri Pirenne (Paris: 1891), ch. 20, 34). This is akin to the better known confusion between *homines* and *omnes*.

138 Hautcoeur, *Église*, vol. 1, no. 621 (pp. 439–40) (1270).

139 Gysseling, *Corpus*, vol. 1/2, no. 609 (pp. 1028–9) (1285).

L. *donare*,[140] *reddere*,[141] *reportare*,[142] *resignare*,[143] *transferre*,[144] compared to F. *raporter*,[145] D. *draghen*.[146] One could claim here that this chaos reflected contemporary reality and that the Latin scribes were not to blame for it. Yet, it would not explain why the vernacular, which was closer to the practitioners of customary law, showed no linguistic hesitation at all. Therefore, even in Latin charters, the scribes sometimes took care to add the term in the vernacular, lest the reader not understand what it was all about. The feudal relief was in Latin *emptio*,[147] *rachatum*,[148] *relevamentum*,[149] *relevatio*,[150] *relevium*,[151] *reliquia*,[152] but in the vernacular *relief* (F)[153] or *cop*/[154]*cope*/[155]*coepe* (D).[156] For clarity's sake, one scribe just abandoned all efforts at finding a suitable word in Latin and used the French word: '*tocius terre mee reliez*' (the feudal reliefs of my whole territory).[157] Another, when describing the relief for non-feudal tenure, clarified the Latin by adding the vernacular equivalent: '*emptionem, que vulgo dicitur cop*' (which the people call *cop*).[158] That he was really thinking with the Dutch vernacular in mind becomes clear when considering his Latin term. The Dutch word for relief was *cop*/*cope*/*coepe* (which in today's Dutch

140 Mussely and Molitor, *Cartulaire*, no. 125 (pp. 133–4) (1267).
141 Hautcoeur, *Église*, vol. 1, no. 91 (p. 93) (1210).
142 Armand d'Herbomez, *Histoire des châtelains de Tournai de la maison de Mortagne* (Tournai: 1895), no. 63 (pp. 70–1) (1239).
143 Vleeschouwers, *Oorkonden*, vol. 2, no. 397 (pp. 428–9) (1262).
144 Mussely and Molitor, *Cartulaire*, no. 125 (pp. 133–4) (1267).
145 Piot, *Cartulaire*, no. 317 (pp. 290–2) (1278).
146 Gysseling, *Corpus*, vol. 1/2, no. 855 (p. 1371) (1289). < Germanic **dragan* (to pull, to carry).
147 Jozef Vermaere, *Abdijorganisatie en domeinexploitatie van de Gentse Sint-Pietersabdij gedurende de dertiende eeuw. Een status quaestionis* (Ghent, unpublished licentiate thesis in history: 1974), vol. 2, 149 (1247–1275).
148 Duvivier, *Querelle*, vol. 2, no. 187 (pp. 306–12) (1253).
149 Hautcoeur, *Église*, vol. 1, no. 175 (pp. 166–7) (1222).
150 Charles Duvivier, *Actes et documents anciens intéressant la Belgique*, vol. 1 (Brussels: 1898–1903), 74–9 (1143–1163).
151 Hautcoeur, *Église*, vol. 1, no. 299 (p. 261) (1240).
152 de Hemptinne and Verhulst, *Oorkonden*, 2/1, no. 157 (pp. 254–5) (1157).
153 Opsommer, 'Splitsing', 79–80 (1284).
154 de Hemptinne and Verhulst, *Oorkonden*, vol. 2/1, no. 186 (pp. 291–2) (1160).
155 Gysseling, *Corpus*, vol. 1/4, no. 1567 (pp. 2354–6) (1297).
156 Gysseling, *Corpus*, vol. 1/3, no. 1305 (pp. 1977–8) (1294). As this example illustrates, spelling in Dutch remained notoriously inconsistent in Flanders until the late nineteenth century.
157 de Hemptinne and Verhulst, *Oorkonden*, vol. 2/1, no. 69 (pp. 116–17) (1134–1143).
158 *Ibid.*, no. 186 (pp. 291–2) (1160).

(*koop*) still means purchase), hence the scribe used the closest equivalent in Latin, *emptio*.[159]

A reference to the vernacular was also helpful when a charter concerned a feudal dower, i.e. in Flanders a life-estate in one half of the fiefs for the widow of a deceased vassal. Scribes either tried to cover all possibilities by using several words in Latin (for example, *dos, dotalitium, donatio propter nuptias*),[160] in the hopes that at least one of them would stick. One charter, after offering two possibilities in Latin, gave up and referred to the vernacular: '*Dote seu dotalitio quod doaire vulgare appellatur*' (*dos* or *dotalitum*, what the people call *doaire*).[161] Once again, the vernacular terminology (F. *doaire*/*douwaire*,[162] D. *bilevinghe*)[163] was standardized. However, it seems that not every scribe was familiar with the right terminology in the vernacular. Some charters in Middle Dutch borrow *douairie*[164] from the French *doaire*,[165] whereas another charter in French copied an imprecise Latin phrase from Roman law: *donne pour neuces*[166] (*donatio propter nuptias*,[167] gift on account of marriage),

159 This confusion between a feudal relief and a purchase is echoed in a message of 1128 of the citizens of Bruges concerning the relief the king of France could ask from a new count of Flanders: '*coemptionem vel pretium*', on which see Galbert of Bruges, *De multro*, 151.

160 Edouard Hautcoeur, *Cartulaire de l'abbaye de Flines*, vol. 1 (Lille: 1873), no. 274 (pp. 294–6) (1289). For an example using even more possible terms, see Ignace De Coussemaker, *Cartulaire de l'abbaye de Cysoing et de ses dépendances (867–XVIIe siècle)* (Lille: 1883), no. 129 (pp. 160–71) (1253).

161 Ghent, State archives, Charters of the counts of Flanders, Collection Saint-Genois, 339 (1284).

162 Hautcoeur, *Église*, vol. 1, no. 716 (pp. 504–5) (1284). < medieval Latin *dotarium* < Latin *dos*.

163 Gysseling, *Corpus*, vol. 1/3, no. 1290 (pp. 1962–3) (1293). Current Dutch *bijleving*; cf. the Dutch word *leven* < Germanic **libēn* (to live). The word in Middle Dutch thus expresses the idea that the dower was a life estate.

164 Gysseling, *Corpus*, 1/2, no. 514 (p. 753) (1284).

165 Cf. the tautology in '*no in bilevinghen no in douarie*' (neither in bilevinghe, nor in douarie); Gysseling, *Corpus*, vol. 1/2, no. 581 (pp. 980–1) (1285).

166 Maurice Vanhaeck, *Cartulaire de l'abbaye de Marquette* (Lille: 1937–1940), I, no. 233 (pp. 223–5) (1269).

167 The charter in French tried to copy a charter in Latin that described the renunciation of a wife, as a potential widow, to her feudal dower. The Latin charter was written by a cleric who used a host of words to cover any possibility, in Vanhaeck, *Cartulaire*, I, no. 229 (pp. 219–21). The French charter tried to follow this, but soon took the easy way out and just stated, 'all other rights she could have'. In fact, these were not relevant. After the appearance of the customary dower of one half of the fiefs in Flanders around 1160, husbands would not award any further rights to endowered wives at marriage, for which see Heirbaut, *Over lenen en families*, 129.

but, conversely, only used one of the proper words to express the idea of a feudal dower).[168]

Making an analysis of the confusion in the Latin sources even more complicated is the fact that sometimes terms may reflect the actual variety of practice. For example, the sources name the man (i.e. the vassal) in Latin as *confeudator*,[169] *feodarius*,[170] *feodatarius*,[171] *feodatus*,[172] *feodalis*,[173] *fidelis*,[174] *homo*,[175] *vasallus*,[176] and *vavassor*;[177] but also in French there is some variety with *foiable*,[178] *hom*,[179] and *vauvasseur*[180] (faithful (person), man, and '*vavassor*'), with the latter, in most cases, indicating a vassal of the lowest rank.[181] In Dutch there is just *man*.[182]

---

168 Cf. Philippe Godding, *Le droit privé dans les Pays-Bas méridionaux du XII*^{e} *au XVIII*^{e} *siècle* (Brussels: 1987), 263.

169 Van Lokeren, *Chartes*, vol. 1, no. 453 (pp. 241–2) (1219).

170 Alphonse De Vlaminck, *Cartulaire de l'abbaye de Zwijveke-lez-Termonde* (Ghent: 1869), no. 18 (p. 16) (1227).

171 Kervyn de Lettenhove, *Codex*, no. 41 (pp. 53–4) (thirteenth century).

172 Vleeschouwers, *Oorkonden*, vol. 2, no. 351 (p. 380) (1255).

173 De Vlaminck, *Cartulaire*, no. 5 (pp. 5–6) (1223).

174 Mussely and Molitor, *Cartulaire*, no. 105 (p. 110) (1254).

175 Duvivier, *Querelle*, vol. 2, no. 7 (pp. 13–14) (1212).

176 *Ibid.*, no. 187 (pp. 306–12) (1253). < medieval Latin *vassus* < Celtic *guas* (servant).

177 Robert Fossier, *Cartulaire chronique du prieuré Saint-Georges d'Hesdin* (Paris: 1988), no. 3 (p. 41) (1161). < *vassus vassorum* (vassal of the vassals).

178 Hautcoeur, *Église*, vol. 1, no. 564 (p. 399) (1264).

179 Vleeschouwers, *Oorkonden*, vol. 2, no. 415 (pp. 450–1) (1266).

180 Thierry de Limburg-Stirum, *Coutumes de la ville d'Audenarde*, vol. 2 (Brussels: 1882–1886), no. 17 (pp. 26–7 (*ca.*1300).

181 The word is, in twelfth century Flanders, linked to ideas of hierarchy, which need to be explored further. It is also less clear what its meaning became in the thirteenth century, when concepts of hierarchy gave way to the idea that all were under the count, so that further distinguishing them no longer mattered. For now, see Dirk Heirbaut, *Graaf en vazallen. Een institutionele analyse van enkele aspecten van de feodo-vazallitische relatie tussen de graaf van Vlaanderen en zijn vazallen van de meerderjarigheid van Boudewijn IV tot Boudewijn IX. (Ca.990–aanvang 1206)* (Ghent, unpublished licentiate thesis: 1988), 277–9.

182 Gysseling, *Corpus*, vol. 1/1, no. 331 (pp. 545–7) (1281). Words like *homo, hom*, or *man* are not necessarily feudal, hence clarifications making clear that the man had a fief, as in '*homo noster feodalis*', for which see Ignace de Coussemaker, *Un cartulaire de l'abbaye de Notre-Dame de Bourbourg (1104–1793)*, vol. 1 (Lille: 1882–1891), no. 157 (pp. 167–8) (1269); '*hommes fievés*', as in Feys and Nelis, *Cartulaires*, vol. 2, no. 320, (pp. 230–2) (1284); or '*man ... van lene*', as in Gysseling, *Corpus*, vol. 1/3, no. 1080 (pp. 1672–3) (1291).

A special case of vernacular clarity versus Latin confusion can be found in the terminology for the fief itself. Compared to French *fief*[183] and Dutch *lene*[184] are several words in Latin, such as *casamentum*[185] or *fiscus*,[186] but most of all *beneficium*[187] and *feodum*[188] (with the variants *feodus*[189] and *feudum*).[190] Originally *beneficium* was more popular, but *feodum* appeared in 1093 at the latest,[191] in all likelihood because clerics became more aware that laymen used another word.[192] Although *feodum* overtook *beneficium* by around 1100,[193] the latter

---

183 First recorded in Gysseling, '*Textes*', no. 8 (p. 197) (1219). The most commonly accepted etymology is that *feodum* was derived from *fehu-ôd* (cattle-good). In an article published in Dutch which never made it into the international literature, Maurits Gysseling, the great specialist of early and high medieval etymology and toponymy in Belgium and Northern France, emphatically rejected this theory. In his opinion, *feodum*, *faw-ôd* (limited possession; *faw*, cf. English few) stands in contrast to allod, *al-ôd* (unlimited possession; *al* cf. English all): see Maurits Gysseling, 'Enkele Oudnederlandse woorden in het Frans', *Mededelingen van de Vereniging voor Naamkunde te Leuven* 29 (1953), 81.

184 First recorded in Gysseling, *Corpus*, vol. 1/1, no. 9 (pp. 44–9) (1253). < Germanic **laih(w)ni* (loan). It is interesting that in German the proto-Germanic word evolved into both *Lehn* (fief) and *Leihe* (tenure), which did not exist in Dutch. Maybe this is due to an earlier and clearer distinction between fiefs and other forms of tenure in Dutch than in German.

185 Eugène Van Drival, *Cartulaire de l'abbaye de Saint-Vaast d'Arras rédigé au XIIe siècle par Guimann* (Arras: 1875), 262 (*ca.*1168).

186 Vercauteren, *Actes*, no. 44 (pp. 119–20 (1110).

187 E.g., Daniel Haigneré, *Les chartes de Saint-Bertin, d'après le grand cartulaire de Dom Ch.-J. Dewitte*, vol. 1 (Saint-Omer: 1886–1899), no. 73 (pp. 26–7) (1058).

188 E.g., Piot, *Cartulaire*, no. 192 (p. 161) (1231).

189 Lille, Archives départementales du Nord, 10 H, 323, pp. 196–7 (1243).

190 Vleeschouwers, *Oorkonden*, vol. 2, no. 266 (pp. 286–7) (1241).

191 Vercauteren, *Actes*, no. 12 (pp. 38–41); no. 16 (pp. 52–3); no. 17 (pp. 54–7). The 1093 charters contain the first undisputed use of *feodum*. For a discussion of earlier, but suspect charters, see Heirbaut, 'Feudalism', 137–8.

192 Cf. late eleventh-century references to popular vocabulary in charters of neighbouring regions: '*beneficium quod vulgo dicitur feodum*' (benefice which the people call fief), for which see Aubertus Miraeus and Johannes Foppens, *Opera diplomatica et historica* (Brussels: 1723–1784), I, no. 28 (p. 515) (1087); or, more dignified: '*beneficium, quod nos laica lingua dicimus feodum*' (benefice which we call in the vernacular fief), for which see William Newman, *Les seigneurs de Nesle en Picardie. Leurs chartes et leur histoire* (Paris: 1971), II, no. 1, (pp. 19–21) (1115). On the expression '*quod vulgo dicitur*', see Michel Parisse, 'Quod vulgo dicitur: la latinisation des noms communs dans les chartes', *Médiévales* 42 (2002), 45–54, which shows that this expression was mainly used when the scribe could not find a good Latin equivalent for an expression which he only encountered in the vernacular.

193 See above, note 157; cf. Galbert of Bruges, *De multro*, ch. 66 (pp. 118–19).

retained some popularity amongst churchmen into the twelfth century.[194] In one case, the preference for *beneficium* may be due to the wish of a monk to make clear that a man held a certain income from his abbey as a benefice and not as a heritable right.[195] By the thirteenth century, it had disappeared, like all other alternatives for *feodum*,[196] and the vernacular term triumphed completely. The example of *beneficium* as opposed to *feodum* shows that the confusion in the sources may sometimes have been by design, as clerics seem to have been well aware of the correct terminology, but were reluctant to use it. After all, as their language helped to distinguish the learned cleric from the laymen, giving in on this point, may have seemed like a capitulation to them.[197]

Terminology without an Equivalent in Dutch

In some cases, the sources from the High Middle Ages offer no Dutch equivalent for Latin and French terminology, e.g.:

- to relieve (a fief): L. *relevare*;[198] F. *relever*.[199]
- fealty: L. *fidelitas*,[200] *fides*;[201] F. *feautei*,[202] *foi*.[203]
- to descend from: L. *descendere*,[204] *movere*;[205] F. *descendre*,[206] *mouvoir*.[207]

194 This should not be exaggerated, as it could happen that churchmen called their church benefice a *feodum*; see Lille, Archives départementales du Nord, 1 H, 631/3137 (1115–1131).

195 Bernard Delmaire, *L'histoire-polyptique de l'abbaye de Marchiennes (1116–1121). Étude critique et édition* (Louvain: 1985), no. 8 (pp. 106–7) (1135).

196 This also helped better to distinguish fiefs from church benefices, for which the word *beneficium* was now reserved; cf. Tournai, State archives, Cartularies, no. 68 fo. 7r (viii) (1221).

197 See more in general, Stéphane Marcotte and Christine Silvi, eds., *Latinum cedens. Le français et le latin langues de spécialité au Moyen Âge* (Paris: 2014).

198 Ghent, State archives, Saint Peter's abbey, 659 (1258).

199 Lille, Archives départementales du Nord, B, 1571, fo. 31v, no. 40 (1260).

200 Galbert of Bruges, *De multro*, ch. 52, (pp. 101–2) (1127). *Fides* mainly occurs in the twelfth century.

201 Lille, Archives départementales du Nord, B, 4047/3121 (1290).

202 Ghent, State archives, Charters of the counts of Flanders, collection Saint-Genois, 635 (1292).

203 Hautcoeur, *Abbaye*, vol. 1, no. 230 (pp. 250–2) (1282).

204 Piot, *Cartulaire*, no. 234 (pp. 204–5) (1239).

205 Van de Putte and Carton, *Hemelsdaele*, no. 10 (pp. 50–1) (1238).

206 Ghent, State archives, Charters of the counts of Flanders, collection Saint-Genois, 887 (1297).

207 Van Lokeren, *Chartes*, vol. 1, no. 904 (p. 425) (1281).

A variant is that Latin and French have the same two words, whereas Dutch has only one, such as 'to abandon (the fief)' (L. *devestire*,[208] *exire*;[209] F. *desvestir*,[210] *issir*;[211] D. *huut ghaen*).[212] This poverty of Dutch seems to have been more due to the lack of contemporaneous texts in Dutch compared with late medieval texts, when there is more material.[213] If a Dutch term is lacking, we do still find the same patterns as when the three languages have an equivalent—confusion in Latin versus clarity in the vernacular—as for example 'to disavow one's homage' (L. *diffiduciare*,[214] *hominium reicere*,[215] *hominium guerpire*,[216] *homagium remandare*,[217] *hominagium reddere*;[218] F. *hommage rendre*).[219] The scarcity of sources in Dutch may explain in one case why Dutch terminology looks more standardized, like 'to split up the fief' (L. *dividere a feodo*,[220] *excerpere a feodo*,[221] *separare a feodo*;[222] F. *dessevrer del fief*,[223] *esrachier del fief*,[224] *estraire del fief*,[225] *oster hors del fief*,[226] *oster et departir del fief*;[227] D. *spliten van den lene*).[228]

---

208 d'Herbomez, *Histoire*, no. 63 (pp. 70–1) (1239).
209 Kervyn de Lettenhove, *Codex*, no. 41 (pp. 53–4).
210 Hautcoeur, *Abbaye*, vol. 1, no. 118 (p. 120) (1258).
211 Piot, *Cartulaire*, no. 317 (pp. 290–2) (1278).
212 Gysseling, *Corpus*, vol. 1/3, no. 1104 (pp. 1702–3) (1292). *Huut ghaen*: cf. current Dutch *uitgaan* (to go out (of)). *Gaan* < Germanic **ge* (to go, to run).
213 For this, see Rik Opsommer, *"Omme dat leengoed es thoochste dinc van der weerelt". Het leenrecht in Vlaanderen in de 14de en 15de eeuw*, 2 vols. (Brussels: 1995).
214 Walter of Thérouanne, *Vita Karoli comitis Flandriae*, ed. Jeff Rider (Turnhout: 2006), ch. 53 (p. 76) (1127). *Diffiduciare* had fallen from grace in the thirteenth century.
215 Galbert of Bruges, *De multro*, ch. 95 (pp. 142–3) (1128).
216 Walter of Thérouanne, *Vita Karoli*, ch. 38 (p. 62).
217 Lambert of Waterlos, 'Annales Cameracenses', ed. Georg Pertz, in *Monumenta Germaniae historica, Scriptores in folio*, vol. 16 (Hannover: 1859), 530–1 (1170).
218 Lille, Archives départementales du Nord, B, 1570, fo. 47v, no. 88bis (*ca.*1226).
219 Frantz Funck-Brentano, *Les origines de la guerre de Cent Ans. Philippe le Bel en Flandre* (Paris: 1897), 216, n. 2 (1297).
220 Mussely and Molitor, *Cartulaire*, no. 69 (pp. 70–1) (1233).
221 *Ibid.*, no. 166 (pp. 188–9) (1284).
222 Frans De Potter and Jan Broeckaert, 'Grimminge', in *Geschiedenis van de gemeenten van de provincie Oost-Vlaanderen* (Ghent: 1864–1900), I, 29 n. 1.
223 Opsommer, 'Splitsing', (pp. 79–80) (1284). *Sevrer* < Latin separare.
224 Hautcoeur, *Abbaye*, vol. 1, no. 264 (pp. 284–7) (1288). < Latin *eradicare*.
225 *Ibid.*, no. 267 (pp. 297–8) (1289). < Latin *extrahere*.
226 Vanhaeck, *Cartulaire*, vol. 1, no. 198 (pp. 190–1_ (1260). Cf. current French *ôter* < Latin *obstare*.
227 Élie Brun-Lavainne, *Franchises, lois et coutumes de la ville de Lille.* (Lille: 1842), 312–14 (1285).
228 Gysseling, *Corpus*, vol. 1/3, no. 1104 (pp. 1702–3) (1292). < Germanic **splitan* (to split).

If Dutch terminology was present, it could have been influenced by French, as was shown above with French *doaire* leading to *douairie* in Dutch. Generally, Dutch terminology was less precise than the French. The French word *relief* was unequivocal, whereas the Dutch *cop/cope/coepe* could mean both relief and purchase. This led to some ambiguity in one text which contains the word *cope* in both of these meanings.[229]

The Importance of Using the Main Language of the Vernacular in the Study of Customary Law

The paragraphs above do not deal with all the intricacies of feudal terminology in Flanders during the High Middle Ages; nevertheless, there can be no doubt that the language which brings us closest to the reality of feudalism in high medieval Flanders was French. There are not enough texts in Dutch, and scribes writing the Latin documents were ignorant of or even hostile to the world of lords, vassals, and fiefs. In short, to study feudalism in Flanders during the High Middle Ages, one should try to start with the sources in the language most used by its practitioners, in this case French. If not, one can easily be led astray by the linguistic chaos exhibited by the Latin sources. The latter show confusion, not because practitioners did not know what to do, but because scribes were unable to report accurately on feudal law in Latin. This calls for caution with theories claiming that feudalism could only come into existence when the learned lawyer appeared on the scene.[230]

A final example will show what can be achieved if one looks at feudal law in Flanders without the clutter of Latin documents, and works only with charters in French. For the rights to a fief, Flemish charters in French very rarely used the word *saisine*,[231] and the terminology of the learned lawyers, namely *dominium utile* and *dominium directum*, was absent.[232] For practitioners in

229 See above.

230 Susan Reynolds, *Fiefs and Vassals: The Medieval Evidence Reinterpreted* (Oxford: 1994).

231 See above.

232 One can find, however, the expression *dominium utile* in a treaty between the countess of Flanders and the count of Holland in 1256, but that was due to the lawyers of the French Crown who had intervened: see Jaap Kruisheer, *Oorkondenboek van Holland en Zeeland tot 1299*, vol. 3 (Assen: 1992), no. 1103 (pp. 23–6), nos. 1107–8 (pp. 31–41). None of the parties seems to have picked up the idea. The German abbey of Kornelimünster, when reporting to the pope on the sale of an allod to an abbey in Tournai, referred to '*omne dominium directum vel utile*': see d'Herbomez, *Chartes*, vol. 2, no. 749 (pp. 213–14) (1275). Once again, this had no influence in Flanders itself.

Flanders the fief was a *hiretage*[233] (L. *hereditas*;[234] Dutch *arve*;[235] heritage), a heritable good which produced *proufis*[236] (profits; D: *bladinghe*,[237] *vrome*).[238] Normally, the vassal who held the fief also received its profits: he was *tenant et prendant*[239] (holding (the fief) and taking (the profits)). However, it was possible that someone else, like his deceased predecessor's widow, had a *viage* (life estate);[240] in such a case, the latter had the profits and the vassal only had the *treffons* (subsoil).[241] *Hiretage* and *proufis* were so crucial that they were the standard for measuring fiefs. A fief's size was expressed by its number of *livrees de terre*[242] (L. *libratae terrae*),[243] i.e. the amount of heritage which yearly produced one pound of profits. The focus on the *livrees de terre* meant that Flemish fiefs were fungible goods. A fief could be replaced by another with the same number of *livrees de terre*, whatever its actual composition.[244] As this example shows, starting from the real terminology of customary law may give us refreshing insights and bring us to a view of feudalism that is different from the classic handbooks or the treatises of the learned lawyers. However, it also makes clear that there was a shared framework.[245] Working with *livrees de terre* would not have been possible without it, as fungibility required consensus on a common standard.

---

233 d'Herbomez, *Histoire*, no. 176 (pp. 235–6) (1280–1290).

234 Georges Espinas, *Privilèges et chartes de franchise de la Flandre*, vol. 1/1 (Brussels: 1959), no. 25 (pp. 49–58) (1220).

235 Gysseling, *Corpus*, vol. 1/1, no. 124 (pp. 244–5) (1272). See above for *arve*, current Dutch *erve* and verb *erven*.

236 Lille, Archives départementales du Nord, B, 1102/4352 bis and ter (between 1276 and 1283). Proufis, cf. English profit < Latin *profectus*.

237 Gysseling, *Corpus*, vol. 1/2, no. 885 (pp. 1371–5) (1289). Cf. current Dutch *blad* (leaf).

238 Gysseling, *Corpus*, vol. 1/1, no. 189 (p. 333) (1277). < Germanic **frumo* (benefit, advantage).

239 Lille, Archives départementales du Nord, B, 402/2109 (1279).

240 Monier, *Lois*, no. 43 (pp. 44–5) (1296). *Viage* = *vie* < Latin *vita* with the suffix *age*.

241 Amaury de Ghellinck d'Elseghem, *Chartes et documents concernant la famille van Vaernewijck*, vol. 1 (Ghent: 1899), no. 23 (pp. 35–40) (1295). Cf. current French *tréfonds* < Latin *transfundus*.

242 Ghent, State archives, Charters of the counts of Flanders, Collection Saint-Genois, 351 (1284).

243 Hautcoeur, *Abbaye*, vol. 1, no. 249 (pp. 267–8) (1285).

244 Lille, Archives départementales du Nord, 4058/4118 (1298).

245 On this, see Heirbaut, 'Spokesmen', 192–208.

Conclusion

When studying customary law, one has to use the language of its specialists and not the Latin of the scribes. However, vernacular texts became available only relatively late. One way around this is by confronting Latin with vernacular terminology, as soon as the latter becomes available, and by paying special attention to the rare references to the vernacular in Latin texts. This article hopes to have proven that this approach is worth trying. The reader should not forget, however, that Flemish feudal law was rather unique: it was precocious and home-grown. The situation may well be completely different in regions where feudalism arrived later and was influenced by learned law.[246]

Bibliography

Manuscripts

Aalst, City archives
Hospital of Our Lady, Charters, no. 2
Brussels, National archives of Belgium
Court of accounts, Accounts in roles, 1000
Court of accounts, Charters of Flanders, series 2, 2013
Ghent, State archives
Abbey of St Bavo, R 31 quire 1
Charters of the counts of Flanders, Chronological supplement, no. 198
Charters of the counts of Flanders, Collection Saint-Genois, nos. 339, 635, 681, 887
St. Peter's Abbey, 659
Lille, Archives départementales du Nord
1 H, 631/3137
10 H, 323
12 H, 2
B, 402/2109
B, 498/3898
B, 498/4213
B, 1101/2828
B, 1102/4352 bis and ter
B, 1250/2197
B, 1292/445

246 See, e.g., Gérard Giordanengo, *Le droit féodal dans les pays de droit écrit. L'exemple de la Provence et du Dauphiné, XIIe–début XIVe siècle* (Rome: 1988).

B, 1561
B, 1570
B, 1571
B, 4047/3121
B, 4058/4118
Namur, State Archives, Charters of the counts of Namur, no. 173
Tournai, State archives
Cartularies, no. 68

Works Cited

Berteloot, Armand. 'Das Mittelniederländische als Urkundensprache im 13. Jahrhundert'. In *Beiträge zum Sprachkontakt und zu den Urkundensprachen zwischen Maas und Rhein*, edited by Kurt Gärtner and Günter Holtus, 173–96. Trier: 1995.

Bertelsmeier-Kierst, Christa. *Kommunikation und Herrschaft. Zum Verschriftlichungsprozeß des Rechts im 13. Jahrhundert*. Stuttgart: 2008.

Boonen, Ute. *Die mittelniederländische Urkundensprache in Privaturkunden des 13. und 14. Jahrhunderts*. Münster: 2010.

Brand, Paul. 'The Languages of the Law in Later Medieval England' In *Multilingualism in Later Medieval Britain*, edited by David Trotter, 63–76. Cambridge: 2000.

Brückner, Thomas. *Lehnsauftragung*. Frankfurt: 2011.

Brun-Lavainne, Élie. *Franchises, lois et coutumes de la ville de Lille*. Lille: 1842.

Carton, Charles and Ferdinand Van de Putte. *Chronique et cartulaire de l'abbaye de Hemelsdaele*. Bruges: 1858.

de Chellink d'Elseghem, Amaury. *Chartes et documents concernant la famille van Vaernewijck*, vol. 1. Ghent: 1899.

de Coussemaker, Ignace. *Documents relatifs à la ville de Bailleul en Flandre*. Lille: 1877–1878.

de Coussemaker, Ignace. *Un cartulaire de l'abbaye de Notre-Dame de Bourbourg (1104–1793)*. Lille: 1882–1891.

de Coussemaker, Ignace. *Cartulaire de l'abbaye de Cysoing et de ses dépendances (867–XVIIe s.)*. Lille: 1883.

de Hemptinne, Thérèse. 'De doorbraak van de volkstaal als geschreven taal in de documentaire bronnen. Op zoek naar verklaringen in de context van de graafschappen Vlaanderen en Henegouwen in de dertiende eeuw'. *Handelingen van het colloquium georganiseerd door de Koninklijke Zuid-Nederlandse maatschappij voor Taal- en Letterkunde en Geschiedenis* 53 (1999): 7–21.

de Hemptinne Thérèse and Verhulst, Adriaan. *De oorkonden der graven van Vlaanderen (juli 1128–1191)*. Brussels: 1988–2009.

de Limburg-Stirum, Thierry. *Coutumes de la ville d'Audenarde*. Brussels: 1882–1886.

de Potter Frans and Jan Broeckaert. *Geschiedenis van de gemeenten van de provincie Oost-Vlaanderen*. Ghent: 1864–1900.

de Reiffenberg, Frédéric. *Monuments pour servir à l'histoire des provinces de Namur, de Hainaut et de Luxembourg*, vol. 1. Brussels: 1844.

de Smet, Joseph-Jean. 'Codex diplomaticus abbatiae Ninoviensis'. In *Recueil des chroniques de Flandre*, vol. 2, 751–983. Brussels: 1841.

de Smet, Joseph-Jean. *Cartulaire de l'abbaye de Cambron*. Brussels: 1869.

de Vlaminck, Alphonse. *Cartulaire de l'abbaye de Zwijveke-lez-Termonde*. Ghent: 1869.

Delmaire, Bernard. *L'histoire-polyptique de l'abbaye de Marchiennes (1116–1121). Étude critique et édition*. Louvain-la-Neuve: 1985.

Deutinger, Roman. 'Seit wann gibt es Mehrfachvasallität?'. *Zeitschrift der Savigny-Stiftung für Rechtsgeschichte, Germanistische Abteilung* 119 (2002): 78–105.

d'Herbomez, Armand. *Histoire des châtelains de Tournai de la maison de Mortagne*. Tournai: 1895.

d'Herbomez, Armand. *Chartes de l'abbaye de Saint-Martin de Tournai*. Brussels: 1898–1901.

d'Hoop, Felix-Henri. *Recueil des chartes du prieuré de Saint-Bertin à Poperinghe, et de ses dépendances à Bas-Warneston et à Couckelaere*. Bruges: 1870.

Dictionnaire du Moyen Français, version 2015 (DMF 2015). ATILF—CNRS and Université de Lorraine, at <http://www.atilf.fr/dmf>.

du Chesne, André. *Histoire généalogique des maisons de Guines, d'Ardres, de Gand et de Coucy. Preuves*. Paris: 1631.

Dunbabin, Jean. *The French in the Kingdom of Sicily, 1266–1305*. Cambridge: 2011.

Duvivier, Charles. *La querelle des d'Avesnes et des Dampierres jusqu'à la mort de Jean d'Avesnes (1257)*, vol. 2, *Preuves (1200–1310)*. Brussels: 1894.

Duvivier, Charles. *Actes et documents anciens intéressant la Belgique*. Brussels: 1898–1903.

Espinas, Georges. *Privilèges et chartes de franchise de la Flandre*, vol. 1/1. Brussels: 1959.

Feys Eusèbe and Aloïs Nelis. *Les cartulaires de la prévôté ou abbaye de Saint-Martin à Ypres (1102–1543)*. Bruges: 1880–1887.

Fossier, Robert. *Cartulaire chronique du prieuré Saint-Georges d'Hesdin*. Paris: 1988.

Fruin, Robert. *De keuren van Zeeland*. The Hague: 1920.

Galbert of Bruges. *De multro, traditione, et occisione gloriosi Karoli comitis Flandriarum*, edited by Jeff Rider. Turnhout: 1994.

Ganshof, François-Louis. *Feudalism*, trans. Phillip Grierson. 3rd edn. Toronto: 1996.

'Gesta episcoporum Cameracensium', edited by Ludwig Bethmann. In MGH SS, vol. 7, 393–525. Hannover: 1846.

Gilliodts-Van Severen, Louis. *Coutume de la Prévôté de Bruges*. Brussels: 1887.

Gilliodts-Van Severen, Louis. *Coutumes des petites villes et seigneuries enclavées*. Brussels: 1890–1893.

Giordanengo, Gérard. *Le droit féodal dans les pays de droit écrit. L'exemple de la Provence et du Dauphiné, XIIe–début XIVe siècle*. Rome: 1988.

Godding, Philippe. *Le droit privé dans les Pays-Bas méridionaux du XIIe au XVIIIe siècle*. Brussels: 1987.

Gysseling, Maurits. 'Les plus anciens textes français non littéraires en Belgique et dans le Nord de la France'. *Scriptorium* 3 (1949): 190–210.

Gysseling, Maurits. 'Enkele Oudnederlandse woorden in het Frans'. *Mededelingen van de Vereniging voor Naamkunde te Leuven* 29 (1953): 81–4.

Gysseling, Maurits. 'Die Einführung des Niederländischen als amtliche Sprache im 13. Jahrhundert'. In *Neerlandica manuscripta. Essays presented to G. I. Lieftinck*, vol. 3, 9–14. Amsterdam: 1976.

Gysseling, Maurits. *Corpus van Middelnederlandse teksten (tot en met het jaar 1300)*, vol. 1. The Hague: 1977.

Haigneré, Daniel. *Les chartes de Saint-Bertin, d'après le grand cartulaire de Dom Ch.-J. Dewitte*. Saint-Omer: 1886–1899.

Hautcoeur, Edouard. *Cartulaire de l'abbaye de Flines*. Lille: 1873.

Hautcoeur, Edouard. *Cartulaire de l'*église collégiale de Saint-Pierre de Lille. Lille: 1894.

Heirbaut, Dirk. *Graaf en vazallen. Een institutionele analyse van enkele aspecten van de feodo-vazallitische relatie tussen de graaf van Vlaanderen en zijn vazallen van de meerderjarigheid van Boudewijn IV tot Boudewijn IX. (Ca. 990–aanvang 1206)*. Ghent: unpublished licentiate thesis, 1988.

Heirbaut, Dirk. 'De procedure tot overdracht van onroerende goederen in het oud-Vlaamse recht: enkele voorbeelden uit de dertiende eeuw'. *Handelingen van de Maatschappij voor Geschiedenis en Oudheidkunde van Gent* 51 (1997): 37–59.

Heirbaut, Dirk. *Over heren, vazallen en graven. Het persoonlijk leenrecht in Vlaanderen, ca.1000–1305*. Brussels: 1997.

Heirbaut, Dirk. 'The Fief-Rente: a New Evaluation based on Flemish Sources (1000–1305)'. *Tijdschrift voor rechtsgeschiedenis* 67 (1999): 1–37.

Heirbaut, Dirk. *Over lenen en families. Het zakelijk leenrecht in Vlaanderen, ca. 1000–1305. Een studie over de vroegste geschiedenis van het leenrecht in het graafschap Vlaanderen*. Brussels: 2000.

Heirbaut, Dirk. 'Finding the Sources of a Non-Bureaucratic Feudalism: the Case of Flanders during the High Middle Ages'. In *Le vassal, le fief et l'écrit. Pratiques d'écriture et enjeux documentaires dans le champ de la féodalité (XIe–XVe s.)*, edited Jean-François Nieus, 97–122. Louvain-La-Neuve: 2007.

Heirbaut, Dirk. 'Rituale und Rechtsgewohnheiten im flämischen Lehnrecht des hohen Mittelalters'. *Frühmittelalterliche Studien* 41 (2007): 351–61.

Heirbaut, Dirk. 'Afstand van Romeinsrechtelijke excepties in Vlaanderen: vroeger dan gedacht'. In *Ius romanum—ius commune—ius hodiernum. Studies in honour of Eltjo J. H. Schrage*, edited by Harry Dondorp *et al.*, 177–85. Amsterdam and Aalen: 2010.

Heirbaut, Dirk. 'Feudalism in the Twelfth Century Charters of the Low Countries'. In *Das Lehnswesen im Hochmittelalter. Forschungskonstrukte-Quellenbefunde-Deutungsrelevanz*, edited by Jürgen Dendorfer and Roman Deutinger, 217–53. Ostfildern: 2010.

Heirbaut, Dirk. 'Zentral im Lehnswesen nach Ganshof: das flämische Lehnsrecht, ca. 1000–1305'. *Zeitschrift der Savigny-Stiftung für Rechtsgeschichte. Germanistische Abteilung* 118 (2011): 301–48.

Heirbaut, Dirk. 'The Spokesmen in Medieval Courts: the Unknown Leading Judges of the Customary Law and Makers of the First Continental Law Reports'. In *Judges and Judging in the History of the Common Law and Civil Law: from Antiquity to Modern Times*, edited by Paul Brand and Joshua Getzler, 192–208. Cambridge: 2012.

Heirbaut, Dirk. 'Feudal Law'. In *Oxford Legal History of Europe* (forthcoming).

Hollyman, Kenneth James. *Le développement du vocabulaire féodal en France pendant le haut moyen âge (étude sémantique)*. Geneva: 1957.

Hyams, Paul. 'Warranty and Good Lordship in Twelfth-Century England'. *Law and History Review* 5, no. 2 (1987): 437–503.

Kadens, Emily. 'De invoering van de volkstaal in ambtelijke teksten in Vlaanderen: een status quaestionis'. *Millennium, tijdschrift voor middeleeuwse studies* 14 (2000): 22–41.

Kamali, Elizabeth. '*Felonia felonice facta*: Felony and Intentionality in Medieval England'. *Criminal Law and Philosophy* 9 (2015): 397–421.

Kervyn de Lettenhove, Joseph. *Codex Dunensis sive diplomatum et chartarum medii aevi amplissima collectio*. Brussels: 1875.

Kruisheer, Jaap. *Oorkondenboek van Holland en Zeeland tot 1299*, vol. 3. Assen: 1992.

Lambert of Ardres. 'Historia comitum Ghisnensium', edited by Johannes Heller. In *Monumenta Germaniae historica, Scriptores in folio*, vol. 24., 551–642. Hannover: 1879.

Lambert of Waterlos. 'Annales Cameracenses', edited by Georg Pertz. In MGH SS, vol. 16, 509–55. Hannover: 1859.

Laske, Caroline. 'Losing Touch with the Common Tongues—The Story of Law French'. *International Journal of Legal Discourse* 1 (2016): 169–92.

Le trésor de la langue française: dictionnaire de la langue du XIXe et du XXe siècle (1789–1960), 16 vols. Paris: 1971–1994, at <ehttp://www.cnrtl.fr/etymologie>.

Lück, Heiner. *Über den Sachsenspiegel: Entstehung, Inhalt und Wirkung des Rechtsbuches*. Dössel: 2013.

Lusignan, Serge. 'Langue et société dans le Nord de la France: le picard comme langue des administrations publiques (XIIIe–XIVe s.)'. *Comptes rendus des séances de l'Académie des Inscriptions et Belles-Lettres* 15 (2007): 1275–95.

Lusignan, Serge. 'A chacun son français: la communication entre l'Angleterre et les régions picardes et flamandes (XIIIe–XIVe siècles)'. In *IIe journée d'études anglo-normandes organisée par l'Académie des Inscriptions et Belles-Lettres*, 117–33. Paris: 2012.

Luykx, Theo. *De grafelijke financiële bestuursinstellingen en het grafelijk patrimonium in Vlaanderen tijdens de regering van Margareta van Constantinopel (1244–1278)*. Brussels: 1961.

Luykx, Theo. *Johanna van Constantinopel. Gravin van Vlaanderen en Henegouwen. Haar leven (1199/1200–1244). Haar regering (1205–1244), vooral in Vlaanderen*. Brussels: 1946.

Marcotte Stéphane and Christine Silvi, editors. *Latinum cedens. Le français et le latin langues de spécialité au Moyen Âge*. Paris: 2014.

Mantou, Reine. *Actes originaux rédigés en français dans la partie flamingante du comté de Flandre (1250–1350). Étude linguistique*. Liège: 1972.

Mantou, Reine. *Chartes en langue française antérieures à 1271 conservées dans les provinces de la Flandre orientale et de Flandre occidentale*. Paris: 1987.

'Miracula Sancti Ursmari in itinere per Flandriam facta', edited by Oswald Holder-Egger. In MGH SS, vol. 15,2, 837–42. Hannover: 1888.

Miraeus, Aubertus and Johannes Foppens. *Opera diplomatica et historica*. Brussels: 1723–1784.

Monier, Raymond. *Les lois, enquêtes et jugements des pairs du castel de Lille. Recueil des coutumes, conseils et jugements du tribunal de la Salle de Lille, 1283–1406*. Lille: 1937.

Mostert, Marco, editor. *New Approaches to Medieval Communication*. Turnhout: 1999.

Mostert, Marco and P. S. Barnwell, editors. *Medieval Legal Process: Physical, Spoken and Written Performance in the Middle Ages*. Turnhout: 2011.

Mussely, Charles and Emile Molitor. *Cartulaire de l'ancienne église collégiale de Notre-Dame de Courtrai*. Ghent: 1880.

Newman, William. *Les seigneurs de Nesle en Picardie. Leurs chartes et leur histoire*. Paris: 1971.

Opsommer, Rik. 'Splitsing van de heerlijkheid Hemsrode (Anzegem) anno 1284: leenrechtelijke bemerkingen'. *Jaarboek van de geschied- en heemkundige kring 'De Gaverstreke'* 15 (1987): 75–80.

Opsommer, Rik. *'Omme dat leengoed es thoochste dinc van der weerelt'. Het leenrecht in Vlaanderen in de 14de en 15de eeuw*. Brussels: 1995.

Parisse, Michel. 'Quod vulgo dicitur: la latinisation des noms communs dans les chartes'. *Médiévales* 42 (2002): 45–54.

Patzold, Steffen. *Das Lehnswesen*. Munich: 2012.

Peters, Ursula. 'Das Forschungsproblem der Vasallitätsterminologie in der romanischen und deutschen Liebespoesie des Mittelalters'. *Beiträge zur Geschichte der deutschen Sprache und Literatur* 137 (2015): 623–59.

Philippa Marlies, *et al. Etymologisch woordenboek van het Nederlands*, 4 vols. Amsterdam: 2003–2009, at <http://www.etymologiebank.nl>.

Pilch, Martin. *Der Rahmen der Rechtsgewohnheiten. Kritik des Normensystemdenkens entwickelt am Rechtsbegriff der mittelalterlichen Rechtsgeschichte*. Cologne: 2009.

Piot, Charles. *Cartulaire de l'abbaye d'Eename*. Bruges: 1881.

Postles, David. 'Seeking the Language of Warranty of Land in Twelfth-Century England'. *Journal of the Society of Archivists* 20 (1999): 209–22.

Prevenier, Walter. *De oorkonden der graven van Vlaanderen (1191–aanvang 1206)*. Brussels: 1964.

Reichert, Winfried. '"In lingua Guallica sive Romana pro commoditate domini": Beobachtungen zur Aufkommen volkssprachiger Urkunden in der Grafschaft Luxemburg'. In *Urkundensprachen im germanisch-romanischen Grenzgebiet*, edited by Kurt Gärtner and Günter Holtus, 369–489. Trier: 1997.

Reynolds, Susan. *Fiefs and Vassals: The Medieval Evidence Reinterpreted*. Oxford: 1994.

Reynolds, Susan. 'The Emergence of Professional Law in the Long Twelfth Century'. *Law and History Review* 21 (2003): 347–66.

Strubbe, Egied. *Egidius van Breedene (11..–1270). Grafelijk ambtenaar en stichter van de abdij Spermalie. Bijdrage tot de geschiedenis van het grafelijk bestuur en van de Cisterciënser orde in het dertiendeeuwsche Vlaanderen*. Bruges: 1942.

Van de Putte, Ferdinand. *Chronique et cartulaire de l'abbaye de Groeninghe à Courtrai*. Bruges: 1872.

Van den Bergh, Laurent. *Oorkondenboek van Holland en Zeeland tot het einde van het Hollandsche huis*. The Hague: 1866–1873.

Van Drival, Eugène. *Cartulaire de l'abbaye de Saint-Vaast d'Arras rédigé au XIIe siècle par Guimann*. Arras: 1875.

Van Mingroot, Erik. 'Kritisch onderzoek omtrent de datering van de Gesta episcoporum Cameracensium'. *Belgisch tijdschrift voor filologie en geschiedenis* 53 (1975): 281–332.

Van Lokeren, Auguste. *Chartes et documents de l'abbaye de Saint Pierre au Mont-Blandin à Gand*. Ghent: 1868–1871.

Vandermaesen, Michel. 'Het ontstaan van enkele "Cartularia van Vlaanderen" in 1336. De grafelijke kanselarij aan het werk'. In *Actief in archief. Huldeboek Hilda Coppejans-Desmedt*, 147–53. Antwerpen: 1989.

Vanhaeck, Maurice. *Cartulaire de l'abbaye de Marquette*. Lille: 1937–1940.

Vercauteren, Fernand. *Actes des comtes de Flandre (1071–1128)*. Brussels: 1938.

Verdon, Laure. 'La paix du prince. Droit savant et pratiques féodales dans la construction de l'état en Provence (1250–1309)'. *Revue historique* 678 (2010): 291–336.

Vermaere, Jozef. *Abdijorganisatie en domeinexploitatie van de Gentse Sint-Pietersabdij gedurende de dertiende eeuw. Een status quaestionis*. Ghent: unpublished licentiate thesis in history, 1974.

Viaene, Antoon. *Veelnamig Vlaanderen. Een historiografisch overzicht van de samenstellingen tot 1800*. Bruges: 1973.

Vleeschouwers, Cyriel. *De oorkonden van de Sint-Baafsabdij te Gent*, vol. 2. Brussels: 1990.

Walter of Thérouanne. *Vita Karoli comitis Flandriae*, edited by Jeff Rider. Turnhout: 2006.

Warnkönig, Leopold. *Flandrische Staats- und Rechtsgeschichte*. Tübingen: 1835–1842.

Warnkönig, Leopold and Albert Gheldolf. *Histoire de la Flandre et de ses institutions civiles et politiques jusqu'à l'année 1305*. Brussels: 1835–1864.

Wijffels, Carlos. 'Getuigenverhoor betreffende de machtsmisbruiken van de baljuw van de heerlijkheid Waasten (1250)'. *Handelingen van de koninklijke commissie voor de uitgave der oude wetten en verordeningen van België* 20 (1962): 319–59.

Wijffels, Carlos. *Analyses de reconnaissances de dettes passées devant les échevins d'Ypres (1249–1291) éditées selon le manuscrit de (†) Guillaume Des Marez*. Brussels: 1991.

CHAPTER 8

Sources of Legal Language: The Development of Warranty Clauses in Western France, *ca.*1030–*ca.*1240

Matthew McHaffie

Introduction

This paper explores the form and language of warranty clauses in the charters of eleventh- and twelfth-century western France, which from the 1030s were sometimes included in records of property transactions.[1] Warranty describes, broadly, the obligations that a principal assumed to defend his or her donee or vendee against third-party challenge; moreover, it is likely that warranty also entailed expectations that should the principal fail to defend a prior transaction successfully, then the ousted donee or vendee acquired a claim for reimbursement or compensation from the principal. Not limited solely to property transactions, warranty obligations also appear in connection with chattels, where vouching a warrantor was an important defence for a purchaser against accusations of theft.[2] The focus here though will be upon warranty of land (or rights therein): that is, the obligations principals undertook to defend and maintain their gifts, sales, or other transactions involving landed property.

The subject of warranty in eleventh- and twelfth-century France has received very little attention.[3] Scholars have instead tended to view warranty as

1 I would like to thank my fellow editors for comments on this paper, as well as Joshua Hey who has discussed aspects of the argument presented here with me. Any errors in fact or interpretation remain my own. The research for this article was funded by The Leverhulme Trust, and written as a Leverhulme Early Career Fellow at King's College, London; I am grateful both to the Trust and to King's for their support. Tegan Currie, as always, has provided moral and editorial support with her characteristic mix of kindness and sternness.

2 See Paul Ourliac and Jehan de Malafosse, *Histoire du droit privé, vol. 2: Les biens*, 2nd edn. (Paris: 1969), 286.

3 See Stephen D. White, *Custom, Kinship, and Gifts to Saints: The* Laudatio parentum *in Western France, 1050–1150* (Chapel Hill: 1988), esp. 36, 53, 194, 202–3 for essential comments on western France; more broadly, see François de Fontette, *Recherches sur la pratique de la vente immobilière dans la région parisienne au moyen âge (Fin X^e^–début XIVe siècle)* (Paris: 1957), esp. 91–101; François Gilliard, 'La garantie du chef d'éviction dans le pays de vaud

 | DOI 10.1163/9789004375765_010

primarily a thirteenth-century development. In part, this is because the evidence for explicit warranty clauses in charters only becomes common after *ca.*1200, whereas the earlier clauses have conversely been viewed as evidence for *voluntary* commitments that were only rarely undertaken.[4] Warranty has often been approached, moreover, from the perspective of the redistribution of alienatory powers within the family: the development of warranty has thus been partially explained as the result of an adjustment away from familial restraints upon transfers of property (seen above-all in the *laudatio parentum*), and towards a property regime that allowed for greater individual agency, and this adjustment occurred only gradually over the course of the later twelfth and thirteenth centuries.[5] Stephen White, however, also noted that the language of thirteenth-century warranty clauses in western France grew out of

---

(du IXe au XVe siècle)', *Mémoires de la Société pour l'Histoire du Droit et des Institutions des anciens pays bourguignons, comtois et romands* 21 (1960), 7–23; François Oliver-Martin, *Histoire de la coutume de la prévôté et vicomté de Paris*, 2 vols. (Paris: 1922–1930), I, 25–36;. See also Jean Yver, *Les contrats dans le très ancien droit normand (XIe–XIIIe siècles)* (Domfront: 1926), esp. 34–46 and Emily Zack Tabuteau, *Transfers of Property in Eleventh-Century Norman Law* (Chapel Hill: 1988), 196–204 for Normandy. Jean-François Poudret, *Coutumes et coutumiers. Histoire comparative des droit des pays romands du XIIIe–XVIe siècle. V: Les biens* (Bern: 2006), includes a discussion of warranty in Swiss customary law, but I have been unable to consult this volume for the present study.

4 Note e.g., White, *Custom*, 53: 'In France during this period [*ca.*1000–*ca.*1200], neither donors nor their lords *regularly* promised that they and their heirs would perpetually warrant, acquit, or defend their gifts against future challenges' (emphasis added); and *ibid.*, 194: 'Thirteenth-century charters included with increasing frequency a kind of clause that did not figure in eleventh- or early twelfth-century documents', referring to warranty clauses binding on the principal and his heirs. One of the questions here centres on whether warranty needed to be explicitly given, or if a donee or vendee could assume that the principal would warrant. The question is unfortunately too complex to enter into in this paper.

5 According to Stephen White, one of the key factors in the emergence of the 'new' and 'fully developed warranty clauses' was the power individuals had to impose warranty obligations on unborn heirs: see White, *Custom*, 194 and 203 (for the quoted words). This change was connected, as well, to the development of the *retrait lignager* and the *réserve coutumière* in the thirteenth century, at the expense of the *laudatio parentum*. As Jean-Louis Thireau has recently argued, however, evidence for the *retrait* and the *réserve* in western France appears much earlier, and co-exists alongside the *laudatio*, and Thireau suggests that the sometimes implicit, sometimes explicit evolutionary narrative of *laudatio* to *retrait* and *réserve* is in need of revision. If Thireau is correct, then the relationship between warranty obligations and familial restraints upon the alienation of property probably also needs re-thinking. See Jean-Louis Thireau, 'Faculté de disposer et protection de la famille dans le très ancien droit coutumier français (X^e–XIIIe siècles)', *Revue historique de droit français et étranger* 87, no. 3 (2009), 337–63.

words used 'since the eleventh century', suggesting a relationship between the old and new and thereby softening the sometimes rigid periodization found in the works of some legal historians.[6] Likewise, Jean-Louis Thireau has also stressed that although warranty clauses became more widespread in the thirteenth century, they did exist in the eleventh and twelfth centuries.[7] Making some sense of the clauses prior to *ca.*1200, and understanding their language and form, thus constitutes one of the primary aims of this present study.

Warranty clauses raise larger questions of interest in a volume about law and language. The first of these questions centres on the interpretation of the sources historians use to study warranty during this period: charters. Such texts were written and preserved by ecclesiastical institutions, often monasteries, meaning the perspective of the sources remains almost exclusively that of churchmen.[8] As a result, it is difficult to know how far ecclesiastical charters can be used to reconstruct wider legal ideas and practices, such as warranty.[9] This is the first problem. Another is that the evidence for warranty clauses such texts do provide displays a staggering diversity in terms of content, form, and language: there is no clear and consistent diplomatic of warranty clauses during this period. Just such a diplomatic would only become apparent in the thirteenth century, owing in part to the changing role of the written word in society.[10] The difficulty lies in attempting to paint a more or less coherent

6 White, *Custom*, 203. For an example of rigid periodization, see, on the Mâconnais, Bernard Vigneron, 'La vente dans le mâconnais du IXe au XIIIe siècle', *Revue historique de droit français et étranger* 36 (1959), 17–47.

7 Thireau, 'Faculté de disposer et protection de la famille', 358.

8 For essential orientation to charters during this period, see Dominique Barthélemy, *La société dans le comté de Vendôme de l'an mil au XIVe siècle* (Paris: 1993), 19–83; *Pratiques de l'écrit documentaire au XIe siècle*, ed. Olivier Guyotjeannin, Laurent Morelle, and Michel Parisse, *Bibliothèque de l'École des Chartes* 155 (1997); Pierre Chastang, *Lire, écrire, transcrire. Le travail des rédacteurs de cartulaires en Bas-Languedoc (XIe–XIIIe siècles)* (Paris: 2001); Nicolas Ruffini-Ronzani and Jean-François Nieus, 'Société seigneuriale, réformes ecclésiales: les enjeux documentaires d'une révision historiographique', in Ecclesia in medio nationis: *Reflections on the Study on Monasticism in the Central Middle Ages/Réflexions sur l'étude du monachism au Moyen Âge central*, ed. Steven Vanderputten and Brigitte Meijns (Leuven: 2011), 77–100 provide an excellent synthesis and discussion of recent charter scholarship.

9 Bruno Lemesle, *Conflits et justice au Moyen Âge. Normes, loi et résolution des conflits en Anjou aux XIe et XIIe siècles* (Paris: 2008), *passim*. See also Dirk Heirbaut's contribution to this volume, for discussion of some of the interpretative pitfalls presented by ecclesiastical charters.

10 Michael T. Clanchy, *From Memory to Written Record: England, 1066–1307*, 3rd edn. (Oxford: 2013), remains the classic; see also the wide-ranging reflections in Paul Bertrand, 'À propos

picture of any given legal idea when the sources we have available present anything but this. This linguistic diversity can be partly attributed to the fact that charters were written in diffuse though privileged centres of documentary production, mostly the *scriptoria* of powerful monastic institutions, and each of these might have had their own styles—perhaps even formularies—for the composition of charters.[11] But the fact remains that how any scribe put a particular legal concept into language was a choice, and one that could be made and re-made time and again. The relationship between law and language in eleventh- and twelfth-century charters was thus highly multifarious.

The circumstances of documentary production lead to a deeper question that the study of warranty clauses might be able to shed light on: the sources of legal language. Eleventh- and twelfth-century law in western France was predominantly oral, unwritten, and what some historians have termed customary.[12] One contributing factor to the emergence of a diplomatic of warranty clauses in the thirteenth century, conversely, was increased familiarity with the texts of written law (especially Roman law) that could serve as a model in the composition of such clauses.[13] The authority of any written clause derived, at least in part, from the relationship written form could establish with formal sources of law, which in the thirteenth century included the texts of the *ius commune* (and the demonstration of the professional skills to interpret them).[14]

---

de la révolution de l'écrit (X[e]–XIIIe siècle). Considérations inactuelles', *Médiévales* 56 (2009), 75–92.

11 See here esp. Olivier Guyotjeannin, '"*Penuria scriptorum*": le mythe de l'anarchie documentaire dans la France du Nord (X[e]–première moitié du XIe siècle)', *Bibliothèque de l'École des Chartes*, vol. 155 (1997), 11–44. On formularies, note the important comments in Sébastien Barret, 'Les actes écrits comme instruments de pouvoir: la contribution des formulaires', in *Chartes et cartulaires comme instruments de pouvoir. Espagne et Occident chrétien (VIIIe–XIIe siècles)*, ed. Julio Escalona and Hélène Sirantoine (Toulouse: 2013), 87–99, esp. 95; Claire Lamy, 'L'abbaye de Marmoutier et sa production écrite (1040–1150): formules en usage au scriptorium monastique et dans les dépendances', in *La formule au Moyen Âge II*, ed. Isabelle Draelants and Christelle Balouzat-Loubet (Turnhout: 2015), 75–90. See also André Marques, in this volume, for formulaic writing in Portuguese dispute texts.

12 Lemesle, *Conflits et justice*, 83ff.; see also White, *Custom*, 40–85.

13 See the comments in Gustave d'Espinay, *Les cartulaires angevins. Étude sur le droit de l'Anjou au Moyen Âge* (Angers: 1864), 279–80; more broadly, Barthélemy, *La société dans le comté de Vendôme*, 73–80 on the emergence of a 'learned style' of documentary production.

14 For a good introduction to the *ius commune*, see Manlio Bellomo, *The Common Legal Past of Europe, 1000–1800*, trans. Lydia G. Cochrane (Washington: 1995); for professionalization see Susan Reynolds, 'The Emergence of Professional Law in the Long Twelfth Century',

When recourse to written law as a formal source of law was minimal, as was the case in the period and region under consideration in this paper, then the relationship between law, language, and legal authority must be understood differently.[15] By examining the form of eleventh- and twelfth-century clauses, and uncovering, if possible, underlying patterns or structures despite linguistic and diplomatic variety, we may be able to adjust our understanding of how such texts mediated the relationship between law and language. Put differently, because warranty clauses were produced in a society characterized by oral and unwritten law, through careful examination of the processes shaping the construction of written warranty clauses, we may be able to apprehend the outlines of these non-written sources of legal language.

This study therefore considers eleventh- and twelfth-century warranty clauses on two levels, that of language and of law, exploring the interaction between them. By examining the formation of warranty clauses, it is possible to apprehend the outlines of common elements that shaped the linguistic choices charter draftsmen made when expressing warranty obligations. I suggest that such choices reflect a 'culture of fidelity' which emerged as the appropriate legal language for warranty, owing, on the one hand, to the relationship between oath-taking and promising warranty, and, on the other, to the orientation of warranty commitments around the practices of the aristocratic elite. Warranty is a large and complex topic, and this article cannot aim at comprehensiveness. The focus remains on law, language, and the relationships between them; this means that some topics such as the operation of warranty in practice, or comparisons with warranty elsewhere, such as in the early Common Law of England, must await further study.[16]

Law and History Review 21, no. 2 (2003), 347–66 and more broadly James A. Brundage, *The Medieval Origins of the Legal Profession: Canonists, Civilians, and Courts* (Chicago: 2008).

15 For discussion on the authority of written documents, see the essays collected in *L'autorité de l'écrit au Moyen Âge (Orient-Occident)*. XXXIXe Congrès de la SHMESP (Paris: 2009).

16 For warranty of land in England, see Paul Hyams, 'Warranty and Good Lordship in Twelfth-Century England', *Law and History Review* 5, no. 2 (1987), 437–503; John Hudson, *The Oxford History of the Laws of England, Volume II: 871–1216* (Oxford: 2012), 345–6; John Hudson, *Land, Law and Lordship in Anglo-Norman England* (Oxford: 1994), 51–8; J. M. Kaye, *Medieval English Conveyances* (Cambridge: 2009), 43–58; and David Postles, 'Seeking the Language of Warranty of Land in Twelfth-Century England', *Journal of the Society of Archivists* 20, no. 2 (1999), 209–22. This present study is deeply indebted to the work that has been done in warranty in the early Common Law.

Overview

This study rests on 325 warranty clauses recorded in charters written and preserved by the ecclesiastical institutions—mostly monasteries—of the Loire valley.[17] The earliest of these clauses survive from the 1030s and 1040s in charters from Marmoutier near Tours, Noyers in the lower Touraine, and Saint-Aubin in Angers.[18] Warranty clauses remain on the whole rare, however, until the 1060s when they start to survive in any significant number, with the extant clauses reaching their apogee in the decades around the year 1100: just under forty per cent of my sample dates to between the years 1080 and 1119 alone, for instance.[19] After *ca.*1140, the number of surviving clauses declines markedly

17 The sources used for the present study are: Paris, Bibliothèque nationale de France, ms. lat. 1930, 'Livre noir de Saint-Florent' (hereafter as *Livre noir*); 'Cartae de rebus abbatiae majoris monasterii in Andegavia', ed. Paul Marchegay, in *Archives d'Anjou*, vol. 2 (Angers: 1850) (hereafter as *MA*); *Cartulaire de l'abbaye de la Trinité de Vendôme*, 5 vols., ed. Charles Métais (Paris: 1893–1904) (hereafter as *TV*); *Cartulaire de l'abbaye de Noyers*, ed. Casimir Chevalier (Tours: 1872) (hereafter as *NOY*); *Cartulaire de l'abbaye de Saint-Aubin d'Angers*, ed. Bertrand de Broussillon, 3 vols. (Angers: 1903) (hereafter as *SAA*); *Cartulaire de l'abbaye de Saint-Vincent du Mans (ordre de Saint Benoît)*, ed. Robert Charles and Menjot d'Elbenne (Mamers and Le Mans: 1886–1913) (hereafter as *SVM*); *Cartulaire du chapitre Saint-Laud d'Angers*, ed. Adrien Planchenault (Angers: 1903) (hereafter as *SL*); *Cartulaire de l'hôpital Saint-Jean d'Angers*, ed. Célestin Port (Paris: 1870) (hereafter as *SJH*); *Cartulaire de Marmoutier pour le Dunois*, ed. Émile Mabille (Châteaudun: 1874) (hereafter as *MD*); *Cartulaire de Marmoutier pour le Vendômois*, ed. Charles Auguste de Trémault (Paris: 1893) (hereafter as *MV*); 'Cartularium monasterii Beatae Mariae Andegavensis', ed. Paul Marchegay, in *Archives d'Anjou*, vol. 3 (Angers: 1854) (hereafter as *RA*); *Cartulaire noir de la cathédrale d'Angers*, ed. Charles Urseau (Paris: 1908) (hereafter as *CN*); 'Cartulaire de Saint-Maur de Glanfeuil', ed. Paul Marchegay, in *Archives d'Anjou* vol. 1 (Angers: 1843) (hereafter as *SMG*); *Grand cartulaire de Fontevraud*, ed. Jean-Marc Bienvenu, Robert Favreau, and Georges Pons, 2 vols. (Poitiers: 2000–2005) (hereafter as *FON*); *Marmoutier: Cartulaire blésois*, ed. Charles Métais (Blois: 1889–1891) (hereafter as *MB*); *Premier et Second livres des Cartulaires de l'abbaye Saint-Serge et Saint-Bach d'Angers (XIe et XIIe siècles)*, ed. Yves Chauvin, 2 vols. (Angers: 1997) (hereafter as *SSE*). All references are to charter numbers, with the exception of *Livre noir*, which refers to folio numbers.

18 *MB* 25 (before 1044), *MD* 97 (1032 × 1037), *MD* 105 (*ca.*1042), *NOY* 10 (1037), *SAA* 940 (1038 × 1055).

19 126 out of 325 clauses fall within this forty-year window. Many charters cannot be dated with precision, and must simply be assigned to the reigning dates of particular abbots, counts, bishops, etc. When only a date range can be supplied for a text, therefore, I have taken the median date of that range when placing the charter within a particular chronological block (so, for example, a text dated 1082 × 1106, for the present purposes, is assigned a date of 1094). I have also, generally, followed dates supplied by the editors

before reaching a nadir in the years between 1180 and 1199, from when I have found only eight examples.[20] We should not attach too much weight as for the popularity of warranty clauses on the basis of these figures, however: they demonstrate rather the overall patterns of documentary survival. At Noyers, for instance, about forty per cent of all acts fall within the period 1080 to 1111; for La Trinité de Vendôme, the period of documentary density covers roughly 1070 to 1105.[21] From the thirteenth century clauses start to survive in greater number again, with thirty such clauses up to this study's terminal date of 1240.

Warranty obligations are found in connection with many types of exchange. The bulk of the evidence is unsurprisingly comprised of gifts, which alone account for over forty per cent of the sample.[22] A further thirty per cent of extant warranty clauses are found attached to quitclaims whereby an individual abandoned challenges (*calumniae*) upon property and undertook to defend the hitherto contested property from external challenge.[23] That nearly one third of the evidence for warranty clauses comes from quitclaims and the techniques actors employed when attempting to settle disputes and restore peace is an important point to keep in mind because it raises the possibility that situations of conflict might have had some prominence in influencing the composition of such clauses. The remaining warranty clauses are found in a number of different types of transaction: about fourteen per cent of the sample concerns sales; just over six per cent concerns confirmations; and the

---

of the cartularies used in this study, correcting only very obvious errors, or following the dating for the charters from the Vendômois, as outlined in Barthélemy, *La société dans le comté de Vendôme*, 84–9 (for Marmoutier) and 103–5 (for La Trinité de Vendôme).

20 See e.g. *MD* 185 (1175 × 1184), *MD* 201 (1192), *MD* 203 (1196), *NOY* 622 (*ca.*1183), *TV* 597 (1190), *TV* 603 (1190), *TV* 619 (1199), and *TV* 624 (1188 × 1200).

21 Chantal Senséby, 'Une notice fausse du cartulaire de l'abbaye tourangelle de Noyers?', *Bibliothèque de l'École des Chartes* 155 (1997), 78; Barthélemy, *La société dans le comté de Vendôme*, 35.

22 Gifts account for 141 of the extant clauses, or about forty-three per cent of the sample. The classification of charters according to type of transaction is an inexact science; these figures are meant to be indicative, rather than precise. The boundaries between gifts and sales, in particular, are notoriously difficult to define for this period, not least when some charters explicitly mention that a property was 'partly' donated, 'partly' sold (*partim ... partim*). On these hybrid transactions, see Barthélemy, *La société dans le comté de Vendôme*, 53–7, esp. 56, and now also Bruno Lemesle, 'Les querelles avaient-elles une vocation sociale? Le cas des transferts fonciers en Anjou au XIe siècle', *Le Moyen Âge* 115 (2009): 337–64.

23 There are 100 warranty clauses included in records of quitclaims.

remaining five per cent includes exchanges and others transactions that are difficult to classify.[24]

The individuals most likely to give warranty were the principals, sometimes acting alone, other times as part of a larger group of kin all agreeing, together, to undertake warranty commitments.[25] For some transactions though, warranty was given only by the principal's kin.[26] Deathbed gifts naturally account for some of these examples as beneficiaries might well have raised their eyebrows at the value of a commitment to defend a transaction made with a principal's dying breath.[27] Another situation that may have encouraged kin-warranty, as opposed to warranty given by the principal, was when women acted as principals.[28] In fact, warranty commitments undertaken solely by women are, on the whole, rare—though not absent.[29]

The other main type of person likely to warranty a transaction was a powerful lord.[30] To take just two examples. Between 1102 and 1113, Hamelin de Méral lay on his deathbed, and asked his lords Guy de Laval and Renaud de Craon to come to his side; once there, Hamelin 'asked them with sobs and tears to grant his alms quit to the monks of Saint-Serge and that each protect

24 Forty-six clauses concern sales; twenty-one for confirmations; and seventeen for the inelegantly labelled 'other'.

25 See *SSE* II, [101] 216 (1113 × 1133) in which Hugh the Young warranted with his two brothers and a cousin. For further examples of groups of kin warranting together, see *FON* 265 (1115 × 1149), *FON* 713 (1125 × 1149), *MV* 3 (1032 × 1064), *RA* 375 (1100), *SAA* 669 (1100).

26 This phenomenon touches on wider questions about the heritability (or not) of warranty obligations, and the relationship between warranty and family structure; unfortunately these issues are too complex to discuss in this paper.

27 See *SAA* 743 (1118) in which Samuel de la Cropte lay on his deathbed, and summoned his nephew, Hugh de Matheflon, to his side, whereupon Hugh agreed to warrant his uncle's gift to the monks of Saint-Aubin.

28 See *SAA* 83 (1082 × 1106) in which Maria and Piscis, her daughter, made a gift to the monks of Saint-Aubin, but the warranty obligations were assumed by Isembard d'Amboise, Maria's son-in-law.

29 For women warranting alone, see *MD* 105 (*ca.*1042), *RA* 225 (1095 × 1100), *SAA* 783 (1100), *SAA* 784 (1110).

30 White, *Custom*, 36 noted warranties given by lords, though also noted that this was not regularly done (*ibid.*, 53); see also Stephen D. White, 'Protection, Warranty, and Revenge in *La Chanson de Roland*', in *Peace and Protection in the Middle Ages*, ed. T. B. Lambert and David Rollason (Durham: 2009), 155–67 for discussion on warranty as a duty lords owe to their men, based off French vernacular literature of *ca.*1100. The classic discussion of the relationship warranty and lordship is now Hyams, 'Warranty and Good Lordship'.

[his gift] in their respective honours'.[31] Or, between 1170 and 1180 Robert de Blou warranted Geoffrey de Saumur's gift 'as the chief and major lord of the fief' (*sicut capitalem et majorem illius feodi dominum*) from which Geoffrey's gift came.[32] Teasing out how to characterize this lordship is a more difficult task: in some cases the warranty of lords was a function of the *personal* lordship between man and lord.[33] In others, though, the intervention of lords was instead a function of territorial authority that need not presuppose any direct, personal relationship between principal and lord, and certainly need not presuppose a relationship of fief-holding.[34] Third-party warranty by lords was a phenomenon that became particular marked in the thirteenth century; just under half of evidence from between 1200 and 1240 concerns warranty of this type, with lords warranting 'as the lord of the fief' (*tamquam dominus feodi*) or because the property came from their jurisdiction (*de cujus fisco*).[35] The imbrication of warranty practices into the frameworks of seigneurial jurisdictions is an important phenomenon, and as I shall suggest later, may have left its mark on aspects of the form warranty clauses took.

Warranty Clauses and the Spoken Word

Surviving warranty clauses record, in the first instance, oaths or other forms of verbalized commitment undertaken by principals or third-parties on their behalf at the occasion of property transactions. Take, for example, the following clause: in 1110 Osanna de Lavazé entered the chapterhouse of Saint-Aubin in Angers and there 'proclaimed ... with a clear voice' (*clara voce ...*

31 *SSE* I, 55: 'rogavit cum gemitu et lacrimis ut elemosinam quam monachis Sancti Sergii dederat concederet quietam et tuerentur unusquisque in honore suo scilicet'.

32 *FON* 838.

33 See e.g. *FON* 939 (second half of twelfth century) in which Geoffrey Poers, Aimeri Poers, and Raoul Poers all warranted the gift of Pierre *Rusticus* because they were 'his liege lords ... and ought to be his warrantors' (*qui erant domini sui lige ... qui debent esse garitores*).

34 In the example cited above (*FON* 838) recording Robert de Blou's warranty, it is significant that Geoffrey de Saumur, the principal, bypassed his immediate lord, Aimeri de Joireau, and sought instead the warranty of the *capitalis* and *major* lord of the fief. On this way of characterizing the 'fief', see in particular Susan Reynolds, *Fiefs and Vassals: The Medieval Evidence Reinterpreted* (Oxford: 1994).

35 See *MD* 232 (1222), *MD* 239 (1224) for the former phrase; see *MB* 234 (1233) for the latter.

protestans) that she would 'acquit' (*adquietaturam*) her gift to the monks.[36] That warranty clauses record spoken commitments can be established in a number of ways. The most direct of these is that many such clauses were introduced by a verb pointing towards spoken commitments. Thus clauses might be introduced by verbs such as *affirmare* (to affirm), *asserere* (to assert), *promittere, spondere* (both to promise), or *testificare* (to testify), all of which clearly refer to speaking.[37] Other verbs such as *constituere* (to decide, agree) or *pangere* (to stipulate) are more ambiguous in their interpretation, but may also imply spoken engagements.[38] Regardless, the promissory verbs of *promittere* and *spondere* were by far the most common means used by scribes to introduce a warranty clause; the other main category of introduction was via a phrase such as 'on the agreement that' (*ea convenientia ut*) or 'on such an agreement that' (*tali pacto ut*), both of which presuppose talking, not least because it is difficult to imagine forming an agreement in silence.[39]

Another indication of the spoken element underlying clauses comes from the rituals attendant upon the giving of warranty. For a start, roughly sixteen per cent of all warranty clauses make references to the warrantor's *fides* or pledge of faith.[40] Between 1093 and 1100, for instance, Vaslin son of Baldric 'gave his pledge of faith' to the monks of Saint-Serge of Angers, thereby strengthening his commitment. The *fides* is further intimated in the use of verbs such as *affidare* or *pleviare* to introduce warranty clauses, the former unambiguously related to the pledging of faith; the latter, in the context of performing warranty, strongly suggestive of such a pledge.[41] Pledging one's *fides* involved not only words, but also gestures, such as the clasping of hands. For example, Geoffrey son of

---

36 SAA 784; see also FON 695 (1144) for a similar formula in a warranty clause (*libera voce … protestatus est*).

37 *Affirmare:* SAA 667 (1082 × 1106); *asserere:* FON 892 (1150 × 1199); *promittere:* FON 180 (1119 × 1125), FON 189 (1109 × 1115), FON 660 (1147 × 1153), *Livre noir*, fo. 89r–v, *Livre noir*, fos. 108v–109r, MV 11 (1072), MV 56 (1066 × 1071), RA 102 (1120); *spondere:* FON 500 (1145 × 1149), *Livre noir*, fos. 104v–105r (1060 × 1067), MA [p.] 29 (1063), MV 60 (1062), SAA 655 (1097), SL 44 (1103); *testificare:* TV 174 (1062 × 1064).

38 *Constituere:* FON 175 (1108 × 1125), FON 838 (1170 × 1180), SSE II, [58] 88; *pangere:* MB 70 (1096 × 1104), SVM 199 (1078 × 1080), SVM 646 (end of the eleventh century).

39 See e.g. FON 265 (1115 × 1149), *Livre noir*, fos. 71v–72r (1076 × 1096), *Livre noir*, fo. 134r (*ca.*1050), MV 3 (1032 × 1064).

40 The *fides* is mentioned in connection to warranty commitments explicitly in fifty-three of clauses. Fontette, *Recherches sur la pratique*, 75–9 noted the importance of the *fides* in later twelfth- and thirteenth-century warranty clauses in the Paris region.

41 Note here Adhémar Esmein, *Études sur les contrats dans le très-ancien droit français* (Paris: 1883), 95–6 on the development of the phrase *plevir sa foi* in connection with the

Harpin 'pledged his faith in the hand of Pierre Gillo'.[42] Clasping hands again points towards the performative dimension of warranty that accompanied the delivery of verbal promises. In some, pledging faith also included osculation, such as when in 1111 Geoffrey, the son of Vicomte Hugh de Châteaudun, 'in his faith kissed the abbot [of Marmoutier]' (*in fide osculatus est*); or in 1118 when Hugh de Matheflon, in warranting his uncle's gift to Saint-Aubin, 'gave a kiss for this matter in the name of his pledge'.[43] The point to stress, again, concerns the performative elements of warranty through which commitments were ritualized and vocalized.

Finally, the spoken promises underlying warranty clauses emerge with especial clarity in the examples that explicitly record oaths sworn by the would-be warrantor. Some clauses were preceded with the verb *jurare* (to swear an oath), whereas others make reference to the *sacramentum*, *juramentum*, or *jusjurandum* (oath) by which a warrantor shored-up his commitment.[44] For example, at some point between 1058 and 1070, one Lunamus gave his warranty to the monks of Saint-Florent as follows: 'he fixed his faith by swearing upon the relics of the saints' (*super sanctorum reliquias jurejando fidem constituit*).[45] Similarly, in 1096 Guy de *Sarciaco*, after selling the fief (*fevum*) he held from Saint-Vincent of Le Mans back to the monks, warranted along with his kin in the following terms:

> they confirmed with an oath sworn upon the text of the Gospel that none of them, nor any man or woman, would ever challenge that at any time or by any trick; if however someone should presume to do so, they would labour with every effort and all urgency, free from wicked intent, to render those properties quit.[46]

---

formation of contract in twelfth-century France; the Latinized *pleviare* is almost certainly related to this.

42 SAA 840 (1154 × 1189), as *affidavit ... in manu*.

43 MD 165; SAA 743. For other examples of osculation, see MV 11 (1072).

44 *Jurare:* SAA 361 (1060 × 1081); *sacramentum:* SL 49 (1150); *juramentum:* MB 176 (1178), NOY 575 (1156); *jusjurandum:* MV 27 (1070), SSE II, [102] 223 (1112) in a verbal form as *subjurejandum*.

45 *Livre noir*, fos. 111v–112r.

46 SVM 317 (1096): 'et super textum sancte Evangelii sacramento firmaverunt quod nullus eorum nec vir nec mulier ullo unquam tempore vel ullo ingenio ibi calumpniam mitterent. Si vero aliquis presumeret, ipsi omni nisu omni instantia absque ullo malo ingenio laborarent ut easdem res quietas redderent'.

These were solemn oaths, sworn on sacred objects.[47] The point is important to underline because it establishes a clear relationship between oath-taking and warranty clauses: any explanations for the forms of warranty clauses must therefore take into account their origins in practices of verbal promises and oath-taking.[48]

This is not to say that every warranty clause records a formal oath; it is more helpful to think in terms of different degrees of formality behind such clauses.[49] Take, for instance, the following three examples. The first dates from between 1110 and 1115, when Fulk de Matheflon warranted his quitclaim to the nuns of Le Ronceray as follows: 'he stated in plain words ... that he would defend the land of Notre-Dame against all men, and accept no custom [from it], to the best of his ability'.[50] My second example dates from between 1070 and 1082, when Aubrey de Laigné 'promised by lawful statement that he would make his [sale] free and quit from all men and challenges'.[51] The final example dates from 1113, when Maurice promised 'to keep safe and defend' properties that he was quitclaiming to Saint-Aubin; then, 'after he promised his faith, Maurice swore an oath in the same chapterhouse over the holy relics about everything for which he had pledged his faith'.[52] The three clauses illustrate well the differing levels of formality to warranty promises, ranging from promises made in plain speech (*planoque predicavit*) to an oath sworn on relics. Quite where Aubrey's 'lawful statement' fits into this is not immediately obvious, but presumably both the content and perhaps a measure of formality transformed

47 For other oaths sworn on relics, see: *SAA* 361 (1060 × 1081), *SAA* 430 (1113).

48 See here Georges Declercq, 'Between Legal Action and Performance: The *firmatio* of Charters in the Early Middle Ages', in *Medieval Legal Process: Physical, Spoken and Written Performance in the Middle Ages*, ed. Marco Mostert and P. S. Barnwell (Turnhout: 2011), 63, 67 for brief comments in his discussion on rituals of touching charters at the occasion of a gift (the *firmatio*) that such rituals may have included an oral statement committing the principal to the execution of the transaction; this practice may parallel the types of oral commitment recorded in eleventh- and twelfth-century charters, and serves as a salutary reminder that the spoken promises under discussion in this paper need not be seen as a novel practice in the eleventh century.

49 I am grateful to Josh Hey for discussion at various points on the comments made in this paragraph.

50 *RA* 130: 'planoque predicavit ... ut terram S. Marie contra homines omens nulla accepta consuetudine pro posse defenderet'.

51 *SSE* I, 145: 'promisit etiam et legali assertione confirmavit ut si in hac ventione calumnia excrevit solidam et quietam ab omnibus hominibus et calumniis faciat'.

52 *SAA* 430: 'hac fide ita promissa, Mauricius omnia de quibus ibi fidem suam dederat, in eodem capitulo, super sanctas reliquias juravit'.

Aubrey's 'statement' into a 'lawful' one. So, not all warranty clauses need necessarily have recorded formal oaths, but they did in the eleventh and twelfth centuries, at least, record spoken promises, some of which took the form of a solemn oath.

An emphasis on the oral practices underlying warranty commitments provides the essential point of departure in their interpretation: our documents record spoken promises.[53] It will hardly come as a surprise, then, that both the form and content of such promises displays considerable variety—as we shall now see.

A Typology of Warranty Commitments

The preceding discussion provides the necessary context in which to begin looking at the warranty clauses themselves. Because such clauses reflected social practices centred on oath-taking and verbal engagements, it should not be surprising that they display marked variety with respect to content, form, and vocabulary. Here I want to construct a rough typology of the different forms of warranty clauses by categorizing them in accordance with the aim any particular clause purported to fulfil.

By far the most common type of clause was for the would-be warrantor to promise to defend his or her gift, sale, quitclaim, etc. For example, between 1084 and 1100, Roscelina and her two sons made a gift to the monks of Marmoutier, and 'promised ... that if a challenge arises, they will acquit it for us [the monks]'.[54] Or, between 1040 and 1060, Hilgod abandoned claims to the church of Naveil he was making against these same monks, and 'with his promise and pledge of faith he would henceforth make it quit against all mortal men and guard and defend it for us [the monks] against the challenge of usurpers (*pervasorum*)'.[55] The content of promises to defend a transaction could vary markedly: some envisaged this defence as something performed in a *curia*, like for example when between 1038 and 1055 one Geoffrey promised the monks of Saint-Aubin he would 'defend [his quitclaim] in court'.[56] Promises of defence may thus

---

53 Note here Barthélemy, *La société dans le comté de Vendôme*, 65: 'Les termes des accords rapportés par les "notices" narratives sont donc ... repris dans des serments'.

54 *MD* 38: 'insuper etiam promiserunt ... quod si aliquando calumnia insurgat, ipsi eam nobis acquietabunt'.

55 *MV* 6: 'ea promisione et ea fide ut abhinc contra omnes mortales illam nobis quietam faciat et a calumnia pervasorum nobis eam tueatur ac defendat'.

56 *SAA* 940: 'defenderet in curia'.

have entailed a commitment to undertake formal proof, either by ordeal, oath, or judicial battle, on behalf of the recipient of a such a promise.[57] Around 1058, Arnoul de *Brisco* promised the monks of Saint-Florent simply that he would defend his gift 'by any proof' (*in omni lege*).[58] The basic component of warranty then, that is to defend one's property transaction, probably had as its core a commitment to turn up in court to help prove a defendant's claims.[59]

Some sense of what else a commitment to defend one's property transaction entailed can be gleaned from promises in which a would-be warrantor sought to limit his liabilities. In 1072, for instance, Thibaud son of Luterius agreed to warrant his quitclaim to the monks of Marmoutier, promising 'to aid us [the monks] to acquit [our properties] against a challenge in any way he is able, except for the payment of money or the waging of a *guerra*'.[60] The monetary liabilities Thibaud sought to avoid are unclear, but may have involved either assuming responsibility for the costs of justice if necessary, such as holding a *placitum*; buying consents from potential challengers; providing pecuniary compensation to an adverse claimant if necessary; or perhaps a combination of these.[61] Making sense of Thibaud's desire to avoid *guerra*, on the other hand, requires little effort: the potential social (to say nothing of personal) costs a *guerra* could entail must have been reason enough to avoid being bound to such an activity by oath.[62] But Thibaud's restrictions also suggest fairly expansive expectations on the part of donees and vendees that warranty included considerable extra-judicial support as well.[63] The limitations Thibaud

57 See *RA* 127 (*ca.*1028).

58 *Livre noir*, fos. 103v–104r.

59 Although space precludes extended discussion on the case material, for examples of warrantors turning up in court to offer testimony and/or oaths in support of their previous grants, see: *FON* 96 (1101 × 1108), *MD* 149 (1095), *NOY* 307 (*ca.*1102), *RA* 226 (*ca.*1100), *SSE* II, [53] 350 (1082 × 1093), *SAA* 364 (*ca.*1090). Note also *FON* 160 (1115), which is discussed briefly in Fontette, *Recherches sur la pratique*, 100–1, as an example of a warrantor offering testimony in court to defend a sale.

60 *MV* 11: 'et promisit ... si aliunde calumnia de illis rebus nobis insurgat ipse adjuvabit nos acquietare calumniam illam omnibus modis quibus poterit excepto per pecuniam dando et per guerram faciendo'. On this agreement, note the brief comments in Barthélemy, *La société dans le comté de Vendôme*, 39, n. 98, 669 and n. 135.

61 See also *SAA* 430 (1113) for another example in which a warrantor stipulated that he would not give money as part of his commitment.

62 On *guerra* in western France during this period, Stephen D. White, 'Feuding and Peace-Making in the Touraine around the Year 1100', *Traditio* 42 (1986), 195–263 remains essential.

63 For two examples of warrantors using force against an adversary to meet warranty commitments, see *Livre noir*, fo. 107r–v (*ca.*1070), and *SAA* 270 (1082 × 1095).

sought to impose on his commitments thus highlights one of the key subjects of negotiation underlying warranty commitments: how to balance the beneficiary's desire, on the one hand, for as complete a commitment as possible with, on the other hand, the would-be warrantor's desire to manage and limit risk. Much of the individuality of warranty clauses in their written form may very well reflect the infinite range of possible solutions to this balancing act.

Ordinarily, commitments to defend a gift, sale, or quitclaim envisaged that such defence would be valid in the event of any challenge: in other words, these engagements were reasonably open-ended with respect to the persons against whom a would-be warrantor would offer his defence. On occasion, however, warranty commitments foresaw specific, named individuals against whom defence was intended. For example, in *ca.*1067 Renaud the *vicarius* of Chaumont promised the monks of Marmoutier that 'he would acquit' his gift of rents to the monks 'against Hugh, a *miles* of Beaugency, who claimed the right to collect them as his own'.[64] Alternatively, a specific individual might be included in a more general statement, like towards the end of the eleventh century when Eudes agreed to warrant 'against Geoffrey and against all mortal men'.[65] Although commitments to defend only rarely include details about specific individuals against whom the promise was directed, such examples provide important evidence for the flexibility of warranty commitments, the recording of which could be tailor-made to the specific circumstances surrounding any particular transfer of property.

A second type of commitment saw that the warrantor would provide material compensation to the beneficiary if he should fail to defend an earlier property transaction successfully. Promises of this sort appear in roughly fifteen per cent of warranty clauses, often as an additional clause to the commitment to defend a transaction.[66] The earliest examples date from the 1050s and concern pecuniary compensation. Thus, in *ca.*1050 Geoffrey 'the Strong' promised the monks of Saint-Florent that if someone should ever challenge the sale he was making to them, 'he would either put an end to (*cessare*)

64 *MB* 45: 'et hoc insuper spopondisse ut adquietaret nobis Rainaldus ipse censum eumdem ab Hugone quodam milite balgenciacensi, qui illum asserebat sibi deberi'.

65 *SVM* 486: 'tali tenore ut nobis de jamdicta ecclesia defensor sit et contra Gaufridum et contra omnes mortales'.

66 In some instances, though, compensation seems to have been the main focus of the commitment: see e.g. *RA* 158 (1170) in which a donor stated that if he could not obtain the consent of his lord, he would provide the nuns with an exchange equivalent to the object of his gift.

that challenge, or return the payment price (*precium*)'.[67] The logic of compensation is self-evident in the case of sales, and commitments such as that made by Geoffrey 'the Strong' sought to mitigate the risk on the part of the purchaser.[68] In the context of donations and quitclaims, principals often committed themselves to compensate the beneficiary monetarily because they had received a pecuniary counter-gift, which thus helped, it seems, to create lasting expectations for both parties.[69] For example, in *ca.*1107 Gautier Britto gave the monks of Marmoutier the right to collect some tithes, and he accepted 60 *solidi* from them, 'on the condition that if any challenge should arise, [he will see to it] that peace is restored within forty days; but if not, he will return without the delay the payment he had accepted'.[70]

Not all commitments to compensate envisaged monetary payments; in fact, nearly half of this type of promise foresaw that compensation would take the form of landed property. The earliest such examples in my sample date from the 1060s. Thus in *ca.*1063, Geoffrey *Papa Bovem* gave land to the monks of Marmoutier 'on the agreement that if ever some challenge for these things should arise and is unable to acquit them for us [the monks], then he will give an exchange for those things (*eorum*) to us in the land of *Gurguenaldo*'.[71] Some provisions for landed compensation amount to what was in effect the naming of real sureties that remained in the possession of the warrantor. The words used in such clauses were *excambium* and *commutatio*,

67 *Livre noir*, fo. 134r.

68 For other examples of pecuniary compensation promised to purchasers, see *Livre noir*, fos. 54v–55r (1051) and *SSE* I, 146 (1074).

69 On this subject, see Barthélemy, *La société dans le comté de Vendôme*, 681–92; and note Yver, *Les contrats*, 39–41. See also Stephen Weinberger, 'Les contre-dons en Poitou et en Provence au XIe siècle: ce qu'il en coûte de faire des affaires', *Provence historique* 210 (2002): 483–96; and the remarks in Chris Wickham, 'Compulsory Gift Exchange in Lombard Italy, 650–1150', in *The Languages of Gift in the Early Middle Ages*, ed. Wendy Davies and Paul Fouracre (Cambridge: 2010), 193–216 are of considerable comparative interest.

70 *Chartes originales antérieures à 1121 conservées en France*, ed. Cédric Giraud, Jean-Baptiste Renault and Benoît-Michel Tock (Nancy and Orléans: 2010), online at <http://www.cn-telma.fr/originaux/index/>, no. 4635 (hereafter as Artem): 'tali conditione ut si aliqua calumnia inde exurgeret, pacem fieri infra XL dies. Sin alias, absque dilatione precium quod acceperat reddere'. The strict time-limit envisaged in this commitment finds an explanation in the fact that Gautier was preparing a journey to Rome; the monks, therefore, likely wanted any potential trouble dealt with quickly, and prior to his departure. For further examples, see, e.g.: *Livre noir*, fos. 104v–105r (1060 × 1067), *NOY* 405 (*ca.*1115), *SAA* 318 (1099), *SSE* I, 6 (1082 × 1093), *TV* 486 (1139).

71 *MA* [p.] 29: 'ea scilicet ratione ut si qua unquam in his calumnia surrexerit a qua nobis illos acquitare non possit, excambium eorum reddat nobis in terra de Guerguenaldo'.

both meaning exchange, though words like *plegium* or *contraplegium* (i.e. real surety), can also be found.[72] Exchanges were sometimes meant to be 'of equal value', 'sufficient', or 'rightful'.[73] Such phrases allude to some formal means of assessing equivalency of value when deciding an exchange, probably before a *curia* or in a *placitum*; this may indicate that from the perspective of those who received promises of warranty, claims for a warrantor's defence against a *calumnia* and claims to receive compensation if that defence failed required separate cases to be made.

A third type of warranty commitment amounted to a promise on the part of the warrantor that he would cause no further trouble to his recipient. One of the earliest clauses from my sample, dating to 1010, took this form when Gautier, a *vassallus*, abandoned claims against the monks of Saint-Florent de Saumur, and promised (*sponsionem fecit*) that 'he would reclaim nothing further' from them.[74] Clauses of this type were uncommon, and where they appear it was often in the context of a quitclaim where, unsurprisingly, a beneficiary might have been especially keen to secure a promise that a former adversary would cause no further trouble.[75] Between 1056 and 1082, for example, Hubert Borellus and his sons brought a challenge against the monks of Saint-Serge for all the possessions the monks held in Hubert's 'fief'; in settling this dispute, however, after abandoning whatever claims they were making, Hubert and his sons 'promised ... to preserve this agreement lawfully, without wicked intent, and to make it pure (*emundent*) from all challenges ... they promised also ... that they would make no further challenge to the monks concerning all these things'.[76] Commitments of this type provide evidence for what Paul

72 For *excambium: SAA* 101 (1082), *SAA* 155 (1160), *SAA* 328 (1060 × 1067); for *commutatio: FON* 265 (1115 × 1149), *RA* 158 (1170), *SVM* 576 (1098), *SVM* 777 (1080 × 1102); for *plegium* or *contraplegium: MD* 241 (1230), *SAA* 155 (1082 × 1106), *SAA* 785 (1110).

73 See e.g. *SSE* II, [56] 369 (1090) for *tantundem valentem* or *TV* 134 (1060) for *tantumdem valentis commutationem*; see *FON* 265 (1115 × 1149) for *sufficienter ... commutacionem*; see *SAA* 155 (1160) for *excambium rectum*.

74 *Livre noir*, fo. 25r–v.

75 For further examples, see: *MB* 176 (1178), *MB* 238 (1238), *RA* 208 (1115), *SAA* 361 (1060 × 1081), *SAA* 669 (1100), *SAA* 896 (1120 × 1127), *SJH* 70 (1215).

76 *SSE* II, [24] 316: 'promisitque audientibus plurimis ipse et filii ejus Robertus et Matheus in capitulo Sancti Sergii ut absque ullo malo ingenio hanc conventionem legaliter conservent et ab omnibus calumpniis emundent. Promiserunt insuper tam pater quam filii ut omnia que monachi in suo fevo vel habere poterunt conservent, et erga monachos Sancti Sergii sint fideles, et calumpniam ulterius eis de omnibus rebus ... non faciant'.

Hyams, in the context of post-Conquest England, termed 'negative' warranty obligations.[77] Their significance lies in the fact that they direct our attention to situations of dispute and the processes of dispute-settlement when thinking about one of stimuli in both the conceptualization of warranty obligations and in writing them down.

A fourth type of commitment can be categorized roughly as protection, and amounted to a promise to allow no harm to befall the warrantee. This type of promise was uncommon. A good example, though, comes from between 1056 and 1082: Harduin and Tescelin (the former's lord) sold a property to the monks of Saint-Serge, and promised to 'make it quit from all challenges'—in other words, they promised to defend their sale with a common type of commitment discussed above.[78] Then, however, the monks gave 12 *denarii* to Roger de Montrevault, the lord of both Harduin and Tescelin, and Roger promised 'that he would never allow Harduin or Tescelin to bring trouble or commit an unjust deed (*injustam rem*) to the monks over that estate nor any other property (*re*)'.[79] The promises given by Harduin and Tescelin on the one hand, and Roger on the other, differed in nature, and this can partly be attributed to the fact that the former acted as principals (i.e. the vendors) while the latter intervened as a third-party. The differences are important however. Whereas the principals promised to acquit their sale, the lord promised that he would allow no harm to befall the monks.[80]

The fifth and final type of commitment I want to mention is one that saw the warrantor promise to acquit the transferred property from any services or dues to which it was liable. Take the following example, dating from between 1156 and 1162: Gérard de Molières, along with his son, made a gift of land to the monks of Saint-Serge, and promised that his son and heir (*ille heres*) who will hold his land after his death 'will wholly acquit the aforesaid alms from all customs and services [to keep it] immune'.[81] Likewise, in 1113 × 1133,

---

77 Hyams, 'Warranty and Good Lordship', 440; see also Fontette, *Recherches sur la pratique*, 85–7 for discussion of similar types of clause in thirteenth-century clauses from the Paris region.

78 *SSE* II, [50] 345: 'tali convenientia ut ipse et Harduinus predictus fidejussores existerent, et de omnibus calumpniis supradictam borderiam quietam et solidam monachis habere facerent'.

79 *Ibid.*: 'tali convenientia promissa ut nullam molestiam aut aliquam injustam rem consentiret a Harduino vel Tescelino monachis aliquando inferre, nec de jam dicta borderia nec de aliqua re'.

80 Not all promises of this type were given by third-parties; see e.g. *SAA* 372 (1082 × 1106).

81 *SSE* II, [58] 92: 'ille heres qui terram jam sepedicti Girardi tenuerit supradictam elemosinam ab omnibus consuetudinibus et serviciis immunem, prorsus adquietabit'.

Bartholomew de Champigné abandoned claims upon rents from the monks of Saint-Serge, and warranted his quitclaim against his own men 'lest on account of this restitution those men disturb the monks'.[82] Protections from excessive or unforeseen burdens upon transferred properties was, as Fontette pointed out, one of the main aims underlying warranty obligations, and a number of our twelfth-century clauses, at least, make it clear that those burdens were connected to the claims for services and customs lords might demand from properties.[83]

The preceding discussion reveals something of the variety in form and content that warranty commitments could take. While the typology I have presented has hermeneutic value, none of the categories should be seen as airtight, and many warranty clauses combined and arranged various types of promise depending on circumstance and need. The image is one of adaptability and flexibility. In part, this must reflect the fact that such commitments were rooted in spoken agreements and oaths, and the variability of the written record therefore was a product of the varied ways in which individuals could form oral agreements. Such a view makes it difficult to know if underlying these commitments there was a coherent idea of warranty: for example, did all promises of defence also entitle the recipient to a claim for compensation if the defence failed? The question may be the wrong one to ask, however. It perhaps makes more sense to see such commitments as part of a conceptual toolbox of warranty from which individuals selected various tools depending on any given situation.

The Language of Warranty

The content of warranty commitments therefore varied according to context and specific needs, and might comprise a number of types of promise that could be combined or kept apart depending on a range of factors that would probably require an individual explanation for every single clause. This same theme of the diversity of warranty commitments can be pursued at the level of language. To begin with the main verbs used to express warranty commitments: I have found around fifty verbs used by scribes when recording warranty clauses. Some of these verbs were generic in meaning, and include: *(ab)*

82 *SSE* II, [97] 202: 'et ipse eos defenderet ne propter hanc redditionem homines illi monachos infestarent'.

83 Fontette, *Recherches sur la pratique*, 94; for other examples of promises of this sort, see *SAA* 669 (1100), *SSE* I, 323 (1096), *SSE* II, [105] 265 (1138 × 1150), *SVM* 810 (*ca.*1100?).

solvere (to free),[84] *(ad)juvare* (to aid, help),[85] *auxiliari* (to aid),[86] *(con)servare* (to keep),[87] *custodire* (to guard),[88] *(de)liberare* (to free),[89] *facere quietum/quietam* (to make quit),[90] *manutenere* (to maintain),[91] *protegere* (to protect),[92] or *tutari* (to keep safe).[93] Alternatively, scribes could opt for more specific verbs when recording warranty commitments. Sometimes, such verbs expressed particular actions a warrantor might undertake in a formal legal setting, like in a *curia* or at a *placitum*. Thus we find, for instance, *denarrare* (to give an account), *(dis) raciocinare* (to deraign), *placitare* (to plead), *probare* (to prove), or, in at least one case, a promise to commit one's self to oath-taking and judicial battle.[94] Other clauses used specialized verbs of exchange, as well, emphasizing the compensatory element to warranty: thus we find verbs such as *commutare* (to exchange), *excambiare* (to exchange), *restituere* (to restore), and also *satisfacere* (to compensate).[95] There were favoured verbs though: *adquietare* (to acquit) and *defendere* (to defend) were each used in seventy-six clauses respectively.[96]

---

84 *Livre noir*, fos. 54v–55r (1051), *Livre noir*, fos. 108v–109r (1062).

85 *Livre noir*, fos. 111v–112r (1058 × 1070), *MB* 112 (1100), *MV* 5 (1056 × 1060), *RA* 95/96 (1080), *SSE* I, 224 (1095 × 1100), *TV* 22 (1040).

86 *RA* 414 (1100), *SAA* 318 (1099).

87 *MD* 165 (1110 × 1111), *NOY* 436 (1120), *RA* 102 (1120), *SAA* 122 (1117), *SAA* 430 (1113), *SSE* II, [13] 4 (1100 × 1110), *SSE* II, [24] 316 (1056 × 1082), *TV* 457 (1102 × 1129), *TV* 330 (1087), *TV* 552 (1144 × 1159).

88 *Livre noir*, fo. 90v (*ca.*1072), *MA* [p.] 36 (*ca.*1070), *MD* 163 (1123), *NOY* 259 (*ca.*1098), *NOY* 556 (1146), *SL* 44 (1103), *SSE* II, [101] 216 (1113 × 1133), *TV* 299 (1080).

89 *Cartulaire de Cormery précédé de l'histoire de l'abbaye et de la ville de Cormery d'après les chartes*, ed. J.-J. Bourassé (Tours: 1861), no. 45 (1070 × 1110), *SAA* 267 (1100s?), *SAA* 269 (1060 × 1067), *SVM* 330 (1158 × 1185), *TV* 125 (1059).

90 *MV* 106 (1060 × 1064), *RA* 327 (*ca.*1110), *SAA* 667 (1082 × 1106), *SVM* 115 (1067 × 1080).

91 'Cartulaire d'Assé-le-Riboul', ed. Bertrand de Broussillon, in *Archives du Maine* III (Le Mans: 1903), no. 9 (1125), *MD* 203 (1196), *TV* 513 (1146).

92 *SSE* II, [13] 24 (1100 × 1110).

93 *NOY* 439 (1121), *SAA* 430 (1113), *SSE* I, 244 (1095 × 1100), *SSE* I, 323 (1096).

94 For *denarrare: SAA* 96 (1100); for *raciocinare: SVM* 576 (1098); for *placitare: SVM* 19 (*ca.*1090); for *probare: Livre noir*, fo. 55r–v (1060 × 1070), *MD* 25 (after 1064), *RA* 127 (*ca.*1028), *SAA* 104 (1039 × 1055); see also *SSE* I, 6 (1082 × 1093): 'ac insuper per fidem suam promisit se absque malo ingenio haec omnia contra omnes calumniatoresueri [*sic*] jurando videlicet ac etiam si necesse esset pugnando'.

95 *Commutare: RA* 158 (1170); *excambiare: TV* 688 (1233), *TV* 699 (1236); *restituere: MB* 96 (1070), *MD* 152 (1096), *SAA* 318 (1099); *satisfacere: NOY* 122 (1085), *NOY* 283 (1100), *NOY* 330 (1105).

96 For *adquietare*, see *inter alia: MV* 53 (1070), *MV* 21A (*ca.*1060), *NOY* (*ca.*1084), *NOY* 231 (*ca.*1094), *SVM* 17 (*ca.*1070), *SVM* 65 (1093 × 1103), *SVM* 199 (1078 × 1080); for *defendere*, see

When describing warrantors with nouns, scribes likewise had recourse to a rich vocabulary, though one that was less extensive than what we have just seen with warranty verbs. I have found roughly twenty nouns, though many of these are clearly related to the verbs used to express warranty commitments. The most common of these are aid or auxiliary (*adjutor* or *auxiliator*), advocate (*advocatus*), defender (*defensor*), surety (*fidejussor*), protector (*protector, tutor*), or witness (*testis*).[97]

Advocate and surety require further comment. *Advocatus* should be understood in its literal sense of someone summoned to speak on one's behalf: in the Loire valley the concept of advocacy was connected to the substantive noun *advocatura*, or a variant, meaning 'advowry'. As Dominique Barthélemy has noted, 'advowry' referred to testimony given in support of a case, and might be given in person or written down (with the implication that the document could then stand-in for oral testimony).[98] Describing warrantors as *advocati* may therefore be part of the same conceptual understanding of warranty when such commitments were expressed with the verb *adquietare*. *Fidejussor*, on the other hand, likely reflects the conceptual slippage in the minds of contemporaries between the practices of personal suretyship and practices of warranty.[99] For example, just over ten per cent of our sample of warranty clauses also saw warrantors give sureties, and an early charter from 1039 or 1040 saw five brothers give sureties (rather than warrant) for the following reason: 'to strive to acquit (*adquietare*) that land for the rest of the days of their lives

inter alia: FON 180 (1119 × 1125), FON 514 (1108 × 1116), MA [p.] 21 (*ca.*1118), MD 185 (1175 × 1184), NOY 102 (*ca.*1083), NOY 252 (*ca.*1096), RA 130 (1110 × 1115).

97 For *adjutor:* FON 660 (1147 × 1153), NOY 494 (*ca.*1134); for *auxiliator:* RA 305 (1080), RA 402 (1085), SVM 656 (1080 × 1102); for *advocatus:* MB 159 (1139); for *defensor:* FON 189 (1109 × 1115), FON 223 (1131), FON 661 (1109 × 1115), NOY 593 (1163), SL 22 (1160), TV 174 (1060 × 1064); for *adjutor:* FON 735 (1115 × 1129), *Livre noir*, fos. 71v–72r (1076 × 1096), NOY 494 (1136), SAA 632 (1107), SSE II, [15] 37 (1062 × 1082), TV 420 (1108); for *fidejussor:* MD 151 (1096), SVM 19 (*ca.*1090), SVM 347 (early twelfth century); for *protector:* SAA 664 (1167), SL 22 (1160), SVM 218 (end of the eleventh century); for *tutor:* FON 500 (1145 × 1149), FON 695 (1144), NOY 544 (1143), NOY 610 (1178), SAA 669 (1100), SSE II, [47] 360 (*ca.*1100); for *testis:* MD 72 (1107 × 1108), TV 603 (1190).

98 See Dominique Barthélmey, 'Une crise de l'écrit? Observations sur des actes de Saint-Aubin d'Angers (XIe siècle)', *Bibliothèque de l'École des Chartes* 155 (1997), 111–13 and examples cited therein.

99 Hyams, 'Warranty', 445, n. 26 noted that suretyship may have been a source of inspiration for warranty practices. The relationship between suretyship and warranty commitments in western France deserves further study, but space precludes discussion here.

from any challenge if by chance one should arise', which directly mirrors the syntax and language of warranty clauses.[100]

One of the more arresting features of the warranty material from western France is the relative lack of evidence for actual warranty language that derives from the vernacular. Only a handful of commitments before *ca.*1200 were expressed with a vernacular-based word like *guarendare* or *garantizare*, like when in 1088 Raoul and Antelmus pledged that 'they would warrant against all challenges as much as they were able'.[101] Warrantors were likewise rarely described as such through vernacular nouns like *guarentus* or *warantus*: there are a handful of examples—the earliest of which date to the 1060s and 1070s—but such uses remain exceptional.[102] Only in the thirteenth century does *garantizare* (or a variant) start to become a regular feature of warranty clauses, like the following example from Saint-Jean l'Hôpital in Angers, where one Aimeri and his heirs agreed that 'we are held to warrant all the aforesaid goods for the aforesaid prior and brothers against Raoul, *miles*, my brother, and against all others, saving the right of the lord king'.[103] Actual warranty language such as this was used in just under sixty per cent of extant clauses post-1200.[104]

The dearth of actual warranty language before 1200 should not be cause for concern. Emily Tabuteau, for example, only found four uses of such language in Normandy prior to 1100; and for England, David Postles has illustrated well a similar linguistic variety to warranty clauses where vernacular language was not a regular feature.[105] That eleventh- and twelfth-century western French

---

100 *MD* 101: 'qui illam videlicet terram ab omni calumnia si forte insurrexerit cunctis diebus vitae suae adquietare satagant'.

101 Angers, Archives départementales de Maine-et-Loire (hereafter as ADML), H 3713, fos. 31v–32r: 'et fidem suam coram legitimis viris plevierunt quod sicut illa dimittebant ita contra omnes calumpnias quoad possent guarentarent'. The earliest example of warranty language I have found comes from *SAA* 104 (1039 × 1055) which uses *guarendare*. For further examples of vernacular warranty verbs, see *RA* 306 (1120), *RA* 376 (1100).

102 *SVM* 17 (*ca.*1070), *NOY* 612 (*ca.*1178), *FON* 939 (1150 × 1199). For *warrantia*, see *MD* 203 (1196). There is also a case in which Goscelin Picher lost his case against Saint-Florent because a court judged he had no claim either by inheritance or warranty (*nec per guarent*): see *Livre noir*, fo. 39r–v (1050 × 1060).

103 *SJH* 107 (1236): 'tenemur garantisare omnia supradicta sepedictis priori et fratribus erga Radulfum militem fratrem meum et erga omnes alios salvo tamen jure domini regis'.

104 See, for example, *MB* 206 (1208), *MB* 238 (1236); *MD* 212 (1202), *MD* 218 (1208), *MD* 219 (1208), *MD* 220 (1210), *MD* 232 (1222), *MD* 239 (1224), *MD* 241 (1230), *MD* 246 (recording two transactions) (1232); *TV* 644 (1204), *TV* 670 (1226), *TV* 679 (1230), *TV* 692 (1236), *TV* 699 (1236).

105 Tabuteau, *Transfers of Property*, 196; Postles, 'Seeking the Language of Warranty'.

warranty commitments were not expressed in the vernacular is significant for another reason, however. Since warranty commitments, as we have seen, recorded verbal promises and oaths, the lack of vernacular words that derive from those of oral practices gives pause for thought. Moreover, because eleventh-century charter production witnessed an expansion in vocabulary, including that coming from the vernacular, we might therefore reasonably expect to see greater borrowing from the vernacular in the construction of new types of clause.[106] Because they did not, however, our evidence thus raises questions about where the language of warranty commitments actually came from? Did the authors of our documents have models from which they could borrow linguistically when expressing warranty commitments in writing, and what might these models have been?

Models

The composition of written warranty commitments displays signs suggestive of influence from a number of different models. In the first instance, sanction and anathema clauses included in charters—especially those dating before *ca.*1000—seem to have helped scribes compose warranty clauses, and parallels can be drawn both in terms of syntax and some vocabulary.[107] The following represents a developed, but typical anathema clause from a charter of Saint-Florent which I quote in the Latin:

> Si quis autem contra hoc testamentum ex parentibus meis aut de heredibus sive coheredibus vel etiam qualiscumque intromissa persona quod fieri non credo aliquid agere vel repetere seu calumpniam inferre

106 Note here Benoît-Michel Tock, 'Les mutations du vocabulaire latin des chartes au XIe siècle', *Bibliothèque de l'École des Chartes* 155 (1997), 119–48; Michel Parisse, '*Quod vulgo dicitur*: la latinisation des noms communs dans les chartes', *Médiévales* 42 (2002), 45–53.

107 On anathema clauses, see now François Bougard, 'Jugement divin, excommunication, anathème et malédiction: la sanction spirituelle dans les sources diplomatiques', in *Exclure de la communauté chrétienne: Sens et pratiques sociales de l'anathème et de l'excommunication, IVe–XIIe siècle*, ed. Geneviève Bührer-Thierry and Stéphanie Gioanni (Turnhout: 2015), 215–38; see also the comments in Benoît-Michel Tock, 'L'acte privé en France, VIIe siècle–milieu du Xe siècle', *Mélanges de l'Ecole française de Rome*. Moyen-Âge 111, no. 2 (1999), 499–537, esp. 514; the overview in Arthur Giry, *Manuel de diplomatique*, new edn. (Paris: 1925), 562–5 remains useful. For the cultural aspects of anathema clauses, see Lester K. Little, *Benedictine Maledictions: Liturgical Cursing in Romanesque France* (Ithaca: 1993).

> voluerit sua repeticio nullum obtineat effectum sed insuper cogente judiciaria potestate auri libras triginta et argenti pondera centum coactus exsolvat et iram Dei omnipotentis incurrat pro cujus amore hanc meam hereditatem tradere volo.[108]

The verb *repetere* (to claim) we have seen in one of the Saint-Florent warranty commitments when Gautier the *vassallus* promised to 'claim nothing further' (*ne amplius repeteret*) from the monks; *repetere* only appears as warranty verb in Gautier's promise, suggesting that in this case, at least, there was a direct borrowing from a verb that features in many Saint-Florent sanctions and one of their early warranty promises.[109] Another Saint-Florent warranty clause dating between 1058 and 1070 shows similar borrowing from anathemas: 'fidem constituit quod per se seu per aliquam *introductam personam* rei predictae nullam ulterius inferret calumniam ...'.[110] Within the corpus of warranty clauses, the phrase *introducta persona*, like *repetere*, only appears in this Saint-Florent clause, again suggestive of borrowing.

Other features of anathema clauses appear to have influenced the composition of a wider selection of warranty clauses. At a basic level, the conditional clause *si quis* is shared across anathema clauses and warranty clauses—though the use of *si quis* to introduce a conditional clause was common outside the context of charter diplomatic as well, so it is difficult to know if, in this case, we are actually observing a process of borrowing. The aspirational phrase of *quod fieri non credo* ('which I do not believe will happen'), or its variant *quod absit* ('God forbid'), common to anathema clauses, also turn up in some warranty clauses. A warranty commitment recorded by the monks of Saint-Vincent of Le Mans dating to between 1067 and 1080, for instance, began 'ut si quando forte *quod fore non credimus* calumpnia surrexerit fratribus loci Sancti Vincentii ...', and charters from Marmoutier and Le Ronceray both included the phrase *quod absit* in some of their warranty clauses.[111]

108 Artem 3449 (1009): 'If any my kin, heirs, co-heirs, or any other person coming into [my inheritance] should act or claim something against this testament, which I do not believe will happen, or should wish to impose a challenge upon it, let his claim obtain no effect and, in addition, under the compulsion of judicial power, let him pay thirty pounds of gold and one hundred of silver, and let him incur the wrath of Almighty God out of love for whom I wish to hand over this my inheritance'.

109 *Livre noir*, fo. 25r–v (1010). For other examples of *repetere* in Saint-Florent anathema clauses, see, e.g., Artem 3355 (1020), Artem 3358 (1050).

110 *Livre noir*, fos. 111v–112r.

111 *SVM* 115, *MD* 97 (1032 × 1037), and *RA* 95/96 (*ca.*1080).

A relationship between anathema and warranty clauses makes sense since both types of clause fulfilled similar purpose, seeking to secure the stability of a transaction over time. If anathema clauses can help account for certain features of warranty clauses, especially concerning syntax, they make it difficult to understand however the relationship between the spoken promises underlying warranty and their written form.[112]

Several additional formulas appear in the drafting of warranty clauses, however, that point towards the practices of oath-taking. One of these is the phrase *pro posse suo* or *in quantum potuerit*, expressing the would-be warrantor's total commitment to fulfilling his promises. The earliest examples of this formula date to the 1060s, but only in the final decade of the eleventh century and into the twelfth does its use appear to have spread more widely.[113] Between 1100 and 1110, for instance, Aimeri and Raoul, in abandoning their claims against the monks of Saint-Florent, 'promised that if anyone should ever challenge [that land], they would defend Saint-Florent to the best of their ability (*pro posse suo*)'.[114] Another formula scribes sometimes included was the phrase *contra omnes homines*, specifying that the would-be warrantor's promise was valid against all men.[115] The earliest uses of this phrase date possibly as early as the 1040s, though the phrase, similar to *pro posse suo*, gained currency from the end of the eleventh century onwards.[116] Finally, a number of clauses include a statement that a promise was made *sine malo ingenio*, or without wicked intent. For example, in 1118 Raoul de Fougères promised the monks of Marmoutier promised that 'he would faithfully and without any wicked intent

112 Though see Laurent Morelle, 'Les chartes dans la gestion des conflits (France du Nord, XIe–début XIIe siècle', *Bibliothèque de l'École des Chartes* 155 (1997), esp. 287–93, for discussion of anathema clauses being read out, part of his larger argument that oral and written should be seen as complementary, rather than antagonistic.

113 See *Livre noir*, fos. 111v–112r (1058 × 1070), *MA* [p.] 36 (*ca.*1070), *MV* 118 (1060 × 1066), *SAA* 288 (1060 × 1087), and *TV* 174 (1060 × 1064) for the early examples.

114 ADML, H 3713 fos. 37r–37rbis: 'et promiserunt quod si quispiam in ea calumpniam mitteret ipsi eam pro posse suo sancto Florentio defenderent'.

115 See also Fontette, *Recherche sur la pratique*, 95: 'la règle générale est, dans la quasi-totalité des cas, que la garantie est accordée *contra omnes* sans exception'.

116 *SAA* 940. Additional eleventh-century examples: *MV* 3 (1032 × 1064), *MV* 6 (1040 × 1060), *MV* 27 (1070), *SAA* 288 (1060 × 1087), *SVM* 17 (*ca.*1070), *SVM* 19 (*ca.*1090), *SVM* 181 (*ca.*1073), *SVM* 182 (1076), *SVM* 377 (1080 × 1102), *SVM* 486 (end of the eleventh century), *SVM* 656 (1080 × 1102), and *SVM* 802 (1090 × 1102). Note also *NOY* 7 (1056 × 1069) for the phrase *contra omnes calumpnias*, rather than *homines* (or variant), or *SSE* II, [15] 37 (1062 × 1082) for a similar formula, expressed as *contra omnes calumpniatores*.

guard (*custodire*)' the properties of the monks.[117] While this formula was not as common as those of *pro posse* or *contra omnes homines*, it does appear in several charters.[118]

Many of these formulas appear in warranty clauses together, giving such examples a distinctive feel. Take the following promise, dated to 1076, when Bernard de *Firmitate* 'agreed faithfully and without wicked intent, and confirmed in accordance with the rites (*rite*) ... promising henceforth that he would be a true and faithful aid to the monks ... against all perfidious men and wicked usurpers'.[119] Several features of this commitment deserve attention. First, the clause makes use of the verb *promittere*, indicating that it bears at least some relationship to the spoken word. Second, it combines two of the formulas I have just mentioned, namely the *contra omnes* and *sine malo ingenio* formulas. Third, it places a premium on fidelity: Bernard agreed *fideliter*, and promised to be a *verus* and *fidelis adjutor*; and it would difficult not to connect the expression *sine malo ingenio* with just such emphasis on fidelity. And fourth, the use of the word *rite* in this clause is arresting, and is strongly suggestive of a highly ritualized practice, characterized by clear expectations—perhaps even templates—as to the types of words Bernard would say.[120]

One such template might have been the oath of fidelity, and extant warranty commitments display marked linguistic similarities to oaths of fidelity. Take for example the oath sworn by Renaud de Château-Gontier to the abbot of Saint-Aubin in 1037, on receipt of some properties from the abbey: Renaud acknowledged that he held these properties 'in the fidelity of homage', and agreed 'to guard and to defend [them] ... as much as he is able, just as a faithful man and friend of the church [ought to do] lawfully'.[121] There are clear parallels

117 Artem 3395. On the Fougères dossier, see Florian Mazel, 'Seigneurs, moines et chanoines: pouvoir local et enjeux ecclésiaux à Fougères à l'époque grégorienne (milieu XIe–milieu XIIe siècle)', *Annales de Bretagne et des Pays de l'Ouest* 113, no. 3 (2006), 105–35.

118 See *MV* 27 (1070), *SSE* I, 146 (1074), *SSE* I, 6 (1082 × 1093), *SSE* II, [24] 316 (1056 × 1082), *SVM* 317 (1096), *TV* 656 (1214).

119 *SVM* 182: 'ipse quoque fideliter et sine malo ingenio annuit et rite confirmavit et ipsius loci ... promittens se deinceps fore verum et fidelem adjutorem monachis ... contra omnes perfides homines et malignos invasores'.

120 The word *rite* is unusual in charters. The only other context in which I have found it concerns accounts of ordeals, where the word *rite* underscores the formal ritualized elements of ordeal, perhaps even pointing towards the use of ritual *ordines*. See Artem 3367 (1066) for an ordeal performed *rite* in the basilica of Saint-Maurice in Angers.

121 *SAA* 1: 'tali quidem conditione ut ipsam dominus ... de abbate ... in fidelitatem hominagii teneat atque tres ejusdem curtis partes ex toto posse suo sicut fidelis homo et amicus ecclesie legitime custodiat et defendat'.

between fidelity and warranty here both in the *pro posse* formula, and in the vocabulary, such as the verbs *custodire* and *defendere*, and the nouns *fidelis* and *amicus*. Another oath of fidelity was sworn to the nuns of Le Ronceray by one Barbot in *ca.*1116, and also exhibits close similarities to the language of warranty commitments: Barbot, upon receiving properties near Angers from the nuns, 'swore liege fidelity upon the demesne altar to the nuns of Notre-Dame against all men and that he would keep faithfully and defend and aid their land and goods as much as he was able'.[122] Here we have both a *pro posse* and a *contra omnes* formula, and the language of Barbot's oath of fidelity likewise displays marked similarities to that found in warranty clauses (*adjuvare, defendere*).

If we cast a slightly wider net, the parallels between warranty commitments and oaths of fidelity becomes even more striking. For a start, Carolingian oaths of fidelity contain much of the same language; thus in 802 when Charlemagne required oaths from all his subjects, the form the oath was to take included a statement that 'henceforth I shall be faithful' (*ab isto die inantea fidelis sum*), and that the oath was sworn 'with a pure mind free from deceit and wicked intent'.[123] Likewise, Occitan oaths of fidelity, studied most recently by Fredric Cheyette and Hélène Débax, include many of the phrases and vocabulary found in western French warranty clauses, and in the handful of actual oaths of fidelity that do survive for this region as well.[124] Nearer to the region under consideration in this paper, the *Conventum* between Hugh de Lusignan and William of Aquitaine in their ongoing dispute about the various obligations each owed the other as result of their fidelity also makes use of the same type of language and stock phrases found in warranty clauses.[125] Finally, Fulbert

---

122 *RA* 74: 'ipse in manu sua ligiam fidelitatem sanctimonialibus S. Marie super altare dominicum juravit contra omnes homines et quod terram eorum, pro posse suo, omnesque res earum fideliter retineret ac defenderet et adjuvaret'.

123 *Capitularia regum francorum*, ed. Alfred Boretius, vol. 1. MGH Legum sectio II (Hannover: 1883), no. 34 (p. 101).

124 Fredric L. Cheyette, *Ermengard of Narbonne and the World of the Troubadours* (Ithaca and London: 2004); Hélène Débax, *La féodalité languedocienne XIe–XIIe siècles. Serments, hommages et fiefs dans le Languedoc des Trencavel* (Toulouse: 2003); see also Hélène Débax, '"Une féodalité qui sent l'encre": typologies des actes féodaux dans le Languedoc des XIe–XIIe siècles', in *Le vassal, le fief et l'écrit. Pratiques d'écriture et enjeux documentaires dans le champ de la féodalité (XIe–XVe s.)*, ed. Jean-François Nieus (Louvain-la-Neuve: 2007), 35–70, for transcriptions of some of these texts.

125 The literature on this text is now vast. See *Le Conventum (vers 1030): Un précurseur aquitain des premières épopées*, ed. and trans. Georges Beech, Yves Chauvin, and Georges Pons (Geneva: 1995); my understanding of the *Conventum* owes much to Stephen D. White,

de Chartres' famous letter on the *forma fidelitatis* emphasised that the *fidelis* ought to 'abstain from evil' (*abstinere a malo*)—similar in sentiment to *sine malo ingenio*—and, moreover, that the *fidelis* should strive to keep his lord safe (*tutum*), offer *auxilium* and *consilium*, and avoid harming his lord.[126]

Uniting these examples was a broad *imaginaire* of fidelity, replete with a rich vocabulary and phraseology. When putting warranty commitments into writing, scribes certainly drew upon this linguistic repertoire. Promises to bring aid (*adjuvare, auxiliari*), or to offer *auxilium* and *consilium*, like in 1080 when Haimo Guischard and his heir promised the nuns of Le Ronceray that they would be 'faithful friends and aids' to the nuns, certainly suggest borrowing from just such a repertoire.[127] Other warranty promises could be built around the verb *tutari*, recalling Bishop Fulbert's admonishment to the prospective *fidelis* to keep his lord *tutum*: Arnaud, for example, between 1095 and 1100, promised the monks of Saint-Serge 'to preserve, aid, and keep safe (*tutari*)' the properties forming the subject of his quitclaim.[128] Perhaps no clearer indication of borrowing from the *imaginaire* of fidelity in the composition of warranty oaths and clauses can be found than when warrantors promise to be a *fidelis* to their warrantee, or agree to undertake their commitments *fideliter* (in the manner of a *fidelis*).[129] While both *fidelis* and *fideliter* were also related to the pledging of *fides*, which as we have seen often accompanied the performance of warranty, they also point to the larger conceptual world of fidelity.[130]

'A Crisis of Fidelity in c. 1000?'. in *Building Legitimacy: Political Discourses and Forms of Legitimacy in Medieval Societies*, edited by Isabel Alfonso, Hugh Kennedy and Julio Escalona (Leiden: 2004), 27–49.

126 *The Letters and Poems of Fulbert of Chartres*, ed. and trans. Frederick Behrends (Oxford: 1976), no. 51.

127 *RA* 305; for verbs using *adiuvare* see: *Livre noir*, fos. 111v–112r (1058 × 1070), *MA* [p.] 21 (*ca*.1118), *MB* 112 (1100), *RA* 95/96 (*ca*.1080); for promises to bring *auxilium*: *RA* 304 (1075), *SAA* 156 (1160), *SAA* 372 (1082 × 1106), *TV* 299 (1080). And for a promise of *auxilium* and *consilium*, *RA* 178 (1080).

128 *SSE* I, 224.

129 For descriptions of warrantors as *fideles*, see *SAA* 273 (1082 × 1106), *SAA* 274 (1082 × 1106), *SSE* II, [24] 316 (1056 × 1082), *SVM* 182 (1076), *SVM* 367 (*ca*.1096); for *fideliter*, see *inter alia*, ADML, H 3713, fo. 30r–v (1087), *MD* 163 (1123), *RA* 102 (1120), *SAA* 122 (1117), *SAA* 896 (1120 × 1127), *SL* 80 (1068 × 1096), *SSE* I, 243 (1093 × 1102), *TV* 417 (1107).

130 It is important to stress that the *fides*—and promises of warranty more broadly—are not identical to oaths of fidelity; but the important point is that warranty clauses display borrowing from the language that characterized oaths of fidelity. The relationship between *fides* and *fidelitas* (as well as their differences) had already been noted by Esmein, *Études sur les contrats*, 95ff. and Yver, *Les contrats*, 46.

All the material discussed thus far is therefore strongly suggestive that when choosing how to formulate and express warranty commitments in writing, scribes drew upon the language and vocabulary that characterized oaths of fidelity. It is likely, moreover, that scribal choice in this regard was influenced in part by changes in practice as to the types of oaths warrantors might actually swear when committing themselves to warranty. Hugh son of Thedolin, in 1059, sold the church of Lancôme to the monks of La Trinité de Vendôme for 27 *livres*; the charter recording this sale includes the following clause:

> Hugh henceforth would drive back any challenge because of that sum of money, except for a case brought by Aubrey de Montoire, his lord from whose fief (*casamento*) that church came. Moreover, it is to be known that Hugh became the man of Abbot Oderic … so that by the true purity of fidelity he would free the church from any challenge, just as he had promised, and see to it that the monks have it quit in perpetuity.[131]

Several points here are worth drawing attention to. The initial agreement to 'drive back any challenge' was introduced by the phrase 'the agreement was such that' (*convenientia talis ut*). This 'agreement' was then strengthened through two acts: Hugh became the man of Abbot Oderic (*devenit homo*), and then swore fidelity (*per veram fidelitatis puritatem*). Barthélemy thought that the phrase *devenit homo* meant that Hugh had performed homage to the abbot, however there need not be any reason to suppose Hugh did anything other than become Abbot Oderic's man, and then swore an oath.[132] What matters for our present purposes is the relationship between agreement and oath: the charter envisages a clear sequence in which Hugh agreed to warrant his sale, and then shored this up through an oath of fidelity that explicitly recalled what he had earlier promised (*sicut promiserat*). So, when the parties concerned sought the type of oath Hugh would swear to secure his promise of warranty, they chose an oath of fidelity.

What factors, if any, drove the desire to model warranty commitments after oaths of fidelity remains a difficult question to answer. The fact that nearly a third of such commitments were promised at the occasion of quitclaims is

131 *TV* 125: 'ac deinceps omnem prorsus propelleret calumniam, propter memoratam pecuniae quantitatem excepta una causa Alberici, senioris sui, de cujus illa ecclesia casamento erat. Interea sciendum est quod idem Hugo devenit homo abbati Odrico … ut per veram fidelitatis puritatem ecclesiam illam ab omni calumnia sicut promiserat, deliberaret atque habendam monachis in perpetuum quietam obtinere faceret'.

132 Barthélemy, *La société dans le comté de Vendôme*, 431–2.

surely one factor. The language of fidelity must have been especially appropriate in contexts where oath-taking centred on the maintenance of good faith. Moreover, promises of this type were also affirmations of friendship—a point that emerges forcefully in those clauses utilizing *amicus*—and served to renew or reform social relationships.[133] Like the ways in which homage was used as a ritual of peace-making, so too must oaths of fidelity have performed a similar role.[134] So, contexts of dispute and peace-making may have made promises of fidelity and good faith seem the natural ones to use as models.

Another factor that surely contributed to the deepening relationship between fidelity and warranty promises was the involvement of powerful aristocrats acting as third-party warrantors. Between 1090 and 1102, for instance, Guérin the monk 'beseeched' William, the lord from whose *casamentum* a donated property came, 'to defend it against all men' (*contra omnes homines defensaret*); such language, reminiscent of that of *fidelitas*, must have been especially appropriate when warranty promises were made by those saturated in a political 'culture of fidelity'.[135] The allure of aristocratic models must have been strong even in cases where non-aristocrats warranted as principals: in *ca.*1093, for instance, Marin promised Marmoutier he would 'defend [rights to wine he abandoned] against all men', and did so in the *camera* of Pierre II the lord of Chemillé, in the presence of Pierre himself.[136] Or between 1093 and 1103, Ermenald warranted Saint-Vincent of Le Mans, giving his pledge (*fides*) 'in the hand' of Hugh, the *dapifer* of the count of Maine, promising 'if a challenge should ever arise we would acquit it as much as he was able, without wicked intent'.[137] When making promises in the presence of the aristocratic elite, and deciding on what type of oath to swear, the oath of fidelity may very

133 For *amicus* in warranty clauses, see: *RA* 305 (1080), *SAA* 328 (1060 × 1067), *SL* 80 (1068 × 1098). Note Stephen D. White, '"*Pactum ... Legem Vincit et Amor Judicium*": The Settlement of Disputes by Compromise in Eleventh-Century Western France', *The American Journal of Legal History* 22, no. 4 (1978), 296, who had suggested that promises of warranty could serve as a means to forge new social relations as an element of restoring peace after disputes.

134 On homage as ritual peace-making, see Paul Hyams, 'Homage and Feudalism: a Judicious Separation', in *Die Gegenwart des Feudalismus / Présence du féodalisme et présent de la féodalité / The Presence of Feudalism*, ed. Natalie M. Fryde, Michel Mollat du Jourdin, and Otto Gerhard Oexle (Göttingen: 2002), 13–50; Barthélemy, *La société dans le comté de Vendôme*, 431–4.

135 *SVM* 802 (1090 × 1102). I take the phrase 'culture of fidelity' from Cheyette, *Ermengard of Narbonne*.

136 Artem 4704.

137 *SVM* 65: 'et si per aliquem insurgeret ipse in quantum posset sine malo ingenio adquitaret'.

well have been the first to come to mind. At any rate, aristocratic practice—in the form of lords warranting themselves, or simply being present when others warranted—appears to have been leaving its mark on the form and language of warranty clauses.

These arguments cannot be pushed too far, not least because the documentary culture of the literate elite can only imperfectly capture processes occurring beneath the level of written language, such as a subtle reorientation in the *types* of oaths and promises individuals might have made when warranting their transactions. Nevertheless, the evidence discussed above is suggestive of a larger trend in which the language of fidelity was coming to shape the drafting of warranty clauses. Through formulas such as *pro posse, contra omnes*, and *sine malo ingenio*, and through a wide vocabulary that included words like *adjutor, adjuvare, auxiliator, custodire, protector, protegere, tueri, tutor*, and above-all *defendere* and *defensor*, warranty clauses reflected a broader 'culture of fidelity'. Although modelling warranty after oaths of fidelity was a process whose outlines we can only apprehend through a glass darkly, that fidelity does seem to have been a model at all is an important conclusion that helps to make sense of eleventh- and twelfth-century warranty clauses.

Conclusions

While much more work remains to be done on the subject of warranty, the preceding discussion offers some suggestions into how warranty clauses in this period brought law and language together. As noted above, one the distinguishing characteristics in eleventh- and twelfth-century western France was the absence of formal written sources of law that could serve to structure documentary culture and legal practice. Models of legal authority were thus unwritten and diffuse, and this, coupled with the varied centres of documentary production (i.e. monastic *scriptoria*), goes a long way towards explaining the diversity in the content, form, and language of warranty clauses. If the preceding arguments that the composition of warranty clauses was modelled, in part at least, after oaths of fidelity is correct, however, it may be possible to say a bit more about the sources of legal language in this period. The fact that nearly one third of warranty commitments were given with quitclaims and the fact that lords warranted their men's transactions, or those of people subject to their authority, both point towards the nexus of disputing and centres of territorial, seigneurial authority as one of the workshops in which the language of warranty clauses was worked out. That disputes stimulated the development of new types of writing and written form has been well-established in recent scholarship;[138] but warranty clauses may provide a way for thinking about the influence of seigneurial jurisdictions upon the ways in which legal language took shape as well. The inclusion of the language of fidelity in the composition of warranty clauses suggests, albeit subtly, that at least one element of charter drafting was orientated around the axes of seigneurial authority and aristocratic practice. Across such axes of aristocratic authority there may have been a more or less shared emphasis by the holders of that authority upon oaths of fidelity as the appropriate means to frame legal commitments. Moreover, that these centres of authority may have shared a common language of fidelity, which was then partially reflected in the drafting of warranty clauses, helps to view such centres as sources of legal language. In a society without written law, the axes of local, jurisdictional authority must have played a prominent role in structuring law and language.[139] Warranty clauses, at the very least then, suggest one way in which we might see the influence of such centres of authority on the form of law and its linguistic expression.

Bibliography

Manuscripts

Angers, Archives départementales de Maine-et-Loire, H 3713 ('Livre blanc de Saint-Florent')

Paris, Bibliothèque nationale de France, ms. lat. 1930 ('Livre noir de Saint-Florent')

Works Cited

Archives d'Anjou, edited by Paul Marchegay, 3 vols. Angers: 1843–1854.

Barret, Sébastien. 'Les actes écrits comme instruments de pouvoir: la contribution des formulaires'. In *Chartes et cartulaires comme instruments de pouvoir. Espagne et Occident chrétien* (*VIIIe–XIIe siècles*), edited by Julio Escalona and Hélène Sirantoine, 87–99. Toulouse: 2013.

Barthélemy, Dominique. *La société dans le comté de Vendôme de l'an mil au XIVe siècle*. Paris: 1993.

138 See Chantal Senséby, 'Des hommes, des écrits et des conflits aux XIe et XIIe siècles dans l'espace ligérien', in *L'Autorité de l'écrit au Moyen Âge (Orient-Occident)*, XXXIXe Congrès de la SHMESP (Paris: 2009), 175–87; Lemesle, *Conflits et justice*, esp. 123–47.

139 For a parallel argument about the importance of local jurisdiction in structuring legal thought and practice, and ultimately the ways in which charter draftsmen chose to represent the legal world around them, see M. W. McHaffie, 'Law and Violence in Eleventh-Century France', *Past and Present* 238, no. 1 (2018), 3–41.

Barthélemy, Dominique. 'Une crise de l'écrit? Observations sur des actes de Saint-Aubin d'Angers (XIe siècle)'. *Bibliothèque de l'École des Chartes* 155 (1997): 95–117.

Bellomo, Manlio. *The Common Legal Past of Europe, 1000–1800*, translated by Lydia G. Cochrane. Washington: 1995.

Bougard, François. 'Jugement divin, excommunication, anathème et malédiction: la sanction spirituelle dans les sources diplomatiques'. In *Exclure de la communauté chrétienne: Sens et pratiques sociales de l'anathème et de l'excommunication, IVe–XIIe siècle*, edited by Geneviève Bührer-Thierry and Stéphanie Gioanni, 215–38. Turnhout: 2015.

Bertrand, Paul. 'À propos de la révolution de l'écrit (xe–XIIIe siècle). Considérations inactuelles'. *Médiévales* 56 (2009): 75–92.

Brundage, James A. *The Medieval Origins of the Legal Profession: Canonists, Civilians, and Courts*. Chicago: 2008.

Capitularia regum francorum, edited by Alfred Boretius, vol. 1. MGH Legum sectio II. Hannover: 1883.

'Cartae de rebus abbatiae majoris monasterii in Andegavia', edited by Paul Marchegay, in *Archives d'Anjou*, vol. 2. Angers: 1850.

Cartulaire de l'abbaye de la Trinité de Vendôme, 5 vols., edited by Charles Métais. Paris: 1893–1904.

Cartulaire de l'abbaye de Noyers, edited by Casimir Chevalier. Tours: 1872.

Cartulaire de l'abbaye de Saint-Aubin d'Angers, 3 vols., edited by Bertrand de Broussillon. Angers: 1903.

Cartulaire de l'abbaye de Saint-Vincent du Mans (ordre de Saint Benoît), edited by Robert Charles and Menjot d'Elbenne. Mamers and Le Mans: 1886–1913.

Cartulaire du chapitre Saint-Laud d'Angers, edited by Adrien Planchenault. Angers: 1903.

Cartulaire de Cormery précédé de l'histoire de l'abbaye et de la ville de Cormery d'après les chartes, edited by J.-J. Bourassé. Tours: 1861.

Cartulaire de l'hôpital Saint-Jean d'Angers, edited by Célestin Port. Paris: 1870.

Cartulaire de Marmoutier pour le Dunois, edited by Émile Mabille. Châteaudun: 1874.

Cartulaire de Marmoutier pour le Vendômois, edited by Charles Auguste de Trémault. Paris: 1893.

'Cartularium monasterii Beatae Mariae Andegavensis', edited by Paul Marchegay, in *Archives d'Anjou*, vol. 3. Angers: 1854.

Cartulaire noir de la cathédrale d'Angers, edited by Charles Urseau. Paris: 1908.

'Cartulaire de Saint-Maur de Glanfeuil', edited by Paul Marchegay, in *Archives d'Anjou* vol. 1. Angers: 1843.

Chartes originales antérieures à 1121 conservées en France. Edited by Cédric Giraud, Jean-Baptiste Renault and Benoît-Michel Tock. Nancy and Orléans: 2010, at <http://www.cn-telma.fr/originaux/index/>.

Chastang, Pierre. *Lire, écrire, transcrire. Le travail des rédacteurs de cartulaires en Bas-Languedoc (XIe–XIIIe siècles)*. Paris: 2001.

Cheyette, Fredric L. *Ermengard of Narbonne and the World of the Troubadours*. Ithaca and London: 2004.

Clanchy, Michael T. *From Memory to Written Record: England, 1066–1307*, 3rd edn. Oxford: 2013.

Débax, Hélène. *La féodalité languedocienne XIe–XIIe siècles. Serments, hommages et fiefs dans le Languedoc des Trencavel.* Toulouse: 2003.

Débax, Hélène. '"Une féodalité qui sent l'encre": typologies des actes féodaux dans le Languedoc des XIe–XIIe siècles'. In *Le vassal, le fief et l'écrit. Pratiques d'écriture et enjeux documentaires dans le champ de la féodalité (XIe–XVe s.)*, edited by Jean-François Nieus, 35–70. Louvain-la-Neuve: 2007.

Declercq, Georges. 'Between Legal Action and Performance: The *firmatio* of Charters in the Early Middle Ages'. In *Medieval Legal Process: Physical, Spoken and Written Performance in the Middle Ages*, edited by Marco Mostert and P. S. Barnwell, 55–73. Turnhout: 2011.

Esmein, Adhémar. *Études sur les contrats dans le très-ancien droit français*. Paris: 1883.

d'Espinay, Gustave. *Les cartulaires angevins. Étude sur le droit de l'Anjou au Moyen Âge.* Angers: 1864.

de Fontette, François. *Recherches sur la pratique de la vente immobilière dans la région parisienne au moyen âge (Fin X^e–début XIVe siècle)*. Paris: 1957.

Fulbert of Chartres. *The Letters and Poems of Fulbert of Chartres*, edited and translated by Frederick Behrends. Oxford: 1976.

Gilliard, François. 'La garantie du chef d'éviction dans le pays de vaud (du IXe au XVe siècle)'. *Mémoires de la Société pour l'Histoire du Droit et des Institutions des anciens pays bourguignons, comtois et romands* 21 (1960): 7–23.

Giry, Arthur. *Manuel de diplomatique*, new edn. Paris: 1925.

Grand cartulaire de Fontevraud, edited by Jean-Marc Bienvenu, Robert Favreau, and Georges Pons, 2 vols. Poitiers: 2000–2005.

Guyotjeannin, Olivier. '"*Penuria scriptorum*": le mythe de l'anarchie documentaire dans la France du Nord (X^e–première moitié du XIe siècle)'. *Bibliothèque de l'École des Chartes*, vol. 155 (1997): 11–44.

Hudson, John. *Land, Law and Lordship in Anglo-Norman England.* Oxford: 1994.

Hudson, John. *The Oxford History of the Laws of England, Volume II: 871–1216*. Oxford: 2012.

Hyams, Paul. 'Warranty and Good Lordship in Twelfth-Century England'. *Law and History Review* 5, no. 2 (1987): 437–503.

Hyams, Paul. 'Homage and Feudalism: a Judicious Separation'. In *Die Gegenwart des Feudalismus / Présence du féodalisme et présent de la féodalité / The Presence of*

Feudalism, edited by Natalie M. Fryde, Michel Mollat du Jourdin, and Otto Gerhard Oexle, 13–50. Göttingen: 2002.

Kaye, J. M. *Medieval English Conveyances*. Cambridge: 2009.

L'autorité de l'écrit au Moyen Âge (Orient-Occident). XXXIXe Congrès de la SHMESP. Paris: 2009.

Lamy, Claire. 'L'abbaye de Marmoutier et sa production écrite (1040–1150): formules en usage au scriptorium monastique et dans les dépendances'. In *La formule au Moyen Âge II*, edited by Isabelle Draelants and Christelle Balouzat-Loubet, 75–90. Turnhout: 2015.

Le Conventum (vers 1030): Un précurseur aquitain des premières épopées, edited and translated by Georges Beech, Yves Chauvin, and Georges Pons. Geneva: 1995.

Lemesle, Bruno. *Conflits et justice au Moyen Âge. Normes, loi et résolution des conflits en Anjou aux XIe et XIIe siècles*. Paris: 2008.

Lemesle, Bruno. 'Les querelles avaient-elles une vocation sociale? Le cas des transferts fonciers en Anjou au XIe siècle'. *Le Moyen Âge* 115 (2009): 337–64.

Little, Lester K. *Benedictine Maledictions: Liturgical Cursing in Romanesque France*. Ithaca: 1993.

Marmoutier: Cartulaire blésois, edited by Charles Métais. Blois: 1889–1891.

Mazel, Florian. 'Seigneurs, moines et chanoines: pouvoir local et enjeux ecclésiaux à Fougères à l'époque grégorienne (milieu XIe–milieu XIIe siècle)'. *Annales de Bretagne et des Pays de l'Ouest* 113, no. 3 (2006): 105–35.

McHaffie, M. W. 'Law and Violence in Eleventh-Century France'. *Past and Present* 238, no. 1 (2018), 3–41.

Morelle, Laurent. 'Les chartes dans la gestion des conflits (France du Nord, XIe–début XIIe siècle'. *Bibliothèque de l'École des Chartes* 155 (1997): 267–98.

Olivier-Martin, François. *Histoire de la coutume de la prévôté et vicomté de Paris*, 2 vols. Paris: 1922–1930.

Ourliac, Paul and Jehan de Malafosse. *Histoire du droit privé, vol. 2: Les biens*, 2nd edn. Paris: 1969.

Parisse, Michel. '*Quod vulgo dicitur*: la latinisation des noms communs dans les chartes'. *Médiévales* 42 (2002): 45–53.

Postles, David. 'Seeking the Language of Warranty of Land in Twelfth-Century England'. *Journal of the Society of Archivists* 20, no. 2 (1999): 209–22.

Poudret, Jean-François. *Coutumes et coutumiers. Histoire comparative des droit des pays romands du XIIIe–XVIe siècle. V: Les biens*. Bern: 2006.

Pratiques de l'écrit documentaire au XIe siècle, edited by Olivier Guyotjeannin, Laurent Morelle, and Michel Parisse. *Bibliothèque de l'École des Chartes* 155 (1997).

Premier et Second livres des Cartulaires de l'abbaye Saint-Serge et Saint-Bach d'Angers (XIe et XIIe siècles), edited by Yves Chauvin, 2 vols. Angers: 1997.

Reynolds, Susan. *Fiefs and Vassals: The Medieval Evidence Reinterpreted.* Oxford: 1994.

Reynolds, Susan. 'The Emergence of Professional Law in the Long Twelfth Century'. *Law and History Review* 21, no. 2 (2003): 347–66.

Ruffini-Ronzani, Nicolas and Jean-François Nieus. 'Société seigneuriale, réformes ecclésiales: les enjeux documentaires d'une révision historiographique'. In Ecclesia in medio nationis: *Reflections on the Study on Monasticism in the Central Middle Ages/Réflexions sur l'étude du monachism au Moyen Âge central*, edited by Steven Vanderputten and Brigitte Meijns, 77–100. Leuven: 2011.

Senséby, Chantal. 'Une notice fausse du cartulaire de l'abbaye tourangelle de Noyers?'. *Bibliothèque de l'École des Chartes* 155 (1997): 61–94.

Senséby, Chantal. 'Des hommes, des écrits et des conflits aux XIe et XIIe siècles dans l'espace ligérien'. In *L'Autorité de l'écrit au Moyen Âge (Orient-Occident)*. XXXIXe Congrès de la SHMESP, 175–87. Paris: 2009.

Tabuteau, Emily Zack. *Transfers of Property in Eleventh-Century Norman Law*. Chapel Hill: 1988.

Thireau, Jean-Louis. 'Faculté de disposer et protection de la famille dans le très ancien droit coutumier français (X[e]–XIIIe siècles)'. *Revue historique de droit français et étranger* 87, no. 3 (2009): 337–63.

Tock, Benoît-Michel. 'Les mutations du vocabulaire latin des chartes au XIe siècle'. *Bibliothèque de l'École des Chartes* 155 (1997): 119–48.

Tock, Benoît-Michel. 'L'acte privé en France, VIIe siècle–milieu du Xe siècle'. *Mélanges de l'Ecole française de Rome*. Moyen-Âge 111, no. 2 (1999): 499–537.

Vigneron, Bernard. 'La vente dans le mâconnais du IXe au XIIIe siècle'. *Revue historique de droit français et étranger* 36 (1959): 17–47.

Weinberger, Stephen. 'Les contre-dons en Poitou et en Provence au XIe siècle: ce qu'il en coûte de faire des affaires'. *Provence historique* (2002): 483–96.

White, Stephen D. '"*Pactum ... Legem Vincit et Amor Judicium*": The Settlement of Disputes by Compromise in Eleventh-Century Western France'. *The American Journal of Legal History* 22, no. 4 (1978): 281–308.

White, Stephen D. 'Feuding and Peace-Making in the Touraine around the Year 1100'. *Traditio* 42 (1986): 195–263.

White, Stephen D. *Custom, Kinship, and Gifts to Saints: The* Laudatio parentum *in Western France, 1050–1150*. Chapel Hill: 1988.

White, Stephen D. 'A Crisis of Fidelity in c. 1000?'. in *Building Legitimacy: Political Discourses and Forms of Legitimacy in Medieval Societies*, edited by Isabel Alfonso, Hugh Kennedy, and Julio Escalona, 27–49. Leiden: 2004.

White, Stephen D. 'Protection, Warranty, and Revenge in *La Chanson de Roland*', in *Peace and Protection in the Middle Ages*, edited by T. B. Lambert and David Rollason, 155–67. Durham: 2009.

Wickham, Chris. 'Compulsory Gift Exchange in Lombard Italy, 650–1150'. In *The Languages of Gift in the Early Middle Ages*, edited by Wendy Davies and Paul Fouracre, 193–216. Cambridge: 2010.

Yver, Jean. *Les contrats dans le très ancien droit normand (XIe–XIIIe siècles)*. Domfront: 1926.

PART 3

Methodology, Interaction, and Language

CHAPTER 9

Law and Language in the *Leges Barbarorum*: A Database Project on the Vernacular Vocabulary in Medieval Manuscripts

Anette Kremer and Vincenz Schwab

Introduction

Linguistic research and the history of law both depend on the same core set of texts from the Middle Ages. Despite the rich variety of sources, the earliest written texts of Old High German have still not been collected systematically, nor have they been made available for the scientific community.[1] This article therefore has a threefold aim. First, after a brief introduction into the traditions of Old High German, we highlight that vernacular words from Germanic legal texts in particular still lack deeper linguistic analysis. Secondly, we shall show the timeline and complex intertextual interactions when the various Germanic tribes first began writing down their customary laws. Thirdly, we shall provide some close analysis of examples found in our sources, through which we show the methods of our work.

We return to the early Middle Ages, when some of the earliest written records of Germanic and Old High German vocabulary start to survive in significant numbers. We have collected these vernacular words from the medieval legal manuscripts of various Germanic peoples, the so-called laws of the barbarians (the *Leges Barbarorum*). The *Leges* include continental Germanic laws, such as the Gothic, Frankish, Saxon, and Upper German laws.[2] Each manuscript was written primarily in Latin, the medieval legal *lingua franca*. Vernacular words were inserted into a Latin text, and had a specific meaning that made sense in the context of the legal practices of various Germanic tribes. Due to the unique features of this genre, legal words constitute a significant portion of the overall vernacular vocabulary of the laws. Some of these issues will be explored in more detail below.

---

1 Heinrich Tiefenbach, 'Volkssprachige Wörter innerhalb lateinischer Texte. Rechtstexte: Leges, Kapitularien, Urkunden', in *Die althochdeutsche und altsächsische Glossographie*, vol. 1, ed. Rolf Bergmann and Stefanie Stricker (Berlin and New York: 2009), 975.

2 Karl Kroeschell, *Deutsche Rechtsgeschichte. Band 1: Bis 1250* (Cologne and Vienna: 2008), 23.

 | DOI 10.1163/9789004375765_011

This article grows out of a research project initiated at the Chair of German Linguistics at the University of Bamberg, Germany, in October 2012, under the supervision of Professor Stefanie Stricker, and is funded by the *German Research Foundation* (DFG). This project collects the vernacular vocabulary found in the Continental West-Germanic laws and aims to analyse it according to a fixed number of formal and semantic criteria. Our main focus is grammatical in orientation: we present detailed analyses of word and inflection classes, inflection forms, morphological structures, and phonological and graphic peculiarities. Thus, we differ markedly from the traditional perspective of a historical lexicology, dealing primarily with semantic analysis.[3]

We plan to make this linguistic material accessible not only for historical linguists, but also for legal historians, cultural scientists, historical lexicographers, and historical grammarians. As a major outcome, we will provide the vocabulary via a web-based platform named LegIT.[4]

---

3 Rosemarie Lühr, 'Zum Sprachtod einer Rechtssprache: Zwei ausgestorbene Wörter aus der Lex Baiuvariorum', in *Germanische Rechts- und Trümmersprachen*, ed. Heinrich Beck (Berlin and New York: 1989), 48. See for example Dagmar Hüpper-Dröge, 'Schutz- und Angriffswaffen nach den Leges und verwandten fränkischen Rechtsquellen', in *Wörter und Sachen im Lichte der Bezeichnungsforschung*, ed. Ruth Schmidt-Wiegand (Berlin and New York: 1981), 107–27; Annette Niederhellmann, 'Heilkundliches in den Leges. Die Schädelverletzungen und ihre Bezeichnungen', in *Wörter und Sachen im Lichte der Bezeichnungsforschung*, 74–90; Dagmar Hüpper-Dröge, *Schild und Speer. Waffen und ihre Bezeichnungen im frühen Mittelalter* (Frankfurt am Main and Bern: 1983); Annette Niederhellmann, *Arzt und Heilkunde in den frühmittelalterlichen Leges. Eine wort- und sachkundliche Untersuchung* (Berlin and New York: 1983); Birgit Meineke, 'Über die Verfahren der Bedeutungsermittlung am volkssprachigen Wortschatz der Leges', in *Bedeutungserfassung und Bedeutungsbeschreibung in historischen und dialektologischen Wörterbüchern. Beiträge zu einer Arbeitstagung der deutschsprachigen Wörterbücher, Projekte an Akademien und Universitäten vom 7. bis 9. März 1996 anläßlich des 150jährigen Jubiläums der Sächsischen Akademie der Wissenschaften zu Leipzig*, ed. Rudolf Große (Leipzig: 1998), 65–72; Gabriele von Olberg, *Freie, Nachbarn und Gefolgsleute. Volkssprachige Bezeichnungen aus dem sozialen Bereich in den frühmittelalterlichen Leges* (Frankfurt am Main and Bern: 1983); Jörg Riecke, *Die Frühgeschichte der mittelalterlichen medizinischen Fachsprache im Deutschen. Band I: Untersuchungen, Band II: Wörterbuch* (Berlin and New York: 2004).

4 The project is still a work in progress, so access to the database is *currently restricted.* For background information about the project and the legal manuscripts, see our website at <http://legit.ahd-portal.germ-ling.uni-bamberg.de>. Further information can be found in Stefanie Stricker and Anette Kremer, 'Das Bamberger LegIT-Projekt. Zur Erfassung des volkssprachigen Wortschatzes der Leges barbarorum in einer Datenbank', *Sprachwissenschaft* 39/3 (2014), 237–263; Stefanie, Stricker, Anette Kremer, and Vincenz Schwab, 'Der volkssprachige Wortschatz der *Leges barbarorum*. Zum Projekt einer Online-Datenbank', in *Weiland Wörter Welten—Akten der 6. Internationalen Konferenz zur Historischen*

Vernacular Vocabulary in Medieval Manuscripts

The first written records of the German language presumably date to the early eighth century, when glosses appeared in Latin manuscripts for the first time. These are Old High German words subsequently added to the Latin text in order to explain the meaning of unknown or difficult Latin words, or to comment on their grammatical form in Old High German dialects.[5] From their beginnings in the eighth century until the thirteenth century, we can find about 28,000 glosses, represented by 250,000 tokens in more than 1,400 manuscripts. Old High German texts did not exist until the end of the eighth century. From the year 800 until 1022 (the year the famous glossator and translator Notker the German of Saint Gall died),[6] there are 125 manuscripts representing seventy-four texts, composed of 11,000 types and 290,000 tokens.[7]

In historical linguistics there has been intensive research on Old High German glosses and texts; its vocabulary has been comprehensively analysed and documented in the Old High German dictionaries and grammar books.[8] In comparison, the results of our recent analysis reveal that the vernacular *Leges* vocabulary (henceforth referred to as inserts or inserted words)[9] appears in about 500 manuscripts. They contain about 1,200 types and 42,000 tokens. While this may seem a small amount (about three per cent of the overall tradition), it nevertheless provides interesting material for linguistic research. On the one hand, the vocabulary in the *Leges* is older than that of the glosses, since its first

---

Lexikographie und Lexikologie (Jena, 25.–27. Juli 2012). Whilom Worlds of Words—Proceedings of the 6th International Conference on Historical Lexicography and Lexicology (Jena, 25.–27. July 2012), ed. Bettina Bock and Maria Kozianka (Hamburg: 2014), 285–94.

5 Stefanie Stricker, 'Definitorische Vorklärungen', in *Die althochdeutsche und altsächsische Glossographie*, I, 31–2.

6 Sonja Glauch, 'Notker III. von St. Gallen', in *Althochdeutsche und altsächsische Literatur. Ein Handbuch*, ed. Rolf Bergmann (Berlin and New York: 2013), 293.

7 Rolf Bergmann, 'Kulturgeschichtliche Aspekte des althochdeutschen Glossenwortschatzes', in *Deutsche Wortforschung als Kulturgeschichte. Beiträge des Internationalen Symposiums aus Anlass des 90-jährigen Bestandes der Wörterbuchkanzlei der Österreichischen Akademie der Wissenschaften Wien, 25.–27. September 2003*, ed. Isolde Hausner, Peter Wiesinger, and Katharina Korecky-Kröll (Vienna: 2005), 49; Jochen Splett, *Althochdeutsches Wörterbuch. Analyse der Wortfamilienstrukturen des Althochdeutschen, zugleich Grundlegung einer zukünftigen Strukturgeschichte des deutschen Wortschatzes. I,1-II* (Berlin and New York: 1993), 1196–1206.

8 E.g. in KFW or in Wilhelm Braune and Ingo Reiffenstein, *Althochdeutsche Grammatik I: Laut- und Formenlehre* (Tübingen: 2004).

9 According to Michael Prinz, 'Vergessene Wörter. Frühe volkssprachliche Lexik in lateinischen Urkunden und Amtsbüchern', *Jahrbuch für germanistische Sprachgeschichte* 1 (2010), 292–3.

appearances in writing date back to the seventh century. Thus they prove that there are lexical records of the German language long before the traditions of glosses and texts had even begun. On the other hand, vocabulary of the *Leges* is rather exceptional, as there are a considerable number of vernacular words documented in the *Leges* manuscripts alone. Due to its antiquity, the formal and semantic analysis of the vocabulary is a challenging task. We shall illustrate some problems below using sample words that have been gathered from the Salian, Alemannic, Bavarian, Lombard, and Frisian laws.

Research on the inserted words has been less active than the research on Old High German glosses or texts. We lack a consistent documentation of the complete vernacular vocabulary,[10] and we are still missing a large number of the vernacular *Leges* words both in standard Old High German dictionaries and in the Old High German grammar books.[11] We aim to fill this research gap by making the *Leges* vocabulary accessible for the *Althochdeutsches Wörterbuch* (KFW; Old High German Dictionary), the *Deutsches Rechtswörterbuch* (DRW, Dictionary of Historical German and West-Germanic Legal Terms), or the *Althochdeutsche Grammatik* (Old High German Grammar), for example.

TABLE 9.1 *Tradition of Old High German*

Tradition	Time period of the tradition	Manuscripts	Vernacular types	tokens	Overall research activities so far
Germanic laws	seventh/eighth c.–eleventh c.	about 500	about 1200	about 42 000	expandable
glosses	early eighth c.–thirteenth c.	about 1490	about 28 000	more than 250 000	intense
texts	end of the eighth c./about 800–mid of the eleventh c.	125 (74 texts)	11 000	290 000	intense

Note: The data published in Stricker *et al.*, 'Der volkssprachige Wortschatz', 285, and Stricker and Kremer, 'LegIT-Projekt', 239 have been updated.

10 Tiefenbach, 'Volkssprachige Wörter', 975; Stricker and Kremer, 'LegIT-Projekt', 238–9.
11 Stricker *et al.*, 'Der volksprachige Wortschatz', 286–7.

The Origins of Germanic Laws and the Legal Tradition of the Germanic Tribes

Initially, the law of each Germanic tribe was customary law. It was 'remembered and passed along through an oral tradition that stretched back for generations'.[12] Accordingly, legal practice was conducted in the vernacular language. There were no written laws until the Germanic tribes made contact with the Roman Empire during the Migration Period. During that time, they adopted the tradition of written legal statutes and the practice of writing down the law from the Romans, who had a well-structured legal tradition and had compiled significant lawbooks as early as the third century.[13] The Roman influence on the various Germanic laws depended on the intensity of the contact between the respective tribes and the Roman Empire. However, we can say that due to the Roman legal standards, the basic character of law of the various Germanic tribes changed considerably by transforming an oral, customary law into a written documentation of legal practice.[14] Thus, the writing down of erstwhile oral law into legal statutes was an appropriate response to the increased desire for legal certainty, an objective sought for by all of the Germanic tribes within their settlement areas.[15]

---

12 Michael Frassetto, *Encyclopedia of Barbarian Europe: Society in Transformation* (Santa Barbara, Denver, and Oxford: 2003), 231.

13 Frassetto, *Encyclopedia*, 232. For more details see for example Johannes Michael Rainer, *Das römische Recht in Europa. Von Justinian zum BGB* (Vienna: 2012); Paul Koschaker, *Europa und das römische Recht* (Munich: 1947); Stefan Esders, *Römische Rechtstradition und merowingisches Königtum. Zum Rechtscharakter politischer Herrschaft in Burgund im 6. und 7. Jahrhundert* (Göttingen: 1997); Peter Stein, *Roman Law in European History* (Cambridge: 1999); Randall Lesaffer, *European Legal History: A Cultural and Political Perspective* (Cambridge: 2010).

14 Frassetto, *Encyclopedia*, 232; Ruth Schmidt-Wiegand, 'Sprache, Recht, Rechtssprache bei Franken und Alemannen vom 6. bis zum 8. Jahrhundert', in *Leges, gentes, regna. Zur Rolle von germanischen Rechtsgewohnheiten und lateinischer Schrifttradition bei der Ausbildung der frühmittelalterlichen Rechtskultur*, ed. Gerhard Dilcher and Eva-Marie Distler (Berlin: 2006), 143; Susanne Hähnchen, *Rechtsgeschichte. Von der Römischen Antike bis zur Neuzeit* (Heidelberg, Munich, Landsberg, Frechen, and Hamburg: 2012), 108ff. See also Karl Kroeschell, *Studien zum frühen und mittelalterlichen deutschen Recht* (Berlin: 1995), 65–88; Georg Scheibelreiter, *Die barbarische Gesellschaft. Mentalitätsgeschichte der europäischen Achsenzeit (5.–8. Jahrhundert)* (Darmstadt: 1999).

15 Astrid Krah, 'Das Bild der Sozialgeschichte in den Leges barbarorum', in *Von den Leges Barbarorum bis zum ius barbarum des Nationalsozialismus. Festschrift für Hermann Nehlsen zum 70. Geburtstag*, ed. Hans-Georg Hermann *et al.* (Cologne and Vienna: 2008), 90.

One of the oldest records of ancient Germanic law is the edict of the Visigothic king Theodoric (*Edictum Theoderici*), which is believed to have been enacted in 458. This law contains written legal statutes for Goths and Romans living in the kingdom of Toulouse. It includes private law, procedural law, and criminal law. The tradition offers six manuscripts written between the ninth and thirteenth century.[16]

The fragmentary law of Theodoric's brother, the Visigothic king Euric, was composed around the same time, approximately 475. The *Codex Euricianus* had been commissioned for Euric's kingdom, which stretched from the south of present day France to some parts of the Iberian Peninsula. It was greatly influenced by Roman law.[17] The Code of Euric is one of 'the most important and influential early Germanic laws'.[18] Today, there is only one manuscript preserved, which was presumably written in the sixth or seventh century.[19]

Based on the Code of Euric, the law of the Visigoths in Spain (*Leges Visigothorum*) was issued in the middle of the seventh century. There are thirty-nine surviving manuscripts from the sixth to the sixteenth century preserving these royal constitutions. The set of laws for the Roman people in the Visigothic kingdom (*Lex Romana Visigothorum*) is considered to have been written down as early as the year 506 and is found in 102 manuscripts, dating from the sixth to the sixteenth century.[20]

The Burgundian laws (*Lex Burgundionum*) were based on ancient Burgundian tribal law and were also influenced by the Law of Euric. The law

---

16 Frassetto, *Encyclopedia*, 232; <http://www.leges.uni-koeln.de/lex/edictum-theoderici/> (accessed 10 January, 2016); <http://www.leges.uni-koeln.de/lex/edictum-theoderici/#mss> (accessed 31 August, 2016).

17 Kroeschell, *Rechtsgeschichte*, 22; Hähnchen, *Rechtsgeschichte*, 109; Clausdieter Schott, 'Der Stand der Leges-Forschung', in *Frühmittelalterliche Studien. Jahrbuch des Instituts für Frühmittelalterforschung der Universität Münster*, ed. Wolfram Drews and Christel Meier (Berlin and New York: 1979), 32.

18 Frassetto, *Encyclopedia*, 232.

19 <http://www.leges.uni-koeln.de/lex/leges-visigothorum/> (accessed 11 January, 2016); <http://www.leges.uni-koeln.de/mss/handschrift/paris-bn-lat-12161/> (accessed 31 August, 2016).

20 Hähnchen, *Rechtsgeschichte*, 109, 111; Schott, 'Stand der Leges-Forschung', 33; Carlos Petit, 'Leges Visigothorum', in *Handwörterbuch zur deutschen Rechtsgeschichte* (*HRGdigital*), ed. Albrecht Cordes, Heiner Lück, and Dieter Werkmüller, 697–9 (accessed 3 January, 2016). <http://www.hrgdigital.de/id/leges_visigothorum/stichwort.html>; <http://www.leges.uni-koeln.de/lex/leges-visigothorum/> (accessed 10 January, 2016); <http://www.leges.uni-koeln.de/lex/lex-romana-visigothorum/> (accessed 11 January, 2016); <http://www.leges.uni-koeln.de/lex/leges-visigothorum/#mss> (accessed 31 August, 2016); <http://www.leges.uni-koeln.de/lex/lex-romana-visigothorum/#mss> (accessed 6 September, 2016).

included the constitutions of the Burgundian kings Gundobad (†516) and Sigismund (†524). It is considered to have been issued between the years 480 and 501 in Lyon, the main residence of the Burgundians. This also applies to the *Lex Romana Burgundionum*, which includes the constitutions of the Roman emperors. The two Burgundian laws are preserved in about 20 manuscripts each written between the seventh and eleventh century.[21]

The Salic Law (*Lex Salica*), which contains civil and criminal law statutes of the Salian Franks, is another example of some of the oldest Germanic laws. It was first written down between 507 and 511 by order of Clovis, the founder of the Salian Empire in northern Gaul. This *Lex* survives in about ninety manuscripts written between the eighth and twelfth centuries, and re-copied in the fifteenth and sixteenth centuries. It is considered to be the most intensely studied of the old Germanic laws.[22]

The law of the Ripuarian Franks (*Lex Ribuaria*) is based on the *Lex Salica*. It represents an updated version for the Frankish people in the Rhineland area (around Cologne), omitting all the statutes for the Roman people included in the *Lex Salica*. King Dagobert was probably responsible for the composition of this ancient law whose origins date back to the first half of the seventh century. The *Lex* is preserved in 52 manuscripts, written between the ninth and the eleventh century, as well as in the sixteenth century.[23]

The *Edictum Rothari*, which was issued in the year 643, is regarded as the first Lombard law committed to writing. In the eighth century, this Edict of the Lombard king Rothar was expanded by his successors into a law called the *Leges Langobardorum*. The *Lombard laws*, which survive in 25 manuscripts

21 Kroeschell, *Rechtsgeschichte*, 22; Hähnchen, *Rechtsgeschichte*, 112; Schott, 'Stand der Leges-Forschung', 35–6; Gerd Kampers, 'Lex Burgundionum', in *Reallexikon der Germanischen Altertumskunde*, vol. 18: *Landschaftsrecht-Loxstedt*, ed. Heinrich Beck, Dieter Geuenich, and Heiko Steuer (Berlin and New York: 2001), 315; Detlef Liebs, 'Lex Romana Burgundionum', in *ibid.*, 322; <http://www.leges.uni-koeln.de/lex/lex-burgundionum/> (accessed 10 January, 2016); <http://www.leges.uni-koeln.de/lex/lex-romana-burgundionum/#mss> (accessed 31 August, 2016); <http://www.leges.uni-koeln.de/lex/lex-burgundionum/#mss> (accessed 31 August, 2016).

22 Kroeschell, *Rechtsgeschichte*, 23; Schott, 'Stand der Leges-Forschung', 36–7; <http://www.leges.uni-koeln.de/lex/lex-salica/#mss> (accessed 11 January, 2016); <http://www.leges.uni-koeln.de/lex/lex-ribuaria/#mss> (accessed 6 September, 2016).

23 Frassetto, *Encyclopedia*, 232–3; Schott, 'Stand der Leges-Forschung', 38; <http://www.leges.uni-koeln.de/lex/lex-ribuaria/#mss> (accessed 10 January, 2016); (accessed 31 August, 2016).

(written between the seventh and thirteenth centuries),[24] were clearly influenced by Roman law as well as by the Visigothic and Burgundian laws.[25]

The oldest and most important Alemannic law is the *Pactus Alamannorum*. It was issued in the first decades of the eighth century and survives in only one manuscript, dating to the ninth or tenth century. The tradition of the *Lex Alamannorum*, in contrast, survives in roughly eighty manuscripts written between the eighth and the eleventh centuries. In addition, a very small number of isolated manuscripts survive from the twelfth, fifteenth, and sixteenth centuries.[26]

The law of the Bavarians (*Lex Baiuvariorum*) is closely related to the Alemannic law; nevertheless we cannot assume that it is a consistent law, since it was influenced by a number of different laws including the Visigothic, the Salian, and the Burgundian laws. It was first written down in the second half of the eighth century. We know of fifty-eight manuscripts written between the ninth and the sixteenth centuries.[27]

The laws of the Frisians, Saxons, Chamavian Franks, and Thuringians are all closely associated with the Imperial Diet of Aachen in the year 802/803. Their redaction was one of the results of the legal reforms of Charlemagne, 'the most prolific legislator that the West had seen since Theodosius', which had been initiated in Aachen.[28] Today there are no preserved manuscripts that include the Frisian law. There is only a print edition from 1557[29] that

24 <http://www.leges.uni-koeln.de/lex/leges-langobardorum/#mss> (accessed 31 August, 2016).

25 Schott, 'Stand der Leges-Forschung', 39; <http://www.leges.uni-koeln.de/lex/leges-langobardorum/> (accessed 10 January, 2016); Walter Pohl, 'Leges Langobardorum', in *Reallexikon der Germanischen Altertumskunde*, vol. 18, 208–10.

26 Vincenz Schwab, 'Volkssprachiger Wortschatz in den oberdeutschen Leges—Altalemannisch und Altbairisch', *Sprachwissenschaft* 39/3 (2014), 266–8; *Leges Alamannorum*, edited by Karl Lehmann, 2nd edn. rev. Karl Augustus Eckhardt, MGH LL nat. Germ. V, 1 (Hannover: 1966), 13–14; <http://www.leges.uni-koeln.de/lex/lex-alamannorum/#mss> (accessed 6 September, 2016).

27 Schott, 'Stand der Leges-Forschung', 40; <http://www.leges.uni-koeln.de/lex/lex-baiuvariorum/> (accessed 10 January, 2016); <http://www.leges.uni-koeln.de/lex/lex-baiuvariorum/#mss> (accessed 31 August 2016).

28 Patrick Wormald, *The Making of English Law: King Alfred to the Twelfth Century, Volume I: Legislation and its Limits* (Oxford: 2001), 45; Kroeschell, *Rechtsgeschichte*, 22.

29 Basilius Johannes (Ioannis) Herold, *Originum ac Germanicarum Antiquitatum Libri, Leges videlicet, Salicae, Allemannorum, Saxonum, Angliorum, Thuringorum, Burgundionum, Francorum, Ripuariae, Boioriorum, Vuestphalorum, Vuerinorum, Frisionum, Langobardorum, Theutonum etc.* (Basel: 1557). See also the version of the Frisian Academy at <http://www.keesn.nl/lex/lex_en_text.htm> (accessed 31 August, 2016).

conserves the criminal-law dominated *Lex*, based on the Alemannic law.[30] The laws of the Saxons, Chamavian Franks, and Thuringians are, conversely, at least sporadically preserved in manuscripts. There are two manuscripts from the ninth and tenth century containing the Saxon law. We know of three manuscripts that include the law of the Chamavian Franks, which was influenced by the *Lex Ribuaria*, the *Lex Salica*, and the *Lex Frisionum*. Two of the manuscripts were written between the ninth and the eleventh centuries; the third one dates to the fifteenth century. The Thuringian law, based on the law of the Ripuarian Franks, survives in only one manuscript from the tenth century.[31]

As shown in figure 9.1 below, all the laws mentioned above had been initially written down between the late fifth century and the beginning of the ninth century. The peak period seems to have been between the first half of the seventh century and the year 803.[32]

The tradition of the manuscripts, however, is not limited to this period ending in 803. We deal primarily with manuscripts written between the eighth and eleventh centuries, and even work with a small number of sixteenth-century manuscripts. The majority of the manuscripts, however, emerged in the ninth century: these were evidently influenced by the legal reforms of Charlemagne, under whom not only were the last four laws shown in figure 9.1 commissioned and put into writing, but, additionally, newer versions of the other laws were also produced.[33] The work of prominent legal historians indicates that

30 Ruth Schmidt-Wiegand, 'Lex Frisionum', in *Reallexikon der Germanischen Altertumskunde*, vol. 18, 319a.

31 Kroeschell, *Rechtsgeschichte*, 22; Schott, 'Stand der Leges-Forschung', 41–2; Ruth Schmidt-Wiegand, 'Lex Francorum Chamavorum', in *Reallexikon der Germanischen Altertumskunde*, vol. 18, 317b–318a; Gerhard Lingelbach, 'Lex Thuringorum', in *Reallexikon der Germanischen Altertumskunde*, vol. 18, 336a; <http://www.leges.uni-koeln.de/lex/lex-saxonum/> (accessed 9 January, 2016); <http://www.leges.uni-koeln.de/lex/lex-francorum-chamavorum/> (accessed 9 January, 2016); <http://www.leges.uni-koeln.de/lex/lex-thuringorum/> (accessed 9 January, 2016); <http://www.leges.uni-koeln.de/mss/handschrift/muenster-sa-msc-vii-5201/> (accessed 31 August, 2016); <http://www.leges.uni-koeln.de/lex/lex-saxonum/#mss> (accessed 31 August 2016); <http://www.leges.unikoeln.de/lex/lex-francorum-chamavorum/#mss> (accessed 31 August, 2016).

32 See also Schmidt-Wiegand, 'Sprache, Recht, Rechtssprache bei Franken und Alemannen', 143.

33 Ruth Schmidt-Wiegand, 'Deutsche Sprachgeschichte und Rechtsgeschichte bis zum Ende des Mittelalters', in *Sprachgeschichte. Ein Handbuch zur Geschichte der deutschen Sprache und ihrer Erforschung*, volume 1, ed. Werner Besch, *et al.* (Berlin and New York: 1998), 77; Wilfried Hartmann, 'Karl der Große und das Recht', in *Karl der Grosse und sein Nachwirken. 1200 Jahre Kultur und Wissenschaft in Europa/Charlemagne and his Heritage.*

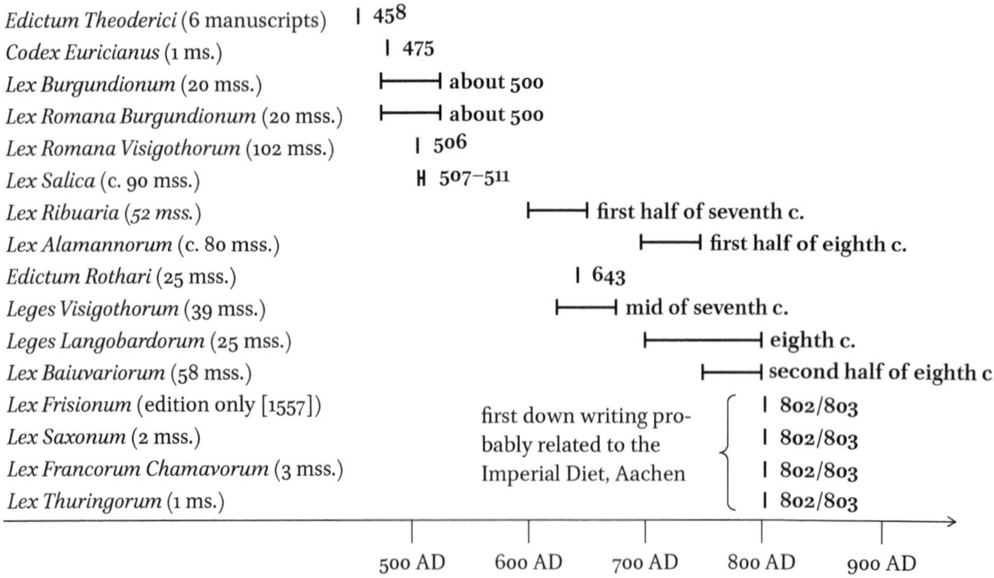

FIGURE 9.1 *Origins of the Germanic laws.*

the great legislative efforts devoted to supplementing missing statutes and to removing contradictory or wrong and inappropriate statements[34] might have been motivated by Charlemagne's 'imperial euphoria',[35] and was an effort to imitate the Roman emperors and their influence and reputation.[36] Wormald, for example, declares that 'barbarian' law-making replicated an archetypical function of Roman imperial sovereignty'.[37] Such a hypothesis is directly related to Einhard's statements about Charlemagne's legal reform in his famous biography, the *Vita Karoli Magni* (*The Life of Charlemagne*).[38] However, Charlemagne's reform measures have frequently been considered a failure,

1200 Years of Civilization and Science in Europe, volume 1: *Wissen und Weltbild/Scholarship, Worldview and Understanding*, ed. Paul Leo Butzer, Max Kerner, and Wolfgang Oberschelp (Turnhout: 1997), 183.

34 Oswald Holder-Egger and Georg Waitz, eds., *Einhardi Vita Karoli Magni* (Hannover and Leipzig: 1911), 33; Karl Ubl, 'Die erste Leges-Reform Karls des Großen', in *Das Gesetz—The Law—La Loi*, ed. Andreas Speer and Guy Guldentops (Berlin and New York: 2014), 75–8; Jennifer R. Davis, *Charlemagne's Practice of Empire* (Cambridge: 2015), 48–9.

35 Wormald, *Making of English Law*, 48.

36 Ubl, 'Die erste Leges-Reform Karls des Großen', 75.

37 Wormald, *Making of English Law*, 64.

38 Holder-Egger and Waitz, *Einhardi Vita Karoli Magni*, 33.

even by his own biographer.[39] This conclusion is based on the fact that hardly any revision marks within the legal manuscripts can be found, and that the new laws did not have major impact on legal practice. Moreover, the manuscripts do not show any obvious traces of uniformity. Thus, to summarise the *status quo*: thus far, present scholarship has not been able to evaluate precisely the degree and extent of editing which was done to the texts of legal materials by Charlemagne's scribes.[40]

The Relationship between Latin and Vernacular in the *Leges Barbarorum*

Most of the legal terms used within the *Leges barbarorum* derive from Indo-European roots.[41] Nevertheless, the terminology developed its specifically legal character in the Proto-Germanic period.[42] In the early Middle Ages, colloquial terms were used in specific contexts and thereby transformed into legal language. This early inventory of legal terminology known from the oldest group of laws, such as the *Lex Burgundionum* (fifth to sixth centuries), the *Leges Visigothorum* (seventh century), and the widely spread *Lex Salica* (sixth to ninth centuries), is expanded by more recent word formations or paraphrases. Recently merging morphological patterns led to an increase in legal terminology in the younger *Leges* texts of the eighth and ninth centuries, but a major portion of the new linguistic inserts was drawn from the pool of pan-Germanic common phrases (such as *bannus, fredum, leudes, mallum, weregeldum*, etc.).[43] Furthermore, the tradition of legal writing has to be understood as a very

39 Holder-Egger and Waitz, *Einhardi Vita Karoli Magni*, 33; Ubl, 'Die erste Leges-Reform Karls des Großen,' 75–8; Wormald, *Making of English Law*, 46.

40 Ubl, 'Die erste Leges-Reform Karls des Großen', 78.

41 There is only a very small set of words with uncertain origin that cannot be traced back to an Indo-European provenience, such as Germ. **aplu-*, OHG. *apful*, ONord. *epli*, for which it has been suggested that it either descends from an inherited word, or shows characteristics of a loan word. See Friedrich Kluge, *Etymologisches Wörterbuch der deutschen Sprache* (Berlin and New York: 2011), 53.

42 Klaus von See, 'Altnordische Rechtswörter. Philologische Studien zur Rechtsauffassung und Rechtsgesinnung der Germanen', *Hermaea. Neue Folge 16* (Tübingen: 1964), 2.

43 Stefan Sonderegger, 'Die ältesten Schichten einer germanischen Rechtssprache. Ein Beitrag zur Quellensystematik', in *Festschrift Karl Siegfried Bader. Rechtsgeschichte, Rechtssprache, Rechtsarchäologie, rechtliche Volkskunde*, ed. Ferdinand Elsner and Wilhelm Ruoff (Zürich: 1965), 419–38, esp. 428–30.

conservative literary genre. Putative old word forms can be found in younger manuscripts, as the scribes did not lightly change original terms.[44]

The integration of vernacular vocabulary into the Latin texts of the *Leges Barbarorum* was accomplished in various ways. The method of embedding also helps determine the functional relationship between Latin and vernacular. Vernacular words potentially occur fully interlaced in the Latin syntax without any visible differentiation between the two tongues, in spite of the etymological disparity. They can either be presented with a German or a Latin inflection:

> *Lex Baiuvariorum* cap. 8.2:
> Si servus hoc fecerit et interfectus cum libera in extraneo fuerit thoro, XX sold. in suo damno minuetur ipsius coniugis *uueragelt*; cetera vero quae remanent, dominus eius cogatur solvere, usque dum repletus fuerit numerus sceleris conpositionis.[45]
>
> If a slave does this and is killed with a freewoman in another's marriage bed, let the *wergild* of that wife be diminished by twenty solidi for her damages; however, let his master be compelled to pay what remains until the amount of the compensation is paid.[46]

Uueragelt is a Germanic word without any display of Latinization. It is presented in its vernacular word form. As a frequently used legal term, it is to be assumed that *uueragelt* nevertheless did not stand out in a way that would have needed any further explanation.[47]

> *Pactus Legis Salicae* cap. 54.2:
> Si quis *sacebarone* aut *obgrafionem* occiderit, qui puer regius fuerit, xiim din. qui f[aciunt] sol[idos] ccc culp[abilis] iudic[etur].[48]

---

44 Tiefenbach, 'Volkssprachige Wörter', 962.

45 *Lex Baiwariorum*, edited by E. de Schwind, MGH LL nat. Germ. I, V, 2 (Hannover: 1926), 354.

46 Translation from *Laws of the Alamans and Bavarians*, trans. Theodore John Rivers (Philadelphia: 1977), 138.

47 Ruth Schmidt-Wiegand, 'Wergeld', in *Germanische Altertumskunde Online* (Berlin and Boston: 2006), at <http://www.degruyter.com/view/GAO/RGA_4861> (accessed 12 January, 2016).

48 *Pactus Legis Salicae*, edited by Karl Augustus Eckhardt, MGH LL nat. Germ. V, 1 (Hannover: 1962), 204.

> If anyone kills a *herald* or a *count*, who is a servant of the king, let him be held liable, if it can be proven that he did this, for 12,000 denarii, which make 300 solidi.[49]

Sacebaro 'herald'[50] and *obgrafionem* 'count'[51] both have Germanic origins, but as a result of their early entry into Latin as loanwords, they both have adapted to the surrounding syntactic context.[52] As Franco-Latin blended, these words were provided with a suitable inflection. To remedy the language gap of non-German speakers in a primarily Romanic population, a context-based paraphrase is given: the comment 'qui puer regius fuerit' shows that *sacebaro* and *obgrafio* had obviously been regarded as foreign words, requiring further explanation for at least one part of the audience. In some cases, it is not possible to decide on whether the word form is German or Latin.

> *Leges Alamannorum* cap. 46:
> De feminis autem liberis, si extra *marcha* vendita fuerit, revocet eam ad pristinam libertatem et cum 80 solidis conponat.[53]

> If, however, anyone sells a freewoman outside the *borders*, let him restore her former freedom to her and compensate with eighty solidi.[54]

Marcha is clearly to be identified as a German word by its phonological representation; the sound shifts from *k* to *ch*. The word form could be a German nominative or accusative singular but it could be an uninflected Latin feminine ending as well. There is no way to tell with certainty.

In all three examples just mentioned, the vernacular words function as phrases within the Latin text regardless of whether or not they are integrated into the syntax. Vernacular words can substitute Latin phrases, as in *marcha*, or they can form an equivalent to a Latin clause, as in *obgrafio* and *sacebaro*. A special type of these equivalent structures even shows an explicit marking

---

49 Translation from *Laws of the Salian and Ripuarian Franks*, trans. Theodore John Rivers (New York: 1986), 101.

50 Ruth Schmidt-Wiegand, 'Sakebaro', in *Germanische Altertumskunde Online* (Berlin and Boston: 2004), at <http://www.degruyter.com/view/GAO/RGA_6436> (accessed 12 January, 2016).

51 DRW, X, 197–8.

52 Tiefenbach, 'Volkssprachige Wörter', 961.

53 *Leges Alamannorum*, 106.

54 For the translation, see *Laws of the Alamans and Bavarians*, 82.

of code-switching.[55] This manner of insertion is mostly used when referring to specialized terminology that is assigned to a specific dialect or technical language.[56] The different ways of marking the vernacular in the Latin text are analysed in the LegIT database and are annotated in detail. About seventy types of integration marker have been identified so far. Besides the marking of a symmetrical relation that is well known from the Glosses (*id/hoc est*), the most common expressions include elements of oral reference like *vocamus, vocant* or *dicimus, dicunt*, and so on.

Such characterisations recall the use of real, spoken language. In fact, this is the highest degree of actual speech that we can get for the Old High German period.[57] The *quod baiuuarii … dicunt* marking, for example, categorizes vernacular inserts as Bavarian tribal language in the *Lex Baiuvariorum*, in contrast to common Frankish terms without a specific introduction that are used in multiple tribal laws, such as the examples mentioned above.

> *Lex Baiuvariorum* cap. 19.2:
> Si quis liberum occiderit furtivo modo et in flumine eiecerit vel in talem locum eiecerit, ut cadaver reddere non quiverit, *quod Baiuuarii murdrida dicunt*, inprimis cum XL sold conponat eo quod funus ad dignas obsequias reddere non valet; postea vero cum suo weregeldo conponat.[58]
>
> If anyone kills a freeman in a secret manner and throws him into a river or throws him into such a place that the corpse cannot be recovered, *which the Bavarians call murdrida*, firstly let him compensate with forty solidi, since he cannot recover the corpse for a worthy burial. After that, however, let him compensate with the wergild.[59]

The German word *murdrida* 'murder'[60] must be considered primary, as it derives from an archaic early Germanic legal tradition, and the Latin text around it merely reflects an attempt to represent the predication. Since there is no

55 Prinz, 'Vergessene Wörter', 305.
56 Tiefenbach, 'Volkssprachige Wörter', 962ff.
57 Gabriele von Olberg, *Die Bezeichnung für soziale Stände, Schichten und Gruppen in den Leges Barbarorum* (Berlin and New York: 1991), 172.
58 *Lex Baiwariorum*, 455.
59 For the translation, see *Laws of the Alamans and Bavarians*, 167.
60 Eckhard Meineke and Andreas Roth, 'Mord und Mordbrand', in *Germanische Altertumskunde Online* (Berlin, and Boston: 2002), at <http://www.degruyter.com/view/GAO/RGA_3786> (accessed 12 January, 2016).

single Latin word that perfectly fits the Germanic legal term, a circumstantial construction of paraphrases has to concern the multiple aspects in the Latin translation. To be qualified as a case of *murdrida*, besides the main aspect of homicide, it is necessary that the offender tries to conceal his crime, abducts the victim's body, and makes it impossible eventually to extradite the corpse.[61]

> *Pactus Legis Salicae* cap 41.10:
> Si quis ⟨uero⟩ Romanum tributarium occiderit ⟨cui fuerit adprobatum⟩, *mallobergo uualaleodi* sunt, MM(D) denarios qui faciunt solidos LXII (semis) culpabilis iudicetur.[62]
>
> If anyone kills a Roman taxpayer, *known in the Malberg* [the language of the court] *as uualaleodi*, let him be held liable, if it can be proven that he did this, for 2000 denarii, which make 62 solidi.[63]

Uuala(h) is a Germanic term for Romanic people;[64] *leod* 'human, man' had long been used not only for a person, but also metaphorically for the monetary fine of a homicide.[65] The introduction *mallobergo* is commonly used in the *Lex Salica* to label technical legal language. That means *uualaleodi* has to be a declaration of a crime in court. It is the *terminus technicus* for the murder of a Roman person.

In summary, the various ways of integrating vernacular into the Latin text produce a very inconsistent picture. Germanic words either kept their vernacular inflection or received a Latin ending. Of course, the age of a word is a consideration to be kept in mind. Latin and Germanic dialects mutually influenced each other, and processes of borrowing can be detected in both directions. A Frankish commonplace like *ueragelt* did not need any further explanation, not even in the seventh century; conversely, if a certain aspect or

---

61 Andreas Deutsch, 'Mord und Mannschlacht im Mittelalter—Zur Terminologie der Tötungsdelikte in vornehmlich frühmittelalterlichen Quellen', *Sprachwissenschaft* 39, no. 3 (2014), 343–70.

62 *Pactus Legis Salicae*, 157.

63 The translation follows *Laws of the Salian and Ripuarian Franks*, 87, modified by Jenny Benham.

64 Frank Heidermanns, 'Leiche', in *Germanische Altertumskunde Online* (Berlin and Boston: 2001), at http://www.degruyter.com/view/GAO/RGA_3303 (accessed 11 January, 2016.

65 Olberg, *Die Bezeichnung für soziale Stände*, 68ff.; Hermann Reichert, 'Leudes', in *Germanische Altertumskunde Online* (Berlin and Boston: 2001), at http://www.degruyter.com/view/GAO/RGA_3337 (accessed 11 January, 2016).

specific contextual meaning needed pointing out, a paraphrase of a Germanic or Latin word could guarantee its understanding.

Furthermore, a well-known Germanic term did not need any accentuation. The most frequently used vernacular inserts do not have any insertion markers in the Latin text. By contrast, terminology that derives from an archaic oral law tradition, or is assigned to a specific tribe or semantic domain, tends to be marked. In our database, the various kinds of embedding are implemented and can be selected in order to focus on specific dialects, on the explicit differentiation between Latin and the vernacular, or to identify distinct legal vocabulary.

Technical Legal Language

Quite a broad range of thematic fields are covered by the early medieval laws. All *lemmata* are annotated by their semantic domain, and an overview of thematic fields can be seen in the database:

The fields include agriculture, everyday life, architecture, craft, warfare, measurement, medicine, myths and religion, names, legal vocabulary, social structure, and, finally, animals. The subclasses of legal terminology are given in detail: legal personality, punishments, elements of crime, trial procedure, and legal rituals. Indeed, more than 240 terms relevant for the history of law appear in this classification. But this chart only contains the types. The frequency of word use ranges from *hapax legomena* on one end, to Frankish commonplaces at the other, with several hundreds of tokens that can be counted several times in several *Leges* texts. *Fredum* (the pacification due that has to be paid to the duke as a fine for the breach of law), for example, appears as the most common vernacular word in the Frankish charters.[66]

The *Lemma* page provides information on morphological structure, dictionary entries, various forms of appearance, and semantic classification. The database also provides links to dictionaries like the DRW (Dictionary of Historical German and West-Germanic Legal Terms), as well as to digital versions of the original documents.

Fredum (as a type) is detected up to nine times in the *Lex Baiuvariorum* and seven times in the *Lex Alamannorum* per every manuscript. After having evaluated eighty-five manuscripts of these two tribal laws, we recorded more

66 Heinrich Tiefenbach, *Studien zu Wörtern volkssprachiger Herkunft in karolingischen Königsurkunden. Ein Beitrag zum Wortschatz der Diplome Lothars I und Lothars II* (Munich: 1973), 56–60.

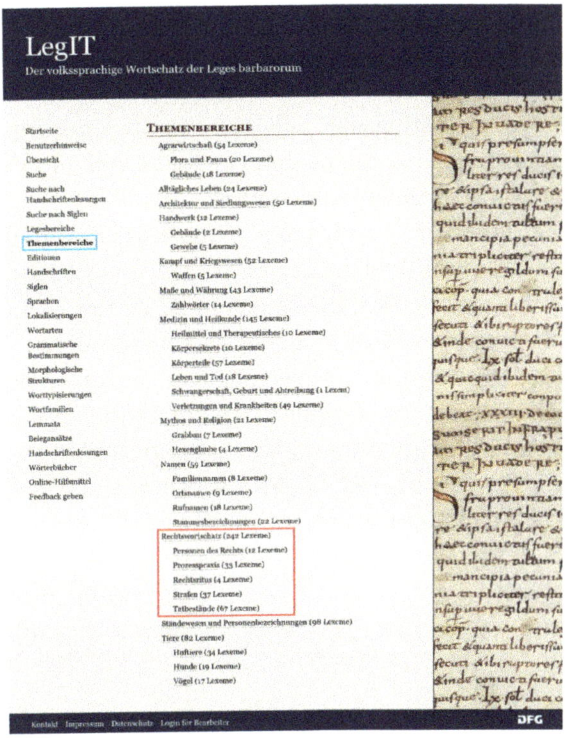

FIGURE 9.2
Overview: thematic fields.
Note: <http://db.legit.ahd-portal.germ-ling.uni-bamberg.de/topics> (accessed 14 January, 2016).

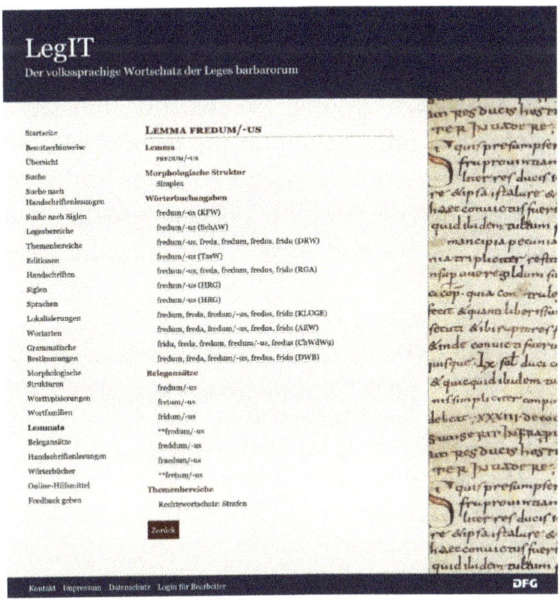

FIGURE 9.3
Overview: Lemma.
Note: <http://db.legit.ahd-portal.germ-ling.uni-bamberg.de/lemmas/5> (accessed 14 January, 2016).

than 500 tokens in various word forms. The word form leads to single tokens, the actual occurrences in the manuscripts. The analysis of manuscripts and information about the codices are of major importance as every written spelling must be interpreted by considering not only the manuscripts, but also their temporal and local genesis. Therefore, the links to digital versions of manuscripts are included (if the codices are available online).

Some written records are unique and occur only once in the entire recorded tradition. Not even one medieval manuscript of the *Lex Frisionum*, for example, has survived from the medieval period—the earliest record of its text is an edition dating to the sixteenth century.[67] Most of its vernacular words only survive to the present through this edition. Conversely, the incompletely preserved *Edictum Rothari* in the manuscript St Gallen, Stiftsbibliothek 730 is the oldest extant copy of the medieval Germanic law.[68] Considering its age, the manuscript represents the oldest document available for a substantial amount of vernacular language, and it also contains the first technical terms.

> *Leges Langobardorum* cap. 14:
> Et si expolia de ipso mortuo tulerit, id est *plodraub*, conponat octugenta solidus.[69]
>
> If they plunder the dead body, that is if they commit *plodraub*, each shall pay eighty solidi as composition for this.[70]

Plodraub, for example, offers the first record of both *plod* (NHG. Blut, Engl. blood),[71] and *raub* (NHG. *Raub*, Engl. *robbery*).[72]

The 'reading' page contains semantics, reading peculiarities, the Latin equivalent, grammatical determination, information on the manuscript and the paragraph within the law where the word is found. The Lombard term *ploderaub*, furthermore, gives an example of how different laws use different legal expressions for a certain crime. The *Edictum Rothari*, preceding the *Leges*

67 Herold, *Originum ac Germanicarum Antiquitatum Libri*.

68 Gustav Scherrer, *Verzeichniss der Handschriften der Stiftsbibliothek von St. Gallen* (Halle: 1875), 236–8. A permalink to the digitized manuscript can be found at <http://www.e-codices.unifr.ch/en/list/one/csg/0730> (accessed 14 January, 2016).

69 *Leges Langobardorum*, edited by George Henry Pertz, MGH LL IV (Hannover: 1868), 455.

70 For the translation, see *The Lombard Laws*, trans. Katherine Fischer Drew (Philadelphia: 1973), 55.

71 KFW, I, 1234–9.

72 Andreas Roth, 'Raub', in *Germanische Altertumskunde Online* (Berlin and Boston: 2003), at <http://www.degruyter.com/view/GAO/RGA_4532> (accessed 11 January, 2016).

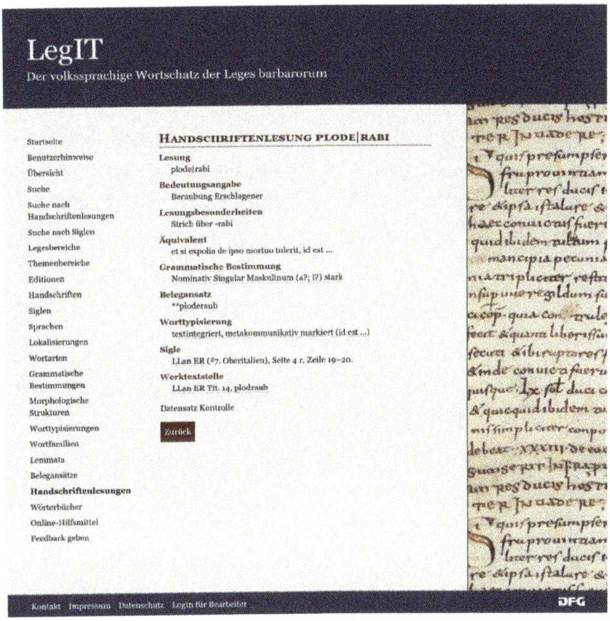

FIGURE 9.4
'Reading' page: plode|rabi. Note: <http://db.legit.ahd-portal.germ-ling.uni-bamberg.de/script_readings/10115> (accessed 14 January, 2016).

Langobardorum, uses *rairaub* (*Edictum Rothari*, cap. 16) for the robbery of a corpse and can be compared with Old Frisian *hrêrâf* (*Lex Frisionum* Add. 3, 75).[73] The Nordic laws instead refer to the same crime by using *valrov* (Gulaþíngslög 178), and under the influence of Nordic models, *walreaf* occurs in Old Saxon lawbooks.[74] *Walaraupa* of the Bavarian Lex (*Lex Baiuvariorum* 19, 4) is etymologically related, but does not refer to action of corpse-robbery, but rather to its object, namely 'the clothing of a dead person'. Trans-Germanic interactions appear alongside the attempts to use expressions that derived from their own legal tradition.[75]

---

73 Heinrich Brunner, *Deutsche Rechtsgeschichte*, vol. 2 (Leipzig: 1892), 145.

74 F. Liebermann, *Die Gesetze der Angelsachsen. Volume 3. Einleitung zu jedem Stück; Erklärungen zu einzelnen Stellen* (Cambridge: 2015 (orig. 1916)), 230. The perspicuous influence of a Nordic model to the younger Old Saxon terminology is stated in Brunner, *Deutsche Rechtsgeschichte*, II, 684.

75 Ruth Schmidt-Wiegand, 'Die volkssprachigen Wörter der Leges barbarorum als Ausdruck sprachlicher Interferenz', in *Stammesrecht und Volkssprache. Ausgewählte Aufsätze zu den Leges barbarorum. Festgabe für Ruth Schmidt-Wiegand zum 1.1.1991*, ed. Dagmar Hüpper and Claudieter Schott (Weinheim: 1991), 181–212, at 193.

Problems and Possibilities of Translating Medieval Law

One of the main problems of dealing with the vernacular of early medieval legal manuscripts is the accurate translation of Germanic words into modern German. Besides the familiar problems posed by any translation from historical sources, the genre of legal sources means one not only has to overcome the cultural gap, but one must also take into consideration the characteristics of technical legal language.

> *Lex Frisionum* cap. 9.1:
> de *farlegani*. si foemina quaelibet homini cuilibet fornicando se miscuerit, componat ad partem regis weregildum suum.[76]
>
> On *fornication*. If a woman fornicates with another man, she pays to the king her wergild.[77]

Farlegani in the headline is a complex word with a verbal basis *liggen* (NHG. *liegen*; Engl. *to lay*). It is common to all Germanic dialects.[78] The prefix is *far-* (NHG. *ver-*, Engl. *for-*).[79] Both constituents can easily be translated into present-day language to produce the following expression: *verliegen*. Using the prefix *ver-*, modern German, besides other semantic functions, describes an expression of opposition, as in *vermessen* 'to measure something wrong', *versprechen* 'to make a slip of the tongue', or *verfahren* 'to lose one's way'. *Verliegen* thus means something like 'to lay wrong'. But this word remains an inadequate translation, which does not match the sociocultural background and legal meaning of *farlegani* all that well. Looking at the Latin context, the proper meaning emerges clearly: *si foemina quaelibet homini cuilibet fornicando se miscuerit* … ('if a woman fornicates with another man').[80] In medieval legal practice, the term *verliegen* means *fornication*.[81] A literal reproduction of the word, which preserves its word formation into the modern German *verliegen*, loses its main semantic aspect because the sexual connotation of *liegen* is no

---

76 *Lex Frisionum*, edited by George Henry Pertz, MGH LL III, 4 (Hannover: 1863), 664.

77 Translated from the Latin by Jenny Benham, in conjunction with the translation published at <http://www.keesn.nl/lex/lex_en_text.htm> (accessed 30 August, 2016).

78 KFW, V, 919.

79 Friedrich Kluge, *Etymologisches Wörterbuch der deutschen Sprache* (Berlin and New York: 2011), 949ff.

80 DRW, III, 425–6.

81 KFW, V, 77.

longer given, and nobody would think of it as a punishable crime. Even though the Germanic elements have counterparts in present-day language, the translator must ignore them, and search out an appropriate legal term instead. The translation of NHG. 'Unzucht'/Engl. 'fornication' breaks the principle of phonological continuance, but can be seen as a present-day semantic correlate to what was predicated by the medieval term *farlegani*.

The main aspects of translating early medieval legal terminology can be described by two conflicting principles: on the one hand, the attempt to preserve phonological continuance, and, on the other, the consideration of semantic change. Only about twenty per cent of the words of the Old High German have phonological correspondents in the present language.[82] And for those that do, they have most likely undergone significant semantic change. The principles of phonological and morphological continuance must often be abandoned; especially technical language depends on the proper use of its terms. A word like *farlegani* may have a phonological counterpart *verliegen* in the present-day language, but this counterpart does not represent the special meaning the term had in its original context, and another lexeme is used nowadays to express the term's specific meaning.

Conclusion

The Bamberg LegIT project collects all Germanic linguistic elements surviving in the medieval legal manuscripts of the *Leges Barbarorum* into a relational database. Vernacular inserts are analysed grammatically, and the user will find etymological information and references to the relevant literature. The linguistic material provides some of the earliest texts of the written Germanic legal tradition. Phenomena like code-switching from Latin to the vernacular are evident when Germanic inserts occur with or without an explicit marking in the Latin syntax. The change of socio-cultural conditions since medieval times has brought about a change of nomenclature as well. Translating technical language from the medieval *Leges Barbarorum* must consider the

82 Ingeborg Köppe, 'Das Fortleben des althochdeutschen Wortschatzes im Neuhochdeutschen und die Bedeutungsermittlung im Althochdeutschen Wörterbuch', in *Bedeutungserfassung und Bedeutungsbeschreibung in historischen und dialektologischen Wörterbüchern. Beiträge zu einer Arbeitstagung der deutschsprachigen Wörterbücher, Projekte an Akademien und Universitäten vom 7. bis 9. März 1996 anläßlich des 150jährigen Jubiläums der Sächsischen Akademie der Wissenschaften zu Leipzig*, ed. Rudolf Große (Leipzig: 1998), 57.

circumstances of that very period, with the aim to identify contemporary equivalents. The compiled data is fundamental to subsequent works on lexicographical and grammatical studies of the Old High German period. It is evident that our research primarily serves historical linguistics, but associated disciplines, such as the history of medicine and the history of law, will also benefit from the LegIT database.

Bibliography

Abbreviations

DRW: Preußische Akademie der Wissenschaften, Deutsche Akademie der Wissenschaften and Heidelberger Akademie der Wissenschaften, editors. *Deutsches Rechtswörterbuch. Wörterbuch der älteren deutschen Rechtssprache*, 13 vols. Weimar: 1932–2014, at <http://www.rzuser.uni-heidelberg.de/~cd2/drw/>.

KFW: Karg-Gasterstädt, Elisabeth and Theodor Frings, editors. *Althochdeutsches Wörterbuch. Bearbeitet aufgrund der von Elias von Steinmeyer hinterlassenen Sammlungen im Auftrag der Sächsischen Akademie der Wissenschaften zu Leipzig*, 7 vols. Berlin: 1952–2016, at <http://awb.saw-leipzig.de/cgi/WBNetz/wbgui_py?sigle=AWB>.

Manuscripts

St. Gallen, Stiftsbibliothek 730, at <http://www.e-codices.unifr.ch/en/list/one/csg/0730>.

Works Cited

Beck, Heinrich, Dieter Geuenich, and Heiko Steuer, editors. *Reallexikon der Germanischen Altertumskunde*, vol. 18: *Landschaftsrecht–Loxstedt*. Berlin and New York: 2001.

Bergmann, Rolf. 'Kulturgeschichtliche Aspekte des althochdeutschen Glossenwortschatzes'. In *Deutsche Wortforschung als Kulturgeschichte. Beiträge des Internationalen Symposiums aus Anlass des 90-jährigen Bestandes der Wörterbuchkanzlei der Österreichischen Akademie der Wissenschaften Wien, 25.-27. September 2003*, edited by Isolde Hausner, Peter Wiesinger, and Katharina Korecky-Kröll, 49–76. Vienna: 2005.

Bibliotheca legum regni Francorum manuscripta, edited by Karl Ubl, assisted by Dominik Trump and Daniela Schulz. Cologne: 2012, online at <http://leges.uni-koeln.de>.

Braune, Wilhelm and Ingo Reiffenstein. *Althochdeutsche Grammatik I: Laut- und Formenlehre*. Tübingen: 2004.

Brunner, Heinrich. *Deutsche Rechtsgeschichte*, vol. 2. Leipzig: 1892.

Davis, Jennifer R. *Charlemagne's Practice of Empire*. Cambridge: 2015.

Deutsch, Andreas. 'Mord und Mannschlacht im Mittelalter—Zur Terminologie der Tötungsdelikte in vornehmlich frühmittelalterlichen Quellen'. *Sprachwissenschaft* 39, no. 3 (2014): 343–370.

Esders, Stefan. *Römische Rechtstradition und merowingisches Königtum. Zum Rechtscharakter politischer Herrschaft in Burgund im 6. und 7. Jahrhundert*. Göttingen: 1997.

Frassetto, Michael. *Encyclopedia of Barbarian Europe: Society in Transformation*. Santa Barbara, Denver, and Oxford: 2003.

Germanische Altertumskunde Online. Kulturgeschichte bis ins Frühmittelalter—Archäologie, Geschichte, Philologie. Berlin and Boston: 2010, at <https://www.degruyter.com/view/db/gao>.

Glauch, Sonja. 'Notker III. von St. Gallen'. In *Althochdeutsche und altsächsische Literatur. Ein Handbuch*, edited by Rolf Bergmann, 293–315. Berlin and New York: 2013.

Hähnchen, Susanne. *Rechtsgeschichte. Von der Römischen Antike bis zur Neuzeit*. Heidelberg, etc.: 2012.

Hartmann, Wilfried. 'Karl der Große und das Recht'. In *Karl der Grosse und sein Nachwirken. 1200 Jahre Kultur und Wissenschaft in Europa/Charlemagne and his Heritage. 1200 Years of Civilization and Science in Europe*, vol. 1: *Wissen und Weltbild/Scholarship, Worldview and Understanding*, edited by Paul Leo Butzer, Max Kerner, and Wolfgang Oberschelp, 173–92. Turnhout: 1997.

Heidermanns, Frank. 'Leiche'. In *Germanische Altertumskunde Online*.

Herold, Basilius Johannes (Ioannis). *Originum ac Germanicarum Antiquitatum Libri, Leges videlicet, Salicae, Allemannorum, Saxonum, Angliorum, Thuringorum, Burgundionum, Francorum, Ripuariae, Boioriorum, Vuestphalorum, Vuerinorum, Frisionum, Langobardorum, Theutonum etc*. Basel: 1557, at <http://www.mdz-nbn-resolving.de/urn/resolver.pl?urn=urn:nbn:de:bvb:12–bsb10144836–2>.

Holder-Egger, Oswald and Georg Waitz, editors. *Einhardi Vita Karoli Magni*. Hannover and Leipzig: 1911.

Hüpper-Dröge, Dagmar. 'Schutz- und Angriffswaffen nach den Leges und verwandten fränkischen Rechtsquellen'. In *Wörter und Sachen im Lichte der Bezeichnungsforschung*, edited by Ruth Schmidt-Wiegand, 107–27. Berlin and New York: 1981.

Hüpper-Dröge, Dagmar. *Schild und Speer. Waffen und ihre Bezeichnungen im frühen Mittelalter*. Frankfurt: 1983.

Kampers, Gerd. 'Lex Burgundionum'. In *Reallexikon der Germanischen Altertumskunde*, vol. 18, 315–17.

Kluge, Friedrich. *Etymologisches Wörterbuch der deutschen Sprache*. Berlin and New York: 2011.

Köppe, Ingeborg. 'Das Fortleben des althochdeutschen Wortschatzes im Neuhochdeutschen und die Bedeutungsermittlung im Althochdeutschen Wörterbuch'.

In *Bedeutungserfassung und Bedeutungsbeschreibung in historischen und dialektologischen Wörterbüchern. Beiträge zu einer Arbeitstagung der deutschsprachigen Wörterbücher, Projekte an Akademien und Universitäten vom 7. bis 9. März 1996 anläßlich des 150jährigen Jubiläums der Sächsischen Akademie der Wissenschaften zu Leipzig*, edited by Rudolf Große, 57–64. Leipzig: 1998.

Koschaker, Paul. *Europa und das römische Recht*. Munich: 1947.

Krah, Astrid. 'Das Bild der Sozialgeschichte in den Leges barbarorum'. In *Von den Leges Barbarorum bis zum ius barbarum des Nationalsozialismus. Festschrift für Hermann Nehlsen zum 70. Geburtstag*, edited by Hans-Georg Hermann, *et al.*, 77–98. Cologne etc.: 2008.

Kroeschell, Karl. *Studien zum frühen und mittelalterlichen deutschen Recht*. Berlin: 1995.

Kroeschell, Karl. *Deutsche Rechtsgeschichte. Band 1: Bis 1250*. Cologne and Vienna: 2008.

Laws of the Alamans and Bavarians, translated by Theodore John Rivers. Philadelphia: 1977.

Laws of the Salian and Ripuarian Franks, translated by Theodore John Rivers. New York: 1986.

Leges Alamannorum, edited by Karl Lehmann, 2nd edn. rev. Karl Augustus Eckhardt. MGH LL nat. Germ. V, 1. Hannover: 1966.

Leges Langobardorum, edited by Georg Henry Pertz. MGH LL IV. Hannover: 1868.

Lesaffer, Randall. *European Legal History: A Cultural and Political Perspective*. Cambridge: 2010.

Lex Baiwariorum, edited by E. de Schwind. MGH, Legum Sectio I, LL nat. Germ. I, V, 2. Hannover: 1926.

Lex Frisionum, edited by Georg Henry Pertz. MGH LL III, 4. Hannover: 1863.

Lex Frisionum. Text and translation, translated by Kees C. Nieuwenhuijsen (no date) at <http://www.keesn.nl/lex/lex_en_text.htm>.

Lieberman, Felix. *Die Gesetze der Angelsachsen, vol. 3: Einleitung zu jedem Stück; Erklärungen zu einzelnen Stellen*. Cambridge: 2015.

Liebs, Detlef. 'Lex Romana Burgundionum'. In *Reallexikon der Germanischen Altertumskunde*, vol. 18, 322–23a.

Lühr, Rosemarie. 'Zum Sprachtod einer Rechtssprache: Zwei ausgestorbene Wörter aus der Lex Baiuvariorum'. In *Germanische Rechts- und Trümmersprachen*, edited by Heinrich Beck, 45–68. Berlin and New York: 1989.

Meineke, Birgit. 'Über die Verfahren der Bedeutungsermittlung am volkssprachigen Wortschatz der Leges'. In *Bedeutungserfassung und Bedeutungsbeschreibung in historischen und dialektologischen Wörterbüchern. Beiträge zu einer Arbeitstagung der deutschsprachigen Wörterbücher, Projekte an Akademien und Universitäten vom 7. bis 9. März 1996 anläßlich des 150jährigen Jubiläums der Sächsischen Akademie der Wissenschaften zu Leipzig*, edited by Rudolf Große, 65–72. Leipzig: 1998.

Meineke, Eckhard and Andreas Roth. 'Mord und Mordbrand'. In *Germanische Altertumskunde Online*.

Niederhellmann, Annette. 'Heilkundliches in den Leges. Die Schädelverletzungen und ihre Bezeichnungen'. In *Wörter und Sachen im Lichte der Bezeichnungsforschung*, edited by Ruth Schmidt-Wiegand, 74–90. Berlin and New York: 1981.

Niederhellmann, Annette. *Arzt und Heilkunde in den frühmittelalterlichen Leges. Eine wort- und sachkundliche Untersuchung*. Berlin and New York: 1983.

Olberg, Gabriele von. *Freie, Nachbarn und Gefolgsleute. Volkssprachige Bezeichnungen aus dem sozialen Bereich in den frühmittelalterlichen Leges*. Frankfurt: 1983.

Olberg, Gabriele von. *Die Bezeichnung für soziale Stände, Schichten und Gruppen in den Leges Barbarorum*. Berlin and New York: 1991.

Pactus Legis Salicae, edited by Karl Augustus Eckhardt. MGH, Legum Sectio I, LL nat. Germ. V, 1. Hannover: 1962.

Petit, Carlos. 'Leges Visigothorum'. In *Handwörterbuch zur deutschen Rechtsgeschichte* (*HRGdigital*), edited by Albrecht Cordes, Heiner Lück, and Dieter Werkmüller, 697–99 at <http://www.hrgdigital.de/id/leges_visigothorum/stichwort.html>.

Pohl, Walter. 'Leges Langobardorum'. In *Reallexikon der Germanischen Altertumskunde*, vol. 18, 208–13a.

Prinz, Michael. 'Vergessene Wörter. Frühe volkssprachliche Lexik in lateinischen Urkunden und Amtsbüchern'. *Jahrbuch für germanistische Sprachgeschichte* 1 (2010): 292–322.

Rainer, Johannes Michael. *Das römische Recht in Europa. Von Justinian zum BGB*. Vienna: 2012.

Reichert, Hermann. 'Leudes'. In *Germanische Altertumskunde Online*.

Riecke, Jörg. *Die Frühgeschichte der mittelalterlichen medizinischen Fachsprache im Deutschen. Band I: Untersuchungen, Band II: Wörterbuch*. Berlin and New York: 2004.

Roth, Andreas. 'Raub'. In *Germanische Altertumskunde Online*.

Scheibelreiter, Georg. *Die barbarische Gesellschaft. Mentalitätsgeschichte der europäischen Achsenzeit* (*5.–8. Jahrhundert*). Darmstadt: 1999.

Scherrer, Gustav. *Verzeichniss der Handschriften der Stiftsbibliothek von St. Gallen*. Halle: 1875.

Schmidt-Wiegand, Ruth. 'Lex Francorum Chamavorum'. In *Reallexikon der Germanischen Altertumskunde*, vol. 18, 317b–18b. New York and Berlin: 2001.

Schmidt-Wiegand, Ruth. 'Lex Frisionum'. In *Reallexikon der Germanischen Altertumskunde*, vol. 18, 318b–20a. New York and Berlin: 2001.

Schmidt-Wiegand, Ruth. 'Sakebaro'. In *Germanische Altertumskunde Online*.

Schmidt-Wiegand, Ruth. 'Wergeld'. In *Germanische Altertumskunde Online*.

Schmidt-Wiegand, Ruth. 'Die volkssprachigen Wörter der Leges barbarorum als Ausdruck sprachlicher Interferenz'. In *Stammesrecht und Volkssprache. Ausgewählte*

Aufsätze zu den Leges barbarorum. Festgabe für Ruth Schmidt-Wiegand zum 1.1.1991, edited by Dagmar Hüpper and Clausdieter Schott, 181–212. Weinheim: 1991 (orig. 1979).

Schmidt-Wiegand, Ruth. 'Deutsche Sprachgeschichte und Rechtsgeschichte bis zum Ende des Mittelalters'. In *Sprachgeschichte. Ein Handbuch zur Geschichte der deutschen Sprache und ihrer Erforschung*, subvolume 1, edited by Werner Besch, Anne Betten, Oskar Reichmann, and Stefan Sonderegger, 72–87. Berlin and New York: 1998.

Schmidt-Wiegand, Ruth. 'Sprache, Recht, Rechtssprache bei Franken und Alemannen vom 6. bis zum 8. Jahrhundert'. In *Leges, gentes, regna. Zur Rolle von germanischen Rechtsgewohnheiten und lateinischer Schrifttradition bei der Ausbildung der frühmittelalterlichen Rechtskultur*, edited by Gerhard Dilcher and Eva-Marie Distler, 141–58. Berlin: 2006.

Schott, Clausdieter. 'Der Stand der Leges-Forschung'. In *Frühmittelalterliche Studien. Jahrbuch des Instituts für Frühmittelalterforschung der Universität Münster*, edited by Wolfram Drews and Christel Meier, 29–55. Berlin and New York: 1979.

Schwab, Vincenz. 'Volkssprachiger Wortschatz in den oberdeutschen Leges—Altalemannisch und Altbairisch'. *Sprachwissenschaft* 39, no. 3 (2014): 266–8.

See, Klaus. 'Altnordische Rechtswörter. Philologische Studien zur Rechtsauffassung und Rechtsgesinnung der Germanen'. *Hermaea. Neue Folge 16*. Tübingen: 1964.

Sonderegger, Stefan. 'Die ältesten Schichten einer germanischen Rechtssprache. Ein Beitrag zur Quellensystematik'. In *Festschrift Karl Siegfried Bader. Rechtsgeschichte, Rechtssprache, Rechtsarchäologie, rechtliche Volkskunde*, edited by Ferdinand Elsner and Wilhelm Ruoff, 419–38. Zürich, 1965.

Splett, Jochen. *Althochdeutsches Wörterbuch. Analyse der Wortfamilienstrukturen des Althochdeutschen, zugleich Grundlegung einer zukünftigen Strukturgeschichte des deutschen Wortschatzes. I,1–II.* Berlin and New York: 1993.

Stein, Peter. *Roman Law in European History*. Cambridge: 1999.

Stricker, Stefanie. 'Definitorische Vorklärungen'. In *Die althochdeutsche und altsächsische Glossographie. Ein Handbuch*, vol. 1, edited by Rolf Bergmann and Stefanie Stricker, 20–32. Berlin and New York: 2009.

Stricker, Stefanie and Anette Kremer. 'Das Bamberger LegIT-Projekt. Zur Erfassung des volkssprachigen Wortschatzes der Leges barbarorum in einer Datenbank'. *Sprachwissenschaft* 39, no. 3 (2014): 237–63.

Stricker, Stefanie, Anette Kremer, and Vincenz Schwab. 'Der volkssprachige Wortschatz der Leges barbarorum. Zum Projekt einer Online-Datenbank'. In *Weiland Wörter Welten—Akten der 6. Internationalen Konferenz zur Historischen Lexikographie und Lexikologie (Jena, 25.–27. Juli 2012). Whilom Worlds of Words—Proceedings of the 6th International Conference on Historical Lexicography and Lexicology (Jena, 25.–27. July 2012)*, edited by Bettina Bock and Maria Kozianka, 285–94. Hamburg: 2014.

The Lombard Laws, translated by Katherine Fischer Drew. Philadelphia: 1973.

Tiefenbach, Heinrich. *Studien zu Wörtern volkssprachiger Herkunft in karolingischen Königsurkunden. ein Beitrag zum Wortschatz der Diplome Lothars I und Lothars II*. Munich: 1973.

Tiefenbach, Heinrich. 'Volkssprachige Wörter innerhalb lateinischer Texte. Rechtstexte: Leges, Kapitularien, Urkunden'. In *Die althochdeutsche und altsächsische Glossographie*, vol. 1, edited by Rolf Bergmann and Stefanie Stricker, 958–75. Berlin and New York: 2009.

Ubl, Karl. *'Die erste Leges-Reform Karls des Großen'. In Das Gesetz—The Law—La Loi*, edited by Andreas Speer and Guy Guldentops, 75–92. Berlin and New York: 2014.

Wormald, Patrick. *The Making of English Law: King Alfred to the Twelfth Century, Volume I: Legislation and its Limits*. Oxford: 2001.

CHAPTER 10

'And Since We are No Lawyers, We Will Void the Lawsuit with Battle Axes'! Voiding a Lawsuit in Old Icelandic Procedural Law

Werner Schäfke

Introduction

One of the well-known peculiarities of the legal system that existed in the Icelandic Commonwealth was that it lacked an executive power.[1] It was one thing for a litigant to be granted justice through a lawsuit, but quite another to obtain that justice: any money or property adjudged to a litigant would have to be wrested from the hands of the opposing party, and this could include a demonstration of power or the use of brute force. Litigants sought out powerful chieftains, not only to enact a judgment, but also to litigate their lawsuits.[2] Judgments were always delivered by panels of judges. In a society without an executive power to protect the law, judges could be threatened by a chieftain's power. This practice was mentioned in many provisions against the disruption of court proceedings found in the law book *Grágás*, and in the many saga episodes that centre on disrupted court proceedings. Another method of using social capital to influence court proceedings, oath-helping, apparently did not exist in the Old Icelandic legal system, as no source names this institution, which was practiced in such places as medieval England, Germany, and Denmark.[3]

The phenomenon in question is thus a type of threat, which is a means of negotiating the perception of one's power. It is more explicit than other types of threat in Old Icelandic literature, as it reveals the character's power resources rather than implying any threatening character traits, such as establishing a

1 See, for example, William Ian Miller, *Bloodtaking and Peacemaking: Feud, Law, and Society in Saga Iceland* (Chicago: 1990), esp. 221–57, with references to further literature.

2 *Ibid.*

3 John H. Baker, *An Introduction to English Legal History*, 3rd edn. (London: 1990), 86–8; Hermann Conrad, *Deutsche Rechtsgeschichte, I, Frühzeit und Mittelalter* (Karlsruhe: 1962), 148; *The Danish Medieval Laws: The Laws of Scania, Zealand and Jutland*, ed. and trans. Ditlev Tamm and Helle Vogt (London: 2016), 22–3.

 | DOI 10.1163/9789004375765_012

love for violence in the character.[4] According to legal sources for the Icelandic Commonwealth, the practice of appearing at court with a group of supporters was illegitimate. Nevertheless, descriptions in saga narratives display a mixture of positive and negative depictions of the practice. This raises the question of society's view of this practice during the Icelandic Commonwealth as it is purported in the high medieval sagas of the Icelanders. The phenomenon of the disruption of proceedings is thus central to the understanding of medieval Icelandic discourse on the function of its society, which is not only interesting, but also represents a special case when compared to other Germanic legal systems, which had a monopoly on violence.

Furthermore, it is interesting that this phenomenon, i.e. voiding a case through a demonstration of power, is expressed in sagas by legal phrases that would otherwise indicate the voiding of a lawsuit through legal means: *at ónýta mál/sǫk fyrir e-u* and *at eyða e-u mál*, both of which can be translated as 'to void someone's lawsuit'. This raises the question of how and why illegitimate legal action was expressed by phrases that would, in other contexts, describe a legitimate legal outcome?

The present article analyses the usage of the two phrases that mean 'to void a lawsuit' in both Old Icelandic legal texts and in sagas. Their basic meaning can be reconstructed from the provisions found in the two main manuscripts of the *Grágás* law book, as well from their usage in saga narratives. Building on this, this article analyses the literary discourse on the voiding of cases by chieftains through the demonstration of their power as a means of influencing court proceedings.

While the provisions in *Grágás* mostly concern judges' refusal to hear or continue a lawsuit, the depictions of case-voiding in saga narratives show how courts could be threatened into obeying a chieftain's agenda. I argue that the literary discourse shows less concern with chieftains influencing the legal system through their power, than it does with the righteousness of the literary character concerned. The literary and the legal discourse both discuss the same problem, but from different angles. While the legal discourse is preoccupied with assuring the functioning of the legal system based upon its own rules, the literary discourse focuses instead on the ideal chieftain, one who would use his power to help his allies and ensure justice. This article will demonstrate how both legal and literary texts can function as supplementary elements in

4 Cf. William Ian Miller, 'Threat', in *Feud, Violence and Practice: Essays in Medieval Studies in Honor of Stephen D. White*, ed. Belle S. Tuten and Tracey L. Billado (Farnham: 2010), 9–27, esp. 16–20.

the reconstruction of Icelandic social history, and can, as well, be used to make visible different constructions of this past.

The Sources for Old Icelandic Legal History and Their Source Value

The Old Icelandic legal system can be primarily understood as the legal institutions and the legal provisions of high medieval Icelandic society from the establishment of the General Assembly (Old Icelandic *alþingi*) *ca.*930 until the end of the Commonwealth in 1262, after which time Iceland came under Norwegian, and, later, Danish rule. Following this 'classical' period, the legal system and its provisions underwent significant change, and constitute a 'post-classical' legal period marked by a greater number of sources.

The 'classical' period is characterized by an acephalic society ruled by chieftains (Old Icelandic *goðar*, sg. *goði*), from which no official law survives. The 'post-classical' society was ruled by the Norwegian monarch, whose laws, *Jónsbók*, survive in many manuscripts, including numerous legal amendments and administrative documents. This article, however, will address the 'classical' period, and the argument it presents is this: it was possible to void a case in the Old Icelandic legal system through threatening judges by bringing supporters to a trial. While this apparently was of concern in legal discourse and considered problematic for the functioning of the legal system, literary discourse, on the other hand, maintained that the ends justified the means, and influencing court proceedings through force was sanctioned if it ensured that substantive law prevailed.

There are three primary sources from the 'classical' period of Old Icelandic legal history: legal texts, the Sagas of the Icelanders, and the Contemporary Sagas.[5] Since the Contemporary Sagas do not mention the legal practice examined in this paper, the following comments focus only on the legal texts and the Sagas of the Icelanders.[6] The primary legal text for this period

5 A thorough and concise discussion of different assessments of the value of all sources for the 'classical' period of Old Icelandic law and its legal system can be found in Jón Viðar Sigurðsson, *Chieftains and Power in the Icelandic Commonwealth*, trans. Jean Lundskær-Nielsen (Odense: 1999), 17–38.

6 There is one example in which one of these phrases referred to the legal practice of case-voiding, but the episode in question does not contain any information regarding the mechanics of voiding this particular case. The example can be found in Kristian Kålund, *Sturlunga Saga efter membranen Króksfjardarbók: udfyldt efter Reykjarfjardarbók* (Copenhagen: 1906–1911), 198–9: 'Enn vigs-mal toc sa maðr, er Sigurðr gricr var callaðr, hann var Odds son; ok vard vnytt fyrir honom, oc vrðv engar bætr eptir Illuga' ('And the homicide case was prosecuted by that

is *Grágás*, which is a collection of legal provisions extant in two different redactions found in two manuscripts, Konungsbók (K) and Staðarhólsbók (St).[7] The degree to which the extant provisions reflect valid legal provisions of the Commonwealth is uncertain. The collection in Staðarhólsbók, for example, was probably created in preparation for *Jónsbók*, a legal compilation for Iceland under Norwegian rule, which synthesized Norwegian law with older Icelandic legal provisions that were necessary to take into account the Icelandic conditions.[8]

While the legal provisions found in *Grágás* are not necessarily reliable, the second genre of source is no less problematic: The Sagas of the Icelanders. This group of about three dozen works has been consulted by legal historians for just about everything that would fall under the rubric 'legal culture' and its depiction in literary sources. The Sagas of the Icelanders are a subgenre of the Icelandic sagas. The Icelandic sagas cover a broad range of narrative texts, from historiographical and historical works to hagiographical and heroic legend. The Sagas of the Icelanders narrate the lives of individuals and the histories of important families or entire areas. They usually cover some or most of the period from the settlement of Iceland (*ca.*874) until around 1050; and although the primary setting for the action is Iceland, they include episodes in Norway or in the Viking colonies in the Atlantic Ocean.

The Sagas of the Icelanders employ a very realistic style, which tempts the modern reader to consider them as realistic depictions of conflicts in Icelandic society:

> They told the tales of their people not as history or literature, but as narratives springing from societal relationships. Their stories are about the conflicts and the anxieties inherent in their society.[9]

Following Byock's reasoning, medieval Icelandic society, its conflicts, and the social institutions for their resolution, are depicted realistically in the Sagas

---

man, who was called Sigurðr the Greek, he was the son of Oddr. But he got his case voided, and no compensations were paid for Illugi'). However, contrary to non-violent disruption of proceedings discussed in this example, the Contemporary Sagas tend rather to depict the practice of scattering a court through the use of violence.

7 GKS 1157 fol., Stofnun Árna Magnússonar í íslenskum fræðum, Reykjavik, and AM 334 fol., Stofnun Árna Magnússonar í íslenskum fræðum, Reykjavik.

8 Lena Rohrbach, 'Matrix of the Law? A Material Study of Staðarhólsbók', in *The Power of Book: Medial Approaches to Medieval Nordic Legal Manuscripts*, ed. Lena Rohrbach (Berlin: 2014), 98–128.

9 Jesse L. Byock, *Feud in the Icelandic Saga* (Berkeley: 1982), 38.

of the Icelanders. On the other hand, the Sagas of the Icelanders are—as is any narrative text—implicitly or explicitly biased. They convey a more or less consistent *opinion*[10] on social structure (including a blatantly affirmative stance), which past audiences (i.e. readers and listeners) may have consciously or unconsciously recognized—or failed to recognize altogether. However, by analysing whether or not a certain societal issue is depicted (or omitted) within a particular literary episode, the discursive position of the work in question can be reconstructed.

Beyond the question of value judgments attached to these issues, it remains unclear which specific period of medieval Icelandic history is reflected in these discursive positions. This is no idle question in the study of Old Icelandic literature, since book culture arrived in Iceland only after its Christianisation around the year 1000 with its first cloisters, and the earliest vernacular text in Latin script (the lost law *Hafliðaskrá*) is thought to have been written in the winter of 1117–1118. However, the earliest manuscripts of the Sagas of the Icelanders date from the thirteenth century, which is also thought to be when most sagas were first written down. What earlier oral stages may have existed has been an ongoing debate since the dawn of modern philology.[11] Moreover, the textual history of the Sagas of the Icelanders did not end in the thirteenth century; manuscript transmission continued in the subsequent centuries, well into the early modern period.

It is unclear what types of society and social conflict are reflected in the sagas: those of the ninth to eleventh centuries, when the sagas are set; those of the arrival of book culture in the eleventh to twelfth centuries; those of the 'writing age' of the thirteenth century; or those of age of manuscript production in the fourteenth and fifteenth centuries? It is most likely a conglomeration, and must be individually determined for each work—or rather, its redaction. Thus, as Sigurðsson states, 'The sagas must be used both as source materials for

10 Cf. Sigurðsson, *Chieftains and Power*, 25, who, from the perspective of historical studies, refers to these depictions as 'knowledge and beliefs'. From the perspective of literary studies, knowledge is always constructed and transmitted through discourse, and thus is found in texts as opinion. If it is transmitted in an illocutionary act that provides information about an authoritative construction of common knowledge about a factual past, it seems to be a viable conclusion to consider it to be 'knowledge that is believed to be referentially true' (*ibid.*, 26). This seems probable, bearing in mind the many factuality signals added to the *syuzhet* (alias *discours, récit*) of the Sagas of the Icelanders.

11 Carol Clover, 'Icelandic Family Sagas (*Íslendingasögur*)', in *Old Norse-Icelandic Literature*, ed. Carol Clover and John Lindow (Toronto: 2005), 239–315.

the society they originated in and as sources for the society they describe', and that society could be thirteenth-, fourteenth-, or fifteenth-century Iceland.[12]

How Did Chieftains Influence Court Proceedings?

Looking at the social structure of the Icelandic Commonwealth, only men of a certain measure of economic power were able to fulfil legal roles, such as functioning as litigators, judges, and panel members. Legal duties were confined to the social class of householders, that is, farmers who owned land or tenants who owned milking stock. Legal duties could also be discharged on behalf of a householder by a representative. The householders were called *bœndr* (sg. *bóndi*) in Old Icelandic. Every individual was required to be attached to a householder, and every household was required to be attached to a chieftaincy (Old Icelandic *goðorð*). However, it was up to the householder to decide which chieftaincy this would be. Only householders could possess a chieftaincy and function as its chieftain (*goði*). Chieftains would normally nominate judges from the ranks of the householders attached to them. Householders could follow their chieftain to an assembly (*þing*), where most courts (*dómar*, sg. *dómr*) were held, to function as the chieftain's assembly participants (*þingmenn*). Both chieftains and assembly participants could fulfil legal roles. This nexus of social power and legal offices is commonly interpreted as a process of householders seeking out the most powerful chieftains, and the power held by a chieftain being dependent on his success as a litigator:

> It was in the farmers' [i.e. householders'] own interest to be thing-men of the goðar who might best care for their concerns, and the more thingmen a goði could enlist the stronger he was at the thing and in any armed conflict.[13]

It seems logical to conclude that the greater the number of supporters a chieftain had—his assembly participants (*þingmenn*) as well as allied chieftains and their assembly participants—then the greater his influence as a litigant in his own affairs as well as a litigator or arbitrator in the affairs of others. Likewise,

12 Sigurðsson, *Chieftains and Power*, 36.

13 Preben Meulengracht Sørensen, *Saga and Society: An Introduction to Old Norse Literature*, trans. John Tucker (Odense: 1993), 38; also referred to in Byock, Jesse L. Byock, *Medieval Iceland* (Berkeley: 1988), 125. Cf. Jón Viðar Sigurðsson, 'Forholdet mellom frender, hushold og venner på Island i fristatstiden', *Historisk Tidsskrift* 74, no. 3 (1995), 311–30, at 325–29.

one can assume that powerful chieftains made for powerful judges who were able to form their opinions more independently of the influence of litigants—but also more in line with their own interests. Both the issue of independence as well as self-interest might explain why decisions were never delivered by an individual judge, but, at ad hoc courts, by a dozen judges and, at most other courts, by thirty-six.[14]

There is, however, only scant reference to textual evidence cited in extant scholarship regarding how chieftains—or any individuals with sufficient power—actually influenced court proceedings. Apart from Preben Meulengracht Sørensen's generic statement quoted above, Jesse Byock refers to two episodes in saga narratives where chieftains directly influenced court proceedings, in addition to one instance of the bribery of a witness.[15]

The scenarios in question, however, often share a common phraseology when it comes to describing the outcome of this influence: *at ónýta mál/sǫk fyrir e-u/at eyða e-u mál* 'to void someone's lawsuit'.[16] This phrase, in the context of individuals influencing the court by virtue of their power, only appears in

14 Split judgements were possible if judges disagreed and there were more than six judges in the minority; the exception is for lawsuits heard before the Fifth Court (*fimtardómr*), where a simple majority decided and lots were drawn in ties for appeal cases or decided in favour of the prosecution in initial cases. There were also numerous members at the Law Council (*lǫgrétta*), which, beyond legislating new laws, decided questions regarding the interpretation of existing laws (comparable to a supreme court), as well as deciding on matters regarding local assembly and communes (comparable to a constitutional court), and deciding on further private and penal matters.

15 Byock, *Feud*, 45–6, discussing *Droplaugarsonar saga*, ch. 5; Byock, *Medieval Iceland*, 213, discussing *Vápnfirðinga saga*, ch. 6; and Byock, *Medieval Iceland*, 132–3, discussing *Njáls saga*, ch. 139.

16 'Bolla þáttr', in *Laxdœla saga*, ed. Kristian Kålund (Halle: 1896), 234–53, at ch. 81; 'Droplaugarsona saga' in *Austfirðinga sǫgur*, ed. Jón Jóhannesson (Reykjavik: 1950), 137–80, at ch. 5 and 6; Forrest S. Scott, ed., *Eyrbyggja Saga: The Vellum Tradition* (Copenhagen: 2003), ch. 19, 29 and 44; Hugo Gering, ed., *Finnboga saga hins ramma* (Halle: 1879), ch. 26; Finnur Jónsson, ed., *Flóamannasaga* (Copenhagen: 1932), ch. 6; Ólafur Halldórsson, ed., *Færeyinga saga* (Reykjavik: 1987), ch. 5; 'Grœnlendinga þáttr' in *Eyrbyggja saga*, Einar Ólafur Sveinsson and Matthías Þórðarson (Reykjavik: 1935), at ch. 5; Jón Helgason, ed., *Hrafnkels saga Freysgoða* (Copenhagen: 1961), ch. 7, 8, 10 and 11; 'Landnámabók' in *Íslendingabók, Landnámabók*, ed. Jakob Benediktsson (Reykjavik 1969), at ch. 79 (67); Einar Ólafur Sveinsson, ed., *Njáls saga* (Reykjavik: 1954), ch. 139; 'Vápnfirðinga saga', in *Austfirðinga sǫgur*, ed. Jón Jóhannesson (Reykjavik: 1950), ch. 6; Finnur Jónsson, ed., *Vatsdœlasaga* (Copenhagen: 1934), ch. 30; 'Víga-Glúms saga' in *Eyfirðinga*, ed. Jónas Kristjánsson (Reykjavik: 1956), 1–98, at ch. 18; 'Vöðu-Brands þáttr', in *Ljósvetninga saga með þáttum*, ed. Björn Sigfússon (Reykjavik: 1940), at ch. 4 and 11.

the Sagas of the Icelanders, and, with the exception of legal texts, it is not used in connection to a lawsuit in other text types.[17] In *Grágás*, the phrase appears in a large number of provisions. There, it is confined to descriptions of plaintiffs' procedural errors that were sufficient to void their lawsuits,[18] or misconduct in any legal duty discharged in a lawsuit that has voided the legal action (but not the plaintiff's lawsuit),[19] the majority of which concern the judge's behaviour.

This paper will examine in detail the episodes supplied by Byock, expanded by episodes referenced in the database of the *Dictionary of Old Norse Prose* and the full-text searchable electronic editions. The individual components of the action will be analysed, as will be the classification of the action in the texts as a legal or illegal measure, and as a morally sound or immoral measure. The conclusion will offer a synthesis of the concept of case-voiding in Old Norse as can be reconstructed from the Sagas of the Icelanders. While the saga episodes discussed below represent a literary discourse, the question remains

---

17 As far as the references in the database of the *Dictionary of Old Norse Prose* are concerned: Den Arnamagnæanske Kommission, Copenhagen, 'Ordbog over det norrøne prosasprog/ A Dictionary of Old Norse Prose'. http://www.onp.hum.ku.dk/ (accessed 24 February, 2016).

18 Here and in the following citations, 'K' refers to the Konungsbók-version of Grágás, and 'S' to the Staðarhólsbók-version. Numbers preceded by '§' refer to article numbers. 'Mistakes in calling [a neighbor] may make a case void', K § 27, p. 64; calling '[r]eplacement of absent neighbor', K § 34, p. 71; 'assembly balking by delay', K § 35, p. 74; 'If a verdict is asked on an irrelevant mater', K § 35, pp. 74–5; prosecutor not removing dismissed judges from court: 'Dismissed judges remain present ...', K § 47, p. 87; 'If a man is summon[s]ed to an assembly to which he does not belong', K § 58, p. 104; 'If a man summons another to an assembly neither belongs to', K § 59, p. 107; 'Errors in procedure make cases void', K § 85, p. 138; 'litigants' disputes over calling of neighbors' and the 'using neighbor-calling against each other', K § 89, p. 152; 'Consequences of not lifting the call', and 'If men conceal or lie about calling', K § 89, p. 153; 'Procedure and penalty if that loss of right [to attend assemblies] is ignored', K § 99, p. 162; 'Atonement claims stand even if a case is spoilt by procedural defects', K § 113, p. 176; 'If a transferred case is not prosecuted', St § 307, p. 219. References are to Andrew Dennis, Peter G. Foote and Richard Perkins, eds. and trans., *Laws of Early Iceland: Grágás, the Codex Regius of Grágás, with Material from Other Manuscripts*, 2 vols. (Winnipeg: 1980–2000); quotations come from the editors' marginal summaries.

19 Two provisions under 'Assembly participants' arrival', K § 56, p. 100; A litigator's '[w]illful neglect of a transferred case' to him, K § 77, p. 123; 'Errors in procedure make cases [i.e. or a defence] void', K § 85, p. 138; litigant's disputes over calling of neighbors and the 'using neighbor-calling against each other', K § 89, p. 152; 'Consequences of not lifting the call', and 'If men conceal or lie about calling', K § 89, p. 153; 'Procedure and penalty if that loss of right [to attend assemblies] is ignored', K § 99, p. 162.

as to whether influence over court proceedings was considered an issue in other discourses. As the types of texts are limited—and there appear to be no surviving administrative documents addressing actual cases of influence over the court—legal texts remain the sole source of further discourse regarding this issue. The following section will therefore examine the legal discourse in *Grágás*, and thus supply a framework for the depiction provided by literary texts.

Legal Provision against Disturbing Court Proceedings

In *Grágás*, the disturbance of court proceedings is considered an offence and is referred to as *þingsafglapan*, usually translated as 'assembly-balking'. *Grágás* contains numerous provisions for assembly-balking (*þingsafglapan*), covering a wide range of possible obstructions of court proceedings, and all penalised by 'lesser outlawry' (*fjǫrbaugsgarðr*), a three-year expulsion from Iceland.[20] The more general provision from *Grágás* that follows below, had it actually been enforced, meant that chieftains would have been threatened with expulsion from Iceland had they behaved in the way many of the characters in the saga episodes cited below did:

> Ef varþing verðr sva af glapat at eigi mego mál lúkaz þar fyrir þeim söcom. þa scal sa er þær sacir átte at søkia stefna þeim er vallda vm þings afglöponina oc lata varða fiorbavgs ɢarð.[21]
>
> If a Spring assembly is balked in such a way that lawsuits cannot be finished because of it, the person who had to prosecute the lawsuits must summon those who are responsible for the assembly-balking and let lesser outlawry be the penalty.

20 The total number of provision is twenty-one: K § 23, K § 25, K § 35, K § 38, K § 40, four provisions under K § 41, K § 58, four provisions under K §117, K § 234, two provisions under K § 244, St § 248, St § 252, St § 406, St § 430. Andrew Dennis, 'Grágás: An examination of the content and technique of the Old Icelandic law books, focused on þingskapaþáttr (the 'Assembly Section')' (unpublished PhD diss., University of Cambridge: 1973), 26 states that '[j]udicial processes are the major concern of both the Alþing and várþing rules'.

21 Vilhjálmur Finsen, ed., *Grágás: Konungsbók genoptrykt efter Vilhjálmur Finsen udgave 1852* (Odense: 1974), K § 58, p. 100.

Assembly-balking by judges, arbitrators, and members of the Law Council is of special concern in *Grágás*, and is included in thirteen of the nineteen more specific provisions.[22] A further three of these nineteen provisions describe scenarios of disturbance at court caused by general riot or an excessively large number of participants.[23] Only three of these nineteen provisions concern litigants.[24] This renders Sørensen's and Byock's inference that judges could have been influenced by the power of the litigants or their litigators probable. It is made even more probable by the fact that, according to the depiction of lawsuits in the Sagas of the Icelanders, it was most desirable to have one's case litigated by the most powerful person available or affordable.

22 Balking by a judge: 'Temporary absence [of assembly members] from the [General] Assembly', K § 23, p. 58; 'If a [challenged] judge refuses to leave [court]', K § 25, p. 61; 'Assembly-balking by delay [of verdict]', K § 35, p. 74; 'Penalty if judges refuse to sum up [prosecution or defence]' (both have to be summed up by one judge each), K § 40, p. 79; 'Asking judges to give judgment, and if only some are willing', K § 41, p. 81; 'If judges are guilty of assembly-balking, the judgment of six or more may stand', K § 41, p. 81; 'Announcement of judgments and assent of judges' (One judge announces the judgement and the others have to assent. If a judge remains silent, this is assembly-balking), K § 41, p. 82; Balking at the Law Council: 'If books do not decide an article of law, the Law Council meets', K § 117, p. 191: 'If some of the men who have seats do not go to their places when they know the Law Council is to be cleared for a meeting, the penalty is lesser outlawry as for other kinds of assembly balking', K § 117, p. 192; 'If members [of the Law Council] balk proceedings' refusing to decide for an opinion in a legal question, K § 117, p. 192; Balking by an arbitrator: 'Arbitrators may select a decider', K § 244, II, p. 205; 'If arbitrators balk a settlement or die', K § 244, II, p. 205; 'If arbitrators balk a settlement', St § 248, II, p. 355; 'Prosecution of a case if private settlement of it is balked', St § 252, II, pp. 356–7.

23 'Penalty for disturbance' (men trampling at each other at an assembly or causing riot at an assembly), K § 117, pp. 189–90; 'Lawspeaker allocates places at Lögberg': 'If men behave so improperly towards the Lawspeaker that they do not let him get to his seat, or those men he has individually named to sit at Lögberg with him, the penalty is lesser outlawry and it is to be prosecuted like other kinds of assembly balking', K § 117, p. 193; 'Balking a meadowland court': 'If of his own accord either of them brings more men to the court than is prescribed, then his penalty is a three-mark fine at the suit of the other, but lesser outlawry if he balks the court and likewise for anyone else who does so. [...] and the same is to apply to all district courts that are balked', St § 406, II, p. 297.

24 'Defence procedure, preliminary': prosecutor delaying the defendant's defence (because this can only start after prosecution has been brought forward completely), K § 38, p. 77; 'If protest against means of proof is regarded as a delaying tactic': 'If the man prosecuting thinks the defendant makes a protest against some formal means of proof, because he wishes to delay judgment', K § 41, p. 81; 'Penalties for balking a communal pasture court': non-attendance or refusal to join court by individuals performing legal duties, St § 430, II, p. 317.

The detailed treatment of the disruptive influence on court proceedings in *Grágás* indicates that this was considered an issue in legal discourse. Since orderly court proceedings are vital for a functioning legal system, the number of provisions and the many different possibilities as to how and when court proceedings might be obstructed are not surprising. Furthermore, the penalty for this offence, lesser outlawry (*fjǫrbaugsgarðr*), was quite severe. Though the actual enforcement of this penalty is uncertain, nor is it clear how often this offence actually occurred and was prosecuted,[25] the harsh penalty set forth in *Grágás* makes it probable that the obstruction of court proceedings was considered a genuine problem for the Icelandic legal system.

While there are two more general provisions for assembly-balking that do not further specify which legal subject was responsible for the balking of a lawsuit,[26] the detailed scenarios for obstruction of court proceedings described in the provisions display a certain resemblance to the saga episodes presented in the following section, in which chieftains influenced judges during court proceedings.

The literary episodes in the following section will be analysed with two questions in mind: First, what specific actions constitute the disruption of court proceedings, according to these texts? Secondly, are these acts judged positively or negatively in the narrative? The answer to the first question sheds more light on what social dynamics the provisions in *Grágás* may have addressed. The answer to the second question shows how these dynamics were framed in two different discourses about the Icelandic Commonwealth: the discourse of legal texts and the discourse of literary texts.

Non-Violent Influence over Court Proceedings

In order to answer the question of which specific techniques of influencing court proceedings are apparently meant in literary discourse by the phrases *ónýta mál/sǫk fyrir e-u* and *at eyða e-u mál*, four examples that provide the

25 Cf. Dieter Strauch, *Mittelalterliches nordisches Recht bis 1500* (Berlin: 2011), 245: 'Der [sc. in *Grágás*] allzu zahlreich angeordnete Lebensringzaun (*fjörbaugsgarðr*, dreijährige Landesverweisung) hätte—wäre er durchgeführt worden—die Inselbevölkerung drastisch verringert und die übermäßige Rechtsfolge des Waldganges, selbst für geringe Vergehen, hätte Herden von Waldmännern mit allen Versorgungsproblemen und Gefahren für die Allgemeinheit schaffen müssen'.

26 Balking of a commune courts (K § 234, II, p. 190); Balking of spring assemblies (K § 58, p. 102).

most information in this regard will be analysed in detail. By looking at acts of influence over court proceedings that have been expressed through another phrase, namely, *at hleypa upp dœminum* ('to scatter the court'), actions that are *not* covered by the other two phrases in literary discourse can be further specified. Alongside the analysis of what these phrases mean, the literary discourse on the interference of court proceedings will be reconstructed through the interpretation of these acts of case-voiding and court-scattering.

The phrases *at ónýta mál/sǫk fyrir e-u* and *at eyða e-u mál* appear several times in the references collected in the *Dictionary of Old Norse Prose* corpus.[27] In one instance, both phrases are used to refer to the same act taken to influence court proceedings, and this act does not differ from actions taken in similar episodes. This indicates that the two phrases were used synonymously. Moreover, these phrases have the same denotative meaning in the literary texts as they do in *Grágás*. They mean on the one hand the result that a lawsuit or a portion of a court proceeding has been nullified, and, on the other, the legal actions that led up to that. We find these meanings, for example, in *Eyrbyggja saga*, in which, at one point, a lawsuit is nullified[28] and, at another point, there is a 'verdict of acquittal' (*bjargkviðar*).[29]

There are, however, a number of episodes in which neither of the phrases exclusively signifies procedural measures. In these cases, the phrases are used in contexts where non-violent force was used to influence court proceedings. These episodes are found almost exclusively in the Sagas of the Icelanders, and always involve chieftains.[30] This usage is part of a literary discourse on the use and abuse of power. While there are many provisions in *Grágás* about judges who are unwilling to fulfil their legal role, the Sagas of the Icelanders present plentiful material as to how judges dealt with court proceedings where litigators arrived with large groups of supporters (*fjǫlmenni*), sometimes identified as 'troops' or 'hosts' (*lið, flokkr*). In this way, the Sagas of the Icelanders offer a supplementary discourse to the one implicit in the many provisions contained in *Grágás*. In only one individual instance do we find a judge using his power to decide a case in his favour, owing to his personal ties to the defendant.[31] His

---

27 Cf. the references above, in nn. 16, 18 and 19; see also *Njáls saga*, ch. 24, 66; ch. 56, 114; ch. 61, 128; ch. 142, 354 and 386.

28 Scott, *Eyrbyggja Saga*, ch. 44, 263.

29 Scott, *Eyrbyggja Saga*, ch. 29, 159.

30 I.e. *goðar*; except in *Færeyinga saga*, where the respective social class are *hǫfðingjar* 'chieftains'.

31 Jónas Kristjánsson, 'Víga-Glúms saga', in *Eyfirðinga sǫgur*, ed. Jónas Kristjánsson (Reykjavik: 1956), 1–98, at ch. 18, 60.

actions, however, are presented in negative terms; in contrast, the non-violent influence of court proceedings is presented in the Sagas of the Icelanders both positively and negatively.

As the following analysis shows, a demonstration of power to influence court proceedings can take one of two types. The demonstration of power is either performed by positively-represented characters to ensure that justice is not obstructed in lawsuits in which the facts are clear and favour their side; or power is demonstrated by negatively-represented characters, leading to injustice. Only in one instance in the Sagas of the Icelanders is the disturbance of legal procedures actually persecuted as *þingsafglapan*.[32]

However, the non-violent demonstration of power is only one end of the scale of measures that could be taken. A second phrase has the specific denotation of violent measures taken to influence court proceedings, and this phrase, *at hleypa upp dœminum* (to break up the court, to scatter the court), delimit the meaning of the two phrases named above, *at ónýta mál/sǫk, at eyða e-u mál*. In the violent episodes in which chieftains intended to void a lawsuit, they simply stormed the court with armed men. There is also an episode in which a demonstration of power turned into open violence. Each of these acts was described by the appropriate phrase.

The following discussion will analyse the usage and value judgments attached to the two synonymous phrases *at ónýta mál/sǫk, at eyða e-u mál* in four saga episodes. Then, an episode featuring both non-violent and violent measures will be analysed in order to highlight the semantic borders between both these phrases, and the third one just mentioned, namely *at hleypa upp dœminum*. The section concludes with an overview of the actors, techniques of disruption, and their valuation conveyed in the analysed episodes.

Example 1: Vápnfirðinga Saga, ch. 6

In *Vápnfirðinga saga*, chapter 6, a chieftain influenced court proceedings through a demonstration of his power in which he brought a large following to the assembly. Although this action was meant to be seen in a negative light, it was ultimately successful. It is not entirely clear just how the case was voided, but it seems probable that the judges did not dare to pass judgement to the disadvantage of the stronger litigant. The lawsuit concerns the dowry of Halla Lýtingsdóttir following her divorce from her husband, the chieftain Brodd-Helgi Þorgilsson. Halla became terminally ill and offered her husband, Brodd-Helgi, the option of divorce. He refused this offer, but immediately became betrothed to a younger woman. Halla then divorced Brodd-Helgi by moving

32 'Vöðu-Brands þáttr', ch. 4, 135.

back to her brother's farm. Halla's brother, the chieftain Geitir Lýtingsson, demanded that Brodd-Helgi return Halla's dowry to him, which Brodd-Helgi would have been required by law to do following the divorce. Instead, Brodd-Helgi refused to acknowledge that Halla had left his farm, and stated that she would return to him. He thus tried to create a legal reality in which she had not effectively divorced him, thereby allowing him to await her death, so as not to have to return her dowry.[33]

Geitir summoned Brodd-Helgi to the local Spring Assembly of the district of Sunnudalr (*Sunnudalsþing*) to conduct a lawsuit over the dowry. At the assembly, of the two large groups of supporters (*fjǫlmenni*), Brodd-Helgi had a larger group than Geitir. When both parties were scheduled to appear in court during the assembly, Brodd-Helgi 'overpowered' (*bera e-n ofrliði*) Geitir:

> Þá stefndi Geitir Brodd-Helga um fé Hǫllu til Sunnudalsþings, ok fjǫlmennti hvárutveggi mjǫk til þingsins, ok varð Helgi fjǫlmennari en Geitir hafði mannval betra. En er at dómi skyldi ganga, þá varð Geitir ofrliði borinn, ok kom <eigi> málinu fram.[34] Ok bauð Geitir málinu til alþingis, ok eyddi Brodd-Helgi þá enn málit ok mest af liðveizlu Guðmundar ins ríka.[35]

> Then Geitir summoned Brodd-Helgi to the Sunnudalr-Assembly about Halla's property, and both of them brought many supporters to the assembly. While Helgi had more supporters, Geitir nevertheless had the better choice of men. And when they were supposed to go to court, Geitir was overpowered, and the case was not brought before the court. Nevertheless, Geitir brought the case before the General Assembly, and Brodd-Helgi voided his case again, mostly due to the support of Guðmundr the powerful.

As a result of Helgi overpowering Geitir, the case could not be heard by the court. If one considered the narrative to take the provisions on assembly-balking from *Grágás* into account, Helgi might be guilty of assembly-balking.

---

33 Byock, *Medieval Iceland*, 212–14.

34 Jóhannesson's edition has 'ok kom Helgi málinu fram' in the main text and offers the reading chosen above with 'eigi' instead of 'Helgi' as a variant reading. The main reading chosen by Jóhannesson, however, is meaningless, since no court proceedings actually taking place are mentioned in this episode, neither for this assembly, nor for following events at the General Assembly mentioned in the sentence cited thereafter above.

35 'Vápnfirðinga saga', ch. 6, 37–8.

However, there are no provisions in *Grágás* that specifically address the situation as presented in the saga narrative, namely, when a defendant hindered the plaintiff's appearance at court. One could only subsume this legal scenario under the more general provisions for assembly-balking by assuming that such behaviour was undesirable. Nonetheless, when Geitir brought the case to the respective court of appeal, the Eastern Quarter's court at the General Assembly (*alþingi*), Helgi was not prosecuted for assembly-balking, despite the fact that this could have been expected had the narrative followed the more general provisions in *Grágás*.

But how is Helgi's behaviour evaluated in the narrative? Is a chieftain's influence over court proceedings through the use of force seen as morally acceptable behaviour for the society depicted in the narrative, or for the implied reader? It appears that Helgi's behaviour is implicitly criticized by the narrative. As the saga relates the story of the alliance (*vinfengi*/*vinátta*, 'alliance, friendship') between the two chieftains and its gradual dissolution into open hostility, they are contrasted with one another. Geitir is depicted as the more cautious character, well-versed in political tactics and jurisprudence. Brodd-Helgi, by contrast, is a bolder, pugnacious figure.[36] Furthermore, Helgi's actions in the lead-up to the lawsuit seem to be viewed as morally negative. Brodd-Helgi's behaviour towards Halla is judged negatively by the people of his district, which was a usual narrative device in the Sagas of the Icelanders to uphold the apparently neutral stance of the narrator.[37] Helgi thus got away with bad behaviour: since his personal character is described in negative terms, using tactics of assembly-balking that border on the illegal, one can only conclude that the text interprets this episode in negative terms.

Example 2: Droplaugarsona Saga, ch. 5

Chapter 5 of *Droplaugarsona saga* describes the impossibility of case-voiding if one had fewer supporters than the opposing litigator. The text's evaluation of influencing court proceedings through a demonstration of power is, again, clearly negative, albeit only if it was done so by an unjust individual. Þorgeirr, the householder at the Hrafnkelsstaðir farm, bought sheep from Þórðr of Geirólfseyr. After Þorgeirr brought his sheep home, they disappeared, and he learned that Þórðr had hidden some at his farm and milked them. Two chieftains litigated the lawsuit. The plaintiff asked Helgi Droplaugarson to prosecute his case. The defendant, Þórðr, was foster father to a child of Helgi Ásbjarnarson, who took over the defence on his behalf.

36 Byock, *Medieval Iceland*, 204–6.

37 'Vápnfirðinga saga', ch. 6, 36–7.

Helgi Droplaugarson appeared at the assembly in the company of two other powerful men, Þorkell Geitisson and Ketill from Njarðvík. They were 'followed by very many people' (*allfjǫlmennir*). In comparison, Helgi Ásbjarnarson did not have enough 'troops' (*lið*) to 'void' (*ónýta*) the plaintiff's lawsuit. Eventually, the men asked for a settlement instead of a judgment, and, being in the position of power, Helgi Droplaugarson agreed, but only on the condition that he be allowed to decide the compensation he would receive (i.e. 'self-judgement' *sjálfdœmi*).

> Síðan fór málit til þings, ok váru þeir Helgi Droplaugarson ok Þorkell Geitisson allfjǫlmennir. Var þar með þeim Ketill ór Njarðvík. Helgi Ásbjarnarson hafði ekki lið til at ónýta mál fyrir þeim. Þá báðu menn þá sættask, en Helgi Droplaugarson vildi ekki nema sjálfdœmi.[38]

> Then the case came before the assembly, and both Helgi Droplaugarson and Þorkell Geitisson had many supporters. With them was Ketill from Njarðvík. Helgi Ásbjarnarson did not have enough supporters to void the case. People then asked them to settle the dispute, but Helgi Droplaugarson did not want anything but self-judgement.

From the way in which the narrative relates the facts, it is clear that the plaintiff had a just cause. Furthermore, before a complaint was filed, the defendant refused to compensate the plaintiff, on grounds that he was foster father to a powerful man's son. This reference to power as opposed to justice is repeated in the assembly scene, where it was precisely Helgi Ásbjarnarson's *lack* of power to influence court proceedings signalled out for mention. Helgi failed to influence the court proceedings because the opposing party demonstrated the combined power of three leaders. It thus seems fair to interpret the scene as a critique of the excessive concentration of power into the hands of an individual chieftain, especially when it was achieved through power networks, such as constructed kinship through a foster-relationship. In contrast, the power demonstrated at court by the plaintiff's litigator and his allies simply ensured justice.

Example 3: Droplaugarsona Saga, ch. 6

Chapter 6 of *Droplaugarsona saga* concerns another lawsuit in which the chieftains Helgi Droplaugarson and Helgi Ásbjarnason faced each other in court. Similar to the previous episode, supporters, if they were on the side

38 'Droplaugarsona saga', ch. 5, 150–1.

of the morally sound individual, were guarantors for the prevention of the obstruction of justice. In this episode, Helgi Droplaugarson was able to defend himself in a lawsuit prosecuted by Helgi Ásbjarnason. Helgi Droplaugarson again showed his strength of numbers before the court, and his actions were depicted as lawful and morally sound. The presence of his supporters only ensured that he could prove the legality of his actions.

The lawsuit arose when Bjǫrn of Snotrunes had an affair with the wife of Þorsteinn of Desjarmýr. Þorsteinn's wife was a close relative of the chieftain, Helgi Droplaugarson. Þorsteinn asked the chieftain for support in this matter and for him to force Bjǫrn to end the affair. Helgi agreed and confronted Bjǫrn; Bjǫrn did not want to end the affair, so Helgi killed him. Since Bjǫrn of Snotrunes had fostered a son of the chieftain Helgi Ásbjarnason, Bjǫrn's widow asked Helgi to prosecute the lawsuit. At court, Helgi Droplaugarson proved the lawfulness of his actions by naming witnesses. Subsequently, Helgi Droplaugarson brought a lawsuit against the late Bjǫrn to have him outlawed posthumously for matrimonial misconduct (*legorð*), but Helgi Ásbjarnason settled the matter through payments.

> Þá gekk Helgi Droplaugarson til dóms og mikit fjǫlmenni með honum. Hann nefndi sér vátta at ónýtt váru ǫll mál fyrir Helga Ásbjarnarsyni, ok kvað þar þá þrjá menn, er þat sá, at Bjǫrn var moldu huliðr. Vann þá Sveinungr eið at stallahring og tveir menn með honum, at þeir sá, at Bjǫrn var moldu huliðr. Nú urðu ǫll mál ónýt fyrir Helga Ásbjarnarsyni.[39]

> Helgi Droplaugarson then went to court with a very large group of supporters. He called witnesses to prove that Helgi Ásbjarnason's complaint was completely without cause, and he called those three men who saw that Björn had been covered with earth. Then Sveinungr and two men swore oaths on the altar-ring that they had seen that Björn had been covered with earth. Now Helgi Ásbjarnason had his whole lawsuit voided.

The case-voiding in this episode was not directly the result of a demonstration of power by bringing the larger group of supporters to court. Instead, the court proceedings followed procedural regulations. The mention of a large group of supporters thus only functions in two respects: First, it indicates that Helgi Droplaugarson was a powerful man; and second, because of his power, there was little chance that proceedings would depart from the legally

39 'Droplaugarsona saga', ch. 6, 152–3.

prescribed path—that is, in Helgi Droplaugarson's favour. This demonstration of power is thus not presented negatively. Throughout the whole dispute, Helgi Droplaugarson acted in accordance with what that narrative depicts as morally sound. He attempted to end the apparently shameful extramarital affair involving his relative. His killing of her paramour was legitimate, and he performed the burial rites as legally obligated. Furthermore, Þorsteinn of Desjarmýr, who asked Helgi Droplaugarson for help, is characterised by the narrator in positive terms, as an 'upright man'.[40]

Example 4: Flóamanna Saga, ch. 6

Ǫrn suspects that Bǫðvarr, a freedman (*leysingi*), has stolen sixty of his wethers. The narrative, however, does not indicate whether this suspicion was justified, since it does not say what actually happened. Bǫðvarr hired Atli Hallsteinsson, a powerful man of aristocratic Norwegian descent, as a litigator. Atli used his power and arrived at the subsequent assembly with 'a large group of supporters' (*fjǫlmenni*) at the opening of proceedings (i.e. before the prosecution was brought forward and would begin the defence). Atli 'voided' (*eyða*) Ǫrn's case 'with very great force' (*hrekja af e-u sem mest*), apparently down to the number of his supporters and their support:[41]

> Erni varð vant um haustit lx. Geldinga, ok hefir eigi góðan róm á Bǫðvari ok berr á brýnn honum, at hann muni tekit hafa. Bǫðvarr duldi þess ok unni honum engra bóta fyrir, þóttiz sitja í trausti ríkra manna.... Um várit stefnir Ǫrn Bǫðvari um stuld. Þykkiz Bǫðvarr sér nú eigi einhlítr um varnir málsins, ok sækir at Atla Hallsteinsson, þvi at hann var honum nær en Hrafn, ok tjár honum málit. Atli segir, at eigi sé ørvænt, at menn finni gagnsakir í máli Arnar. Eptir þat tók Atli við ǫllu fé Bǫðvars með handsǫlum.... Á þingi er mál búit til sóknar á hendr Bǫðvari, ok kom málit í dóm. Þá gekk at dómum Atli með fjǫlmenni, ok bad Ǫrn fella niðr málit,—'elligar mun ek ónýta þat fyrir þér'. Ǫrn kvaz ætla, at eigi mundi

40 'Droplaugarsona saga', ch. 5, 151: 'Þorsteinn var þó vel at sér' ('However, Þorsteinn was an upright man').

41 This is apparently also implied by Ǫrn when he mentions that Atli will only succeed in voiding the case through *ofríki* 'overwhelming force'. A clear example that voiding a case through *ofríki* means hindering the opposing party from attending court proceedings by barring their way to court with a large following of supporters is found in Helgason, *Hrafnkels saga*, ch. 8, 21. In the episode in *Hrafnkels saga*, the interpretation of assembly-balking follows the pattern of the episodes discussed here. Assembly-balking is viewed negatively, as is the balking chieftain, and the outcome is considered unjust in the narrative.

> ónýtt verða, nema með ofríki,—'má vera', segir Ǫrn, 'at torsótt verði at eiga við jarlborna menn sem þú ert, Atli; hygg ek (at) meir eyðir þú málit fyrir fégirni þína en réttindi, sem frædr þínir hafa gǫrt'. Við þessi orð varð Atli reiðr mjǫk ok eyðir málit fyrir Erni ok hrekr hann sem mest af málinu.[42]
>
> In autumn, Ǫrn was missing 60 wethers, and he did not have a high opinion of Bǫðvarr, and told him to his face that he must have taken them. Bǫðvarr denied this and did not concede him compensation for it, because he thought himself to be under the protection of powerful men.... In spring, Ǫrn summons Bǫðvarr to the court for theft. Bǫðvarr does not consider himself without the need for help of others regarding his defence in the lawsuit, and he seeks Atlí Hallsteinsson, because he was closer to him than Hrafn, and relates the case to him. Atli says that it would not be unlikely, if one found counter-suits to Ǫrn's lawsuit. After this Atli took all of Bǫðvarr's possessions in trust.... At the assembly, the lawsuit is prepared for prosecution against Bǫðvarr, and the case comes to court. Then Atli came to the court with many supporters, and asked Ǫrn to drop the suit, 'or I will void it'. Ǫrn said he meant that it would not be voided, except with violence,—'it can be', said Ǫrn, 'that it might get difficult to deal with men of noble birth like you, Atli. I reckon that you are trying to void this case because of your greed rather than for justice, as your kin has done'. Atli became very angry because of these words and voided Ǫrn's case and, with very great force, drove Ǫrn to drop it.

Atli's noble birth was noted by Ǫrn as a reason for his use of force to influence court proceedings. The implication is that the use of force to influence court proceedings was a tool of powerful men who did not respect the proper functioning of the Commonwealth's legal system. Atli's status as an aristocrat would associate him more with the rivalling aristocratic social structure in Norway, which formed a usual foil for saga narrative to the acephalic Icelandic society.

Between Non-Violent and Violent Force: Færeyinga Saga, ch. 5

In chapter 5 of *Færeyinga saga*, two of the householder Hafgrímr's servants (*heimamenn*, sg. *heimamaðr*) commenced 'a comparison of persons' (*mannjafnaðr*). Eventually, one, Eldjárn kambhǫttr, wounded the other, Einarr. In return, Einarr incapacitated Eldjárn. Since Eldjárn was a servant at Hafgrímr's farm, he enjoyed his protection (*grið*), and Hafgrímr took up

42 Jónsson, *Flóamannasaga*, ch. 6, 9.

a lawsuit against Einarr. Einarr's brothers, the chieftains (*hǫfðingjar*, sg. *hǫfðingi*) Brestir and Beinir, took up Einarr's defence. Brestir offered Hafgrímr a settlement, but Hafgrímr said he would only accept it if he would be granted self-judgement. Brestir rejected this, and Hafgrímr summoned Einarr to the Straumsey Assembly. Both parties arrived at the assembly with 'a large group of supporters' (*fjǫlmenni*). Just as Hafgrímr was about to file his complaint, Brestir and Beinir entered the court, backed by their 'troops' (*flokkr*), and filed a countersuit against Eldjárn for wounding an innocent man. Since Eldjárn was then sentenced to outlawry, Hafgrímr's suit became void.

> nu koma huorir tueggíu til þíngs ok fíolmenna en er Hafgrimr gekk at domum ok ætlade at hafa fram malít a hendr Æinare þa geingu þeir brædr at ödrum megin Brestir ok Bæinir medmyklum flokki ok vnyttí Brestir malít firir Hafgrimi ok ohelgade Kambhȯtt at fornnum landz lȯgum er hann barde saklausann man ok hleypti upp domínum firir Hafgrimi en þeir sottu Elldíarnn til vtlegdar ok fullra sekta.[43]

> Now both arrive at the assembly with a large group of supporters, and just as Hafgrímr entered the court and intended to file the lawsuit against Einarr, Brestir and Beinir entered at the other side with large troops, and Brestir voided Hafgrímr's case and outlawed Kambhǫttr according to the old laws of the land, since he [sc. Eldjárn kambhǫttr] smote an innocent man and he [namely, Brestir] violently broke up Hafgrímr's court and they prosecuted Eldjárn to be condemned to exile and full outlawry.

Brestir and Beinir are characterized positively, and described as 'excellent men'.[44] Brestir, in addition to his extreme strength, skill in combat, and beauty,[45] was also considered wise and knowledgeable in legal affairs.[46] His brother Beinir was characterized as his equal in most respects.[47] They were both retainers and close allies of Jarl Hákon Sigurðarson (*ca.*937–995), the last pagan king of Norway (*ca.*975–995).[48] The lack of any explicit characterization of their brother Einarr by the narrator, though, makes it apparent that he is merely a functional character in their conflict with another powerful figure.

---

43 Ólafur Halldórsson, ed., *Færeyinga saga* (Reykjavik: 1987), ch. 5, 11.
44 *Ibid.*, ch. 5, 9: 'ágætir menn'.
45 *Ibid.*
46 *Ibid.*, ch. 5, 11: 'Brestir var vítr madr ok lȯgkęnn'.
47 *Ibid.*, ch. 5, 9.
48 *Ibid.*

Their opponents, on the contrary, are described throughout the text in negative terms. While powerful, wealthy and valiant, Hafgrímr is, in clear contrast to Brestir, described as impetuous and unwise.[49] His farmhand Eldjárn receives even more clearly a negative description. The narrator attributes a long list of pejorative characteristics to him: thus he was 'foolish' (*heimskr*), 'abusive' (*illorðr*), 'malicious' (*illgjarn*), 'without virtues' (*dáðlaus*), 'aggressive' (*tilleitinn*), 'dishonest' (*lyginn*), and 'slanderous' (*rógsamr*).

Given the clear view that Brestir and Beinir were the protagonists in this case, the addition of the phrase '*ok hleypti upp domínum firir Hafgrimi*' ('and he [namely, Brestir] violently broke up Hafgrímr's court')[50] seems unnecessary in this context. Unlike the episodes discussed above, Brestir and Beinir could have proceeded without violence. One can only conclude that it was not the use or avoidance of violence *per se* that was evaluated either positively or negatively, but rather, the just intentions of the characters. In these episodes, the legal system was just one possible instrument available to the protagonists to ensure justice.

If one considers how the use of violence to influence court proceedings (*at hleypa upp dœminum*) was understood in the Sagas of the Icelanders, it also follows that it was not violence, but just intentions that were central to literary discourse. For example, in chapter nineteen of *Eyrbyggja saga*, there is no clear evaluation of the parties involved in the scattering of a court.[51] The two parties attacked each other as one party attempted to scatter the court by force. The positive valuation lies with the chieftain Snorri goði, who broke up the second fight that erupted at the court, and arranged an agreement. The narrative at this point cites skaldic verse praising him because he succeeded in parting the combatants and arbitrating a solid settlement.[52] The violent breaking up of a court even takes on a comic dimension in chapter thirty of *Vatnsdœla saga*. Here, the elderly Þorsteinn and his hot-headed son Ingólfr deliberated over how to continue their lawsuit against Ingfólfr. Þorsteinn's conclusion was that 'since we are no lawyers, we will void the lawsuit with battle axes!'[53] At the assembly, father and son stormed the court and scattered it by force.

---

49 *Ibid.*, ch. 5, 8.

50 *Ibid.*, ch. 5, 11.

51 Scott, *Eyrbyggja saga*, ch. 19, 42.

52 *Ibid.*, ch. 19, 44.

53 Jónsson, *Vatsdœlasaga*, ch. 30, 85: 'ok þótt er vér sém eigi lǫgmenn, þá munu vér eyða málit með øxarhǫmrum'.

Conclusion

The semantics of the phrases *at ónýta mál/sǫk fyrir e-u* and *at eyða e-u mál* can be divided into two forms of usage. The first is purely legal, signifying the nullification of a court action or a whole lawsuit. The second usage implies the non-violent use of force to influence court proceedings, as opposed to use of violence. Violent force as means of influencing court proceedings, however, is represented by a different phrase, namely, *at hleypa upp dœminum*. The use of this same phrase both in *Grágás* and in literary texts that devote key scenes to the influence over court proceedings shows, in a remarkable way, how deeply literary discourse concerned itself with the legal system, as well as with a broader discourse on how that legal system ought to function effectively within its social context.

The examination of legal texts and relevant saga episodes in conjunction lends credence to the idea that the obstruction of court proceedings was a problem for the Icelandic legal system. Such obstruction seems to have played an important role in legal discourse, and was considered a problem that was required regulation through many detailed provisions.

The way in which literary discourse approached the matter stands in contrast to this legal discourse. In literary discourse, court-influencing is described in two different ways, according to the aims of the influencing litigator or litigant. If the aims were to ensure justice, then bringing many supporters to the court was depicted as a means to prevent the obstruction of justice. If the litigator or litigant's goals were born purely out of a desire to gain power or profit, and their cause was not to ensure justice, then court-influencing emerges in a negative light.

There are no cases in the corpus where influencing the court by force to ensure justice was done was depicted negatively. Nor are there cases there are no cases where the court was about to deliver a legal sentence that was immoral, and hence force was required to ensure that moral, as opposed to legal justice, was done. The literary discourse was thus less concerned with the chieftain's powerful position, and more, instead, with the promotion of the ideal of chieftains who acknowledged the Commonwealth's legal system—and supported its functioning with the power they possessed.

We thus have two different discourses on the functioning of the Icelandic Commonwealth's legal system, the legal and the literary. In the legal discourse, *Grágás* may reflect most closely the learned legal view of the thirteenth century, since it can be assumed that it was written down in preparation for the law code *Jónsbók*, instituted by the king of Norway.[54] It thus seems unsurprising that

54 Rohrbach, 'Matrix of the Law'.

the dynamics of court proceedings that were a result of the Commonwealth's oligarchic social order are framed as problematic.

The literary discourse reconstructed here through the Sagas of the Icelanders, however, is more difficult to pin down to a specific moment in time. The manuscripts in question are spread over several centuries, which means that historical readers would have interpreted the stories differently, from century to century. Regardless, the Commonwealth's legal system is not depicted as defective, nor or as subverted to chieftains' power, nor indeed does the view in the sagas foreshadow the bloody conflict of the Age of the Sturlungs. This literary discourse merely underscores the relevance of chieftains who possessed a sense of moral justice. Such a view does not seem readily to reflect the post-Commonwealth construction of a memory of the Icelandic Commonwealth as a failed state. Nor does this view suggest that the monopolization of power in the hands of the King of Norway rescued a failed Icelandic Commonwealth. We find, rather, a romanticized picture, demonstrating how power in the hand of oligarchs could ensure moral justice. In one of the episodes, it was even a Norwegian aristocrat, who had settled in Iceland, who upset the rule of law—explicitly so because of the behaviours learned in the Norwegian social structure (see above, *Flóamanna saga*, ch. 6), as opposed to that of Iceland.

Individuals from different centuries may have ascribed a range of meanings to this literary discourse that evaluates legal culture and procedure, but the *literary* discourse does not reflect the *legal* discourse—wary of the abuse of power in the Commonwealth—that we find in *Grágás*. It remains difficult to determine whether these sagas bear traces of twelfth-century social order, as literature commissioned by chieftains, or were a romanticized retrospective look by the Icelandic service aristocracy's powerful families at the morally sound behaviour of their ancestors; these stories may very well have served both ideological purposes.

The reconstruction of the larger interpretative frameworks attached to the phrases analysed in this article also shows why the same phrases were used in such different ways in sources such as *Grágás,* on the one hand, and the Sagas of the Icelanders on the other. The analysis here indicates that the Sagas of the Icelanders presented the act of influencing a court by use of force as a practical, legitimate practice, presenting it as a legal practice by expressing it through the language of legal discourse.

Bibliography

Manuscripts

Reykjavik, AM 334 fol., Stofnun Árna Magnússonar í íslenskum fræðum.

Reykjavik, GKS 1157 fol., Stofnun Árna Magnússonar í íslenskum fræðum.

Works Cited

Den Arnamagnæanske Kommission København. 'Ordbog over det norrøne prosasprog/ A Dictionary of Old Norse Prose', at <http://www.onp.hum.ku.dk/>.

Baker, John H. *An Introduction to English Legal History*, 3rd edn. London: 1990.

Beck, Sigríður. 'Frá goðum til yfirstéttar: 1220–1387'. In *Þriðja íslenska söguþingið 18.–21. maí 2006*, edited by Benedikt Eyþórsson and Hrafnkell Lárusson, 234–44. Reykjavik: 2007.

Benediktsson, Jakob, editor. *Íslendingabók, Landnámabók*. Reykjavik: 1969.

Byock, Jesse L. *Feud in the Icelandic Saga*. Berkeley: 1982.

Byock, Jesse L. *Medieval Iceland*. Berkeley: 1988.

Conrad, Hermann. *Deutsche Rechtsgeschichte, vol. I, Frühzeit und Mittelalter*. Karlsruhe: 1962.

Clover, Carol. 'Icelandic Family Sagas (*Íslendingasögur*)'. In *Old Norse-Icelandic Literature*, edited by Carol Clover and John Lindow, 239–315. Toronto: 2005.

Dennis, Andrew. *Grágás: An Examination of the Content and Technique of the Old Icelandic Law Books, Focused on þingskapaþáttr (the 'assembly section')*. Unpublished PhD diss., University of Cambridge: 1973.

Dennis, Andrew, Peter G. Foote, and Richard Perkins, editors and translators. *Laws of Early Iceland: Grágás, the Codex Regius of Grágás, with Material from Other Manuscripts*, 2 vols. Winnipeg: 1980–2000.

Finsen, Vilhjálmur, editor. *Grágás: Konungsbók genoptrykt efter Vilhjálmur Finsens udgave 1852*. Odense: 1974.

Gering, Hugo, editor. *Finnboga saga hins ramma*. Halle: 1879.

Halldórsson, Ólafur, editor. *Færeyinga saga*. Reykjavik: 1987.

Helgason, Jón, editor. *Hrafnkels saga Freysgoða*. Copenhagen: 1961.

Jóhannesson, Jón, editor. *Austfirðinga sǫgur*. Reykjavik: 1950.

Jónsson, Eiríkur and Finnur Jónsson. *Hauksbók udgiven efter de arnamagnæanske Håndskrifter No. 371, 544 og 675, 4° samt forskellige Papirshåndskrifter af det kongelige nordiske Oldskrift-Selskab*. Copenhagen: 1892–1896.

Jónsson, Finnur, editor. *Flóamannasaga*. Copenhagen: 1932.

Jónsson, Finnur, editor. *Vatsdælasaga*. Copenhagen: 1934.

Kålund, Kristian. *Laxdœla saga*. Halle: 1896.

Kålund, Kristian. *Sturlunga Saga efter membranen Króksfjardarbók: udfyldt efter Reykjarfjardarbók*. Copenhagen: 1906–1911.

Kristjánsson, Jónas, editor. *Eyfirðinga sǫgur*. Reykjavik: 1956.

Miller, William I. *Bloodtaking and Peacemaking: Feud, Law, and Society in Saga Iceland*. Chicago: 1990.

Miller, William I. 'Threat'. In *Feud, Violence and Practice: Essays in Medieval Studies in Honor of Stephen D. White*, edited by Belle S. Tuten and Tracey L. Billado, 9–27. Farnham: 2010.

Rohrbach, Lena. 'Matrix of the Law? A Material Study of Staðarhólsbók'. In *The Power of Book: Medial Approaches to Medieval Nordic Legal Manuscripts*, edited by Lena Rohrbach, 98–128. Berlin: 2014.

Scott, Forrest S., editor. *Eyrbyggja Saga: The Vellum Tradition*. Copenhagen: 2003.

Sigfússon, Björn, editor. *Ljósvetninga saga með þáttum*. Reykjavik: 1940.

Sigurðsson, Jón V. 'Forholdet mellom frender, hushold og venner på Island i fristatstiden'. *Historisk Tidsskrift* 74, no. 3 (1995): 311–30.

Sigurðsson, Jón V. *Chieftains and Power in the Icelandic Commonwealth*, translated by Jean Lundskær-Nielsen. Odense: 1999.

Sørensen, Preben Meulengracht. *Saga and Society: An Introduction to Old Norse Literature*, trans. John Tucker. Odense: 1993.

Strauch, Dieter. *Mittelalterliches nordisches Recht bis 1500*. Berlin: 2011.

Sveinsson, Einar Ólafur and Matthías Þórðarson, editors. *Eyrbyggja saga*. Reykjavik: 1935.

Sveinsson, Einar Ólafur, editor. *Njáls saga*. Reykjavik: 1954.

The Danish Medieval Laws: The Laws of Scania, Zealand and Jutland, edited and translated by Ditlev Tamm and Helle Vogt. London and New York: 2016.

CHAPTER 11

Biblical Analogues for Early Anglo-Saxon Law

Carole Hough

Introduction

Religious influence on Anglo-Saxon law is taken to begin with the late seventh-century codes of Kings Wihtred of Kent and Ine of Wessex,[1] where such topics as church dues, infant baptism, and Sunday observance first appear.[2] The only earlier extant laws, those issued by King Æthelberht of Kent towards the end of the sixth century or the beginning of the seventh,[3] and a supplementary set issued by his successors Hlothhere and Eadric in the mid seventh century, deal exclusively with secular concerns. With the exception of the opening sequence of Æthelberht's code, inserted to make provision for the Roman missionaries whose arrival in the late sixth century acted as the catalyst for its promulgation in written form, his laws had clearly been in oral circulation long before the conversion to Christianity. The main analogues for these early Kentish laws are found on the continent, where comparison with other barbarian codes both aids interpretation and points towards a common ancestry.

Aids to interpretation are much needed, since the early Kentish laws offer many challenges. Difficulties arise partly from the high proportion of *hapax legomena*, and partly from the elliptical phraseology, which assumes much background knowledge on the part of the reader or listener.[4] As Whitelock explains:

---

1 I am grateful to participants at the conference on *Law and Ritual in the Middle Ages*, held in Leeuwarden from 22–23 September 2016, for their feedback on this paper.

2 It is less certain whether references to ecclesiastical penance appear as early as this. The issues are discussed in Carole Hough, 'Penitential Literature and Secular Law in Anglo-Saxon England', *Anglo-Saxon Studies in Archaeology and History* 11 (2000), 133–41, which at 139 concludes that 'there is little evidence of a close link between the penitentials and secular law in early Anglo-Saxon England'.

3 The dating evidence is discussed in Carole Hough, 'Legal and Documentary Writings', in *A Companion to Anglo-Saxon Literature*, ed. Phillip Pulsiano and Elaine Treharne (Oxford: 2001), 170–3.

4 A list of *hapax legomena* in the Kentish laws is compiled by Patrizia Lendinara, 'The Kentish Laws', in *The Anglo-Saxons from the Migration Period to the Eighth Century: An Ethnographic*

 | DOI 10.1163/9789004375765_013

> The translation of the Anglo-Saxon laws has its special difficulties. They are frequently, especially in the earlier times, very briefly and even cryptically expressed, being composed for persons familiar with the general circumstances and thus requiring guidance on a particular issue only.[5]

The absence of surviving case law drawing on the extant legislation closes off that potential route to interpretation, and also leaves it uncertain whether the laws were actually put into practice.[6] The same applies to a large extent even to later Anglo-Saxon law, including the great *domboc* issued by Alfred the Great towards the end of the ninth century. As well as incorporating the laws of Ine, the *domboc* contains a Prologue which draws extensively on Mosaic law and situates the Anglo-Saxons, like the Israelites, as the chosen people of God.[7] Alfred's *domboc* is thus taken to represent the first link between Old English and Old Testament law. The purpose of this paper is to suggest that such links may already appear in Æthelberht's code, and to discuss some of the implications for our understanding of early Anglo-Saxon legislation.

Anglo-Saxon and Continental Law

The suggestion is not entirely new. The Anglo-Saxon laws stand apart from their continental cousins by being written in the vernacular language, Old English, rather than in Latin, and the reasons for this have been much debated. Indeed, since the three Kentish codes survive only in the twelfth-century *Textus Roffensis* manuscript (Rochester, Cathedral Library A.3.5), it has even been suggested that they may originally have been issued in Latin, and only later translated into Old English.[8] This is not widely accepted, however, and

---

Perspective, ed. John Hines (Woodbridge: 1997), 223–4, followed by two further lists of words of limited occurrence, at 224–5.

5 Dorothy Whitelock, ed., *English Historical Documents: Volume I, c. 500–1042*, 2nd edn. (London: 1979), 365.

6 Surviving records of case-law are brought together in Patrick Wormald, 'A Handlist of Anglo-Saxon Lawsuits', *Anglo-Saxon England* 17 (1988), 247–81. Most date from the later Anglo-Saxon period, while the early material deals with civil rather than criminal justice—'inasmuch as the distinction exists under early medieval conditions', as Wormald points out, at p. 279.

7 The role of Mosaic law in Alfred's *domboc* is examined in detail in Patrick Wormald, *The Making of English Law: King Alfred to the Twelfth Century, volume I: Legislation and its Limits* (Oxford: 1999), 416–29.

8 Lendinara, 'The Kentish Laws'.

more recent research has supported a Kentish original.[9] Nevertheless, the motivation for the use of the vernacular remains uncertain, and continues to be discussed. According to Wormald:

> Three likely and complementary reasons suggest themselves. The first is that no one at Æthelberht's court was sufficiently *au fait* with both Kentish law and Latin prose to make the necessary conversion. Second, it might be guessed that Gregory's Rome already had a 'Byzantine' toleration for vernaculars, … A third factor, subsuming the two others, was that the language of the *Cantwara* was not cramped by the cultural ascendancy of Latin, as Frankish or Lombardic were so soon as their speakers were established within Roman frontiers, and as trans-Rhenan tongues must have been by Frankish ascendancy.[10]

While these are cogent suggestions, there is an alternative approach. More than half a century ago, Wallace-Hadrill tackled the issue from the opposite direction, asking not why the Anglo-Saxon laws were written in the vernacular, but why the continental laws were not. Discussing the Lombard text issued in 643 and known as Rothar's Edict, he wrote:

> The Edict is written not in Lombardic but in Latin. The reason for this may be that Lombardic was not a literary language; Latin was the language of Western law. On the other hand, the Lombards were a proud people still. They did not love the Romans or the Greeks. The Kentish kings had managed to record their laws in their vernacular; and it is not, I think, absolutely certain that the Frankish kings had not done likewise. The true reason may be that the actual work of compilation was done by, and for the benefit of, clerks to whom that great exemplar, the Mosaic law, was known only from the Latin Bible. Behind the barbarian laws lies the Book of Deuteronomy.[11]

The final sentence in particular offers a penetrating insight which has not yet been fully taken on board in scholarship on early English law. This is in

---

9 Lisi Oliver, *The Beginnings of English Law* (Toronto: 2002), 17; Carole Hough, 'The Earliest English Texts? The Language of the Kentish Laws Reconsidered', in Textus Roffensis: *Law, Language, and Libraries in Early Medieval England*, ed. Bruce O'Brien and Barbara Bombi (Turnhout: 2015), 137–56.

10 Wormald, *Making of English Law*, 101.

11 J. M. Wallace-Hadrill, *The Barbarian West, 400–1000*, 3rd edn. (London: 1967), 55.

contrast to research on continental and later English legislation, where Biblical parallels underpin some important studies. For instance, Elsakkers identifies parallels between abortion law in Exodus 21:22–23 and *Leges Visigothorum* 6.3.2 as evidence for a Gothic version of Exodus;[12] Oliver suggests that Exodus 21:19 helps to explain a ruling relating to leg wounds in *Pactus Alamannorum* 11.3;[13] and Jurasinski discusses Sabbath observance in Frankish and late-seventh-century Anglo-Saxon legislation in relation to the Heptateuch.[14] Given the close relationship between Anglo-Saxon and continental Germanic law, it seems likely that the Kentish codes may also repay comparison with Biblical models. If Old Testament precepts do indeed underlie the barbarian laws from which the earliest Anglo-Saxon legislation evolved, they may provide important comparative material for interpretation as well as impacting on the evidential value of the laws for Kentish society.

Æthelberht's Law-Code

Before attempting to identify signs of Biblical influence, it is necessary to differentiate between elements of Æthelberht's code that may have been inspired by the Roman missionaries under Augustine, and elements that predate their arrival. The organisation of the laws may fall into the former category. Thus whereas Howlett argues that Æthelberht's code comprises ten parts, 'presumably in imitation of the Decalogue', this structure and its motivation need not predate the process of committing the laws to writing.[15] Indeed, it cannot do so, since the first of the ten parts is the section providing for the missionaries, and Howlett himself takes the 'Biblical style' (based on chiastic patterning) that he identifies throughout the code to stem from Roman influence.[16]

The legislative content of the code, on the other hand, is a different matter. There is widespread agreement that the laws must have circulated orally for

12 Marianne Elsakkers, 'Gothic Bible, Vetus Latina and Visigothic Law', *Sacra Erudiri* 44 (2005), 37–76.

13 Lisi Oliver, *The Body Legal In Barbarian Law* (Toronto: 2011), 120.

14 Stefan Jurasinski, *The Old English Penitentials and Anglo-Saxon Law* (Cambridge: 2015), 100–9.

15 D. R. Howlett, *British Books in Biblical Style* (Dublin: 1997), 258.

16 *Ibid.*, 257: 'Since Bede states explicitly that these laws imitate Roman models and their heading states that they derive from the time of the Roman Saint Augustine of Canterbury, it is not surprising that they exhibit Biblical style'.

some considerable time before being written down. Parallels between Kentish and continental Germanic law can only be accounted for on the assumption that the early Anglo-Saxon settlers brought with them a legal tradition that was preserved in oral tradition before the introduction of literacy. Corroborative evidence is provided by the mnemonics discussed by Oliver, and by the absence of chapter numbers in the manuscript, which, as I have suggested elsewhere, 'may reflect an original conception not as a written text but as a spoken utterance, where the visual clues provided by chapter numbers would be irrelevant'.[17] The subject matter of the laws can therefore be dated well before the arrival of Augustine, so that any parallels with Deuteronomy or other books of the Bible stand apart from missionary influence.

One such parallel has already been identified by Oliver, who points out that early continental case-law and legislation repeatedly establishes a terminus of forty days for legal processes such as witness statements.[18] She goes on to observe that

> the regulation on payment for homicide in early seventh-century Kent was that the first twenty shillings of the wergild must be paid at the open grave, but the kin-group then had forty days to pay the remaining eighty. The forty-day time period may be biblically inspired.[19]

If her suggestion is correct, the Biblical inspiration must be taken to reflect a phase of influence predating the promulgation of Æthelberht's code in writing. This may provide a context for further links between early Kentish and Old Testament law.

Laws Concerning Women

Some of the most problematic clauses in Æthelberht's code are in the section concerned with women and marriage. Relatively straightforward is Æbt 77, referring to the marriage contract:

> Æbt 77. Gif man mægþ gebigeð ceapi geceapod sy, gif hit unfacne is; gif hit þonne facne is, ef þær æt ham gebrenge 7 him man his scæt agefe.

17 Hough, 'Legal and Documentary Writings', 171. See further Oliver, *Beginnings of English Law*, 36–41.

18 Oliver, *The Body Legal*, 38–9.

19 *Ibid.*, 39.

> If anyone pays for a girl, the bargain is to stand, if there is no fraud; if however, there is fraud, she is to be taken back home, and he is to be given back his money.[20]

Although the nature of the fraud is not specified, no huge leap of imagination is required to deduce that it refers to a bride who is found not to be a virgin. The idea is a commonplace in many ancient legal systems: 'Laws permitting the return of non-virginal spouses are found throughout the Indo-European world'.[21] The fact that it features in both Mosaic and Kentish law may therefore be no more than coincidence. Indeed, even in the Heptateuch there is no explicit statement that a non-virginal bride can be repudiated. Rather, the idea is implicit within a sequence of verses from Deuteronomy 22:13–21, dealing with the procedures for establishing whether or not such a charge is justified, and the appropriate penalties in the event of either a malicious or a well-founded accusation. Similarly, the reference to a bride-price, which first appears in Exodus 22:16, is common to many other legal systems besides those of early Judaism and Anglo-Saxon Kent. More specific parallels are needed to support the notion of Biblical influence on Æthelberht's code.

Moving on to Æbt 82, we find another legal commonplace.

> Æbt 82. Gif man mægþman nede genimeþ, ðam agende L scillinga, 7 eft æt þam agende, sinne willan ætgebicge.
>
> If anyone takes a girl by force, [he is to pay] 50 shillings to her guardian, and afterwards buy the guardian's consent.

Again, the notion of recompense for rape is hardly earth-shattering, and neither is the idea that the person responsible should have to marry the girl whose marital prospects would otherwise be seriously compromised. The occurrence of the same idea in Deuteronomy 22:28–9 might therefore again be coincidence:[22]

---

20 Unless otherwise stated, texts and translations are from the edition presented in Carole Hough, 'Women and the Law in Seventh-Century England', *Nottingham Medieval Studies* 51 (2007), 207–30. All clause numbers are from F. Liebermann, *Die Gesetze der Angelsachsen*, 3 vols. (Halle: 1903–16).

21 Oliver, *Beginnings of English Law*, 107–8.

22 All Biblical quotations and layout are from Robertus Weber, *Biblia Sacra: Iuxta Vulgatam Versionem*, 2 vols., 2nd edn. (Stuttgart: 1975), which is also available online (http://

> 28 si invenerit vir puellam virginem quae non habet sponsum et adprehendens concubuerit cum ea et res ad iudicium venerit
> 29 dabit qui dormivit cum ea patri puellae quinquaginta siclos argenti et habebit eam uxorem quia humiliavit illam non poterit dimittere cunctis diebus vitae suae
>
> If a man happens to meet a virgin who is not pledged to be married and rapes her and they are discovered, he shall pay her father fifty shekels of silver. He must marry the young woman, for he has violated her. He can never divorce her as long as he lives.

However, what may be suggestive is the recurrence of the figure fifty, especially as it seems out of proportion to other penalties in Æthelberht's code. 50 shillings was the amount payable for loss of an eye (Æbt 43) or a foot (Æbt 69), and it was also half the wergild of a freeman (Æbt 21). In the context of an addition to the standard bride-price, indicating that the woman has lost out neither on her chances of marriage nor on the associated financial settlement, it seems rather high, so it may be worth considering the possibility that the amount might simply echo the figure of 50 shekels of silver in Mosaic law.

The abduction sequence continues in Æbt 83 and 84, running in direct parallel with Deuteronomy 22 since the penalty for rape of a virgin is immediately followed by the penalty for rape of a girl engaged to be married.

> Æbt 83. Gif hio oþrum mæn in sceat bewyddod sy xx scillinga gebete.
>
> If she is betrothed to another man at a [bride] price, he is to pay 20 shillings compensation.
>
> Æbt 84. Gif gængang geweorðeþ xxxv scilł, 7 cyninge xv scillingas.
>
> If she is assaulted on the road, 35 shillings, and 15 shillings to the king.

The term *gængang* is one of the most problematic in Old English, as reflected in the entry for the term in the *Dictionary of Old English*:

> 1. legal term of uncertain meaning, with interpretations based on whether or not the sentence is interpreted as independent of, or a continuation of,

www.latinvulgate.com/). Biblical translations are from the New International Version (https:www.biblegateway.com).

> the preceding two sentences; if the sentence is independent, suggestions include '(the offence of) waylaying (on the open road)'; if the sentence is a continuation, 'attack, fight (on the open road)' related to an abduction mentioned earlier; or 'return (of an abducted woman to her guardian or fiancé)'; or 'meeting (between an abductor and a woman who came willingly to meet him)'.[23]

The main issues have been extensively canvassed by myself and others, and need not be revisited here.[24] However, one point that may have been overlooked in previous discussions is the significance placed on the location of a sexual attack in Deuteronomy 22:23–7.

> 23 si puellam virginem desponderit vir et invenerit eam aliquis in civitate et concubuerit cum illa
> 24 educes utrumque ad portam civitatis illius et lapidibus obruentur puella quia non clamavit cum esset in civitate vir quia humiliavit uxorem proximi sui et auferes malum de medio tui
> 25 sin autem in agro reppererit vir puellam quae desponsata est et adprehendens concubuerit cum illa ipse morietur solus
> 26 puella nihil patietur nec est rea mortis quoniam sicut latro consurgit contra fratrem suum et occidit animam eius ita et puella perpessa est
> 27 sola erat in agro clamavit et nullus adfuit qui liberaret eam

> If a man happens to meet in a town a virgin pledged to be married and he sleeps with her, you shall take both of them to the gate of that town and stone them to death—the young woman because she was in a town and did not scream for help, and the man because he violated another man's wife. You must purge the evil from among you. But if out in the country a man happens to meet a young woman pledged to be married and rapes her, only the man who has done this shall die. Do nothing to the woman; she has committed no sin deserving death. This case is like that of someone who attacks and murders a neighbor, for the man found the young

23 DOE, s.v., *gēan-gang*.

24 Christine Fell, 'An Appendix to Carole Hough's Article "A Reappraisal of Æthelberht 84"', *Nottingham Medieval Studies* 37 (1993), 7–8; Hough 1993; Carole Hough, 'Alfred's Domboc and the Language of Rape: A Reconsideration of Alfred ch. 11', *Medium Ævum* 66 (1997), 1–27, at 15–16; Oliver, *Beginnings of English Law*, 108–9.

woman out in the country, and though the betrothed woman screamed, there was no one to rescue her.

Here there is a legal distinction between adultery in the town, where a woman could be held responsible for not summoning help, and rape in the country, where no help would be available. This might just have a bearing on the additional penalty in Æbt 84 for an attack on the road, where again it seems unlikely that help would be to hand. Indeed, penalties for robbery on the road in other laws within the same code (Æbt 19 and Æbt 89) show that it was regarded as a location vulnerable to crime.

Laws Concerning the Unfree

Following directly on from the abduction sequence is a clause relating to adultery with the wife of an *esne* or unfree servant:

> Æbt 85. Gif man mid esnes cwynan geligeþ be cwicum ceorle ii gebete.
>
> If anyone lies with the wife of an unfree servant during the husband's lifetime, he is to pay 2 [shillings] compensation.

Here the problematic phrase is *be cwicum ceorle*. The literal meaning is transparent—'while the husband is alive'—but to the best of my knowledge no-one has succeeded in making sense of this in the context of the law. If the husband were not alive, the woman would be a widow, and subject to different regulations. If she has a husband, it stands to reason that that husband must be alive. I have suggested elsewhere that the phrase is a legal formula, as it also occurs in the eleventh-century laws of Cnut, with the Latin equivalent in Salic and Ripuarian law.[25] Where the formula originates, however, remains a mystery.

It is interesting to note in this connection that Exodus 21:2–3 refers to time-limited slavery, and addresses the position of the wife of such a slave. The man goes free after six years, together with his wife if he was already married at the beginning of his period of servitude:

> 2 si emeris servum hebraeum sex annis serviet tibi in septimo egredietur liber gratis

25 Hough, 'Women and the Law', 227–8. The laws in question are II Cnut 53; *Pactus Legis Salicae* 15, *Capitula Legi Salicae Addita* V, 133 and *Lex Ribuaria* 39.

> [3] cum quali veste intraverit cum tali exeat si habens uxorem et uxor egredietur simul
>
> If you buy a Hebrew servant, he is to serve you for six years. But in the seventh year, he shall go free, without paying anything. If he comes alone, he is to go free alone; but if he has a wife when he comes, she is to go with him.

The following verses outline different scenarios, where a slave marries after entering servitude, or where a daughter is sold into slavery by her father. The emphasis throughout is on protecting the rights of the woman. Could this have a bearing on Æbt 85? Time-limited slavery would fit with the half-free status of the *esne*, so the law might be intended to differentiate between the position of a woman whose husband dies within the six years, and one who can expect to be manumitted alongside him in the course of time.[26] How relevant this is to early Kentish society is of course a separate matter, and raises another issue. In the absence of other contemporary documentation, Æthelberht's laws are extensively quarried for information relating to pre-Christian Kent. If they contain in part a garbled version of Old Testament law, their value as historical evidence may be seriously compromised.

Æbt 85 acts as a transition between laws concerning women and laws concerning the unfree. Æbt 87 reads as follows, with alternative translations from successive editions:

> Æbt 87. Gif esnes eage 7 foot of weorðeþ aslagen, ealne weorðe hine forgelde.
>
> Wenn eines Lohnknechts Auge und Fuse abgehauen warden, entgelte ihn [den Thäter dem Herrn] ganz mit [Knechts-]Werth. (Liebermann)[27]
>
> If the eye and foot of a servant are destroyed [by blows], his full value shall be paid. (Attenborough)[28]

---

26 The phrase *ii gebete* might thus refer to two-fold compensation, as understood by previous scholars, on which see Hough, 'Women and the Law', 228. Simple compensation may be payable for adultery with an ordinary slave-woman; double compensation for adultery with one whose term of slavery was time-limited by that of her husband.

27 Liebermann, *Die Gesetze der Angelsachsen*, I, 8.

28 F. L. Attenborough, *The Laws of the Earliest English Kings* (Cambridge: 1922), 17.

> If a servant's eye or foot is destroyed, the full value is to be paid for him. (Whitelock)[29]

> If a servant's eye or foot becomes struck off, let him pay him [i.e., the servant's master] the entire worth. (Oliver)[30]

Discussion focuses on the tironian sign, which can represent either 'and' or 'or'. Although Liebermann translates as 'und', his notes state that '"und" hier = "oder"',[31] so Attenborough is alone in taking the law to refer to the destruction of both organs. In my view, such a reading is supported by the equation mentioned above, whereby the personal injury tariff sets compensation for both an eye and a foot at the same value as the wergild of a freeman.[32] However, my purpose here is to challenge the assumption, made explicit by the explanatory glosses provided by Liebermann and Oliver, that the servant's value is to be paid to his master by the perpetrator of the injuries. Who is more likely to beat a servant than his master? If a slave is maimed through a beating, his master has simply damaged his own property. The situation is different with regard to a servant, who would lose his ability to support himself. Again, we turn to Exodus 21, where verse 26 reads as follows:

> 26 si percusserit quispiam oculum servi sui aut ancillae et luscos eos fecerit dimittet liberos pro oculo quem eruit

> An owner who hits a male or female slave in the eye and destroys it must let the slave go free to compensate for the eye.

The verb *forgyldan* in Æbt 87 has a range of meanings, including 'to pay for, redeem, release', a sense attested exclusively in the legal register.[33] It may be possible that in this context it refers to the master's obligation to remit the servitude of a servant maimed through a beating, or even an obligation to pay that servant his own value.

Coincidentally, this clause has sparked a suggestion of Biblical influence from a different angle. Oliver comments:

29 Whitelock, *English Historical Documents*, 394.
30 Oliver, *Beginnings of English Law*, 81.
31 Liebermann, *Die Gesetze der Angelsachsen*, III, 16.
32 See above, 293.
33 DOE, s.v., *forgyldan*, 4.a.

> The parallel with the biblical collocation of 'the halt and the blind' is interesting, but since there is no other biblical reference in this text of which I am aware, I hesitate to make much of it.[34]

Taken alongside other potential Biblical analogues, the idea may appear more persuasive.

Finally we turn to two clauses from an earlier section of Æthelberht's code, again dealing with penalties for sexual relations with slaves.

> Æbt 14. Gif wið eorles birele man geligeþ xii scilł gebete.
>
> If anyone lies with a nobleman's serving-maid, he is to pay 12 shillings compensation.
>
> Æbt 16. Gif wið ceorles birelan man geligeþ vi scillingu*m* gebete. Aet þære oþere ðeowa'n' L scætta. Aet þare þriddan xxx scætta.
>
> If anyone lies with a freeman's serving-maid, he is to pay 6 shillings compensation. For a slave of the second [class], 50 *sceattas*. For one of the third [class], 30 *sceattas*.

Out of around thirty attestations of OE *birele*, these are the only two to refer to women. Hence whereas the main definition provided in the DOE entry (s.v. *byrle*) is the literal 'one who pours out drink, cup-bearer', a secondary definition 'referring to a woman: cupbearer, or perhaps more generally, serving-maid' is created to accommodate the occurrences in Æthelberht's laws.[35] Equally strikingly, they are also the only two to refer to low status. Other quotations in the DOE entry are to high-status officials, including cup-bearers at the great feasts in *Beowulf* and (metaphorically) *Andreas*, the cup-bearer of a bishop in Gregory's *Dialogues*, those officiating at the wedding feast in John's Gospel where Jesus turned water into wine, and so on. Glosses use the term as an equivalent to Latin *pincerna* 'butler' and (as *yldest byrla*) *magister calicum* 'chief cupbearer', while the importance of the role is also reflected in a quotation from the will of King Eadred, bequeathing eighty *mancuses* of gold to the holder of such an office. This is not the kind of official we would expect to find in the household of an Anglo-Saxon *ceorl*.

---

34 Oliver, *Beginnings of English Law*, 115.

35 DOE, s.v. *byrle*.

One of the other quotations in the DOE entry is from the Old English translation of the *Heptateuch*, recounting the episode where Joseph interprets the dreams of his fellow-prisoners in Egypt. Here Genesis 40:9 reads as follows:

> Gen 40.9: þa rehte þæra byrla ealdor him his swefn, & cwæþ: ic geseah wingeard … & Pharaones drincefæt on minre handa, & ic nam þa winberian & wrang on þæt fæt & sealde Pharaone.
>
> So the chief cupbearer told Joseph his dream. He said to him, 'In my dream I saw a vine … Pharaoh's cup was in my hand, and I took the grapes, squeezed them into Pharaoh's cup and put the cup in his hand'.

Is it more plausible that the lowest class of Kentish freeman structured his household along similar lines to that of an Egyptian Pharaoh, or that the legal reference may have been inspired by the Biblical account? These questions have no definitive answers, but they are questions that do not appear to have been asked before. The issue of ecclesiastical influence on early Irish law has been significantly reassessed in recent scholarship, and it may be time to do the same for early Anglo-Saxon law.[36]

Old English Words for Law

Finally I should like to touch briefly on the Old English words for law itself. It is well known that before the introduction of the Old Norse loan-word *lagu*, the etymon of PDE *law*, during the late Anglo-Saxon period, Old English differentiated between established law, known as *æ*, and new law, known as *dom*. Hence the preamble to the mid-seventh century laws of the Kentish kings Hlothhere and Eadric presents the new decrees as *domas*, intended to supplement the existing *æ* represented by Æthelberht's code:

> Hloþhære 7 Eadric Cantwara cyningas ecton þa æ, þa ðe heora aldoras ær geworhton, ðyssum domum þe hyr efter sægeþ.
>
> Hlothhere and Eadric, kings of the people of Kent, augmented the laws which their predecessors had made by these decrees which are stated hereafter.

---

36 See e.g. Donnchadh Ó Corráin, Liam Breatnach, and Aidan Breen, 'The Laws of the Irish', *Peritia* 3 (1984), 382–438.

On the basis of a solid corpus of around 1,300 occurrences, DOE identifies the primary meaning of *ǣ* as divine and secular law, with a secondary meaning in relation to marriage:

1. law (divine and secular), statement of law (written or customary), code of behaviour; also figurative
2. marriage (freq. in Ælfric); some of the citations are ambiguous and may be taken as forms of ǣwe noun 'wife, married woman'

With the exception of the early seventh-century laws, all occurrences of sense 1 appear to refer to divine law. Indeed, Wormald observes that only in the seventh century does the term appear to have a general legal sense.[37] However, there may be another way of looking at it. Rather than assuming that seventh-century legislation uses this frequently attested term in an otherwise unrecorded sense, we might consider the possibility that here too, it refers to divine law.

Conclusions

The main conclusions of this paper are twofold. On the one hand, potential analogues with Mosaic law may help to throw light on the interpretation of some problematic clauses in early Anglo-Saxon legislation. On the other hand, the same analogues not only cast further doubt on whether the laws were actually applied, but also undermine their evidential value for early Kentish society. How likely is it that the Anglo-Saxons would have been following Old Testament law? The surviving codes may have less to do with contemporary reality than we thought. As reflected in the quotation from Whitelock above, it has been considered axiomatic that interpretive cruxes stem from the fact that modern scholars lack the background knowledge available to the Anglo-Saxons.[38] If the argument put forward in this paper is correct, it may be possible that the Anglo-Saxons didn't understand them either.

Bibliography

Abbreviations

DOE: *Dictionary of Old English A–G*, version 2.0. CD-ROM, 2008.

37 Wormald, *Making of English Law*, 95, n. 330.

38 See above, at n. 5.

Works Cited

Attenborough, F. L. *The Laws of the Earliest English Kings*. Cambridge: 1922.

Elsakkers, Marianne. 'Gothic Bible, Vetus Latina and Visigothic Law'. *Sacra Erudiri* 44 (2005): 37–76.

Fell, Christine. 'An Appendix to Carole Hough's Article "A Reappraisal of Æthelberht 84"'. *Nottingham Medieval Studies* 37 (1993): 7–8.

Hough, Carole. 'Penitential Literature and Secular Law in Anglo-Saxon England'. *Anglo-Saxon Studies in Archaeology and History* 11 (2000): 133–41.

Hough, Carole. 'Legal and Documentary Writings'. In *A Companion to Anglo-Saxon Literature*, edited by Phillip Pulsiano and Elaine Treharne, 170–87. Oxford: 2001.

Hough, Carole. 'A Reappraisal of Æthelberht 84'. *Nottingham Medieval Studies* 37 (1993): 1–6. Reprinted in Hough (2014), 150–157.

Hough, Carole. Women and the Law in Seventh-Century England. *Nottingham Medieval Studies* 51 (2007): 207–30. Reprinted in Hough (2014), 46–72.

Hough, Carole. 'Alfred's Domboc and the Language of Rape: A Reconsideration of Alfred ch. 11'. *Medium Ævum* 66 (1997): 1–27. Reprinted in Hough (2014), 169–202.

Hough, Carole. *"An Ald Reht": Essays on Anglo-Saxon Law*. Newcastle upon Tyne: 2014.

Hough, Carole. 'The Earliest English Texts? The Language of the Kentish Laws Reconsidered'. In Textus Roffensis: *Law, Language, and Libraries in Early Medieval England*, edited by Bruce O'Brien and Barbara Bombi, 137–56. Turnhout: 2015.

Howlett, D. R. *British Books in Biblical Style*. Dublin: 1997.

Jurasinski, Stefan. *The Old English Penitentials and Anglo-Saxon Law*. Cambridge: 2015.

Lendinara, Patrizia. 'The Kentish Laws'. In *The Anglo-Saxons from the Migration Period to the Eighth Century: An Ethnographic Perspective*, edited by John Hines, 211–30. Woodbridge: 1997.

Liebermann, Felix. *Die Gesetze der Angelsachsen*, 3 vols. Halle: 1903–1916.

Ó Corráin, Donnchadh, Liam Breatnach, and Aidan Breen. 'The Laws of the Irish'. *Peritia* 3 (1984): 382–438.

Oliver, Lisi. *The Beginnings of English Law*. Toronto: 2002.

Oliver, Lisi. *The Body Legal in Barbarian Law*. Toronto: 2011.

Wallace-Hadrill, J. M. *The Barbarian West 400–1000*, 3rd edn. London: 1967.

Weber, Robertus. *Biblia Sacra: Iuxta Vulgatam Versionem*, 2 vols., 2nd edn. Stuttgart: 1975.

Whitelock, Dorothy. *English Historical Documents* c. *500–1042*, 2nd edn. London: 1979.

Wormald, Patrick. 'A Handlist of Anglo-Saxon Lawsuits'. *Anglo-Saxon England* 17 (1988): 247–81.

Wormald, Patrick. *The Making of English Law: King Alfred to the Twelfth Century, Volume 1: Legislation and its Limits*. Oxford: 1999.

Index

www.ingramcontent.com/pod-product-compliance
Ingram Content Group UK Ltd.
Pitfield, Milton Keynes, MK11 3LW, UK
UKHW022224051026
15624UKWH00002B/342

9 789004 342675